Health IT JumpStart

The Best First Step Toward an IT Career in Health Information Technology

Patrick Wilson

Scott McEvoy

WILEY

John Wiley & Sons, Inc.

Acquisitions Editor: Mariann Barsolo
Development Editor: Mary Ellen Schutz
Technical Editor: Patrick Conlan
Production Editor: Liz Britten
Copy Editor: Kim Wimpsett
Editorial Manager: Pete Gaughan
Production Manager: Tim Tate
Vice President and Executive Group Publisher: Richard Swadley
Vice President and Publisher: Neil Edde
Book Designer: Judy Fung
Compositor: Kate Kaminski, Happenstance Type-O-Rama
Proofreader: Sheilah Lewidge; Word One, New York
Indexer: Ted Laux
Project Coordinator, Cover: Katherine Crocker
Cover Designer: Ryan Sneed
Cover Image: © Sarah Fix Photography Inc. /Getty Images

Copyright © 2012 by John Wiley & Sons, Inc., Indianapolis, Indiana

Published simultaneously in Canada

ISBN: 978-1-118-01676-3

ISBN: 978-1-118-20394-1 (ebk.)

ISBN: 978-1-118-20396-5 (ebk.)

ISBN: 978-1-118-20395-8 (ebk.)

For general information on our other products and services or to obtain technical support, please contact our Customer Care Department within the U.S. at (877) 762-2974, outside the U.S. at (317) 572-3993 or fax (317) 572-4002.

Wiley publishes in a variety of print and electronic formats and by print-on-demand. Some material included with standard print versions of this book may not be included in e-books or in print-on-demand. If this book refers to media such as a CD or DVD that is not included in the version you purchased, you may download this material at http://booksupport.wiley.com. For more information about Wiley products, visit www.wiley.com.

Library of Congress Control Number: 2011938576

10 9 8 7 6 5 4 3 2 1

Dear Reader,

Thank you for choosing *Health IT JumpStart*. This book is part of a family of premium-quality Sybex books, all of which are written by outstanding authors who combine practical experience with a gift for teaching.

Sybex was founded in 1976. More than 30 years later, we're still committed to producing consistently exceptional books. With each of our titles, we're working hard to set a new standard for the industry. From the paper we print on, to the authors we work with, our goal is to bring you the best books available.

I hope you see all that reflected in these pages. I'd be very interested to hear your comments and get your feedback on how we're doing. Feel free to let me know what you think about this or any other Sybex book by sending me an email at nedde@wiley.com. If you think you've found a technical error in this book, please visit http://sybex.custhelp.com. Customer feedback is critical to our efforts at Sybex.

Best regards,

Neil Edde
Vice President and Publisher
Sybex, an Imprint of Wiley

To our families, without whose love and support this book would not have been possible.

—PW and SM

To Gina, the best spouse for life's adventures. To Mom and Dad whose commitment to Christ, continuous learning, and lives of adventure were passed on to their kids and grandkids.

—PW

Acknowledgments

When writing a book, you always think about who you are going to personally thank. Well, they haven't given us enough pages to do that for everyone, so we want to thank the following folks who have made a lasting impact on our lives.

Patrick Wilson would like to thank the following folks. The Burckhardt's, Brown's, and Boucher's: You invested time praying and playing with the Wilson kids no matter how unique we were. Ernie Ruiz: With your guidance, we built so many projects together including a shuttle simulator for my eighth-grade science fair. Mike Wood and Mrs. Caetano: You made science a blast, literally. Doug Canby: No matter what crazy camp I wanted to go to, you would help me work with Rotary to find funding. Wayne and Sheila Wiebe: You let me participate as a member of your family and I am forever grateful. Mark Hayward: As my history and English teacher, you taught me that life is precious and to pursue my dreams (I still owe you that Volvo). Tina Darmohray: You instilled in me the drive to finish school. Your mentoring was instrumental in my career choices, and school has opened up many doors. Jennifer and Chris Stone, my flight instructors: You gave me the freedom of flight. JR Taylor, Denise Taylor, and Marty Martinez: you gave me the training necessary from day one to handle any parachute emergency. Pastor Verne: You have always been around to answer any philosophical question—or just to beat me at tennis. Dave Fry: Thank you for your ongoing mentoring in information security. Karon Head: thanks for all the help in keeping work interesting and fun. David Runt: Thanks for giving me the opportunity to grow at CCHS. Blythe and Bob at CompTIA: your ongoing support serves the entire HIT VAR community. Marc Miyashiro, Lance Mageno, and Earle Humphreys: Thank you for providing guidance on the many topics of healthcare IT. Lastly, thanks to all who have allowed me to participate in their lives; each experience has helped shape who I am today.

The accomplishments listed in my bio would not have been possible without unwavering support from my family, faith, parents, mentors, and business partner. Thanks to my wife, who endured long weekends, put up with calls from the editor hunting for me, and maintained the home front while I was working or writing. To my kids, who can now finally have the full attention of their father as they grow into adulthood. To my parents, who gave me space to be my own person. You had your hands full. I want to thank my pastors, who prayed and worked with me to maintain some semblance of balance in my life. Thanks to my Bible Study members, who pitched in and opened their home or led the group as I traveled. To my brother and sister, who supported me, even if their brother took a briefcase to school. Thanks to God, who gave us all unique abilities to serve and meet the needs of others.

Scott McEvoy would like to thank his lovely wife, Sharon, and his wonderful daughter, Patty, for their patience during this project and for providing the support necessary to enable him to complete this endeavor. He would also like to thank his colleagues, clients, current and previous co-workers, as well as friends for their contributions to this work.

And there are some folks we both would like to thank. We can't leave out some of the wonderful staff at medical practices who have chosen to work with us. Patty and Michelle, not only are you awesome to work with, but you gave up precious time to give feedback on the book. Dr. Cook, Dr. Jacobs, Dr. Freinkel, Dr. Tremain, Dr. Pramanik, and Dr. Bronge: Each of you provided valuable feedback on the book's content. The information you have shared will help so many other IT professionals and the practices they serve.

We would like to thank the good folks at Sybex and Wiley for giving us the opportunity to write this book. Pete Gaughan and Mariann Barsolo were instrumental in helping us with the concept and worked very hard to bring the concept to fruition. Without Mariann's tireless effort, this book may not have gotten off the ground, much less made it to the printing presses. We also want to give a special thank you to our developmental editor, Mary Ellen Schutz, for her patience and skillful handling of these first-time authors. I can't think of a better person to bird-dog me (PW) and keep me on task and point. Without her tutelage, this book would not be what it is—and our formatting errors would have certainly put us in mortal danger (the term *hit men* was used frequently) with the rest of the production team. That said, let us acknowledge and thank the rest of the production team, including our technical editor Patrick Conlan, production editor Liz Britten, copyeditor Kim Wimpsett, compositor Kate Kaminski, proofreader Sheilah Ledwidge, and indexer Ted Laux. Their efforts truly made an improvement and provided polish to the finished product.

About the Authors

Patrick Wilson has been intrigued by the amazing potential of technology, patient care, and customer service for more than a decade and has been passionate about computer applications for more than 32 years. His dad, an educator and blogger (www.grandadscience.com), brought home the first personal computer in the county when Patrick was just four years old. This early start fueled his lifelong passion for technology and also provided him with a keen understanding of both legacy systems and bleeding-edge technology. A 17-year veteran of the computer industry, Patrick currently serves as the assistant director of IT, security, and infrastructure for Contra Costa County Health Services (CCHS). CCHS consists of a 160-bed hospital, three large clinics, 25+ smaller clinics, a health plan, public health, hazardous materials, and environmental health. Previously, Patrick headed up the IT organizations for several Silicon Valley startups, including Global Network Manager, serving as the director of IT and CTO. In 2006, Patrick cofounded Vital Signs Technology, Inc. with Scott McEvoy, which serves the technology needs of small to midsized medical practices on the West Coast.

Patrick has a bachelor's degree in business from Western Baptist College. He is a CISSP, MCSE + Security, CompTIA Security+, certified in Homeland Security CHS-I, and a Microsoft Small Business Specialist. He also has federal certifications from CERT and FEMA. Patrick lives in Northern California with his wonderful (and patient) wife and two awesome kids. His hobbies include spending quality time with his family, flying, and skydiving—of course, never both at the same time.

Scott McEvoy is a seasoned IT professional from the fast-paced startup world and has held a number of roles, including systems and network administrator, IT manager, and senior director of World Wide Information Systems. As the director of IT at Vitria Technology (Red Herring: Number 2 in their Digital Universe Top 50 Private Companies of 1999), he helped the company grow the employee base from 50 to more than 1,500 in a little over two years. Tiring of Silicon Valley, Scott took his leadership skills and his passion for a good wine to Jackson Enterprises where he directed the IT Operations team of Kendall-Jackson for the corporate headquarters, affiliated wineries, and distributors. In 2006, Scott cofounded Vital Signs Technology with Patrick Wilson and set out to develop technology solutions targeting healthcare and emerging technology companies. He is among a limited number of healthcare professionals in the United States who has a CPHIMS certification. He has installed EMRs from single-doctor practices to multi-site medical groups. His early involvement with a public health record company has allowed them to grow with reduced security risks to the patient data in the organization's custody.

Scott has a bachelor of business administration degree in MIS from Pace University, as well as a number of vendor certifications from nearly all major technology companies including Microsoft, Cisco, Juniper, and CPHIMS. Scott lives in Northern California with his lovely wife and daughter. In his spare time, he enjoys cooking and hiking with his family, SCUBA diving, practicing karate, and participating in his daughter's school activities.

Contents

Introduction

Let's take a second to thank you for embarking on this journey with us. We hope that the subject matter and content provided in this book will have a positive impact on your career, employer, and patients served by the work you accomplish. Businesses are in dire need of trained professionals who understand the healthcare delivery system and healthcare technology, and we expect this book to help those looking to enter that market. At publication time, government calculations on labor project that there will be a 30.3 percent increase in healthcare jobs: physicians, nurses, technologists, administrators, and IT staff. In other words, the increase is expected to add 4.7 million new healthcare jobs by 2014 (www.bls.gov/oco/oc01002.htm).

Where are all the jobs coming from? Well, recent regulations stemming from the American Recovery and Reinvestment Act (the ARRA stimulus bill) are a significant driver for the rapid push for developing competent IT professionals focused on Health IT, also known as Healthcare IT. The federal government is expected to invest $27.3 billion, and the private sector will invest nearly twice that amount to meet the stimulus reimbursement requirements. Later, we will dive into the technical details of the stimulus funding, but for now we just want to share that the funding is broken into three different phases, each requiring different electronic health record (EHR) capabilities and reporting requirements. The requirements to meet reimbursement, which significantly impact technology purchase decisions, are not yet finalized; therefore, it is necessary to have trained staff members who can anticipate the expected regulations and implement robust solutions. Nearly two-thirds of the regulations have not yet been developed to meet the reimbursement requirements by 2015. Even as we go to press, the head of the Office of the National Coordinator was expected to agree to delay phase 2 requirements for ARRA funding by two years until 2014.

With the government funding part of the EHR deployment, many physicians, private practices, and hospitals are utilizing that funding to radically change how care is delivered. In the not-so-distant past, a physician would appear in the exam room with a chart in one hand and a pen in another. With the new funding and implementation of an EHR, those days are soon to be but fond memories. Medical practices, hospitals, and long-term healthcare providers are businesses, and most businesses (excluding nonprofits) are created to make a profit. Businesses expect a long-term improvement in patient outcomes and a lower cost of service delivery. Additionally, medical practitioner reimbursements are being reduced by payor organizations such as Medicare, Aetna, and HMOs. Technology, though a cost to the organization, is expected to drive down costs by reducing waste (such as repeated labs and incomplete image studies) and increasing the visibility of care across all locations a patient receives care. Lastly, patients now expect access to their health information so they can make more informed decisions, track medication usage, and provide home care.

The federal Medicare program will start penalizing doctors financially for not utilizing electronic health records (EHR) by 2015. However, given the complexity, the lack of trained implementers, and the criticality of patient care, the jury is still out on what the adoption rate for an EMR will be. Some doctors are electing to stop taking Medicare patients, set themselves up for retirement, or possibly go into a true private practice where patients pay a fee for the service delivered. No matter how many medical practices adopt EMR systems, it is clear that there are not enough properly trained staff to support the number of future implementations. An opportunity of epic proportions awaits those willing to learn about the intersection of healthcare and technology.

Who Should Read This Book

This book is for anyone who wants to learn about healthcare IT, medical workflow, and regulatory compliance in healthcare, including:

- IT professionals who are looking to leverage their existing knowledge and expand into healthcare
- Students who want to explore the technical aspects of healthcare delivery
- Medical office managers who want to know about IT and regulatory compliance
- Healthcare professionals who want to expand their role in the medical practice

We did not write the book from the perspective of teaching the reader how to paddle but rather how to take the right line down the rapids—and what to do if your raft takes on too much water. As such, it is most beneficial if you have at least a basic understanding of network, system, and hardware technologies.

What's Inside

Here is a glance at what's in each chapter:

Chapter 1: Healthcare Ecosystem: Past, Present, and Future   begins with a look back at the healthcare environment and the events and technological advances that helped shape our current healthcare delivery system. We introduce terms and concepts such as *business associate*, *meaningful use*, *provider*, and *payer* that are referenced throughout this book.

Chapter 2: Building Relationships and Continuing Education   provides insight into resources, such as associations, user groups, communities, and organizations, that are useful in learning about healthcare and making connections within the industry.

Chapter 3: Healthcare Lingo   introduces medical terminology and the acronyms commonly used in healthcare environments. At the end of this chapter you will know WHO, MA, PA, PACS, CAH, and many more terms.

Chapter 4: HIPAA Regulations   covers the Health Insurance Portability and Accountability Act of 1996 in depth and helps lay a foundation for understanding one of the most important regulations in healthcare.

Chapter 5: HITECH Regulations   provides an in-depth discussion of the Health Information Technology for Economic and Clinical Health Act and includes the information that is necessary to keep you and your clients from running afoul of the law.

Chapter 6: ARRA Funding   covers the American Recovery and Reinvestment Act of 2009 that is fueling the nation's investment in electronic medical and health records (EMR/EHR) and the requirements that are necessary for demonstrating meaningful use of those records in order to collect on these funds.

Chapter 7: PCI and Other Regulations   examines additional regulations affecting the healthcare industry, imposed by credit card companies, as well as state and federal governments, to ensure that personally identifiable information remains secure and protected.

Chapter 8: Operational Workflow: Front Office   provides insight into a medical practice's day-to-day business operations. In this chapter, we discuss the basic workflow involved in a patient visit and the impact it has on patient satisfaction and business operations.

Chapter 9: Operational Workflow: Back Office   discusses the administrative functions of the medical practice. These functions include the billing, coding, claims, and collections processes that are so important to the viability of the medical practice.

Chapter 10: Operational Workflow: Nursing   looks at the clinical workflow from the nursing perspective and the impact that technology has on patient care. We also look at key concepts and technologies that are shaping the future of nursing.

Chapter 11: Operational Workflow: Clinician   provides perspective into the medical practices workflow from a physician's perspective. In this chapter, we examine the challenges and complications that impact the physician, which in due course impact the entire organization.

Chapter 12: Clinical Applications   provides an overview of the clinical and diagnostic applications commonly found in a medical practice and includes a discussion of the technical nuances of supporting these applications.

Chapter 13: Administrative Applications   discusses the nonclinical applications that are critical to the business and the impact these applications have on operational efficiency.

Chapter 14: Tying It All Together with Technology   is a practical discussion of what it takes to successfully deploy technology solutions in a medical practice, taking into account technical challenges, regulatory compliance, and interactions in a healthcare environment.

Chapter 15: Selecting the Right EHR Vendor   discusses the challenges of the EHR selection process, as well as strategies for helping your client make an informed technical and business decision when selecting an EHR system.

Making It Meaningful

When working in healthcare, you will come to realize that very few practices are alike. Many practices, however, face the same struggles. Some of the struggles are based on the size of the medical practice, the number of offices, and how the entity receives their funding. To drive home these differences, we have built a few case studies that will be referenced throughout the book. Spend time becoming familiar with each scenario. The scenarios illustrate how healthcare IT is delivered differently based upon the end user. Understanding how to implement protections for a small office with a single physician is different than understanding how to secure a small hospital. To help guide those thoughts, we created three fictitious healthcare businesses, which will be used throughout the book. The entities are made up, but the scenarios and solutions are based on our experience and expertise.

Dr. Multisite   This scenario presents a single physician with three offices; one office is owned, and two are shared spaces. As an allergist, he has to have access to refrigerators at each location to house the vials for shots. The offices are open every day, but he is on premise one full day a week in the two remote locations and three days in the main office. He has nursing staff at each site. They borrow Internet connectivity from the two shared spaces, *and* he travels with the WiFi access point to save money on purchasing a second.

Middleton Pediatrics   This midsized medical practice has ten physicians, five office locations, a dated infrastructure, and a 30 percent employee turnover, and it is still on paper charts. Email access is through an internal Exchange Server running on Small Business Server. The system acts as their firewall as well. The five office locations are connected via IPSec VPN tunnels, and the server acts as their authentication machine for the workstations using Active Directory. They currently provide access to their patients using a DSL connection straight to the Internet without any security.

North Community Hospital and Clinics   The acute-care facility has 160 beds audited by the Joint Commission, and they have an emergency room (ER). They have an IT staff of 50 to support the hospital and 30 ambulatory care facilities. The facilities are located in under-served and high-crime areas. The security of the PCs in the exam rooms is questionable. The larger clinics have armed security officers. The hospital has a lab, radiology, intensive care unit (ICU), post-anesthesiology care unit (PACU), ER, and six operating rooms. They are looking to consolidate their 14 business applications into a single system, which will allow portal access to patients and community providers. Their timeline is 18 months for installation. They have no wireless infrastructure, and a third of their computers are too old to handle the new system.

We look forward to using the scenarios throughout the chapters to help you learn valuable lessons about the various ways that technology and services are delivered. We do caution that these are scenarios and should be used only as guidance when providing IT services to a similar-sized entity. We also include terms-to-know and review questions which we hope will help you gauge your understanding of the material.

How to Contact the Authors

We welcome your feedback about this book or about books you'd like to see from us in the future. You can reach us by writing to info@hitjumpstart.com. For more information, visit our website at www.hitjumpstart.com, "like" our Facebook page (HIT JumpStart), or follow us on Twitter (@hitjumpstart) or LinkedIn (HIT JumpStart).

Sybex strives to keep you supplied with the latest tools and information you need for your work. Please check the book update page at www.sybex.com/go/healthitjumpstart. We'll post additional content and updates that supplement this book should the need arise.

Chapter 1

Healthcare Ecosystem: Past, Present, and Future

You are about to embark on a journey that is more fluid and dynamic than rafting down the class 5 Kern River (recently voted the most dangerous white-water rapids in the United States). With regulatory compliance changing annually and new technologies available daily, navigating healthcare technology is a bit of a challenge. We are honored to be your guides down this class 5 river. Taking the time to pick up this book shows your commitment to learning and drastically increases your odds of success.

This chapter provides you with a solid foundation and shows where you are headed on this journey. Understanding how the healthcare ecosystem has taken shape over the centuries, today's challenges, and finally what the future holds is the goal of this chapter. As a primer to healthcare, it introduces you to the way computers are used in healthcare, the unique lingo of healthcare, government regulations that affect how our care delivery system works, and medical practices workflows.

Healthcare Primer

History is not just for liberal arts majors. Understanding how the healthcare vertical has matured from guessing about how our bodies work to mapping the human body will give you an appreciation for the advances made in the past century. These technical advances are just the beginning of what we can expect in the future with the help of knowledgeable professionals such as you. Add to this the fact that moral obligation and biblical integrity concepts permeate the fiber of the medical profession, and you will begin to understand why this brief introduction to the history and core values of modern medicine are vital to your ability to work effectively in healthcare IT.

Pre-twentieth Century Healthcare

History demonstrates that patient care has come a long way since early civilizations such as the Egyptians, all the way to the time of Napoleon and his advancement into the Russian winter with hundreds of thousands of soldiers.

Early Egyptian medicine is considered to have started circa 3,000 B.C. The Egyptians continued to advance the practice of medicine through 600 A.D. The earliest recorded physician was Hesy-Ra, an Egyptian who practiced in about 2700 B.C. and served King Dojser. Medical practices at the time were based on the flow of the Nile. The body was deemed to have channels that carried air, water, and blood throughout the body. Egyptian physicians followed washing protocols to keep themselves healthy. In a 1973 study, the British found that more than 60 percent of the pharmaceuticals given to early Egyptian patients had a positive effect.

This knowledge was transferred throughout the ages. Hippocrates (460–370 B.C.) used a lot of the Egyptian knowledge to form his work in medicine. Hippocrates believed that when a change disrupted the balance within the body, the result would be a disease. The forces that must be aligned were known as the four basic fluids, or *humors*: blood, phlegm, black bile, and yellow bile. Later, in Greece, these humors were later linked to the basic elements of air, water, fire, and earth. The early work of Hippocrates lasted until the nineteenth century when Louis Pasteur and Robert Koch found the actual methods for disease transmission and that microorganisms caused illness, not an imbalance of the four humors.

The work of Hippocrates had a lasting effect in the medical community. Each doctor today swears to a Hippocratic oath. Though over time, some U.S. states have chosen to change portions of the oath to support their law of euthanasia. The following modern version was crafted in 1964 by the former dean of the School of Medicine at Tufts University:

I swear to fulfill, to the best of my ability and judgment, this covenant:

◆ *I will respect the hard-won scientific gains of those physicians in whose steps I walk, and gladly share such knowledge as is mine with those who are to follow.*

- *I will apply, for the benefit of the sick, all measures [that] are required, avoiding those twin traps of overtreatment and therapeutic nihilism.*

- *I will remember that there is art to medicine as well as science, and that warmth, sympathy, and understanding may outweigh the surgeon's knife or the chemist's drug.*

- *I will not be ashamed to say "I know not," nor will I fail to call in my colleagues when the skills of another are needed for a patient's recovery.*

- *I will respect the privacy of my patients, for their problems are not disclosed to me that the world may know. Most especially must I tread with care in matters of life and death. If it is given to me to save a life, all thanks. But it may also be within my power to take a life; this awesome responsibility must be faced with great humbleness and awareness of my own frailty. Above all, I must not play at God.*

- *I will remember that I do not treat a fever chart, a cancerous growth, but a sick human being, whose illness may affect the person's family and economic stability. My responsibility includes these related problems, if I am to care adequately for the sick.*

- *I will prevent disease whenever I can, for prevention is preferable to cure.*

- *I will remember that I remain a member of society, with special obligations to all my fellow human beings, those sound of mind and body as well as the infirm.*

- *If I do not violate this oath, may I enjoy life and art, respected while I live and remembered with affection thereafter. May I always act so as to preserve the finest traditions of my calling and may I long experience the joy of healing those who seek my help.*

Clearly, Hippocrates had a profound impact on patient care. He spent a great deal of time making sure that doctors of his time had bedside manners. He established the Hippocratic School of Medicine and is believed to have documented 70 medical works. His legacy is found in terminology diagnosis (Hippocrates fingers), in medical schools, and across most aspects of healthcare.

Following Hippocrates a few hundred years later was Galen. He fathered the notion of thorough research through observation and investigation. He was trained in Smyma and Alexandria in Greece. Initially, he served as a physician to the gladiators. He was one of the prominent sports and royalty doctors of his time. Although his initial theories relied heavily on his understanding of the humors espoused by Hippocrates, he later spent time researching the anatomy of humans and animals. Galen documented his research for future generations. His theories and documentation of the physiology of a human lasted until William Harvey wrote *De Motu Cordis* in 1628. Galen's understanding of how the brain controls muscle movement still holds true today. Though there is a deeper understanding of exactly how this occurs, he was correct in how the brain operates.

Galen, a thorough observer, was able to track diseases and the course of symptoms. One of the diseases he tracked was the Antonine plague. This plague affected nearly 50 percent of the Roman population and caused more deaths than any other outbreak during the third century. Based on Galen's documentation of the symptoms, many believe that the Antonine plague was actually smallpox. Galen could predict whether the patient would survive based on the symptoms. His accuracy was phenomenal given the crude tools when compared to today's lab and diagnostic equipment.

Clinical and diagnostic advances faltered for many centuries. It wasn't until the 1800s that a number of technological advances were made in diagnosing patients, protecting them, and advancing the art of surgery. In 1816, prior chief physician at Salpetriere Hospital René Theophile Hyacinthe Laennec engineered the first stethoscope. To prevent sticking his ear directly to the chest of a patient being seen for heart disease, he used a tightly wound piece of paper to listen to the heart. One end of the piece of paper was held to her chest while the other end was placed near his ear. George Cammann invented the stethoscope as you know it today in 1852. It is said that the next great medical diagnostic invention was the use of X-rays for diagnostic imaging.

Around the same time, Napoleon was preparing his advance into Russia. Napoleon's army of nearly 600,000 men was vaccinated for smallpox and other known diseases. However, that would not protect them from the spread of typhus. Even though Napoleon had championed sterile medical care for his military, those precautions could not stop the spread of the plague. Just five months into the war, Napoleon was left with just 40,000 of the original army and returned to Europe. (He would later die from the disease.) His army returned to central Europe and spread the disease.

Napoleon traveled with a well-equipped medical facility. He brought the brightest and best surgeons and physicians to treat the wounded. Unfortunately, his medical staff did not understand how the disease was spreading. He had sterile areas and treatment suites but not an understanding of communicable diseases. Typhus, known as war fever, was feared even as recently as World War II. The allies used DDT (now known to cause a great number of diseases such as cancer) to delouse the habitats that the Allied forces stayed in. Now, DDT is no longer used because of its known side effects.

In the mid-1800s, John Snow first used statistical analysis to monitor communicable disease. Had he worked alongside Napoleon and his team, there might have been a different outcome for the 450,000 soldiers. Snow used statistical analysis to correlate an outbreak of cholera in London. The outbreak killed more than 340 people in just four days. When looking at the common factors among the deaths, he found that all had taken water from the same well pump. Even with the data to prove his theory, the local community would not take him seriously. To prevent additional deaths, he stole the handle to the pump on Broad Street. His work was the genesis of utilizing math in the treatment of patient care. Now, instead of using paper, we utilize databases with structured data with specialized analysis tools to look for trends. Utilizing robust, secure, and highly available computer systems to uncover medical trends can cut the time of treatment and recovery and can improve patient outcomes.

Advances in the science of medicine continued to occur throughout the century. In the mid-1800s Carl Zeiss started producing his lenses for microscopes and the study of the human body. Initially tissue was magnified and studied. Later, fluid would be examined for disease. The Zeiss Company is still in existence and continues to make lenses for medical equipment. Its latest equipment is connected to computers that are used for diagnostics.

Operating techniques also improved significantly. Probably the most important was the work done by Horace Wells, who in 1844 used nitrous oxide to dull the pain of a dental patient, himself. Horace tried utilizing nitrous oxide on a patient in neck surgery, but it failed to numb the area causing great discomfort to the patient. Dentists now had a method for reducing the pain experienced by their patients, but most other surgeons had no other practical methods to reduce their pain. John Snow, of statistical analysis fame, found that chloroform worked very well on patients. By 1853 chloroform was being used as an anesthesia for surgery and childbirth. He even administered chloroform to Queen Victoria during labor. Now mobile anesthesia carts, medication-dispensing systems, and computer-controlled airflow systems are used in operating rooms and ambulatory care settings, as well as at the local dentist's office. By the end of the nineteenth century, medical science had made vast strides, highlighted by statistical analysis for communicable disease, physicians' new capabilities to listen to a patient's heartbeat and lungs, and other areas of medical relevance. (And, of course, we are all thankful for the work done by Wells to reduce the pain of visiting a dentist.)

Advances continued through the twentieth century. The advent of X-ray technology diagnostic imaging allowed for the internals of the patient to be viewed without subjecting them to surgery. The heart valve and heart replacement were introduced. The past shows that techniques mature over time and ultimately are improved as advances in computer technology happen. There is no end in sight for the integration of techniques and technology.

Healthcare and Religion

As we mentioned earlier, moral obligation and biblical integrity concepts permeate the fiber of the medical profession. As authors, we clearly understand that science has generated a plethora of new techniques based on the inquisitive mind for discovery. Though many discoveries focus mainly on helping humans live better and longer, some scientific discoveries, such as DTD treatment for typhus or shock treatment for mental health patients, had a negative effect on human life. You should be aware that some doctors believe that the use of computers has a negative impact on patient care and therefore resist using them, because it is the doctor's oath to do no harm.

Western medicine has its origins based on the work of Hippocrates and the biblical influences and principle of "treat your neighbor as yourself." The focus on the health of the neighbor and "hurt no one" has served as the foundation for clinical care. Hospitals and shelters were created by churches and missionaries worldwide. In response to a Bible passage (Zechariah 7:10, which reads, "Do not oppress the widow, orphan, the stranger, or the poor, and do not think in your hearts of doing evil to another"), religious organizations throughout Europe founded hospitals designed to give care to refugees, shelter those who were cast out by their families (the blind, mentally challenged, visibly scarred, mentally ill), and provide care packages and medications to those who could not afford the care. Additionally, when expanding north from Mexico, the Spaniards placed missions throughout the West. To this day, a number of religious organizations have missionary arms whose sole mission is to continue that long lineage. Even the Geneva Code of Ethics includes special provisions for medical personnel and chaplains. They are not to be treated as prisoners of war but as retained personnel, which allows them to continue their professional responsibilities. This unique approach, not shared by all cultures, places high value on the protection of human life and respect of the person.

Earlier societies and even some religious groups continue to hold the belief that being sick or having an illness has a direct correlation between a behavior and punishment. This punitive thought pattern has caused religious organizations and churches to split. Establishing these unfounded relationships between an illness and failure to uphold a moral code has had many believers and nonbelievers questioning why they must bear the pain of the illness they have. Luckily, science started to connect the dots between the illness and its root cause. Although there is now an understanding of the cause of most illnesses, the moral obligations of doctors have not changed. They continue to say the Hippocratic oath and swear to do no harm. As an engineer in the field working around patients, you must be sensitive to their religious beliefs as well. As you have probably been told, religion and politics are two topics not typically brought up in the workplace. In a clinical setting, it is imperative to understand the religious underpinnings and carefully navigate that with the patient and clinician.

payer systems
A payer system is an insurance company that provides coverage to a subscriber for their clinical care. Large payer systems are Cigna, Aetna, Kaiser Permanente, and Blue Cross.

With the advent of the separation of church and state, the landscape of how healthcare was provided to the community started to change. Churches started operating clinics and larger hospital systems to support widows, orphans, and the underprivileged. To cover those who were financially able to pay and who wanted coverage, *payer systems* developed across the country. Prior to the existence of healthcare payers, patients had to seek free care or have money to pay for medical care.

History of Managed Healthcare and Healthcare Insurance

Managed healthcare started in the early 1900s. Medical insurance and managed care are intended to reduce the cost of provisioning healthcare across the population being managed. The managed care was a model created by a number of large companies. Examples of these companies include Kaiser

Permanente and the Western Clinic located in Washington State. Monthly premiums in the early 1900s were roughly $.50 to $1.50, which was nearly 2 percent of a person's income. To give you some perspective, the average worker in 1910 made $400 a year. A modern healthcare IT professional can make that in less than an eight-hour day.

In 1929, a managed care pioneer by the name of Michael Shadid began a cooperative health plan for rural farmers in Elk City, Oklahoma. The members who enrolled in his plan paid a predetermined fee and received medical care from Dr. Shadid. In the same year, the Ross-Loos Medical Group was established in Los Angeles; it provided prepaid services to county employees and employees of the city's Department of Water and Power. Its members paid a premium of $1.50 a month. In 1982, the Ross-Loos Medical Group came to be known as CIGNA Healthcare.

Blue Cross had its genesis as a local prepaid medical system for a group of roughly 2,000 teachers in Dallas, Texas. Known as Baylor Health, it also had a hospital in Dallas, Texas. Blue Cross was initially used for acute care. Not until the advent of Blue Shield was ambulatory care covered. That hospital was known as Contractors General Hospital.

In 1933, Sidney Garfield and a number of his peers began providing healthcare coverage for those workers who were building portions of the Los Angeles aqueduct. He set up the business by contracting with the insurance companies that were providing workers' compensation insurance. This allowed the insurance company to have a known cost for covering the insurance and Dr. Garfield and his associates a way to provide services to those who needed it. These services initially were only for injuries suffered while on the job. The employees were able to augment their health benefits to cover other illnesses. (In our research, it is not clear whether families were allowed to receive coverage like many workers enjoy today.)

When Henry J. Kaiser, of Kaiser Steel fame, started building the Grand Coulee Dam, he wanted to provide health benefits for his staff. Kaiser looked for help from Dr. Garfield, and they insured 6,500 steel workers and their families. Nearing the end of the dam project, after World War II, Kaiser Foundation medical plans were made available to the public at large. The foundation continues to expand to this day by providing the publicly available medical insurance and coverage at reasonable prices. By the mid-1950s, the plan had half a million members. Kaiser Foundation health plans now provide healthcare coverage for millions of American.

Over the same period, several other prepaid group insurance plans developed. The Group Health Association (GHA) in Washington, DC, a nonprofit consumer cooperative, was founded in 1937 to lower the rate of mortgage loan defaults that resulted from crippling medical expenses. Other similar organizations included the Health Insurance Plan (HIP) of Greater New York, founded in 1944 to cover city employees, and the Group Health Cooperative of Puget Sound, in Seattle, Washington, formed after World War II in 1947 by 400 families, each contributing $100.

With World War II raging in the 1940s, labor was in short supply, and the government imposed wage controls. To address the labor shortage, employers began to offer health insurance as a fringe benefit to attract the best employees. The government sought to encourage this new development, offering businesses income tax exemptions for healthcare-related expenses. This began the current trend of the employer as a health insurance supplier.

Initially, Blue Cross charged the same premium to everyone, regardless of sex, age, or preexisting conditions. This may have been because Blue Cross was a quasiprofit organization, created and run by hospitals whose focus was signing up new hospital patients. This changed as more private insurers entered the market. Profit-driven organizations revamped the way they charged their insured and began basing rates on relative risk. In this way, they were able to charge the riskiest potential customers higher rates or avoid insuring them altogether. To survive in the fluid healthcare market, Blue Cross adopted the same rating systems. In time, it lost its tax advantage, and today, it is virtually identical to most other health insurance companies.

Healthcare coverage continued to expand, and greater populations were being served. To control costs, the payer organizations started to expand and purchase smaller insurance providers. Right now, insurance carriers cannot provide the same coverage across state lines. Soon, that will be changing under the new Patient Protection and Affordable Care Act. With payers able to spread costs across larger population groups, healthcare costs are expected to drop. The act also limits the amount of profit and administrative costs for an insurance carrier to 20 percent of the premiums. How this will be audited has yet to be determined.

Patient Protection and Affordable Care Act

Sometimes referred to as Obamacare, the premise of the act is that by providing coverage for a greater number of Americans, the cost of everyone's healthcare will be reduced. When uncovered patients often seek treatment in a emergency room setting, the cost of the care skyrockets. If preventative care is given, then the costs to the system are less.

With consolidations in payers, the healthcare ecosystem must look to technology to facilitate the actuarial tables necessary for the calculations. Additionally, both payers and clinical providers have concluded that the use of information technology improves patient care and can reduce the cost of that care. Given the capabilities of electronic medical record (EMR)/electronic health record (EHR) systems, the federal government bought into the same idea. The feds even included funding for EHR systems in the recent American Recovery and Reinvestment Act of 2009 (ARRA) bill. This has spurred a lot of interest. The use of technology in healthcare dates back nearly 50 years. The next section gives you a brief history of computer use in healthcare.

Computer Use in Healthcare

The ultraconservative arena of healthcare has been slow to adopt the use of technology. Although there will always be researchers innovating and pushing the envelope, remember that it took nearly 7,000 years for medical professionals to become willing to even dissect a cadaver. However, most physicians are aware that a great number of the advances would not have been possible without computers and the researchers who program and use them. Today, even the retina can be scanned in the ophthalmologist's office without great cost to the doctor or the patient.

Homer R. Warner, one of the fathers of medical informatics, founded the Department of Medical Informatics at the University of Utah in 1968, and the American Medical Informatics Association (AMIA) has an award named after him on the application of informatics to medicine. The first known use of computers in healthcare was for a dental project led by Robert Ledley, D.D.S., at the National Bureau of Standards. In 1960, he started the National Biomedical Research Foundation (NBRF). The purpose of the foundation was to promote the use of computer technology and other electronics in biomedical research. One of the early projects to come out of NBRF was a system that analyzed chromosomes. In 1965, his team released *Atlas of Protein Sequence and Structure*. By the mid-1970s, the NBRF had developed a complete CT scanner. Dr. Ledley continues as president and director at the NBRF.

Databases and Operating Systems

Neil Pappalardo, Robert Greenes, and Curtis Marble developed the Massachusetts General Hospital Utility Multi-Programming System (MUMPS) at Massachusetts General Hospital in Boston. By the 1980s, the MUMPS operating system was the most commonly used operating system supporting clinical applications. This is also one of the only operating systems we have never used. We have seen a number of operating systems, just not MUMPS. Most applications written for MUMPS require a terminal emulator to connect to. A terminal emulator was OK in the 1970s, 1980s, and 1990s, but not anymore. The operating systems most commonly used now have a graphical interface allowing for windows, mouse controls, and other methods for communicating with the computer. Therefore, the U.S. Department of Veterans Affairs (VA) developed a graphical frontend called the Computerized Patient Record System (CPRS). The VA migrated off the MUMPS database operating system in favor of InterSystems Caché for the more recent VistA electronic medical record system.

The U.S. Department of Veterans Affairs

The VA is one of the world's largest integrated healthcare delivery systems, serving 4 million military veterans and employing nearly 200,000 employees. The veteran population is so large that it has taken nearly 25 years to develop an integrated system. To give you some perspective, the VA has 160 hospitals, 800 clinics, and approximately 130 nursing homes. The challenges are daunting, but the VA is an example of the proliferation of technology within the healthcare setting. Maintaining information about the treatment of America's heroes is a huge and important endeavor. Currently, the federal government has given providers just five years to develop a similar level of integration.

EHR and EMR
The terms are typically used interchangeably, though there is a critical difference. An EMR is the electronic medical record, which is used only by the provider delivering the services. An EHR is an electronic health record that is shared across the boundaries of the provider delivering the services.

In the 1970s, a growing number of commercial vendors began to market practice management and EMR systems. Although many products exist, only a small number of health practitioners use fully featured EHR systems.

Electronic medical records are not the only technology being implemented in the healthcare setting. EMR systems must run on some computing platform. Roughly 300 EMR packages are available in today's marketplace. Some, presumably, are shuttering the shop because they are unable to meet the regulatory compliance requirements. Others have become obsolete. The early EMR packages are simply so old that the operating system they were written on is no longer supported or in existence. Each of the major EMR vendors now write code that can be installed on IBM AIX, Oracle Solaris, HP-UX, Windows Servers, and the various Linux ports. When reviewing whether an EMR vendor is capable of delivering innovative technology, look at the underlying operating systems. Knowing which operating systems support the package provides a glimpse into the vendor's R&D budget, as well as a glimpse into your ongoing maintenance costs.

Clinical Application Platforms

clinical application platforms
Clinical application platforms are the underlying technology used in the delivery and support of health information systems and clinical applications.

Clinical application platforms are the underlying technology used in the delivery and support of health information systems and clinical applications. When implementing any technology solution, it is important to begin with a solid foundation and have the ability to build upon that foundation in the future. Healthcare providers may tell you that they want to use best-of-breed solutions or state-of-the-art technology to ensure they have the ability to deliver the best possible care to their patients. You should be aware that these solutions are not always the best solution. Make sure that the existing platform supports the solution, whether requested or proposed. If it does not, be sure that the healthcare provider understands the consequences of adopting incompatible solutions.

Real World Scenario

The Heterogeneous Hospital

In one hospital setting we work in, we have multiple operating systems, including IBM AIX, Oracle Solaris, HP-UX, and multiple versions of Windows and Linux serving different needs. The business units chose to use best-of-breed applications, with little to no analysis of the ongoing support costs. Having nine operating systems to support increases the time required to patch the operating systems, increases the possibilities of vulnerabilities because the underlying system may no longer receive patches, and increases the training costs to keep staff current.

Operationally, the Unix operating system staff must attend three training classes every other year. The Windows staff needs recurring training every few years based on Microsoft's release schedule. Staff is also limited in vacation time because of the specialization of each staff member. Outside their area of expertise, each engineer can provide only backup for common problems and cannot perform more technical upgrades.

Application upgrades are also problematic, because they require patching more than one system and ensuring that they can talk with each other. During one upgrade, staff didn't include a test case for transferring patient last names from the admitting system to the scheduling system. After upgrading, the scheduling system changed the last names of all new patient admits to "No Name." The scheduling system vendor knew of the problem but forgot to include a patch with the upgrade package. Clearly an embarrassing situation for the team, it proves that there are unanticipated costs with using different systems for each phase of delivering patient care.

The Data Storage System

The data storage system is the lifeblood of patient data. Without the data storage system, there is nothing to work and report from. Nothing will limit your career in the healthcare field faster than buying insufficient disk space. When an application fails because it ran out of disk space, you could have just killed a patient because access to information about drugs they were allergic to wasn't available to medical staff. It is therefore of utmost importance to understand the tolerance for downtime. A recent installation that we worked on required 99.9999 percent uptime and a recovery point objective of a few minutes, with a recovery time objective from the worst-case scenario of six hours. Having clear business objectives allows technical staff (such as yourself) to make the best decisions with the data you have.

Gone are the days when information was stored on internal disks or even directly attached disk storage systems. To meet the uptime and consolidation requirements, a number of organizations are consolidating on appropriately sized disk arrays attached to either a Fibre Channel fabric or an IP-based network. iSCSI disk access over a local area network (LAN) or virtual local area network (VLAN) has advantages of running on a single network architecture instead of requiring a fiber fabric and LAN network. The Fibre Channel with virtual storage area network (VSAN) access has advantages, because it is easier to maintain than a LAN and was specifically built for moving data. Whether you choose a LAN/VLAN/iSCSI or a Fibre Channel/VSAN solution, administrators must be made fully aware of the nature and sensitivity of the data, isolate the data storage, and secure it properly.

With the data storage systems becoming more and more complex, it is important to utilize as few disk vendors as possible. Some disk vendors do not support certain operating system releases, applications, or SAN network technologies. You can reduce the number and severity of implementation issues by building a supported technologies list and providing that information when the business is doing its application discovery. (This suggestion applies to all the technology utilized.)

Wireless

COWs
COWs are mobile computing platforms that move between rooms, sometimes even with the physician from exam room to exam room.

Another technology in high demand within the healthcare market is wireless. To meet the demand of consumer device sprawl by the physicians in the medical facilities, wireless is now becoming as important as the LAN connectivity for the workstations. Also, computers on wheels (COWs) become a work hazard when physically attached to a network. Draping Ethernet cables is not an option, because the cable itself becomes an occupational hazard. (You will learn more about wireless in Chapter 14, "Tying It All Together with Technology.")

With information now available at the physicians' fingertips, there is a growing demand for supporting tablets and, more specifically, for supporting Android and Apple iPad devices. Doctors and other clinicians are no longer willing to sacrifice the comfort and convenience they experience in their private lives, especially as consumer-grade systems become more powerful and robust. Think about it. Carrying a five-pound laptop through a day of rounds actually puts a significant amount of stress on the arms and upper body. Prior to recommending a device, we recommend that you walk around with it and use it while standing for the better part of a day.

Software Applications

To reduce costs, many organizations are moving away from choosing just best-of-breed line-of-business applications. The information technology departments are becoming involved in the decision earlier in the process to prevent going with technology that has no possibility of interfacing with the other production applications within the business. Most business are choosing to add modules within the current production systems to reduce the ongoing operating and support costs. Other health systems are using the promise of ARRA funding as a reason to rip out what they have and replace it with a completely new system that includes the functionality of an entire line-of-business application.

To meet the timeline demands and still keep the business operational, the production and replacement system must be up and running simultaneously. This need can create administrative nightmares, such as staff being off-site training on the new system when a production system goes down. Typically a system is phased out over a period of a year, so operating system patches will need to be applied. Make sure as you lead the change or switch-over that appropriate staffing levels are maintained and that staff is properly trained. Few businesses will allow a doubling of staff to maintain the infrastructure.

Imaging Devices and Other Diagnostic Tools

A picture archiving and communication system (PACS) is a tool used mostly by imaging departments. Within the imaging department there are a number of diagnostic tools. For imaging the brain, there are CT scanners, MRI scanners, and nuclear medicine scanners. When capturing these studies on the patient, the images are sent to the PACS. The radiologist then reviews the image and dictates or writes notes on what was uncovered. The image is then archived for later retrieval by the physician who ordered the study. Accessing the images typically via a web interface allows patients to view the image along with the doctors.

Cardiology EKGs, wound pictures, and other diagnostic images can also be sent to the PACS server. To interface with the imaging device, though, a common format was needed that included demographic information about the patient and information about what part of the body was imaged. PACS technology is advancing quickly. A recent imaging system from Agfa allows for the importation of all DICOM-compliant images, stores them in a searchable database, and allows the doctors to view the image without any specialized software.

Another imaging device is the ultrasound. The ultrasound device is the only diagnostic imaging device that doesn't use radiation. Ultrasound data is sent to the PACS system utilizing DICOM imaging as well.

As you continue your career in healthcare, you will soon realize that downtime, patches, and systems maintenance are difficult to schedule because of patient safety concerns. Upgrading workstations in an emergency room (ER) for Microsoft Windows patches is costly. The doctors, nurses, and patients do not appreciate having their computers rebooted to support the management of the system. Therefore, it is of utmost importance that systems are selected with more than just their clinical functionality. Make sure that the system has a minimal client install, preferably a zero footprint.

Healthcare IT Lingo

As more technology is embraced, each medical practice needs to rethink how they interact with their patients. Similarly, you need to understand the healthcare lingo in order to interact with the medical practice. If you take the opportunity to join HIMSS, take a look at its dictionary of common healthcare terms. HIMSS is a phenomenal resource for technical and medical jargon. Without its conscientious and consistent upgrading of its technical dictionaries, many IT professionals who would dare enter the healthcare IT market would be lost. Chapter 3 covers much of the language of healthcare. For now, make sure you understand the terms we present in this section.

Modern medicine has its roots in Latin, so if you know Latin, you should be good to go. However, because many of us never learned Latin, choose a method that is most appropriate for your learning style and learn the terminology. In Chapter 3, we will provide tricks to remember the basics. We are not trying to make you doctors, where you are able to understand every word, but having a basic vocabulary will help when communicating with the physicians and installing the EMR systems. For those who prefer to learn via audio, we recommend finding an MP3 program or visiting iTunes U. There is also a great deal of medical training available from Stanford, UCONN, University of Boston, Harvard, and many others.

Lingo is not just confined to the medical diagnosis, medication, or procedures; it includes a number of procedural and diagnostic codes that facilitate billing, clinical care, continuity of care of the patient, and public heath tracking.

Diagnostic and Procedural Codes

ICD-9 and the new ICD-10, or international classification of diseases, are the codes used when billing insurance companies and payers such as Medicare and Medicaid. The latest release known as ICD-10 is replacing ICD-9 on October 1, 2013. The new classification takes into account new procedures and diseases that are billable. Insurance companies pay based on the ICD code. If the medical practice has a poor coding method, then the practice is losing money. If you work on optimizing the billing process, the practice can increase revenue.

With the upcoming requirement to use ICD-10 on October 1, 2013, there will be an increase of nearly ten times the number of codes. With the newer codes, insurance companies will have more granularity.

Another system for tracking patient interaction is known as *Common Procedural Terminology (CPT)* codes. When seeing a patient, doctors enter their CPT codes into the EMR and EHR systems. The EMR/EHR system translates the CPT codes to ICD codes, which are necessary for completing billing transactions. Take some time to learn the major code groups and how they are broken down.

Other Healthcare IT Concepts

Just like the transition from Internet Protocol version 4 (IPv4) to IPv6, if you know the underlying reason of how and why a healthcare IT system works, you will be able to understand and serve the market.

Business Associate   A *business associate* is a third-party person or entity that must use, create, or disclose protected health information while rendering services on behalf of the healthcare provider or institution.

Clearinghouse   A *clearinghouse* is an entity that processes information received in any form from another entity and converts nonstandard data elements or transactions into standard data elements or transactions, or vice versa.

Covered Entity   A *covered entity* is a healthcare provider, health plan, or clearinghouse (insurance, EDI, or other). Kaiser Permanente or a local county hospital system are examples of a covered entity that has more than one role in the healthcare ecosystem.

De-identified Data   After an expert examines data classified as individually identifiable data and determines the likelihood that the information could be used to identify an individual is "very small" and documents and justifies that determination, the data can be classified as de-identified. *De-identified data* may *not* include name, phone number, email address, SSN or medical serial numbers, or any human features such as photo, fingerprint, or retinal scans.

Disclosure   *Disclosure* is the release of identifiable health information, regarding a patient's encounters or treatment.

Electronic Data Interchange   The automated exchange of data and documents in a standardized format is known as *electronic data interchange (EDI)*.

Electronic Data Repository   A structured data repository, typically stored in a relational database, that stores all aspects of clinical in-patient and out-patient care data is known as an *electronic data repository*. This data repository can include clinical decision support systems, order entry tracking, and medication tracking. These systems typically exist for reporting or additional functionality not found in the other line-of-business applications that have only a subset of the data.

Electronic Master Patient Index   An *electronic master patient index (eMPI)* is a database that contains a unique identifier for every patient in the enterprise.

Encounter   A visit between a patient and healthcare system provider of healthcare services to treat a medical condition or conditions is known as an *encounter*.

Formulary Coverage   The medication that is covered by the insurance company is known as *formulary coverage*. Prescribing medication not on the formulary list will increase the cost for the patient.

Informed Consent   Healthcare providers are legally required to explain the risks, protections, purpose for, and potential benefits of a particular medical procedure to a patient or their representative prior to performing any medical procedure.

Meaningful Use   The final rule released by Centers for Medicare and Medicaid Services (CMS) on July 19, 2010, specifies the minimum objectives and criteria of EMR/EHR systems used by the eligible physician prior to receiving payment from Medicare.

Medicare—Title 18   Medicare (also known as Title 18) is a federal program for the elderly (65+) and disabled, regardless of financial status.

- ◆ Part A provides insurance for hospital stays.
- ◆ Part B provides formulary coverage.
- ◆ Part D provides medication coverage through a private third party.

There is currently no Part C. Count it as a reprieve from legislation, not a screwup on the authors' part.

Medicaid—Title 19   Medicaid (also known as Title 19) refers to the federal and state programs that cover some or all of the medical costs for low-income or special-needs citizens (blind, geriatric, permanently disabled). It can also include members of families with dependent children.

Pay-for-Performance   Financial incentives for medical providers to reach certain performance metrics or benchmarks are known as pay-for-performance (P4P).

Privacy Notice   This is a companywide notice that describes how the company, practice, or covered entity will treat protected health information.

Government Regulations

HIPAA
HIPAA is a federal law that includes required and addressable security rules for medical records in the United States.

Many medical practices and the ancillary IT consulting businesses would not be focusing on healthcare technology had there not been a recent push by the federal government for EHRs and EMRs for all Americans. The market started to open up with the creation of the *Health Insurance Portability and Accountability Act (HIPAA)*. When most Americans hear HIPAA, they think privacy and security. The HIPAA security rules are only a few pages long. Those pages include a laundry list of required and addressable security rules. These regulations are broken up into three distinct categories: administrative, physical, and technical.

To fill the holes that were uncovered in the HIPAA regulation and in an effort to keep patient information private, the ARRA legislation of 2009 created a set of laws known as *Health Information Technology for Economic and Clinical Health (HITECH)*. These new regulations define how HIPAA security and privacy audits will be handled. The regulations also require that the business associates of a covered entity must follow HIPAA regulations and specify that a breach of more than 500 records requires immediate notification to the U.S. Department of Health and Human Services (HHS) and the media.

Government regulation has been a constant force since 1933 when Medicare, Medicaid, and Social Security were created and the government put its purse strings into healthcare. Medicaid provides fallback insurance for individuals in need, while Medicare is for senior citizens. Given the rising costs of healthcare, the government steps in from time to time to try to reduce the effects of large insurance companies. For you, the most recent healthcare reform and ARRA legislation is the biggest boon you will probably ever see.

HIPAA

The 1996 regulation officially known as HIPAA added regulations surrounding the protection of electronic health information, portability of care to prevent coverage lapses, and administrative simplification. In addition, it clarified an insurance option that granted tax write-offs for employers who provided portability in healthcare coverage provided to their employees. Under the *Consolidated Omnibus Budget Reconciliation Act of 1985 (COBRA)*, a person who receives healthcare through their employer and is laid off can continue to receive the same medical coverage, although they are required to pay the full premium amount themselves. HIPAA is comprised of five titles. Figure 1.1 provides an overview of each title and the provisions of that title.

Administrative, physical, and technical safeguards are the groupings outlined within HIPAA. Each group has its own set of rules and standards that can be either addressable or required.

> **Administrative Safeguards** *Administrative safeguards* are the actions, policies, and procedures a covered entity uses to manage security measures that protect electronic public health information (ePHI) and manage the conduct of the covered entity. The required safeguards are risk analysis, risk management, sanction policy, system logging and review, assigned security responsibility, workforce security, data recovery planning, disaster recovery planning, emergency mode operation, isolating healthcare clearinghouse, and incident response and reporting.

> **Addressable Safeguards** *Addressable safeguards* are authorization and supervision, termination procedures, workforce clearance, access authorization, access establishment, security awareness and training, testing and revision, and assessment of the criticality of applications and their databases.

HITECH
HITECH defines how HIPAA security and privacy audits and breaches are handled.

Figure 1.1   HIPAA titles and provisions

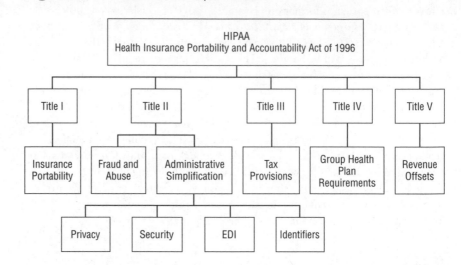

Physical Safeguards   *Physical safeguards* are the physical measures, policies, and procedures a covered entity implements to protect a covered entity's systems, related buildings, and equipment. The physical safeguards are typically seen as the least daunting to review. They include standard facility access controls, workstation use, workstation security device, and media controls. Addressable standards are contingency operations, facility security plan, access control and validation procedures, maintenance records, accountability, data backup, and storage.

Implementing physical safeguards can be complex and include monitoring user access, having audit control, and utilizing off-site storage for backup. There seems to be less covered here, but a great deal of capital is spent in this area. Do not skimp in recommendations. If you are a Certified Information Systems Security Professional (CISSP), use your background to make recommendations that can be successfully managed to completion. Physical security such as unauthorized access to a data center or the theft of drives from a data center can land you on the front page of the newspaper.

Technical Safeguards   *Technical safeguards* are the technology and policies and procedures used by the covered entity to protect electronic protected health information and control access to it.

The technical safeguards section is where technology, training, and policies can really help a business secure their data. These safeguards include access control, audit controls, integrity, person or entity authentication, mechanism to authenticate ePHI, unique user identification, emergency access procedures, and transmission security. The following are the addressable technical safeguards: automatic logoff, encryption and decryption, integrity controls, and encryption of data in motion.

Real World Scenario

Security Can Impede Adoption

Knowing what the healthcare practitioner faces in terms of regulatory compliance is crucial. Things as simple as implementing automatic logoff can reduce their productivity by a patient a day. That can be approximately $300 in lost revenue, which equates to $6,000 per month—an amount equal to the pay for one medical assistant. Armed with that knowledge, implement technologies that support your clients' workflow, not impede it.

HIPAA also requires additional operational oversight requiring a covered entity to comply with these safeguards. These requirements give the ability for a covered entity to terminate a contract with a business associate based on a data breach or failure to take reasonable steps to comply with the intent of the law. In addition, the business associate must do the following:

◆ The business associate must implement administrative, physical, and technical safeguards that reasonably and appropriately protect the confidentiality, integrity, and availability (CIA) of ePHI.

◆ The business associate must ensure that any agent of the business associate will do the same.

◆ The business associate must report to the covered entity when a breach occurs.

◆ The business associate must authorize the termination of the agreement by the covered entity if the business entity has violated a material term of the contract.

◆ The business associate must implement reasonable and appropriate policies and procedures to comply with the standards.

◆ The business associate must maintain the policies in written form, not verbal.

◆ The business associate must maintain a written record of the action, activity, or assessment.

◆ Records must be kept for six years.

◆ The document must be made available to whom the document pertains.

◆ The documents must be periodically reviewed.

HITECH

The HITECH legislation, which is part of the ARRA, adds more regulations that affect the healthcare continuum. Business associates are now required to be HIPAA compliant. The penalties for noncompliance or breaches were increased to a maximum of $1.5 million, and *protected health information* was defined. HITECH was signed into law as part of the ARRA on February 17, 2009.

HHS is now responsible for the following:

◆ Imposing penalties when violations occur because of willful neglect

◆ Conducting periodic audits of covered entities and their business associates

◆ Asking for criminal penalties now applicable

Additionally, covered entities and business associates can now be prosecuted by a state attorney general. The attorney general can step in when the resident of the state has been harmed by the criminal negligence of a covered entity or business associate. Previously, HIPAA stipulated a maximum penalty of $25,000 could be levied on the covered entity and did not carry any criminal penalties.

What other items changed? Unsecured, protected health information is now defined. Breached entity protection is provided through a safe harbor clause when the breached data is encrypted using technology approved by HHS. Predefined incident response plans are now required. Be very aware of this new provision, because it can affect the amount of quality time you spend with your friends and family.

The safe harbor statute states that if data is secured using a specified HHS technology, the breached entity is not required to report it. To be considered encrypted, the data must be unusable, unreadable, or indecipherable. To be considered encrypted, the data must be unusable, unreadable, or indecipherable. Let's repeat, for the sake of importance: protect yourself and your customers from the embarrassing act of unintentional disclosure of patient data. To claim safe harbor, the data must meet National Institute of Standards and Technology (NIST) guidelines as follows:

◆ Data in motion follows FIPS 140-2.

◆ Data at rest follows NIST SP800-111.

◆ Data to be disposed of follows NIST SP800-88.

◆ Data in use currently does not have NIST guidelines.

FIPS
FIPS stands for federal information processing standard.

In addition to breach notification, provisions defining the proper disclosure of the patient data were expanded. Patients now have the right to request an audit trail of all their public health information (PHI) disclosures. The audit trail must include the information about the data disclosed and the entities to whom their PHI was disclosed. Each patient can request this information for the past three years. The only effective way to generate this audit trail is to have access controls and logging for any business process that touches patient data.

Both the covered entity and their business associates are required to comply with audit requests.

To have an understanding of these regulations, you must first read them. We will cover audit trails in greater detail in Chapter 7, "PCI and Other Regulations." There are a significant number of nuances that if not known or addressed can cause issues at the time of an audit.

Privacy, Security, and Audit Resources

We recommend reading the seven pages of safeguards. If you have additional time, then review the privacy part of the HIPAA act, though it is roughly 30 pages.

- **U.S. Department of Health and Human Services:** www.hhs.gov

- **Federal Advisory Committee Blog:** http://healthit.hhs.gov/blog/faca

- **Combined regulation of all rules:** www.hhs.gov/ocr/privacy/hipaa/administrative/combined/index.html

---

Meaningful Use

Meaningful use is a term defined in the HITECH Act that outlines the necessary metrics that a medical provider must meet to be eligible for the distribution of ARRA funds. Although, as of this writing, meaningful use has not been completely defined, as a healthcare IT provider, you must verify that the EHR that will be deployed is certified. To give a short briefing, the following is an extract:

Stage 1   Stage 1 (2011) focuses on capturing patient visit information electronically in a coded (ICD-9, ICD-10, SNOMAS) format that allows the provider to track key clinical indicators, coordinate care across multiple providers, and generate Public Health and Quality of Care Measures (measures) reports.

Stage 2 and Stage 3   Currently the Center for Medicare and Medicaid has proposed 25 objectives/measures for EPs and 23 objectives/measures for eligible hospitals that must be met to be deemed a meaningful EHR user. The Federal Register (1852–1854) outlines the following goals for Stage 2 and 3:

Federal Register
The Federal Register is the daily publication for rules, proposed rules, and notices of the federal government.

"Our goals for the Stage 2 meaningful use criteria, consistent with other provisions of Medicare and Medicaid law, expand upon the Stage 1 criteria to 41 and encourage the use of health IT for continuous quality improvement at the point of care and the exchange of information in the most structured format possible, such as the electronic transmission of orders entered using computerized provider order entry (CPOE) and the electronic transmission of diagnostic test results (such as blood tests, microbiology, urinalysis, pathology tests, radiology, cardiac imaging, nuclear medicine tests, pulmonary function tests and other such data needed to diagnose and treat disease). Additionally we may consider applying the criteria more broadly to both the inpatient and outpatient hospital settings.

"Our goals for the Stage 3 meaningful use criteria are, consistent with other provisions of Medicare and Medicaid law, to focus on promoting improvements in quality, safety and efficiency, focusing on decision support for national high priority conditions, patient access to self management tools, access to comprehensive patient data and improving population health."

ONC
The Office of the National Coordinator for Health Information Technology is the federal entity responsible for coordinating nationwide efforts to implement and use the most advanced health information technology and the electronic exchange of health information.

Some physicians have already deployed EHR systems to meet the demands of their practices. The new government regulations have a high barrier of entry. For instance, all EHR applications must be qualified. To qualify for payments, the practice must deploy a certified solution. The Office of the National Coordinator for Health Information Technology (ONC) selected two authorized testing and certification bodies—Certification Commission for Health Information Technology (CCHIT) and the Drummond Group Inc (DGI). These organizations will have the authority to certify EHR systems based on the final meaningful use guidelines. Because of the cost of accreditation, there will surely be consolidation within the EMR/EHR space. The certification body would be strained if even half of the more than 1,200 vendors of EHR software applied for that accreditation.

This begs the question, "What do I do with a customer who has an EHR that doesn't meet meaningful use?" They are out of luck for the most part. Hospitals and larger practices that have built their own EHR can validate that they meet the required functionality.

The CCHIT website lists EHRs that were certified under the older criteria; however, that list is not definitive for the 2011 requirements. Some EHR favorites are not listed, so it is important to check the certifications frequently.

Table 1.1 lists the available meaningful use objectives necessary to meet reimbursement requirements. You can study them in greater depth at the following location:

https://www.cms.gov/EHRIncentivePrograms/30_Meaningful_Use
.asp#BOOKMARK4

Table 1.1   CCHIT Meaningful Use Objectives and Measures

Objective	Measure
Record patient demographics (sex, race, date of birth, etc.)	More than 50 percent must be in structured data.
Record vital signs	More than 50 percent must be in structured data.

Table 1.1   CCHIT Meaningful Use Objectives and Measures *(continued)*

Objective	Measure
Maintain validated current and active problem diagnoses	More than 80 percent must be in structured data.
Track active medication list	More than 80 percent must be in structured data.
Track active medication allergy list	More than 80 percent must be in structured data.
Record smoking status for patients older than 13	More than 50 percent must be in structured data.
Patient records for private practice	Provide clinical summaries to patients to more than 50 percent of all office visits within three business days.
Patients records for acute-care setting	Provide an electronic copy of hospital discharge instruction for 50 percent of all patients.
When requested, provide a patient with an electronic copy of their record	Within three business days, patients must receive their record.
Individual physicians (nonhospital) electronically prescribe medication	More than 40 percent of all prescriptions are sent electronically.
CPOE for medication order entry	More than 30 percent with at least a single medication must have their medication ordered using CPOE.
Drug-to-drug and drug-to-allergy interaction checking	Enable adverse drug and drug allergy information for the entire reporting period.
Test data interchange with at least one authorized entity	Complete at least a single EHR transaction to test this data interchange.
Implement at least one clinical decision support rule	Enable one support rule.
Conduct a security review of patient data and the security of it	Conduct a security risk and vulnerability analysis and mitigate as appropriate.
Report clinical quality measures to state or CMS	For 2011, provide written attestation of clinical quality measures. In 2012, these measures must be sent electronically.

Table 1.1 CCHIT Meaningful Use Objectives and Measures *(continued)*

Objective	Measure
Menu Set	
Implement drug formulary checks	Implement a drug formulary check system with at least one internal or external for the entire reporting period.
Incorporate lab results into the EHR	More than 40 percent of all lab results must be entered into the EHR as structured data.
Reduce patient disparities by generating reports looking for specific conditions	Generate at least one listing of a specific set of conditions.
Use EHR to identify educational resources for patients	More than 10 percent of the patients receive relevant educational resources.
Perform medication reconciliation between the different care settings	Medication reconciliation is completed for at least 50 percent of transferred patients.
Summary of care for patients to a referring provider	50 percent of the patients who are transitioned to another care provider receive a care summary.
Submit immunization information electronically	Perform at least one test submission.
Data regarding disease surveillance data to a public health system	Test at least one test data submission.
Document advance directives for patients 65 years or older	More than 50 percent of patients 65 years of age or older have either a yes or no regarding having an advanced directive.
Submit reportable lab results to a public health agency electronically	Perform at least one test of data submission.
Send reminders for preventive follow-up care	Send more than 20 percent of the patients 65 years or older or 5 years or younger appropriate reminders.
Provide a patient portal	More than 10 percent of patients within four days of the data are updated within the EHR.

To receive ARRA dispersements, the EHR chosen must be a qualified electronic health record (qEHR). The ONC will make the final rule based on feedback from the industry. So, why are doctors more willing to implement qEHR packages? The government is helping fund some of the expenses. Table 1.2 lists the payment breakdown.

Table 1.2   qEHR Payment Breakdown

Year	Payment Amount
Year 1	$15,000 (If payment year is 2011 or 2012, the amount is $18,000.)
Year 2	$12,000
Year 3	$8,000
Year 4	$4,000
Year 5	$2,000

In addition to this revenue, providers that serve in a health professional shortage area can receive a bump of 10 percent on these payments. Please remember, though, that these payments are taxable.

Providers that choose not to implement EHR will see a decrease in their Medicare fee schedule from 1 percent per year to a maximum of 5 percent. This will drive adoption of EMR in medical practices that have a high Medicare patient volume. In the industry, this is known as a high medical panel.

Barrier Profile Tool

As a trusted advisor, it is your responsibility to understand the particulars of their workflow. Without that understanding, the practice you are preparing to serve might lose a great deal of money. The particulars include staff training; communication barriers; workflow challenges, such as a single doctor with six offices; technical skill of staff; lack of standards; and a lack of HIPAA and HITECH compliance.

Each of these issues will require attention to remediate. In time, you will start to formulate and ask better questions. Document the process from start to finish in that particular office. Bring in practice management consultants who can provide additional guidance outside your area of expertise.

Understanding the workflow is so critical that a group called the Delmarva Foundation actually built a Barrier Profile tool. The organization has spent considerable time collecting the right questions to ask. Though the tool could be customized to include a scoring system, for now it will at least get the juices flowing for what needs to be covered when talking with the doctors and office staff.

Workflows in Medical Practice

Understanding the workflows and processes within the medical practice will increase the likelihood of success of both your client and your business. With your baseline knowledge of the workflow, you will be more prepared to address current challenges and identify solutions. We will spend four chapters discussing workflow (Chapters 8 through 11). For workflow scenarios that we do not cover, spend some time looking at the HIMSS site. Its documentation on ambulatory care practices is the best we have found. Depending on your focus, the customer and practice interactions may change. When studying the medical practice, pay attention to the touch points between the customer and business, between the business and its business associates, and between the provider and payer. When these interactions can be standardized or automated, that is where you'll find the biggest bang for the buck.

Let's take a look at a few of these processes.

Scheduling a New Patient

More than likely at some point you have sought the services of a doctor, and you are aware as to how they schedule appointments. For an average patient, scheduling an office visit takes about 12 minutes. In addition to coordinating schedules, information regarding new insurance is often obtained. For new patients, there are additional forms that might be mailed so that the patient doesn't have to fill them out upon arrival. For specialists, they might provide instructions to the patient about restrictions on taking medications prior to their visit.

Once the patient is scheduled, their insurance must be validated. The office staff generally completes this task prior to the patient's arrival. If there are issues with the patient's health insurance, the staff will try to resolve any problems prior to their scheduled appointment. As you can see, the process is more involved than simply asking to see the doctor at 5 p.m. on Friday.

After waiting for some period of time, the patient arrives to see the doctor. For some specialties, it could take months to get an appointment. For others, such as your general practitioner, it should be just a day or two.

An Office Visit

Here are some interesting facts about an office visit. A 15-minute office visit actually takes 72 minutes to complete. This includes a period of sitting in the waiting area, being triaged by a nurse, being visited by the doctor, then receiving discharge information from the nurse, scheduling any appropriate follow-up appointments, and finally paying any additional fees.

Upon arrival, the patient will check in with the front-office staff. The staff is already armed with the copayment amount. Because many Americans change their jobs frequently, the front-office staff will confirm that the system has the latest insurance information. If any additional paperwork needs to be completed, the patient is asked to complete these forms in the waiting area.

At this point, the staff will scan in any relevant information from previous visits, assuming this is the first time the patient has seen the doctor since the EHR implementation. The insurance card is also scanned into the system on the patient's first office visit.

Within this simple doctor's office visit, there are a number of regulations that must be considered. First, because it is a medical office, both HIPAA and HITECH must be followed. In the state of California, for example, the SB1389 privacy law must also be adhered to. If a credit card transaction occurs, more than likely PCI-DSS must be followed. Lastly, the interaction has caused FTC red flag rules. Because there is a copay amount, the medical practice is loaning the patient money until the insurance claims are paid out. This should be a simple transaction between the patient and the medical office. You can see how quickly this simple visit becomes complicated.

Often the next interaction is when the nurse will come to the waiting area and call your name. In certain confidential settings (STD clinics and anonymous testing centers), providers are not allowed to address a patient by name. Once the nurse gets your attention, they will guide you into the exam rooms and record your weight. Weight and height help the doctor calculate your body mass index, which helps them predict future health risks.

After the weigh-in, the vital signs are taken and recorded. The nurse may use a tablet or other computing device to input the data into the EHR. Once the nurse has assessed the patient's initial condition, they leave the exam room, and the patient waits for the doctor's arrival. If there are additional items to address, the nurse will take care of them prior to leaving. If the right questions are not asked or documented, the doctor will have to reexamine the patient, which only wastes valuable time.

After a period of time, the doctor enters the exam room and greets the patient. After washing his or her hands, the doctor will proceed to ask the patient questions while reviewing and tapping away at the EHR. If the EHR template for the visit is properly configured, the doctor may spend more time examining the patient than fiddling with the EHR system. If the system is relatively responsive, the doctor may also make small talk while conducting the exam. If the system is nonresponsive or acting up, the doctor's frustration with using the EHR system may be released toward either the patient or the office staff.

Once the data is collected within the EHR application, quality metrics can be calculated. For patients with chronic diseases, the medical practice can track which treatments are working and which are not. If necessary, the doctor will prescribe medications and enter this data into the system. Most modern EHR systems will then automatically send the prescription to the pharmacy of the patient's choice. Sometimes, there is a batch job that runs several times a day to push the data to the pharmacy. After a few more minutes, the doctor wraps up the appointment and leaves the exam room.

Though it appears straightforward, the previous example was for a general practitioner. If additional tests were needed, then they would have been ordered at that time. If a breathing test or perhaps a skin test in an allergy office was ordered, then the doctor would temporarily leave the exam room and return later to analyze the data and final results. If the testing systems are electronic, it is possible to directly input the data into the EHR system.

After the doctor completes the examination, the nurse reviews the notes from the doctor. They may have discharge orders to communicate with the patient and may hand out informational pamphlets that the doctor wants the patient to read. To be a complete medical record, even a pamphlet on diabetes care must be entered into the system in order to correctly document the educational component of care.

Once the nurse completes these tasks, the patient checks out at the front desk. This could entail scheduling another visit, getting directions to a lab, or making any additional payments. Now the encounter for this patient visit is complete.

Though it has taken a few pages to outline the flow of a standard office visit, please be aware that this is just general guidance. It is to give you context for the remainder of the book. Not knowing the basic workflow can impact how you would create solutions. Without a thorough understanding of the particular practice or hospital system you are working with, implementing IT for IT's sake will reduce your positive impact in the organization.

Monitoring and Diagnostic Equipment

When working around diagnostic imaging systems, it is important to understand the potential health issues. First and foremost, never enter an area without the proper training or attire. The information presented here cannot be construed as safety training. Please see your employer for their complete training. If you are not comfortable with the training you received, do not work around diagnostic equipment—particularly diagnostic imaging equipment. When serviced and used properly, safety is maintained, but the inverse is also true.

Radiation

A CT scan of the abdomen and pelvis exposes you to a radiation dose of 10mSv. This is one exposure is comparable to three years of just general radiation exposure. An X-ray of the chest is just 0.1mSv, which is comparable to ten days of exposure of natural radiation. To protect yourself from these imaging systems, it is always best to minimize the amount of time exposed to the system. Moreover, the effects of the X-ray or other radiation falls off rapidly as the distance between the diagnostic device and yourself increases. Additionally, wearing a leaded apron is a generally accepted practice for all X-ray general use. When using fluoroscopy, leaded glasses and thyroid shields are also suggested. CT scanning, fluoroscopy, interventional radiology, and nuclear medicine use the highest doses of radiation.

Currently, there are no studies that demonstrate that low-dosage radiation causes cancer. However, at moderate and higher levels of radiation, it has been shown that cancer has been induced. When radiation causes cancer, it falls into two general classes. Skin effects and hair loss is classified as deterministic radiation. A stochastic effect is cancer. For example, a patient getting high-dosage CT scans multiple times a year will generally experience deterministic radiation. However, higher dosages of radiation when used for imaging the brain or thorax might result in cancer. The jury is still out on whether low-level radiation exposure is harmful.

Magnetic Fields

Be very careful around MRI systems. Most MRI systems are never turned off because it takes roughly three hours to make them functional. Because of the strength of the magnetic field, never work or even walk around the device. The smallest amount of metal can go flying across the room. Employees who have a screw to strengthen a bone, a camera in their pocket, and even someone with a PC in their hand can see it fly across the room and attach itself to the magnet. The event would make the self-aligning iPad2 case look like child's play.

For years, diagnostic equipment did not communicate with other systems. The information from the diagnostic image, an X-ray, for example, would be studied by the radiologist. The findings from the study would be manually entered into the patient record system. In the next section, we will cover how these diagnostic systems now communicate in real time with other patient care systems. Getting the right information to the right people at the right time is what data exchange is all about.

Data Exchange

To work effectively in healthcare IT, you need to understand how data is exchanged between providers, clearinghouses, and the future Nation Health Information Network. Table 1.3 describes the standard types of data interchange.

Table 1.3   Standard Data interchange Types

Data interchange Type	Description
Flat file	Typically comma- or pipe-delineated files that are shared via email or FTP.
HL7 or Health Level 7	A common method for exchanging data between clinical systems. A clinical application has information on admits, discharges, and transfers (ADTs). The admit is a fundamental event in an acute-care facility like a hospital.
X.12	Typically used to transfer financial information.
X12N	A subset of the X12 family that focuses directly on insurance transactions.
Diagnostic Imaging and Communications in Medicine (DICOM)	A standard for storing, printing, transmitting, and archiving imaging data. It's often used in a radiology department to associate images with a particular patient. Without an ADT feed from the admitting system, the radiology tech must type in the patient demographics. Doing this can cause an increase in medical errors.
XML	An extensible markup language. This is a file format that encodes documents with tags. Very much like HTML, it allows for the developer to choose the encoding. Data can be exchanged using web service calls, Simple Object Access Protocol (SOAP), and other methods.

Spend some time reviewing the data exchange technologies that will have the greatest impact on the consulting and implementation practice your business will be building. For example, if you will not be working with a hospital or radiology practice, it may not be necessary to study the DICOM format in depth.

International Classification of Diseases Code Sets

The International Statistical Classification of Diseases and Related Health Problems (most commonly known by the abbreviation ICD) provides codes to classify diseases and a wide variety of signs, symptoms, abnormal findings, complaints, social circumstances, and external causes of injury or disease. The World Health Organization (WHO), operating under the United Nations umbrella, acts as a coordinating authority on international public health and publishes the ICD. By classifying diseases and other health problems, these codes provide a basis for compiling and tracking mortality and morbidity statistics by WHO member states.

The adoption of new code sets is required periodically. Earlier code sets might not reflect the currently diagnosable diseases or the treatments a provider might be able to give. Just as a dictionary periodically adds or removes words based on their frequency of use—words such as *Internet*, *intranet*, *email*, and others would not have been used at all when the dictionary was originally released—so the transaction and code sets are updated to reflect latest trends. For example, the last version of the ICD-9 diagnosis code set had just 13,000 codes. ICD-10 has roughly 68,000 diagnostic codes. For procedural codes, ICD-9 had 3,000, while the ICD-10-PCS has 87,000.

The administrative simplification portion of HIPAA requires that covered entities apply and use eight electronic transactions and defines the code sets to be used for those transactions. Table 1.4 lists the transactions and code set used for each transaction.

Table 1.4   Transactional Code Sets

Transaction	Code Set
Healthcare claims	X12N 837
Eligibility inquiry and response	X12N 270/271
Referral certification and authorization	X12N 278
Healthcare claim status and response	X12N 276/277
Enrollment and disenrollment in a health plan	X12N 834
Healthcare payment and remittance advice	X12N 835
Premium payments and payroll deduction	X12N 820
Coordination of benefits	X12N 837

Table 1.5 lists the diagnostic, service, and procedural code sets.

Table 1.5   Diagnostic, Service, and Procedural Code Sets

Code Set	Used For
International Classification of Diseases, 9th Edition, Clinical modification, Volumes 1 and 2	Diagnosis codes (to be replaced with ICD10-CM no later than October 1, 2013)
International Classification of Diseases, 9th Edition, Clinical modification, Volume 3	Procedure codes for inpatients (To be replaced with ICD10-PCS no later than October 1, 2013)

Table 1.5   Diagnostic, Service, and Procedural Code Sets *(continued)*

Code Set	Used for
Code on Dental Procedures and Nomenclature	Dental procedure codes
Health Care Financing Administration Common Procedure Coding System	Physician and other health services, equipment, supplies, and other items used in providing services
Current Procedural Technology, 4th edition	Physician and other healthcare services

EDI reduces the costs of doing business. It reduces the cost of having staff open, sort, scan, and store the received mail. When processing the transaction manually, a greater error for over- or underpayments can occur. Patients can even die. EDI is not meant just for the business-side transactions. Lowering costs across the care continuum was the major reason for simplifying the HIPAA administration. The lack of a common and shared code was a major obstacle, which is why government interaction was needed.

An important identifier in all of these transaction sets is the national provider ID. In the past, health plans would assign a unique identification number for each health provider. In some cases, the payer even required a different identifier for each location. Providers spent an enormous amount of dollars and time resubmitting claims because these provider IDs were unique to each payer. The nation provider identifier (NPI) is a unique ID to the provider but is not generated by a health plan. This number, as created by the government, is for use by not only the provider but all health plans and clearinghouses. An NPI is a 10-digit number with a validating check digit at the end. No information about the provider is included in the NPI. Doing so would have created an administrative burden for both providers and payers if physicians became specialists or if they changed how they practice medicine either privately or in a hospital setting. To receive an NPI, the physician applies online at https://nppes.cms.hhs.gov.

Keeping Current

This book is designed to build upon the technical foundation that you have laid for yourself over the years. To keep current, it is important to join the career- and business-enhancing organizations that specialize in healthcare. Their websites and local and national meetings bring relevant and current information to you. Take some time to add a few to your RSS feeds or bookmark them. Some of the associations require membership. HIMSS, CompTIA, and MGMA are well worth the cost.

CompTIA has a healthcare IT community that is focused on training and legislative leadership. During some meetings, we have met with senior congressional staff to discuss the value of the ARRA funding, why jobs were not being created as quickly as anticipated, and how legislators could use the power given to them by the people to meet the demands unique to healthcare.

Another excellent organization is the Healthcare Information and Management Systems Society (HIMSS). The organization has a plethora of information regarding healthcare in the United States and even overseas. The yearly conference is attended by nearly 30,000 people a year. If you are located outside the United States, look for a similar organization in your locality.

To understand how the operations side of a medical practice works, take the time to review the information at the Medical Group Management Association (MGMA). You can apply for a five-day trial membership to see whether the information is relevant to what you want to learn. This site is loaded with information about the internal operations and benchmarks for medical practices. Most office managers of large medical practices belong to this organization. Here you will get a pulse on their business challenges.

The majority of installations, as well as many healthcare devices, use operating systems from Microsoft. The Microsoft Healthcare Users Group (MS-HUG) is another excellent resource. This group focuses on operating systems, best practices, and practice management software.

Lastly, search for the county medical associations representing the counties for which you want to deliver services. You can often join as a business member and obtain access to the local doctors' directory for a fee (typically about $100). Find out how the associations communicate with their members. If the association publishes a monthly magazine or newsletter, ask the editor whether you can contribute an article.

- ◆ *Privacy and Information, Security Law Blog*: www.huntonprivacyblog.com
- ◆ *Life as a healthcare CIO*: http://geekdoctor.blogspot.com
- ◆ *Health IT Buzz*: http://healthit.hhs.gov/blog/onc

The healthcare vertical is by far the most exciting market we have ever been involved with. The constant change, the funding sources, and the unique people we meet keeps the job interesting and challenging. Over the next chapters, we will cover in greater detail the brief descriptions that we provided here. Next we will explain in greater detail the associations where a professional can get information to keep up to date on the changes, understand best practices, and possibly meet others who can be mentors as you enter this exciting space.

Terms to Know

administrative safeguards

physical safeguards

payer system

COBRA

electronic record or data
repository

encounter

meaningful use

Medicaid—Title 19

privacy notice

addressable safeguards

technical safeguards

HIPAA

electronic data interchange (EDI)

electronic master patient index
(eMPI)

informed consent

Medicare—Title 18

pay-for-performance (P4P)

Review Questions

1. Hippocrates and Galen are best known for their contributions to
   _____.

   A. Early medical practice

   B. Their contributions to Bible study

   C. Ohms law and its practical uses

   D. Socialized medicine

2. When was COBRA coverage, as we know it today, established?

   A. 1933

   B. 2010

   C. 1996

   D. 1985

3. HIPAA has how many titles?

   A. 3

   B. 4

   C. 5

   D. 6

4. What are the three types or classes of safeguards for HIPAA?

   A. Administrative, technology, physical

   B. Physical, operational, technology

   C. Administrative, technical, physical

   D. Tactical, privacy, security

5. Which of the following standards is not used in electronic data interchange?

   A. HL7

   B. FIPS-140

   C. DICOM

   D. Flat file

6. HITECH includes provisions to increase financial penalties for security breaches affecting data to what amount and criminal penalty?

   A. $25,000 maximum fine per incident, criminal penalties for negligence

   B. $1 million maximum yearly fine, only civil penalties

   C. $1 million maximum fine per incident, criminal penalties

   D. $1.5 million maximum fine per year, criminal penalties

7. Which type of diagnostic imaging equipment causes no known harm to the patient?

    A. CAT

    B. MRI

    C. Ultrasound

    D. Nuclear Med

8. Which legislation requires that business associates comply with HIPAA?

    A. HIPAA

    B. ARRA

    C. HITECH

    D. Sarbanes–Oxley

9. How many core meaningful use objectives must be met by a eligible provider?

    A. 15 core and 10 from the menu set

    B. 10 core and 15 from the menu set

    C. 15 core and 15 from the menu set

    D. 15 core and 10 from the menu set

10. What healthcare society was formed specifically for healthcare information management professionals?

    A. HIMSS

    B. CompTIA

    C. HITRUST

    D. MS-HUG

Chapter 2

Building Relationships and Continuing Education

Connecting with others is an important aspect of learning. This connection is especially important given the diverse nature of the healthcare industry. Though you can choose to go about it on your own, we strongly discourage it. To understand the regulations affecting healthcare, you would have to read more than 5,000 pages of regulations and have decades of experience in multiple industries along with a whole lot of free time to devote exclusively to studying healthcare IT. We suspect that you don't fall into this category or you wouldn't have picked up this book.

Having gone through the learning curve, we'll share some of the many resources we use to learn and keep current. We will look at just a few of the top resources where we have found the most concise and relevant information. Many of the organizations we cover in this chapter have web-based learning, face-to-face meetings (regionally or nationally), podcasts, and white papers. We hope to help you choose by pointing you to a number of associations and groups that can meet your training and professional development needs.

MGMA

If membership in any of the associations is recommended, we suggest joining the *Medical Group Management Association (MGMA)*. The information and training you will find there gets you inside the head of the medical practice manager. At a recent conference a group of panelists from top HIT VARS agree that the MGMA is one of the top memberships to have, and maintain for anyone who wants to learn HIT. The cost of the MGMA membership is on par with the cost of HIMSS. Currently, MGMA offers a five-day free trial of its membership. Setting up a membership on a trial basis allows you to view the content and make sure that the information is relevant to the areas you want to study. If the target of your training is an acute-care facility, some of the training will have less relevance. Billing practices and coding standards will be similar, but front- and back-office workflow can be very different between acute and ambulatory care. You can join the MGMA as a consultant or student.

MGMA was designed to connect medical managers with other medical managers and develop best practices. The MGMA also holds educational seminars for its members regarding regulations, industry best practices, EMR, ARRA funding, and a number of other topics. Members can participate in ongoing training online and in person. Much of its training is done locally. Attending local training puts you into the same room as one of the key decision makers in the medical practices. Whether doctors would agree, the practice managers are the glue of the organization. They keep the practice from breaking apart, and keep it pointed in the right direction. Learning side by side with those who you later will be supporting has its benefits. Asking questions of the medical practice managers will help you help them.

Training is just one benefit of membership. Online at the MGMA website, members gain access to business best practices, EMR selection guides, how to interview an IT provider, and other material. Exposure to training from the MGMA gives more than just a sneak peek into how medical practices operate. They have research on which metrics, when monitored, can take a practice from merely making ends meet to being highly profitable. Some of the metrics they suggest measuring include number of days on delinquent accounts, number of visits per doctor, productivity reports based on physician, coding reports to verify compliance with coding standards, and many others.

Yearly the MGMA hosts a convention. Not only can you use the convention to learn what medical practices are doing, it is a great opportunity for a number of reasons. Meeting with vendors who are selling into the same market can build some synergies. As with any conference, the conference organizer is always looking for presenters. Though you may not be ready for delivering the keynote address at this point, as a constant learner (as anyone in this profession is), speaking at a conference can be within reach. Document a deployment and create a case study on it.

HIMSS

The *Health Information Management System Society (HIMSS)*, www.himss.org, is a nonprofit organization based in Chicago, Illinois. Internationally, HIMSS has offices in Brussels; Washington, DC; Singapore; and Leipzig. The organization primarily focuses on IT systems and associated management systems designed to accommodate the delivery of healthcare.

HMSS was founded in 1961 on the belief that implementing healthcare was complex, with an original primary purpose "to promote the continual improvement of hospital management systems through organized programs of research, education, and professional practice." Members believed that by combining their collective expertise and experience, best practices could be uncovered. These best practices could then be shared with other member organizations, and the collective intelligence of the group would be raised, ultimately ending in better patient care and better outcomes.

Currently, HIMSS has more than 30,000 members, more than 470 corporate members, more than 85 501(c)3 nonprofit members, and 1,500 certified healthcare professionals who have passed their rigorous Certified Professional in Healthcare Information and Management Systems (CPHIMS) exam. With that breadth of membership, HIMSS is looked to for framing public policy, providing professional training and development, and providing up-to-date research for its membership to meet the vision and mission statements by improving the quality, safety, access, and cost-effectiveness of patient care. To meet the training and knowledge transfer goals of the organization, HIMSS created the Dorenfest Institute for Health Information (DIHI), an online-based training, research, report, and white-paper repository for healthcare technology information. Annually since 1998, DIHI releases reports on clinical, financial, and hospital IT.

Access to the online training and research can meet many of your needs. For those who need live interaction, HIMSS has more than 50 chapters internationally. Chapters are located regionally and are in nearly 40 states and a number of countries. Local chapters bring live training and professional networking on a quarterly basis at a minimum. With the recent regulatory changes, chapters are meeting more frequently to get information out to membership. At just $140 a year for membership, HIMSS is a tremendous bargain. We recommend skipping a lunch a month to pay for it. Student membership is just $30 a year.

HITRUST

Regulations abound in healthcare. Here is just a short list of the ones that apply to medical practices in California: HIPAA, SOX, FTC Red Flag Rules, SB 1386 (California breach law), HITECH, GLB, ISO 2700X, and PCI-DSS. Each regulation, accreditation, law, and rule has unique requirements. Whatever system you establish to meet those requirements, security should be at the core of your framework, not a passing thought after installation. Because of the complexity of security and the myriad of regulations, it has always been thought of as too big to really tackle. To reduce the number of gray hairs healthcare security professionals end up with, the *Health Information Trust Alliance (HITRUST)* converged all of them into one framework. The *Common Security Framework (CSF)* is an information security framework that harmonizes the requirements of existing standards and regulations, including federal (HIPAA, HITECH), third-party (PCI, COBIT), and government (NIST, FTC). HITRUST has a goal that "…an organization's adoption of the CSF will establish confidence in its ability to ensure the security of *[Protected Health Information] PHI*."

HITRUST is not an association in the terms of membership. It is led by industry veterans and governed by an executive council. The council is made up of industry veterans who are in the best position to lead HITRUST to the rapid adoption that it is currently receiving. HITRUST bills itself as a "collaboration with healthcare, business, technology and information security leaders." It has developed from this collaboration a CSF, which can be used no matter the size of the organization. Additionally, CSF can be used by third parties for assessments and accreditation. The CSF provides covered entities and third-party auditors with the needed structure, detail outlines, and, when necessary, clarity when trying to make security deployable in an organization.

The CSF (which is roughly 470 pages as of this writing) was created by the team at HITRUST and reviewed by its council and industry experts. Though relatively new, the CSF is starting to become an industry standard. If by chance you are being tasked with developing a security plan for any covered entity, here is the place you should best start. If you are working in conjunction with a hospital or a practitioner, the CSF is free to use. If you are a consultant, pricing for use of the CSF starts near $2,000 depending on the size of the organization. For more information, go to www.hitrustalliance.com.

MS-HUG

Much of the world's infrastructure runs on Microsoft server, networking, database, and infrastructure technologies. By bringing teams of individuals together to form a user group, Microsoft facilitates the open collaboration among the group. This ultimately improves the capabilities of the underlying technologies as best practices, research, and technology solutions are shared among group members. The *Microsoft Health Users Group (MS-HUG)*, www.mshug.org, joined forces with HIMSS in 2003 when HIMSS created an alliance program with large vendor-driven healthcare user groups. Both Microsoft and Cisco user groups are managed by HIMSS, with a careful eye to serving HIMSS's members.

The mission of MS-HUG is to "be the healthcare industry forum for exchanging ideas, promoting learning, and sharing solutions for information systems using Microsoft technologies." Members make up an international community of healthcare thought leaders and IT experts. Resources from global healthcare leaders focus on the international applicability of Microsoft solutions. Clearly, healthcare technologies cross boundaries in our global economy. As healthcare IT needs become more prevalent in the international community, MS-HUG will be right there in support of IT leaders.

Members (membership is included in the yearly membership with HIMSS) gain direct access to Microsoft resources. These resources are the cream of the crop. They are available, typically at a moment's notice, to provide system architect guidance for projects you might encounter in your future healthcare work. Online resources include a robust community of thought and technical leadership outside of Microsoft. As with any community-driven user group, it is only as strong as its members. Ultimately, MS-HUG allows any HIMSS members to share ideas on the delivery of healthcare and the implications on systems and network infrastructure. Membership at this time hovers around 5,000 technically savvy leaders with a global reach.

MS-HUG leverages its diverse membership to provide guidance on product use and development. Made up of more than just global CIOs, active participants include IT practitioners, independent software vendors (ISVs), solution providers, and other HIMSS members. With real-world experience, members can help drive reasonable standards to meet the needs of the majority of healthcare entities.

In addition to standards, Microsoft has invested heavily in training MS-HUG members. A yearly conference is held in Redmond, Washington, where industry leaders share their experiences, industry stalwarts explain possible regulatory changes, and visionaries share what they believe will happen in the short and long term. To supplement the annual conference, MS-HUG provides a number of webinars, online training sessions, and other training material.

Cisco Connected Health

Cisco partnered with HIMSS to form a community (*Connected Health*) that is dedicated to sharing best practices for better healthcare. The best practices include networking technologies, voice, converged networks, data automation, security, and a number of other areas. Given Cisco's presence in the healthcare market, this group has a lot to say and a lot of resources backing it. Once membership is approved, members gain access to the vast arm of the Cisco healthcare and technology experts. In addition to Cisco experts, the forums are littered with members who have experimented with nearly any imaginable network topology and system configuration—and most importantly, they lived to tell about it. Open and nearly uncensored information sharing is a huge plus for such a challenging market. Cisco also provides members of Connected Health with first access to training and announcements of new technologies.

Just in case interactive information sharing is not the style best suited for your learning, Cisco invests yearly in a number of intriguing white papers. The white papers are much more than another marketing brochure on why Cisco believes it is number one. The papers dive into highly technical challenges that face most infrastructure teams in healthcare. Cisco doesn't want those in charge of healthcare technology to struggle with implementing it.

During Cisco's annual Community for Connected Health Summit, attendees are exposed to new products, training, and best-practice topics. The solution sharing among peers is powerful and very useful in growing attendee knowledge and business opportunities.

To keep Cisco partners and HIMSS members trained to meet the needs of the national and international health markets, Cisco also provides ongoing training. Members receive reduced pricing to attend training events, allowing you and your organization to eclipse the competition.

With an understanding of today's reduced budgets and time commitments, Cisco has invested in online training, as well. Webinars can be delivered to desktops, notebooks, and even mobile devices. Training topics include security, network performance, selling correct solutions, and (of course) network design training. Online, you will find a vast amount of information on the www.connectedforhealth.com website. News alerts help you keep tabs on what might be impacting the healthcare ecosystem. These alerts include industry trends and impact to training. Another area of the site is dedicated to case studies. These case studies share the experiences of both customers and the installation team. You can also access the area configured for best-practice guides.

Cisco has invested a great deal of resources to make a positive impact for their partners who are looking to expand into healthcare, and those who are already doing it. When looking for technical training in the healthcare, www.connectedforhealth.com is a great place to start. Make sure you sign up for the HIMSS membership first.

CompTIA Health IT Community

The *Computer Technology and Information Association (CompTIA)* grew out of an industry need for a trade association. The initial goal of the association was to assist with the creation of part commonality. Back in the early days of computing, parts were not interchangeable between different manufacturers. If you bought an IBM computer, you were stuck with buying only IBM replacement parts. Companies such as Apple have found that controlling the manufacturing is profitable, but even Apple has common interfaces now to connect other equipment (USB, FireWire, and the like).

CompTIA is also one of the largest technical certification companies in the world. Many technologists either know of its certifications or have them. The CompTIA A+ certification is one of the most sought after certifications for professionals seeking entrance into the IT support world. Employers also use the exam as a litmus test when hiring.

Continuing with its history of supporting the industry with a certified workforce, CompTIA has invested heavily in the health IT space. As an organization, members work with CompTIA's membership and industry stalwarts such as Intel, gloStream, Ingram Micro, TechData, and others to deliver healthcare IT training to local partners and their national conventions. Bringing together industry giants allows CompTIA to bring a unique perspective to the health IT community.

CompTIA also produces an annual market research report, *Heathcare IT Market: Insights and Opportunities*. In 2010, it reported that more than half of the healthcare provider community spent more on IT hardware and services than in the previous year. Additional research uncovered that 77 percent of the doctors are constantly looking at ways to improve patient care, while just 35 percent of those are looking at implementing new IT hardware to improve patient care. Forty-three percent are looking at deploying an EMR within the next 18 months. Of the physicians looking to install EMR, up-front costs, the complexity of the EMR, and security are all major inhibitors to purchasing an EMR.

CompTIA recently brought together industry experts to develop training around the complexities of the healthcare industry. The outcome of their work was a number of documents available to members.

The *10 Week Guide to Healthcare IT* leads the reader through an educational study program on their way to being HIT savvy. Another document, *Healthcare IT: An Overview of Ambulatory Workflow*, describes the front-office, clinical, back-office, and revenue collection cycle of an ambulatory care practice. *Quick Start Guide: 7 Steps to Healthcare IT* describes how to find the niche (security, EMR deployment, hardware installation, and so on) and how to define the approach if you want to start a business, not just a career. The last four steps in the quick-start guide include finding areas for increased productivity in clinical workflow, understanding and maintaining competence regarding regulatory compliance, creating a culture of security, and finding places for continuing education. *Solution Provider Self-Assessment Tool for Healthcare* is an Excel spreadsheet that walks a VAR through a document process on assessing a medical practice.

CompTIA also understands that its market is the IT professional who is constantly on the go. To provide educational content for those professionals, CompTIA produces video training and audio training on healthcare IT, the regulatory space, and the unique characteristics of a medical practice. Included with the video content are study guides that support the learning experience.

If learning online is not the best method for your style, CompTIA holds one-day training boot camps. Each boot camp covers the training material in an interactive way. The documents used are the ones that are found listed earlier, but as adult learners, it is very effective to meet with your peers and work through use cases and scenarios. By the end of the training, the attendees walk away with the beginnings of a business plan.

To help facilitate interactions with healthcare industry expects, CompTIA holds monthly webinars. Webinar topics include selling an EMR to an ambulatory care provider, ARRA funding, HITECH compliance, and many others.

"Driven by the members and for the members" is one of the core philosophies of CompTIA. One of the methods CompTIA used to meet the goals was the creation of communities of business professionals who share similar business goals. These peer-to-peer communities meet monthly. In addition to healthcare IT, there are communities for service providers, small-business owners, managed service providers, security, and others.

 Real World Scenario

Setting Public Policy

CompTIA also has a public policy group. This group is tasked with providing feedback on proposed legislation, helping to set small-business administration goals, and even helping get legislation written. On a recent healthcare IT community call, two of the attendees were from the U.S. House of Representatives' Committee on Small Business. On the call, they asked why there wasn't the huge upswing in tech spending or healthcare jobs as expected when the ARRA funding was enacted. They proactively listened, took the concerns of the healthcare community, and reported back to the U.S. House of Representatives.

Ultimately, CompTIA will be offering a healthcare IT certification. It will be based on the training and input from industry experts. There will be strata certifications that will allow the certification holder to show their differing levels of expertise. These tests are expected to be available in 2011.

Local Communities

Nearly all counties in the United States have medical associations. If you live in a sparsely populated area, the association might serve a number of communities. Located at www.ama-assn.org/ama/pub/about-ama/our-people/the-federation-medicine/state-medical-society-websites.shtml is a list of all state medical societies. You can find regional information from many of the state sites, and you can find a list of specialties and their associate societies.

We are not aware of any national listing of local medical associations, though its creation would be very beneficial.

Some local medical associations allow vendors and consultants to become nonvoting members. The association uses corporate membership as a method for funding its organization. Depending on the membership level allowed to nonclinicians, member contact information is either included as part of the membership fee or sold at an additional cost.

Magazines are a staple for most medical associations. For example, the one in our local vicinity is called the ACCMA. The magazine is published on a monthly basis. Advertising space is available for purchase if you find that you want to build a solution that warrants marketing in the magazine.

When looking for free advertising, contact the editor and offer to write a column on technology and how it can meet the needs of the practice. Most articles are required to be vendor neutral, but an article on virtual desktops, security tools, or even outsourcing an email server are topics that practitioners would possibly find interesting. Remember that messaging is key here. Present yourself and business as a trusted advisor for healthcare IT.

Fees will vary by location for the association.

Regional Extension Centers

Over the past few years, we have spoken about healthcare IT and what a company or individual must learn to be a serious contender in this market. When describing the complexities of deploying an EHR, we use the analogy of JFK's decision to send a man to the moon and return him safely. The complexities of sending a man to the moon is on par with the installation of an EMR package and health information network (HIN). The space program, however, had an advantage. It had a singular, well-defined goal that was funded by one organization. The move to a national health network is less clearly defined, has multiple sources of funding (private, state, and federal funds), and is being pursued by multiple organizations at the local, state, and federal levels. The primary players in this are the local physicians who are being hit with a carrot-and-stick approach: Here's some money to help you get started, and by the way, if you are not done in a few years, we are going to start taking money away from you. The physicians recognize the value of the end goal—the national health network—but are faced with a myriad of decisions regarding technology and implementation that they are not prepared to make. The mandate to deploy an EHR system or face payment penalties of up to 5 percent hasn't endeared physicians to the technology.

Federal stimulus dollars created regional extension centers (RECs) to provide an unbiased partner in deploying EHRs. They are intended to ease the transition to new technology and prevent reductions in Medicare and Medicaid reimbursements, especially for those practices in underserved areas. The RECs are expected to reach out to more than 100,000 physicians. However, there are no ground rules on how they must operate, so each one is unique. Since they all are operating under the shared goal of deploying EHRs, many of them share a number of similarities. Each REC typically provides the following:

◆ Training events

◆ Guidance on selecting the right EHR funding model (ePrescribing over ARRA funding)

◆ Information on how to connect to a health information exchange (HIE)

◆ Education on how to maintain patient privacy

◆ Procedures to secure an EHR system

health information exchange
A health information exchange (HIE) is the transmission of healthcare-related data among facilities, health information organizations (HIOs), and government agencies according to national standards.

To assist in providing training for their constituents, they typically hold healthcare IT summits, trade shows, and other social events. The government hopes that these events will improve physician buy-in. By sharing how to effectively select, implement, and use EHRs to improve quality and care, the REC expects to see higher EHR adoption rates. Without the physician buy-in and deployment in EHR systems, there is a belief that the quality and value of healthcare within the United States will decline.

To reach the efficiency goals of an EHR deployment, practices will have to redesign how they provide care. Many practices will need help from seasoned EHR consultants. RECs provide the consultants or recommend consultants who can provide the detailed workflow analysis. This analysis is a time-consuming task and should be done by trained consulting staff. It is critical that each practice has its unique workflow requirements uncovered prior to deploying the product. The work of what each employee does, as well as the work they will do after the implementation, now must be documented. Once the deployment occurs, billing, care, and scheduling processes will change. In addition, if not enough information is entered into the system, the physician will not meet meaningful use objectives.

Project and implementation management is another area RECs are meant to address. The REC should be capable of providing implementation support over and above what a typical EMR vendor would be capable of doing. Providing project management and project oversight also helps the practice contain the costs of an EHR project. When selecting the vendor, the REC helps the physician choose the product based on the best product fit and lower cost of ownership. Ownership in a medical EHR is not cheap. Implementation costs, software maintenance, support contracts, and even travel expenses add up quickly during an install.

RECs are important to the healthcare IT professional for multiple reasons. First, if you are working with smaller practices, you will most likely run into the REC because the medical practice will have contacted them for support. A REC can also be an avenue for employment. Clearly, there is not enough healthcare IT professionals to serve the market. The EHR vendors are struggling to maintain staff, hospitals are facing similar issues, and consulting firms are unable to maintain deep benches of professionals. Lastly, another angle to work with the EHR is supporting its training objectives. As a healthcare IT professional, you can give talks on deploying technology in healthcare settings, speak of the challenges with building interfaces, or write articles for its newsletters.

Blogs Worth Reading

With information changing at such a rapid pace, one of the greatest publishing tools created in the past decade was the blog. Although there are many blogs, there are few great ones. Our short list is as follows:

www.huntonprivacyblog.com   The Privacy and Information Security Law Blog is written by the attorneys from the Hunton & Williams LLP law firm. They are known as one of the premier privacy law firms in the world. Lisa J. Sotto, an attorney with the firm, wrote *Privacy and Data Security Law Deskbook*. This book is worth the read and provides a foundation during the first read for healthcare IT professionals, and the more you read it, the deeper your understanding. Their breadth of coverage gives you a glimpse into laws created locally and at the state, national, and international levels. We have not found another blog that has the reach of this one and its concise information regarding privacy or information security law affecting more than just the healthcare space.

hipaahealthlaw.foxrothschild.com   The HIPAA, HITECH & HIT Blog is written by the attorneys at Fox Rothschild, LLP. As the title suggests, this blog focuses on just law that affects the healthcare vertical in the United States. Its topics include EHR, HITECH, meaningful use, HIE, security breach notifications, and identity theft. The attorneys' knowledge allows healthcare IT professionals to learn about legal topics without having to read the gory details of the legislation. The coverage of how to respond to data breaches or not passing a security audit provides important insights on building corrective action plans. The blog also has a lot of data points for those IT professionals looking to build a presentation regarding security violations or why funding security is important.

geekdoctor.blogspot.com   The Life as a Healthcare CIO blog is written by John D. Halamka, MD, who is the CIO of Harvard. The blog provides a unique view of an emergency room physician who is at the bleeding edge of technology. Following his exploits can provide a few minutes of entertainment and a great deal of insight. The IT leadership that he provides supports 3,000 doctors, 18,000 faculty, and 3 million patients. Over the course of his blog, he writes about providing secure access to clinicians using consumer-grade products, the Virtual Lifetime Electronic Record (which is part of the VA Healthcare System), and even IT governance. His blog provides the healthcare IT professional with a broad view of a practicing clinician and CIO of a large academic and clinical setting.

www.candidcio.com   The Candid CIO blog is written by Bill Weider, CIO of Ministry Health Care and Affinity Health System. The health system is located in Wisconsin. His blog posts share his experiences as a healthcare CIO. (He shares similar views with the authors regarding a number of topics. This validates our experience in healthcare with a larger organization.) In a post on November 28, 2010, he talks about the challenges that a hospital faces when trying to keep teams motivated when installing an EHR. He writes about the big picture, leadership that can motivate, and communicating the right message to the right audience.

safetynethospital.blogspot.com   Doing Common Things Uncommonly Well is written by Anna Roth, CEO at Contra Costa Regional Medical Center (CCRMC). Though one of this book's authors, Patrick Wilson, may be biased because he works with Roth, she is well respected in her field. She provides insights into how technology can improve patient care. She writes about how to look at the delivery of healthcare through the eyes of the patient, not just the employee. Roth is also a fellow at the Institute for Healthcare Improvement. The team at CCRMC has become a model hospital in how operational improvements can increase patient satisfaction, reduce costs, and provide better quality of care.

blogs.msdn.com/b/healthblog   The HealthBlog is written by Bill Crouse, MD, Microsoft's worldwide health senior director. Crouse's blog posts include titles such as "Aligning Properly Places Incentives to Improve Health and Healthcare Services" and "Connecting Care, Sharing Information Between Healthcare Providers, Patients and Families," and his writing is not full of Microsoft product marketing. His position within Microsoft exposes him to a number of issues facing the healthcare market that IT professionals can learn from.

curinghealthcare.blogspot.com   The Curing Healthcare Blog is written by Steve Beller, a clinical psychologist, researcher, and CEO of National Health Data Systems, Inc. His post "Constructing the Ultimate EHR" is a thoughtfully constructed write-up on how EHRs can improve the care received by patients. He writes about how using the best EHR will allow for data integrity checks, focusing on whole-person care (not focused on just the ailment being treated by a particular specialist), handling images of all types, building a lifetime medical record, and implementing controls for securing the exchange of patient data. In early 2010, he wrote a series of posts about how private health records could be used to best serve the customer and ultimately improve patient outcomes.

www.hl7standards.com/blog/   The HL7 Standards Blog is written by the team of professionals at Corepoint Health. Data interchange of course is a focus of the blog. The recent post on the difference between X12 and HL7 was eye-opening. As authors we always think of the details and protocols as they relate to getting workflow done. In his April 12, 2011 post, the author Christopher Stehno states what should be blatantly obvious. The difference is that HL7 transactions are used for day-to-day events that happen rapidly where the entire "story" is not necessary. This might be moving a patient from one room to another. X12, on the other hand, is meant to handle transactions that require the entire story. This story could be the insurance billing necessary for a medical practice to be paid. To complete an X12n transaction, an acknowledgment must be received prior to moving to the next transaction.

www.medgadget.com   The medGadget Blog is written by a group of doctors and biomed engineers and focuses on the latest and greatest trends. A blog post on April 15, 2011 was interesting about a sufferer of asthma. There is a GPS tracking system that traces symptoms based on location to see whether a particular area triggers a greater sensitivity in the patient. This blog posts new information almost daily. This site will give a healthcare IT professional a leg up in knowing the medical device trends. These trends can provide for future career growth because you will understand how computers, handhelds, and other digital devices are changing the way healthcare is delivered.

ehrmentor.blogspot.com   This is our site for consolidating information and ideas specifically for healthcare IT professionals.

Active participation in these groups will help you grow your knowledge in the healthcare IT space.

Blogs are always being updated and changing, and, depending on the blogs you subscribe to, can give you a view of what clinicians, industry experts, and patients are thinking.

The more you give to the community, the more you will receive in return. The need for healthcare IT professionals is staggering. Sharing in the right way will not harm you or your business. Peer groups do more than get together for beverages; they are popular because you can learn and share about real-world experiences.

Listing resources is also very dangerous. We have taken the liberty to share with you the resources, associations, and membership that have served us well when building our knowledge. A couple of the memberships are what we consider mandatory (HIMSS, MGMA), while others are nice-to-haves depending on what your ultimate focus is (VAR, employee for a practice, and so on). You will have to gauge which memberships are important for you. And our disclaimer is "Your mileage may vary."

Real World Scenario

Walking a Mile in the Patient's Shoes

Recently a colleague of ours was diagnosed with cancer. His wife, a business consultant, used blog posts as a way to communicate what they were going through and how others could help them as they went through this journey. He was able to get to the right doctors, and after aggressive treatment, he is now cancer -free. The wife writes emotionally about what she faced, as well as humorously about how life became much more complicated, and the relationships that were built.

It is important for IT professionals to understand what patients and clinicians are experiencing: the frustrations of dealing with voice recognition software, scheduling systems that were down more than they were operational, and even guest wireless access provided to the patients that allowed them to connect during long chemo treatments. Improperly deployed and tested technology can negatively impact the experience and care a patient receives. In one instance, a colleague tried to schedule an appointment, but the actual primary care physician wasn't listed as their primary doctor, so they couldn't schedule an appointment. After reaching a live operator, the operator changed the primary care doctor but had to wait until the data upload later that night before being able to schedule the appointment.

However, access to a guest wireless network allowed both the patient and his wife to work, respond to emails, watch videos, do clinical research, and even update their Facebook page. The wireless network provided freedom to the patients. No longer were they confined to the chairs and to the magazines the doctor subscribed to. That guest network was important to the quality of care.

Knowing that we are ultimately supporting the care of fellow human beings with technology is important. The way we deploy technology can make extremely painful experiences and time-consuming procedures more bearable to patients and their families.

Terms to Know

HIMSS	MGMA
HITRUST	CompTIA
regional extension center	

Review Questions

1. Which national organization would you look to when trying to understand back-office procedures?

    A. HIMSS

    B. MGMA

    C. REC

    D. HITRUST

2. The healthcare market is constantly changing. What association or society can help keep the IT staff up-to-date?

    A. HIMSS

    B. MGMA

    C. HITRUST

    D. REC

3. Medical providers have been given a team of local EMR experts to go to for help. What is the group called?

    A. HIMSS

    B. MGMA

    C. REC

    D. HITRUST

4. What alliance has developed a framework for security audits?

    A. HIMSS

    B. MGMA

    C. HITRUST

    D. REC

5. Which vendor sponsored or managed group focuses on the delivery of the medical information across multiple methods such as video, network, and voice?

    A. Cisco Connected Health

    B. MGMA

    C. HIMSS

    D. MS-HUG

6. Healthcare IT is a growing market. Which association is best set up to certify beginning healthcare IT professionals?

    A. CompTIA

    B. MGMA

    C. MS-HUG

    D. HITRUST

7. A medical specialty is hard for you to understand. What local resource would be the best to find out more about that specialty?

    A. AMA

    B. Local medical association

    C. Public health department

    D. MS-HUG

8. Which association hosts the largest IT meeting annually?

    A. REC

    B. HIMSS

    C. HITRUST

    D. MGMA

9. What resource would be used when looking for a personal view on a topic?

    A. MS-HUG

    B. Cisco Connected Health

    C. HITRUST

    D. Blog

10. Is HITRUST a common security framework based on three tiers of provider sizes?

    A. Yes

    B. No

Chapter 3

Healthcare Lingo

Language is a key method of interaction between two or more humans. Ever try to communicate with someone who doesn't speak the same language as you and remember how frustrating that was? Language barriers only complicate understanding. Healthcare professionals need fewer barriers, so we have written this chapter to expose you to the lingo of the healthcare market. We are not experts in Latin, though we did study it for fun while working at Vitria Technologies. We will expose you to the high-level Latin terms, industry terms, and other terminology used differently in the medical community. For example, in normal networking terms, IDS stands for intrusion detection system. When working in the medical field, IDS stands for integrated delivery system, which is therefore how we'll use it in this book.

Medical Terminology

English is considered to be one of the hardest languages on the planet. Many scholars believe it is the most difficult because of the number of words that sound similar or are spelled the same but have different meanings. For example, if we said the word *red*, you might hear the word *read*. The first being a color, while the second is the act of being informed through the act of reading. These are two distinct meanings of a similar sounding word. Another example is the printed word of read, and read. The first being the act of interpreting the printed word. The later being the act of reading. Even in print, there are opportunities for misunderstanding. The medical community cannot live with such inconsistencies.

Latin and Greek are used as the basis for nearly all medical terminology. The human body, human conditions, and treatments are very complex. They need a language that supports this complexity—now, as well as in the time of Hippocrates. Most terms in medical vocabulary are made of three parts: the root of the word, a prefix, and a suffix. Figure 3.1 shows the structure of medical terms. (We'll tell you more about Latin and Greek later in this chapter.)

Figure 3.1   Medical word structure

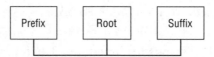

Reliance on a specific language that is clear and concise is important for accurate and effective communication. As stated earlier in the chapter, medical terminology has its roots in Latin and Greek. The human body, its conditions, and its treatments are very complex. The early physicians needed to have a language that supported this complexity, as well as one that was spoken and written during their time of discovery. Now, the terminology didn't stay stagnant over the past centauries, so the terminology is ever expanding. As new treatment, ailments, and conditions present themselves, there will be a need to add definitions to the medical terminology. For now, though, the use of Greek and Latin has provided for a solid foundation.

Medical vocabulary is typically made of three parts: the root of the word, a prefix, and a suffix. English medical terms are often built from the Latin and Greek terms. When combining a suffix and the root word, if the suffix starts with a consonant, the letter *o* is added between the suffix and root. For example, let's look at the word *nephrology*. *Nephr* is the root word, which is used when identifying the kidney. The suffix -*logy* is used to add the meaning "the study of." However, pronouncing the word *nephrlogy* would be challenging in the English language. Adding the trailing *o* to the root allows for the word *nephrology* to flow from the tongue.

The rules for modifying the prefix are easy: We are not aware of any.

There are a plethora of medical suffixes. The most common are defined in Table 3.1.

Table 3.1   Medical Suffixes

Suffix	Meaning
ian	Specialist in the study of
iatrics	Medical specialty
iatry	Medical specialty
ics	Medical specialty
ia	The exaggerated feeling of
ism	Impaired control
ac	Pertaining to the heart
ar	Pertaining to muscles
ary	Pertaining to diet
ic	Pertaining to a measurement
oid	Toxin or poison
ory	Respiratory systems

Medical language has many more suffixes, but these are the ones you will most like run into. Learning the language of healthcare will improve your ability to deliver timely IT service and help with your understanding when medical staff is trying to communicate with you.

The most common prefixes we have run into are defined in Table 3.2.

Table 3.2   Medical Prefixes

Prefix	Meaning
Ante	Before
Dextro	Right
End	Inside
Hyper	Excess
Hypo	Under
Leuk	White
Melan	Black
Mon	One
Pan	All
Pseudo	False
Sinister	Left

Now, there are plenty more of the prefixes—enough to keep a student busy for a few months learning them all. Our goal was to present the ones we most frequently run into.

Thus ends our broad overview of the lingo used within the healthcare environment. We learned much of what we know regarding the healthcare language by listening to MP3s. You might be able to learn using the same tactic. You're not becoming a doctor, so knowing every word is not essential.

You don't need to speak Greek or Latin to succeed in this vertical. But you do need to understand that the technologies used specifically in the healthcare vertical have their own lingo and that certain terminology is based on color codes.

Color Codes

color codes
Color codes alert you to dangerous situations. Knowing their meanings can save lives, including your own.

Color coding is used across many industries and used in everyday life. Red is used for stop signs, for taillights in a car, to indicate the end of the runway, and for code conditions in a hospital or ambulatory care setting. One of the most critical issues with using *color codes* is that when they are not standardized, errors can happen and cause loss of life. The Hospital Association of Southern California (HASC) was the first to take a stab at standardizing the color codes. These codes were meant to be adopted by hospitals in order to be better prepared in the event of an emergency.

In 1999, the HASC formed a security task force to come up with standardized color codes for the type of emergencies that a hospital faces during the day. You can find these codes at www.hasc.org/download.cfm?ID=29042.

- **Red** for fire
- **Blue** for adult medical emergency
- **White** for pediatric medical emergency
- **Pink** for infant abduction
- **Purple** for child abduction
- **Yellow** for bomb threat
- **Gray** for a combative person

elopement
The term *elopement* means to escape. Just like when couples run off to elope, patients have been known to run off from the hospital.

- **Green** for patient elopement
- **Silver** for a person with a weapon and/or hostage situation
- **Orange** for a hazardous material spill/release
- **Triage Internal** for internal disaster
- **Triage External** for external disaster

These codes are constantly being reviewed to make sure they are consistent with the National Incident Management System (NIMS), Hospital Incident Command System, and Joint Commission. Over the years, additional codes have been added such as green and code Triage (which of course isn't a color).

In the highly competitive healthcare market, staff is not always going to work at one particular healthcare facility for the length of their career. In fact, many hospitals must outsource some on-call nursing staff to augment their staff and deal with fluctuations in patient count. It is easy to see that using different color codes across the multiple medical systems these employees work in would cause confusion.

Prior to performing work in a medical environment as an IT professional, take the time to ask whether the codes that are in use conform to the HASC guidelines. If they don't, take the time to learn the differences. It may just save the life of a patient, fellow co-worker, or even yourself.

Real World Scenario

Heard It on the Overhead

Knowing the codes might not seem necessary for an IT professional. To give some credence to knowing the codes, we'll share an experience that happened to one of the authors in early 2011.

About five minutes into the Super Bowl (with a house full of people), the HVAC system at the hospital burst. We got the call and headed over to the facility. Upon arrival, we found a few cleaning staff using water vacuums to suck up the fluid on the floor. Until the stationary mechanics arrived, on-site medical staff called a Code Orange (a hazardous material spill/release) for that area of the hospital. Luckily, we knew what that code meant and directed other personnel away from the area until the HVAC engineers confirmed that the fluid was not harmful.

The water damaged the phone system, which took nearly four hours to return to operation. During that time, a Code Gray (a combative person) was called when a psych patient became combative. The local security staff was promptly dispatched to bring the situation to a satisfactory resolution. Even though we were recovering the phone in the area where the Code Gray was called, we continued to work on returning the phone system to normal because we would not have been able to provide capable assistance. The code was called off within five minutes.

Understanding how to respond to code alerts is important. As important is understanding the vertical lingo used when working within the healthcare environment.

Healthcare Terminology

First we'll cover the organizations in the healthcare ecosystem. Then we'll introduce terms related to the business itself or processes within a healthcare business. Finally, we'll talk about well-known acronyms that can cause confusion for IT professionals changing from one vertical to another.

Government, Private, and Nonprofit Entities

While working within the medical community, you will run into acronyms for government, private, and nonprofit entities.

American Medical Association (AMA)   The American Medical Association is the national association for physicians, medical residents, and first-year medical students. Though only approximately 20 percent of doctors are members of the association, it does represent 135,000 practicing physicians. Unfortunately, unless you become a medical student at a minimum, you cannot join.

American Nurses Association (ANA)   The American Nurses Association represents the interests of 3.2 million nurses based in the United States. Their work involves providing resources to nurses to improve clinical outcomes and supporting the migration to electronic charting. They are leading the front when pushing for nurse informatics.

Critical Access Hospital (CAH)   To be a critical access hospital, the facility must meet the following CMS requirements.

- ◆ The hospital is located in a state that has established with CMS a Medicare rural hospital flexibility program, has been designated by the state as a CAH, and is currently participating in Medicare as a rural public, nonprofit or for-profit hospital.

- ◆ The hospital was a participating hospital that ceased operation during the 10-year period from November 29, 1989 to November 29, 1999.

- ◆ The hospital is a health clinic or health center that was downsized from a hospital, is located in a rural area or is treated as rural, is located more than a 35-mile drive from any other hospital or CAH (in mountainous area the mileage is 15 miles), maintains no more than 25 inpatient beds, maintains an annual average length of stay of 96 hours per patient for acute inpatient care, and complies with all CAH Conditions of Participation, including the requirement to make available 24-hour emergency care services 7 days a week.

Additionally, a CAH can have up to 10 beds for rehab or psychiatric care.

CMS Certification Number (CCN)   A CMS certification number is the hospital identification number that is tied to their Medicare provider agreement.

Center for Disease Control and Prevention (CDC)   The Center for Disease Control and Prevention is a government entity that is part of the Department of Health and Human Services. The group's mission is to create the expertise, information, and tools that people and communities need to protect their health.

Center for Medicare and Medicaid Services (CMS)   The Center for Medicare and Medicaid Services is another government agency, though its charter is to support the Medicare and Medicaid needs of the United States. Additionally, the Office of the National Coordinator (ONC) works within the CMS organization. The ONC is responsible for the meaningful use definition, the National Health Information Network (NHIN), and the national health information technology plan.

U.S. Food and Drug Administration (FDA)   The U.S. Food and Drug Administration has been tasked with assuring the safety and security of human and veterinary medications, implants, medical devices, food supply, and radiation-emitting devices.

Federal Fiscal Year (FFY)   When our federal government creates a budget, it is done across a time period called the Federal Fiscal Year. The FFY runs from the first day in October to the last day of September. The fiscal year identifier is for the year the budget ends. So if the budget ended on September 30, 2011, the budget is identified as FFY11.

Health Information Technology Policy Committee (HITPC)   The federal government has asked for recommendations when developing policies that affect the nation's health information network. This includes data interchange, certification criteria, and other standards. The committee that heads those policy discussions and recommendations is called the Health Information Technology Policy Committee.

Health Professional Shortage Areas (HPSAs)   Health Professional Shortage Areas are geographic or demographic populations that are underserved. This could be an area where the percentage of citizens per physician is too high. Though there might be enough physicians in a community, there may be a medically underserved population (MUP) that reflects that there are not enough providers to meet the needs of a particular socioeconomic, cultural, or linguistic group.

Joint Commission on Accreditation of Healthcare Organizations (JCAHO)   JCAHO ("jay-Ko"), the former Joint Commission on Accreditation of Healthcare Organizations, is now known as the Joint Commission. The Joint Commission has accredited more than 19,000 healthcare organizations in the United States. Its goal is to improve healthcare by providing quality improvement recommendations based on their audits. At a minimum, losing Joint Commission accreditation could mean the hospital won't receive federal reimbursement for Medicare or Medicaid services rendered, but most likely an unaccredited hospital would be shut down.

Medicare Care Management Performance Demonstration (MCMP)   As part of the Medicare Prescription Drug, Improvement, and Modernization Act of 2003 (MMA), the Secretary of Health and Human Services was required to create a pay-for-performance program with physicians to meet the needs of Medicare patients by adopting health information technology. The Medicare Care Management Performance Demonstration provides a reimbursement for participating physicians who meet or exceed the guidelines of promoting continuity of care, stabilizing medical conditions, reducing adverse outcomes, and minimizing or preventing episodic chronic conditions that previously resulted in an emergency room visit or hospitalization.

National Health Information Network (NHIN)   The National Health Information Network is the ultimate goal of the EHR funding. This information interchange location will be similar to an ATM. The patient's provider can go to a computer terminal, authenticate, and then pull down the necessary information regarding the patient being seen.

Notice of Proposed Rulemaking (NPR)   A Notice of Proposed Rulemaking is used to inform the public that the federal government is looking to add, change, or remove a rule or regulation. These notices typically include a comment period when the public can voice their concerns.

Medicare Physician Quality Reporting Initiative (PQRI)   The Medicare Physician Quality Reporting Initiative is an incentive payment program for physicians who see Medicare patients. This program requires that physicians report on the quality metrics that are published yearly by CMS.

World Health Organization (WHO)   The World Health Organization provides leadership on health issues at an international level. This includes setting standards, setting evidence-based policy, and supporting countries that need assistance uncovering health trends.

Healthcare Business Processes

The following acronyms are related to the business process.

Adopt, Implement, or Upgrade (A/I/U)   This is used to indicate the adoption, implementation, or upgrade of an EHR/EMR to meet the requirements of ARRA incentive payments.

Clinical Documentation Architecture (CDA)   Clinical Documentation Architecture is a standard from the HL7 group meant to specify the encoding, semantics, and structure for exchanging clinical documents. The CDA became available in HL7 v3. This reference architecture will become more important to be familiar with as disparate EHR applications are required to exchange data.

Clinical Decision Support System (CDSS)   A clinical decision support system is an application written to help clinicians make better treatment or care plans. Clearly, physicians do not have the time to review all the clinical data available in a treatment and outcomes database. In early CDSSs, information was fed into the application, and the application outputs the next best steps for patient care. This could include care or treatment. Since clinicians have attended typically decades of college, they were not comfortable with technology dictating the next steps. Refinements to CDSSs now do more analysis on the data regarding the patient and compare their demographics, lab results, and other clinical criteria. From there the clinician can see many options for treatment or care and select the most appropriate for clinical care. The options that are not applicable to the case are removed from the system. This allows the system to constantly learn.

Continuity of Care Records (CCR)   These are documents shared across clinical boundaries to support the ongoing care of a patient. The record is typically transmitted electronically. Even if it is not sent electronically, the record contains sections on insurance, allergies, problem lists, diagnosis, patient demographics, and care plan.

Computerized Physician Order Entry (CPOE)   This is a requirement to meet the ARRA funding reimbursement. The types of orders entered by the physician include labs, radiology, pharmacy, and therapy. The idea is that physicians typically have illegible handwriting, which is a problem when the pharmacist is trying to interpret the doctor's dosing directives.

Real World Scenario

Early Editions of CPOE

A local children's hospital was going through their first installation of a CPOE system. When we spoke to an NICU physician, she stated that the hospital was expecting a 60 percent reduction of bad medication orders in just the first month of utilization. During a recent encounter with the new CIO, we found out that they are experiencing a nearly 98 percent error rate in order entry.

While there we noticed that there was a un-secured wireless network. This network was implemented to support the physicians, and the rollout of CPOE. When we noticed that the wireless was unsecured, we spent a few minutes with the physician showing her the clear-text orders going from the workstation to their clinical system. Although the hospital got the CPOE system right, they hadn't provided the appropriate security to protect the network.

About two weeks after the IT team made contact with us. The team was interested in learning how to secure the environment without being intrusive to the physicians. In the end, time was spent with their IT folks and helped them improve the security of the wireless network.

Days in Account Receivable (DAR)   Days in account receivable is a financial measurement used by a hospital to gauge cash flow. If this number goes too high, then the business is effectively providing loans to their patients.

Discharged Not Final Billed (DNFB)   This is a key indicator in how efficient the billing department is. Hospitals track and review the number of days from the patient being discharged and the final billing being coded, and this time period is called a discharged not final billed. Reducing the number of days a patient's billing sits in a DNFB improves the bottom line and cash flow of the organization.

Diagnosis-Related Group (DRG)   A diagnosis-related group is a classification system/framework that hospitals use to classify cases into one of a possible 500 or so groups. The group is based on an ICD code. The reason for the grouping is to allow hospitals and payers to understand what hospital resources, including human, medication, and supplies, are used within those groups.

ePrescribing (eRx)   ePrescribing is a national patient safety initiative meant to reduce medication errors by making eprescriptions more accessible to the population as a whole.

Fee for Service (FFS)   When a doctor or other medical staff sees a patient, it is typically based on a fee-for-service model. This means that each service provided in the visit is paid for individually. The fees, therefore, are separate and unbundled. Other payment models exist, such as pay-for-performance (P4P).

Health Information Exchange (HIE) and Health Information Network (HIN)   The ultimate goal of the surge in healthcare informatics is the end state of having a health information exchange. An HIE is a system of interconnects where information is shared across a number of entities. The goal is to have local HIE exchanges first to work out the kinks. From there, a regional HIE would share information about the patients who are most likely to be seen. Then, there will be the national HIE called the Health Information Network.

Health Level Seven (HL7)   This is a method for exchanging data about a patient in near real time. HL7 has multiple versions currently available. Most U.S. medical practices and hospital systems use HL7 v2.5 and v3.0. Earlier releases will be phased out, especially with the advent of the ARRA funding. The funding forces EHR vendors to support customers who are migrating off their dated infrastructure. Please note that migration is typically a complex endeavor. Many old HL7 interfaces must be rewritten to support the newer formats.

Intensive Care Unit (ICU)   This is an area where patients with acute trauma are being treated. This includes patients who require ventilators or breathing or feeding tubes or are in a medically induced coma. ICUs typically have more advanced types of technology than in any other patient area. Being able to monitor medication, vital signs, and other critical body functions from a central location is typically another differentiator in an ICU wing.

Integrated Delivery Network (IDN)   This is a group of ambulatory care facilities and private providers working together to provide continuity or continuum of care for a specific geographic area or market. One of the goals of an IDN is to reduce the cost of care for a particular patient population. Financial capitation, optimum use of resources, and improved patient access are all perceived benefits of a IDN.

Long-Term Care (LTC)   LTC facilities are exactly what you would perceive them to be. These are care facilities that provide medical services and, in many instances, nonmedical services for patients who have chronic illness or a disability and, therefore, cannot care for themselves. Many long-term facilities have on-site medical staff. They also typically have staff to help keep the patients bathed and assist with normal daily activities, such as taking medicine.

Medical Assistant (MA)   This is an employee who handles routine clinical and clerical tasks.

Master Person Index (MPI)   This is a database that contains a unique ID for all patients who have ever used the healthcare facility. The MPI typically includes enough demographic and personal information to validate that only one record exists for the patient. Additionally, if the MPI is extended to meet other reporting needs, it might have other core data elements such as the type of service rendered, patient disposition, and aliases they have used.

Metropolitan Statistical Area (MSA)   When you read or hear this term, think of it as a geographical region with a high population and critically close economic ties. These areas are defined by the U.S. Office of Management and Budget. The Bureau of Labor and Census Bureau utilizes the statistical areas as a way to identify statistical trends. MSAs are used by Medicare for competitive bidding.

Neonatal Intensive Care Unit (NICU)   This is an ICU for babies. Monitoring and trending are important uses of technology in the NICU. In some cases, a baby's weight gain is measured in grams, so the equipment must be able to measure and capture that data. Connecting weigh tables, vital sign monitoring devices, and other care systems to a central monitoring station allows for clinical staff to be alerted promptly of any measurement abnormalities.

Pay for Performance (P4P)   This is a payment model used where services are bundled and the medical provider is paid based on outcome, quality, and efficiency.

Physician Assistant (PA)   This is a clinician who practices medicine under the supervision of a physician or surgeon. PAs typically provide diagnosis and preventative care for patients that the doctor has asked them to handle. In some cases, such as rural clinics, a PA may be the only medical clinician in the area. In this case, they are required to confer with a physician as required by their state laws. Since doctors are becoming scarce, PAs are becoming a more prevalent fixture in the care setting.

Picture Archiving and Communication System (PACS)   Imaging systems need to have a system to share the pictures with the appropriate staff no matter their proximity to the actual imaging equipment. To meet the need, an imaging center deploys a PACS. Radiologists are one of the most costly employees in a clinical setting. To reduce the amount of time spent tracking down jackets of images, to improve diagnosis, and to reduce the amount of film storage, imaging centers rely on the features available when working with a PACS system. Also, remember that a PACS system uses the DICOM file format for transmitting imaging data.

Personal Health Record (PHR)   The PHR is a new phenomenon. A PHR is utilized by patients who want to track their own medical information outside the provider's EMR or paper-based system. For many chronic patients, they want to track their own medical information because of the number of medications, procedures, or therapies they are on or have received. Patients with hypertension, heart problems, or dialysis are good candidates for a PHR. Additionally, the patient now has the power to manage their own health information no matter their location.

Regional Health Information Organizations (RHIO)   RHIOs became a hot topic around 2005. After much effort was put into trying to define, develop, and operationalize them, only a few survived. In California, the first RHIO, CalRHIO, died in January 2010. An RHIO exists to exchange data between provider boundaries to support regionally acceptable goals while providing privacy and security of the information. For IT professionals, the three of the pillars of the RHIO (which are the most challenging to accomplish) are the security of the RHIO, the privacy of the data, and interoperability. There is a boatload of money to be made to the group that solves those problems.

Registered Nurse (RN)   This is the largest occupation within healthcare, based on statistics from the Bureau of Labor. There are roughly 2.6 million nurses servicing patients. Nearly 60 percent of RNs are hospital-based. RNs are critical in the care continuum, because they are the faces of the care setting. They are also a group that must be managed when deploying an EMR. The nursing staff typically has competing needs when charting patients' vital signs, chief complaints, problem lists, allergies, and the like. An ER nurse needs to be able to triage the information quickly with the least amount of interference from a computing platform. Typically, nurses in other areas of the hospital will be less sensitive to the amount of time it takes to enter and access data.

Real World Scenario

Knowledge of the Tools

Bear with me (Patrick Wilson) as I explain why knowing the technical tools are critical in the clinical settings.

More than a decade ago, one of my kids was born. As a parent of a newborn and enjoying (at the time) two jobs, I was not necessarily the most awake person as I attempted to change diapers for the first time. I tried to find a moist cloth to clean him, but there were only dry cloths. I rang the nurse desk and asked what I should do since I didn't have the right cloths.

Giggling on the other end, the nurse said, "Reach in front of you. See the faucet? Rotate the right handle 90 degrees and place the dry cloth under the water. That will cause the cloth to be wet."

She hung up and probably was laughing her head off with the other ladies.

You will have similar issues when you work with clinical nursing staff. You know the tools, but they might not. Be patient with them as they type, ping, or work to resolve an application problem with you. Your knowledge of the environment and tools must be translated into plain English whenever you assist the medical staff, or they will become frustrated with the technology and the staff supporting it. Keep communication clear and concise. Use terminology they understand, describe each task in detail, and explain the steps required to complete it. And lastly, make sure the phone is on mute if you are about to chuckle about the situation.

Situation, Background, Assessment, Recommendation (SBAR)
Communication is critical among professionals, no matter the vertical. To improve communication in a clinical setting, a framework called SBAR was designed. When communicating with clinical staff as an IT professional, you can use this framework to make sure all the appropriate information is reviewed. In complex situations, this can be a time-saver. The staff understands the SBAR framework, and as an IT professional, you can glean the appropriate information without having to go out on limb to discover a way to pry the information from the staff.

Real World Scenario

Systemwide Information Flow Stops

Recently, a medical system where we provide services had a systemwide PACS outage. This affected the entire emergency room workflow, interrupted the work of the radiologists, and meant that the clinical staff members who needed to review images throughout the clinics and hospital were unable to function. We got a call midmorning, and the conversation started off something like this: "What is the current situation of the down PACS machine? We need an assessment of the recovery time ASAP, and what are your recommendations for continuing workflow? Lastly, we will need to know why the [insert explicative here] system went down so it won't happen again. RIGHT!?"

The clinical staff was thinking about workflow decisions that had to be made immediately. Patients were in critical condition, and without the ability to collect and read particular radiology images, they could not be treated. The right person to read the images was at another location and was not receiving the data. Was the best option for the emergency room staff to send patients via ambulance to another hospital? This was an expensive option but one that must be made if necessary. Operationally, the clinical staff was thinking in the SBAR format. The PACS administrator and the vendor engineer were thinking in terms of "How do we fix this outage now?"and weren't providing the answers staff wanted.

We, the vendor, and our on-site systems staff worked out a communication plan where information flowed from them to us. We could then format the information in a consumable way for the clinical staff, give them an initial briefing, and provide updates every 15 minutes.

So, as we received information about the status of the system, we would translate it. Initially, the vendor and the on-site PACS administrator reported that "The system is experiencing an indexing problem. There are images in the cache queue that are not being transmitted to archive. This is causing the database to get backlogged and not transmit images for current radiology studies. Once we start the reindexing and push the log jam through, the system will be more responsive. However, the system's performance will be impacted until that occurs. Current reindexing rates are five studies per minute. There are 4,500 that are stuck. We still don't know if that will fix it, though it is our best shot."

Using the SBAR format, we reported by email to clinical staff. The message looked like this:

Situation   Images unavailable available through the PACS system.

Background   Unknown root cause, but initial troubleshooting with vendor points to a broken database used to reference images.

Assessment   Treat system as being down. We estimate the system completely operational in 15 hours based on the recovery steps. The system will be partially available during recovery. Not all studies available. Images are still correctly assigned to the right patient.

Recommendation   Work with current downtime procedures if image or study is not available. Use your best clinical judgment on patient movement.

Update frequency   15 minutes.

The email went out every 15 minutes with current information. The organization also has an operational alerts system. Updates were added there, as well.

What happened when there was no change in the update? Well, our professional communication tactic was talk with the charge nurse and head clinician. From there, when necessary, we worked out a modified update schedule. Without information flowing up to the clinical staff, the IT department's relevance diminishes tremendously in their eyes.

When we spoke with the radiologists a week after the incident, we talked about the challenges they face when a critical system goes down. First, they wanted to make it clear that IT professionals are not in the business of making life and death calls for patients on a moment's notice. Second, the clinical staff must make workflow decisions with the latest information they have. Lastly, the physicians lose respect with the IT staff when information doesn't flow. As physicians, they understand that the IT staff has to troubleshoot the system, just like the human body, but IT professionals must not become so focused on their job that they are not able to communicate their status to others. When communication gaps happen, the medical staff questions the competency of the IT team and raises those issues with the CEO of the hospital. Communication must be constant, consistent, and in a format that the medical staff can understand.

Skilled Nursing Facility (SNF)   An SNF can also be referred to as a convalescent home. This is where a patient who needs constant care, typically for the remainder of their life, will live.

Strengths, Weaknesses, Opportunities, Threats (SWOT)   SWOT is an analysis tool used by many when looking to either expand or exit a business. Healthcare facilities use a SWOT analysis to see what type of services they might be best suited to deliver. Another use is for outlining the reasons to deploy an EMR solution. A well-documented SWOT analysis will help the organization select the right application vendor and lead to a better outcome for the dollars spent.

Terms You Thought You Knew

The following terms are utilized differently in healthcare than they are in normal circles of technology.

Computer-Aided Detection/Diagnosis (CAD)   This is used extensively in the radiology imaging environment. For many of us in the computer field, the acronym CAD refers to computer-aided design. There is no designing in the healthcare vertical acronym. Even online knowledge services such as Wikipedia refer to CAD only as computer-aided design. CAD systems in the healthcare vertical are used to search images for abnormalities and bring it to the attention of the physician, surgeon, or radiologist.

Integrated Delivery System (IDS)   This is used interchangeably with an integrated delivery network (IDN). For those of us in information security, we know an IDS as an intrusion detection system.

Primary Care Physician (PCP)   This is the doctor assigned to a patient. Based on a patient's medical insurance, the PC is selected for them. In some cases, the PCP is selected by the individual. In either case, the PCP is meant to be the general practitioner who knows the patients care across all continuums. A PCP for us techies, though, refers to the priority code point, which is the priority field within an 802.1q tagged frame.

Request for Information (RFI)   This is another acronym that has mixed use in the medical and IT verticals. Both verticals use RFI to gather information about a particular technology or vendor solution. However, those in security also know it as remote file inclusion. This is a vulnerability where a file can be added to a website and then run remotely as though the server administrator wanted it to run.

Terms to Know

integrated delivery system (IDS)	computer-aided detection (CAD)
primary care physician (PCP)	Lain root words
Greek root words	color code
registered nurse (RN)	physician assistant (PA)
situation, background, assessment, recommendation (SBAR)	

Review Questions

1. What color code is used when alerting for a bomb?

   A. Yellow

   B. Blue

   C. Red

   D. Green

2. What color code is used for a person bearing a weapon?

   A. Green

   B. Black

   C. Red

   D. Gray

3. In healthcare what does the acronym IDS stand for?

   A. Intrusion Detection System

   B. Intravenous Delivery System

   C. Integrated Delivery System

   D. Incident Detection System

4. What vowel is used to combine a medical root word and a suffix?

   A. A

   B. E

   C. I

   D. O

5. What does the suffix *ology* mean?

   A. The study of

   B. To understand

   C. More than one (trilogy)

   D. To remove

6. If the root word *pod* means foot, adding the suffix *-iatry* would create a word meaning what?

   A. Surgery on the foot

   B. Removal of the foot

   C. A doctor specializing in the foot

   D. Specializing in the foot

7. An abduction of an infant or child is what color code?

    A. Blue

    B. White

    C. Green

    D. Pink

8. What languages are used for most medical terminology?

    A. Hebrew and Arabic

    B. Latin and Greek

    C. French and German

    D. English and Chinese

9. What is the best reason for having a standardized color coding system?

    A. Allows for staff to work in different settings or facilities

    B. Improves productivity

    C. Reduces mistakes

    D. All of the above

Chapter 4

HIPAA Regulations

Prior to utilizing computers, massive amounts of paperwork were transferred between the different players in the healthcare ecosystem. The Health Insurance Portability and Accountability Act of 1996 was the beginning step for putting patient information into an electronic format. Hospitals had been using computers to track patient movement, to improve patient outcomes by using diagnostic imaging hardware, and to provide decision management for people with chronic diseases. But with the number of payers and providers, something had to change in the workflow. Fraud could easily happen with providers asking for reimbursement of services not rendered. Payers could underpay providers. With the federal government being a large payer of services rendered to the public, Congress decided to reduce the administrative burden of providing and paying for services. The result was HIPAA. Without the invention of the Internet, data communications (modems), and useful practice management software running on computers, the administrative simplification requirements would not have been possible. If you're getting into the healthcare IT field now, you'll benefit from all that has been learned in the last few decades.

HIPAA Overview

HIPPA is hundreds of pages, and healthcare IT professionals should be concerned with some key items. This includes the privacy rule, which states what a *covered entity* is allowed to do with the information it collects on patients. The security rules include administrative safeguards to protect patient information by requiring the covered entity to follow certain business practices such as hiring and termination processes. The physical safeguards are meant to protect the physical building and the covered entity's physical assets. Technical safeguards utilize technology to deter unauthorized access to protected health information (PHI). A group health insurance plan with 50 or more subscribers, a healthcare professional, or a clearinghouse are regulated as covered entities. HITECH expands compliance to *business associates*—any person or other business performing activities on behalf of the covered entity that require access, use, or disclosure of protected health information. Business associates are not members of the covered entity's staff.

Given the breadth of information here, you must ask yourself how you are going to remember it all. Of course, we always remember those things that are important to us. We remember our names, our spouse's birthday, and, if married, our anniversary. The information presented in this chapter covers the meat of the HIPAA regulations that affect the confidentiality and privacy of your protected information and that of your employers. This chapter will also lay a foundation for your career in what many consider to be the hottest career for the next decade. Be patient, because there is a lot of information here. Remember, careers can be decided in just a day, though working in the health IT field typically requires a lifelong journey of learning.

Real World Scenario

Technical Knowledge Misapplied in a Medical Practice

Recently, Patrick visited a local allergist. When he arrived, he noticed that they had a wireless network that was secured with Wired Equivalent Privacy (WEP). The security used by WEP now can be broken in just a few minutes. As a patient of the practice, he was concerned about the privacy and security of his personal information. Although the technician who installed the wireless system did so successfully, the end result was a vulnerable network that could lead to protected health information being inappropriately accessed.

Continues

> When the doctor came into the room to examine him, Patrick mentioned that he was worried about the security of his patient data. He spent a few minutes explaining the different levels of security for wireless. He explained WEP, WPA, WPA-PSK, WPA2, and WPA2-PSK vs. using no wireless protection at all. On top of the technical explanation, he also reminded the doctor that a breach of protected health information can cost $25,000 or more. At that time, HITECH was not yet conceived; had it been, the fines could be up to $1.5 million and jail time. The physician quickly understood that Patrick was not trying to show his network prowess but had a desire to protect patient information (especially his own). As a business, we went on to work with their IT department to secure the wireless network.
>
> Regardless of who is responsible for managing the underlying technology, it is our responsibility as information technology professionals to help keep patient data secure. The security of the patients is important, because it has a direct correlation to the financial viability of the medical practice. We have a moral and ethical responsibility to help other IT professionals keep information secure.

The HIPAA law has many faces. Let's look at them so you are aware of their contents and what applies to your career in healthcare IT.

HIPAA Elements

A legislative package as large as HIPAA is typically broken up into more consumable chunks. The chunks are called *titles* for this legislation. Not all five titles have a direct correlation to information technology, but we will cover all of them briefly so that you have some basic information. Knowing the intricate details of Title III, Title IV, and Title V will not advance your career unless you are a contestant on *Jeopardy*.

Title I is meant to help the many Americans who are not able to obtain insurance independently through their employer. When their employment ends, those with chronic diseases or ailments are not able to as easily obtain insurance.

Title II is the most relevant piece of the legislation to your career. This part of the HIPAA legislation provides for fraud reform and administrative simplification. Yes, you read that right—the government wrote a document to provide for administrative simplification. The simplification area covers electronic data interchange, national provider indicators, privacy, and security. Before diving deep into this title, let's look at the other titles.

Title III creates allowances for certain medical insurance and made changes to the health insurance law. Tax-deferred savings accounts to cover medical expenses are identified here. Self-employed individuals can also now deduct 80 percent of the cost of their health coverage. Also, Title III provides the way companies write off company life insurance policies. Section E of this title covers state insurance pools.

Title IV provides for the application and enforcement of Group Health Plan Requirements and addresses issues found with the Consolidated Omnibus Budget Reduction Act (COBRA), which is the mechanism by which former employees can continue to carry group health insurance by paying their own premiums. Although we are not sure how allowing the carryover of insurance enables budget reconciliation, we do know that without COBRA many people who find themselves without work would not be able to obtain insurance even once they returned to a company providing a healthcare benefits package. Ex-employees cannot continue coverage indefinitely. Most insurers and businesses limit the length of time of ongoing coverage to 18 to 36 months, depending on the circumstances. As with anything in life, a COBRA plan is not free. In fact, a business has the right to extent coverage at a cost of up to 102 percent of the plan's actual cost. Though 2 percent is not a lot, it can be a great deal to those who are not employed.

COBRA generally requires that group health plans sponsored by employers with 20 or more employees in the prior year offer employees and their families the opportunity for a temporary extension of health coverage (called *continuation coverage*). In certain instances where coverage under the plan would otherwise end, such as via a layoff, termination, leave of absence, or other qualified circumstances, COBRA allows these former employees to continue their coverage.

COBRA, however, didn't provide for true portability of the insurance coverage from one carrier to another. Many insurance companies will not insure customers who have preexisting conditions such as diabetes, heart issues, and the like. The preexisting conditions could also be exempted from coverage under the new health insurance policy. The key here is that the coverage cannot lapse for longer than 63 days or more. A break in coverage nullifies the certificate of coverage.

HIPAA requires that employers give the departing employee evidence of their prior coverage. This document is known as the Certificate of Group Heal Plan Coverage and shows that there has been coverage for the preexisting condition. The new policyholder is then required to accept a credit of coverage to nullify any preexisting conditions in the policy. Although the certificate information differs from state to state, you can find many examples on the Internet. Make sure you select the correct state prior to using one of these examples in your work.

Title V covers revenue offsets. Company-owned life insurance can no longer deduct the interest on loans. Individuals who lose their U.S. citizenship must now pat taxes on the health coverage benefits they receive. There are a number of other tax-related items in this part of the legislation. Since we are not CPAs, we will leave that area alone.

Title II: Administrative Simplification and Fraud Prevention

The area affecting the information technology professional is covered in Title II, which contains the meat of the act. Table 4.1 is a snapshot of the areas that are covered.

Table 4.1   Title II, "Preventing Health Care Fraud and Abuse; Administrative Simplification; Medical Liability Reform"

Subtitle or Part	Section
Subtitle A—Fraud and Abuse Control Program	Sec. 201. Fraud and abuse control program. Sec. 202. Medicare integrity program. Sec. 203. Beneficiary incentive programs. Sec. 204. Application of certain health anti-fraud and abuse sanctions. Sec. 205. Guidance regarding application of healthcare fraud and abuse sanctions. Sections 201–205 identify the fraud and abuse controls and sanctions for committing Medicare fraud.
Subtitle B—Revisions to Current Sanctions for Fraud and Abuse	Sec. 211. Mandatory exclusion from participation in Medicare and state healthcare programs. Sec. 212. Establishment of minimum period of exclusion for certain individuals. Sec. 213. Permissive exclusion of individuals with ownership or control interest in sanctioned entities. Sec. 214. Sanctions against practitioners and persons for failure to comply with statutory obligations. Sec. 215. Intermediate sanctions for Medicare health maintenance organizations.

Table 4.1   Title II, "Preventing Health Care Fraud and Abuse; Administrative Simplification; Medical Liability Reform" *(continued)*

Subtitle or Part	Section
	Sec. 216. Additional exception to anti-kickback penalties for risk-sharing arrangements.
	Sec. 217. Criminal penalty for fraudulent disposition of assets in order to obtain Medicaid benefits.
	Sections 211–217 outline the exclusion periods for different types of individuals and entities that commit the fraud.
Subtitle C—Data Collection	Sec. 221. Establishment of the healthcare fraud and abuse data collection program.
Subtitle D—Civil Monetary Penalties	Sec. 231. Social Security act civil monetary penalties.
	Sec. 232. Penalty for false certification for home health services.
Subtitle E—Revisions to Criminal Law	Sec. 241. Definitions relating to federal healthcare offense.
	Sec. 242. Healthcare fraud.
	Sec. 243. Theft or embezzlement.
	Sec. 244. False statements.
	Sec. 245. Obstruction of criminal investigations of healthcare offenses.
	Sec. 246. Laundering of monetary instruments.
	Sec. 247. Injunctive relief relating to healthcare offenses.
	Sec. 248. Authorized investigative demand procedures.
	Sec. 249. Forfeitures for federal healthcare offenses.
	Sec. 250. Relation to ERISA authority.
	Sections 241–250 make changes to federal criminal law regarding healthcare fraud, theft, and false statements. Interfering with investigators and laundering money round of the criminal law changes.

Table 4.1   Title II, "Preventing Health Care Fraud and Abuse; Administrative Simplification; Medical Liability Reform" *(continued)*

Subtitle or Part	Section
Subtitle F—Administrative Simplification	Sec. 262. Administrative simplification.
PART C—Administrative Simplification	Sec. 1171. Definitions. Sec. 1172. General requirements for adoption of standards. Sec. 1173. Standards for information transactions and data elements Sec. 1174. Timetables for adoption of standards. Sec. 1175. Requirement. Sec. 1176. General penalty for failure to comply with HIPAA requirements. Sec. 1177. Wrongful disclosure of individually identifiable health information. Sec. 1178. Effect on state law. Sec. 1179. Processing payment transactions. Sec. 264. Recommendations with respect to privacy of certain health information.
Subtitle G—Duplication and Coordination of Medicare-Related Plans	Sec. 271. Duplication and coordination of Medicare-related plans.
Subtitle H—Patent Extension	Sec. 281. Patent extension.

One might ask why all of this legislation is necessary. When the analysis was done by the U.S. Senate, they found that nearly 31 cents of every dollar spent on healthcare was spent on administrative tasks or fraudulent reimbursements for services not rendered. With nearly 20 cents of every healthcare dollar being used to pay for administrative tasks such as insurance benefits checking and payment management, these costs are a significant part of healthcare costs that could be reduced if the tasks were automated. If administrative costs were reduced, the savings could be significant. The other 11 cents is spent on fraud or services that were rendered but not necessary. Americans spend more than a $1 trillion annually, which means more than $310 billion don't go to delivering patient care. If the $310 billion could be reduced by 10, 20, or even 30 percent, those public funds could be used to care for Medicare and Medicaid subscribers.

Both the U.S. House of Representatives and Senate directed the Department of Health and Human Services to develop national standards for healthcare transactions, electronic identifiers, national doctor provider numbers, and much more. Many of those data interchange requirements are already in place. Ultimately, these nationally identifiable code sets allow for better fraud detection, better analytics on public health outbreaks, better care for patients, and better outcomes for those seeking care. Transactions for billing can be scrutinized for fraudulent charges. Even better for the physicians, they receive payment faster.

Doctors, hospitals, and insurance businesses are not the only ones committing this fraud. During economic downturns, many people cannot afford healthcare. Being creative, families started fraudulently sharing their insurance with others. This is prevalent in community-based hospital systems and in prison systems. When a patient is seen, it is imperative that the provider properly identify who is actually receiving care. There are stories of an extended family sharing a single insurance card across 70+ family members.

Real World Scenario

Patient Fraud Causes Near Fatal Allergic Reaction

A patient recently entered a hospital setting using a insurance from another close family member. The patient's insurance had lapsed, and because of the criticality of the presenting symptoms, medical staff started taking action to save the patient's life. The cardholder's medical record was opened, and the prior medical history was pulled up. Additional information, such as the cardholder's drug allergies, was pulled as well. The family member who brought the patient to the ER did not notify the attending physician that the insurance card presented was not that of the person being treated. However, amazingly the treating physician had seen the actual insurance card holder a few weeks prior. After a thorough work-up, family history, and medication history, the physician found that a medication which they were treating the patient with would cause a drug-drug interaction that could have been fatal. The patient was thankful that the physician caught this, and was apologetic about using the wrong insurance. To prevent fraud, some health plans are starting to require positive ID of the patient when the patient is over 18. This verification doesn't help the younger populations, but is a step in the right direction.

So, how can compliance to administrative simplification directives reduce the amount of fraud? With the data being collected through clearinghouses, the workload of each physician can be tracked. Billing against patients who are deceased is typically prevented, and the services delivered to a single patient can be better managed. To get there, though, a number of healthcare management systems must be updated or replaced. The billing system and systems that exchange information electronically with the billing system must be changed. This is where we step in as healthcare IT professionals.

Even manual processes have changed. Now, prior to dispensing medication, a nurse checks each patient for the *five rights*:

- Right patient
- Right medication
- Right frequency
- Right dose
- Right method of dispensing (oral, shot, and so forth)

By going through the manual procedure of asking the patient questions, medications are given to the right patient all the time. This procedure reduces waste, improves patient care by preventing death or other symptoms caused by incorrect medication, and ultimately saves money for the payers (which ultimately should make it back in lower insurance premiums to insurance subscribers).

The HIPAA laws apply to only a select group of businesses—covered entities.

Covered Entities

Legislation seems to always apply to a group that doesn't necessarily want to be legislated. In the case of Title II of the law, those who must comply with it are referred to as *covered entities*. This piece of information is a foundational definition of knowledge for compliance.

There are three major types of businesses or entities, along with their business associates, covered by HIPAA: health plans, healthcare providers, and healthcare clearinghouses. Full definitions of these entities are provided by HHS here:

www.hhs.gov/ocr/privacy/hipaa/understanding/summary/privacysummary.pdf

Health Plans Health plans for individuals and groups that provide or pay the cost of medical care are covered entities. Included are health, dental, vision, and prescription drug insurers, as well as health maintenance organizations (HMOs), Medicare, Medicaid, Medicare+Choice and Medicare supplement insurers, and long-term care insurers.

Healthcare Providers Every healthcare provider that electronically transmits health information is covered by the HIPAA transaction rule.

Healthcare Clearinghouses Clearinghouses are businesses that convert nonstandard data sets to standard data sets, or vice versa. Companies typically included in this type of service include billing services or community health management information systems. Other businesses are covered, though there are too many to list here.

Business Associates   A business associate is a person or organization that is not part of a covered entity's workforce that performs certain functions that involve the use or disclosure of individually identifiable health information. Business associate services to a covered entity are limited to legal, actuarial, accounting, consulting, data aggregation, management, administrative, accreditation, or financial services.

Any covered entity that uses a business associate to perform services covered under the law must have a written contract that covers the work being done by the business associate. The covered entity must require certain safeguards to protect the PHI used by the business associate. Additionally, the agreement requires safeguards on the individually identifiable health information used or disclosed by its business associates. Moreover, a covered entity may not contractually authorize its business associate to make any use or disclosure of protected health information that would violate the rule. Covered entities that have an existing written contract or agreement with business associates prior to October 15, 2002, which was not renewed or modified prior to April 14, 2003, were permitted to continue to operate under that contract until they renew the contract or April 14, 2004, whichever came first. You can view sample contracts at www.hhs.gov/ocr/hipaa/contractprov.html.

Figure 4.1 is a graphical representation of the decision tree that can help you see whether the business you are working with or for is a covered entity.

Figure 4.1   Covered Entity

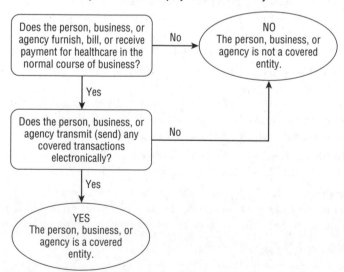

Privacy Rule

Given that information is now required to be sent electronically to receive payment, Congress added language to make sure that the information would be kept private. Maintaining privacy is one of the biggest challenges of healthcare security teams. The privacy rule, which was finalized after receiving 52,000+ comments, was released on December 28, 2000. Call it a belated Christmas present. The rule went into effect April 14, 2003 (for smaller plans, 2004), and all covered entities must comply. In response to public feedback, there was another round of modifications to the privacy rule in March 2002. The *final* regulations were released on August 14, 2002. These rules are part of 45 CFR Part 160 and Part 164.

These rules set standards that are meant to address how individually identified health information is used, stored, and released (disclosed) by covered entities. Further into the privacy rule, this individually identifiable health information is called *protected health information*. Business associates are covered under the privacy rules. The agreements between covered entities and their business associates must clearly delineate what the business associate is allowed to do with the information and what process will be followed when the information is lost, stolen, or no longer needed. The privacy rule refers to individually identifiable health information transmitted by a covered entity in any form as PHI. Protected health information is actually more easily understood when you know the definition of de-identified data.

De-identified Data

To support the needs of public health organizations, there was a need to identify what constituted de-identified data. De-identified data must not include names, phone numbers, dates related to an individual, phone numbers, fax numbers, email or web addresses, license or passport numbers, device identifiers on equipment, SSN or Medical record numbers, IP numbers, pictures, visit information, or any human features such as photos, fingerprints, retinal scans, or any other individually identifiable information.

Although the information is protected, there are times when it might make sense to disclose patient information to others. These disclosures happen in the course of doing business. Information may be disclosed to the patient, disclosed to facilitate payment for services, disclosed to provide an opportunity to agree or object to a course of treatment, or disclosed to allow treatment of the patient. Disclosure for the public interest and the release of a limited data set for the purposes of research also is allowed.

Prior to issuing the privacy rule required by HIPAA, state law was the only way to legally provide protection for PHI. Now that there is a national standard, it is much easier for businesses to work across state lines. Inside the

Health and Human Services division of the federal government, the Office for Civil Rights (OCR) is responsible and accountable for implementing and enforcing the privacy rule. The OCR receives and responds to privacy complaints and enforces civil fines if the covered entity fails to comply with the privacy rule.

The goal is to protect individually identifiable information—securely protect it from anyone without a need to know. Protection must be provided whether information is in the form of data that is stored electronically, the spoken word, in written records, or in any other form (skywriting, we guess). Securing data to the point that the provider is unable to access it to provide care is not the intent of this rule, but insurance companies should receive what is necessary to pay the insurance claim and nothing more unless prescribed by law.

Today, there are now more hands on an individual record than ever before. Years ago when a patient would visit the doctor, only four or five people would access the record. The record would be handled by the front-office staff, the intake nurse, the doctor, possibly the checkout staff, and the billing staff. Now, a patient cannot be guaranteed that their information is viewed only by the office staff and doctor. Information is likely to change hands many times and often is moved from the practice to an outside billing firm, insurance clearinghouses, research facilities, and other third parties.

Additional security controls to meet the privacy concern of doctors who treat highly sensitive diseases, cancer, and maliciously stereotyped illnesses are always recommended. In these settings for patient care, additional precautions must be taken so that the name of a patient suffering from cancer, HIV, or other sometimes-embarrassing conditions or diseases is kept safe. Inappropriate release of this type of information could harm a patient's career, increase insurance rates, and be embarrassing for their family. Although all protected health information needs to remain private, this type of data is particularly sensitive; as an IT professional, take the time to secure these systems and the data.

We recommend full disk encryption for the drive or drives in the workstations and servers. The password should be greater than 16 characters since anything less is cracked within a few hours with the right tools. Additionally, we do not recommend wireless networks for these settings. Wireless adds an additional entry point from physical spaces that the covered entity doesn't control—like the parking lot. Backups of the servers and workstations (if applicable) should be encrypted. This is a strong *should*. The simplicity of encrypting the tapes can prevent you from ruining someone's life and identity. Lastly, we suggest that the server be in a physically secure location with limited access and that each entry to the server location be documented. Sometimes this is impractical; however, these measures are strongly recommended (for a reduced likelihood of lawsuits).

Under the privacy rule, the covered entity is allowed to use or disclose PHI for payment, care coordination, treatment of the patient, and other healthcare operations activity, such as case management and patient outcome quality indicators. Healthcare operations are far-reaching because the data can be used for business planning (adding a surgery center to reduce costs), fund-raising for the hospital or clinic, facilitating medical review audits, and credentialing (certain credentialing bodies require that a number of procedures or cases be handled by a provider to keep their credential or licensing). However, before doing certain activities or data mining with someone's PHI, the hospital or clinical practice must ask for the right to use the data in such a manner. A covered entity must obtain the written authorization for the use of the patient's information if that information is going to be used for anything other than treatment, payment collection, or healthcare operations. Additionally, a patient cannot be denied treatment for not waiving their right to privacy for the allowed areas. Hence, a patient seeking a kidney transplant can't be denied the treatment just because they will not authorize the use of their information for marketing purposes that benefit the hospital.

The written authorization is called a *privacy notice* or *privacy practices notice*. Each covered entity is required to distribute and have patients sign these notices that outline the reasons the patient's information would be disclosed to a third party. How the organization protects the patient's PHI, how changes to the notice will be communicated, and how the covered entity will comply with the provisions of the privacy practices must all be included in the notice. If the covered entity fails to maintain the privacy of the patient or uses the information for other means, the patient must be notified of how to bring about a complaint. A person associated with the covered entity must be named, and contact information for the OCR must be provided.

So, you might wonder who a patient would contact with their complaint. The privacy rule requires that every covered entity have a named privacy officer. This individual is responsible for responding to, remediating, and managing the complaints. The privacy officer is also responsible for maintaining and documenting the privacy notices for the covered entity. Typically the privacy officer is also responsible for training the employees on their responsibilities for protecting patient information. In larger workforces, the privacy officer typically has a team or a computer-based training system to train and track compliance to workforce training.

privacy officer
This individual is responsible for responding to, remediating, and managing PHI privacy complaints.

To reduce the amount of data that is constantly shared across business units within an organization or from covered entities to business associates, the entity where the data originated must share only the minimum necessary. This is accomplished by having policies in place to reduce the amount of data disclosed and to periodically review the data being disclosed. Only in rare circumstances, such as a patient changing physicians, can a covered entity ask for an entire medical record.

Fines are used to ensure compliance. Covered entities that fail to comply with their published privacy notices can incur fines that range from $100 per violation up to a maximum yearly fine of $25,000. The Office of Civil Rights has the option to refrain from levying a fine when the practice did not cause the violation by willful neglect or lack of due diligence and the covered entity remediated the issue within 30 days of notification of the violation.

On top of the civil fines, there are also criminal penalties associated when a covered entity or person knowingly discloses PHI in violation of the HIPAA rules. For these violations, the fine is $50,000, and a one-year prison sentence can go along with it. These penalties increase to $100,000 and five years in prison when the person or covered entity received the information under false pretenses. An example of this would be pretexting. Pretexting occurs when the person with the information you want believes they are communicating with a person who should have a right to know. Hewlett-Packard and its board got slammed when they used private investigators to obtain phone records of other board members from phone companies. Lastly, if the goal was to transfer, sell, steal, or use the PHI for personal gain, commercial advantage, or malicious harm, the fines are $250,000 and 10 years in prison.

Real World Scenario

UCLA Employee Goes to Jail

Huping Zhou was sentenced to four months in prison after pleading guilty to four misdemeanor counts of breaching the privacy of high-profile patients and even the records of his supervisors, and fellow staff.

In October 2003, Zhou found out that UCLA was getting ready to terminate his employment based on performance. Once he found that out, Zhou chose to illegally access medical records of his supervisors and co-workers. Since access wasn't immediately terminated, he continued to use his access to view records of Drew Barrymore, Arnold Schwarzenegger, Leonardo DiCaprio, and others. Over the period of three weeks, he accessed and reviewed patient information that he should not have been reviewing.

Zhou claimed he was not aware it was federal crime to access the medical records that he didn't have a right to access. All staff members of a covered entity are supposed to operate under the minimal amount necessary guidelines.

Why is Mr. Zhou's case important? He was the first-prosecuted case under the HIPAA legislation. Remember, you can do jail time under HIPAA—and now with HITECH, you can receive even stiffer penalties.

The privacy rule is just the tip of the iceberg. Regulations are supposed to provide guidance for protecting PHI. However, there are a number of methods.

HIPAA Security

Sanctions within the administrative simplification provisions, which include the HIPAA security rules, are summed up in just seven pages of the HIPAA legislation. The security rule is broken into six sections. Each of these sections has standards. All covered entities must be comply with these standards. Each section also has implementation standards.

Implementation Specifications

Implementation specifications come in two different flavors—required and addressable. A *required implementation standard* is, of course, required. For an *addressable implementation standard*, a covered entity must actually complete an assessment. After the assessment is completed, the specification standard must be complied with by having a "reasonable and appropriate" safeguard in place. There is no definition of reasonable and appropriate, and this ultimately is a way out for a covered entity. The covered entity can decide that there are no reasonable and appropriate measures, but they must document this decision.

Though there is no definition for "reasonable and appropriate," the law provides guidance. This guidance has five contributing factors: cost, size, technical infrastructure, probability, and resources.

Cost Sometimes implementing a safeguard can be cost-prohibitive. An example is 164.310(d)(2)(iv) Data Backup and Storage. Though it is imperative to back up their data, a business can spend a great deal of money creating an exact real-time copy. A real-time copy of data can cost 10× more. Having real-time replication across two data centers can cost millions. Most physicians don't have millions of dollars to build out that level of redundancy. Depending on the level of redundancy and time-to-recover objective, there are great vendors to choose from. First, we always recommend building the operating system used by the application in a virtual environment. Extracting the hardware layer from the server makes it much easier to back up and recover. We have had great success with eFolder for file backups and system backups. Backup Exec is another option when not trying to back up a virtual environment, though it is a bit clunky. Commvault is another vendor doing exceptionally well in the Windows Server backup and recovery space. It has a method for backing up virtual environments that supports the quick portability of the data.

Size Another factor used when deciding whether the safeguard is reasonable and appropriate is the size of the organization. HITRUST has considered both revenue or the number of employees as the basis for the compliance consolidation guidance. The larger entities should have a well-planned and executed data infrastructure. Segmenting the networks from the data services, business network, human resources network,

implementation specification
An implementation specification is a detailed method that a covered entity can utilize to become compliant with a particular standard.

external vendor network, and segments that have PHI can increase the complexity and time to hack the environment. Allowing outbound traffic from the data center only to specific locations is important as well. We also recommend allowing only the necessary ports in and out of the data center to specific machines and having physically secured space for the servers. Smaller entities should have at a minimum the servers with PHI on a different network segment. This is accomplished by connecting them in most cases to a different port on the firewall and assigning the port a different IP range. No matter the size, we recommend using OpenDNS to filter outbound DNS requests. This can reduce the number of virus and malware infections the customer experiences.

Technical Infrastructure   Technical infrastructure is a huge component in understanding how an addressable implementation specification can be met. One of the requirements is Password Management 164.308(a)(5)(ii)(D). Password management is much easier for those who have an authentication database system such as Active Directory, Lightweight Directory Access Protocol (LDAP), or other authentication services. With smaller offices or with systems that allow anonymous access (Windows 95, Windows 98, and others) password management must happen on each computer. Covered entities must document the procedures and policies that are in place to meet the specification. We will discuss the many alternatives for accomplishing the safeguards required under HIPAA later in the chapter.

Probability   Covered entities must also look at the probability and criticality of potential risks to electronic private health information (ePHI). The potential for stolen data in a network that allows open access to ePHI will be higher than the probability of being breached in a system with controls that limit access.

With addressable implementation specifications, a response that explains how the covered entity meets the specification is required. The organization must document compliance measures, track all changes, and keep records of who approved the document and changes for at a minimum of seven years. This will come in handy if you are ever asked why a particular policy is in place or who requested a change that ultimately led to a breach of PHI.

Now that we've covered the differences between a required and addressable implementation specifications, let's review the specifications that must be complied with.

Understanding Implementation Specification Terms

Before diving completely into the implementation specifications, we must cover a few definitions. The following list is a compilation of the actual language from the HIPAA regulatory text. It simplifies confusing verbiage that we found needed clarification in our training classes and in our work with our customers. As always, we are not providing legal guidance. The full text is here:

`http://ecfr.gpoaccess.gov/cgi/t/text/text-idx?c=ecfr&sid=94244a6ea462 29b6ccc3bb47a405272d&rgn=div5&view=text&node=45:1.0.1.3.75&idno=45`

Access The ability or means necessary to read, write, modify, or communicate data or otherwise use any system resource. Per the federal regulations, this definitions does not apply to 164 subpart D or E.

Administrative Safeguards Administrative actions, policies, and procedures to manage the selection, development, implementation, and maintenance of security measures to protect ePHI and to manage the conduct of the covered entities' workforce.

Authentication The corroboration that a person is who they say they are.

Availability Data that is accessible and usable when requested by an authorized user.

Confidentiality Data that is not made available to an individual or process without appropriate authorization.

Disclosure The release, transfer, provision of, access to, or divulging in any manner ePHI outside the entity holding the information.

Electronic Media Removable or transportable digital memory medium. In addition, the transmission media such as Ethernet, fax, WiFi, and the like.

Encryption Use of an algorithmic process to transform data into a form where there is a low probability of decrypting the contents.

Facility The physical premises and the interior and exterior of a building or buildings.

Information System Interconnected set of information resources under the same direct management control that share common functionality. A system typically includes hardware, software, information, data, applications, communications, and people.

Integrity The state of data or information that has not been altered or destroyed in an unauthorized manner.

Malicious software Software designed to damage or disrupt a system.

Password Confidential authentication information composed of a string of characters.

Physical safeguards Physical measures, policies, and procedures that protect a covered entity's electronic information systems, related buildings, and equipment from natural and environmental hazards and unauthorized intrusion.

Protected Health Information   Individually identifiable health information that is transmitted by electronic media, maintained in electronic media, or transmitted or maintained in any other form or medium.

Security Incident   The attempted or successful unauthorized access, use, disclosure, modification, or destruction of information or interference with system operations.

Technical Safeguards   Technology and the policy and procedures for its use that protect health information and control access to it.

User   Person or entity with authorized access.

Workstation   Electronic computing device—for example, a laptop or desktop computer—or any other device that performs similar functions, and electronic media stored in its immediate environment.

Now that we have reviewed the most critical definitions, let's dive into the actual implementation specifications.

Implementing Safeguards

The goal of the implementation specification is for covered entities to ensure the confidentiality, integrity, and availability of all ePHI that it has created, maintains, transmits, and receives. Covered entities must use the following safeguards to reasonably protect ePHI from any reasonable threat to the security, integrity, and confidentiality of the protected information. Compliance is not just a matter of the covered entity; each employee and business associate of the covered entity must take seriously these mandates to protect the integrity, confidentiality, and availability.

All of the implementation specifications are split into three separate domains:

◆ Administrative safeguards

◆ Physical safeguards

◆ Technical safeguards

Administrative Safeguards

Administrative safeguards are the actions, policies, and procedures that manage security measures that protect ePHI and manage the conduct of the covered entity. Physical safeguards are the measures, policies, and procedures that protect a covered entity's systems, related buildings, and equipment. Technical safeguards include the technology, policies, and procedures that are used to protect ePHI. The technology safeguards should also assist in controlling access to the ePHI.

Under the HIPAA law, the administrative safeguards for security can be found in chapter 164.308. The actual implementation must comply with the specifications included there. The specifications are identified as either required or addressable. Remember that the measures taken to comply with addressable specifications must be documented. A covered entity must explain whenever they determine that a particular specification is not reasonable and appropriate for the covered entity. As part of the assessment process, the covered entity is required to implement an equivalent alternative measure whenever they find that a particular specification is not reasonable and appropriate. Alternative measures must be reasonable and appropriate.

Table 4.2 lists the required administrative safeguards and security management processes. The first four processes are meant to create enforceable policies and procedures to prevent, alert, detect, and minimize the damage of a particular incident, as well as correct security violations. Table 4.3 lists the addressable administrative safeguards.

Table 4.2   Required Administrative Safeguards

Safeguard	Specification	Suggestions
Risk analysis	Conduct an accurate and thorough assessment of the potential risks and vulnerabilities to the confidentiality, integrity, and availability of electronic protected health information held by the covered entity.	We utilize Nmap to assess what is on the network and respond to port queries. Nmap is also good at identifying the type of operating system. Metasploit is used to see what vulnerabilities exist across a multitude of applications. Commercial tools from Solarwinds, Retina, and others are useful for collecting very similar data in a easier manner without a Unix background.
Risk management	Implement security measures sufficient to reduce risks and vulnerabilities to a reasonable and appropriate.	Many covered entities just purchase a book of policies and never truly get them ingrained into the organizational fabric and culture. Assist the customer by making the policies meaningful and applicable to their organization.
Sanction policy	Apply appropriate sanctions against workforce members who fail to comply with the security policies and procedures.	Verify with the covered entity that the policies dealing with security and privacy include a termination clause. We find too many of our customers with only disciplinary language and not including termination.

Table 4.2   Required Administrative Safeguards *(continued)*

Safeguard	Specification	Suggestions
Information system activity review	Implement procedures to regularly review records of information system activity, such as audit logs, access reports, and security incident tracking reports.	Baselining system activity immediately when a system goes live gives you the capability to monitor changes in performance and access variances. For example, why is an employee accessing the EHR system when they are not on shift? Has their account been hacked? Are they looking for information they do not have the clinical need to be viewing? A challenge to meet this requirement is to collect the data in a central repository. Each EHR application collects audit data in different formats and at different intervals, and some cannot report the data in real time. Utilizing a security event information management (SEIM) such as nitro security or splunk can facilitate the analysis of the collected logs. After configuration, we recommend that a report regarding access activities be sent out weekly at a minimum, preferably daily. The more frequent the abnormal report is reviewed, the more quickly violations or breaches can be identified and dealt with.
Assigned security responsibility	Each covered entity must have at least one individual charged as the security official. In some organizations this might be the CISO, HIPAA security officer, and/or HIPAA privacy officer.	To meet this specification, the CE must document a security officer. As a professional, you can come in and help provide training to that individual or provide augmented staffing to play that role in the organization.
Workforce security	Implement policies and procedures to ensure that all members of its workforce have appropriate access to electronic protected health information.	To meet the demand that all employees have their own logon accounts, we recommend deploying an LDAP solution. Active Directory (AD) from Microsoft is a foundational software system many of us have already deployed outside or even within healthcare. If AD is not an option, then look for an open source LDAP authentication mechanism for the organization.
	Not all providers are independent of the health plan. When health plans are owned or operated by the same entity, there must be checks and balances. These balances reduce the likelihood of corruption or impropriety. Health care providers cannot share certain information regarding patients with the health plan. If a procedure is deemed too costly, the plan can be reviewing that information and simply not allow it at their hospital.	The minimum necessary is a method for restricting access to the software and data to only the portion the user needs to perform their role. We have found that in small physician offices, role-based access control doesn't work because of the number of jobs a single employee might have. In a larger organization using a single clinical application or EHR system, role-based access control can work because the role can be set up once and affect access from more applications.

Table 4.2   Required Administrative Safeguards *(continued)*

Safeguard	Specification	Suggestions
	Workforce security is much more than just making sure that the appropriate staff have just the information that they need to complete their jobs. In addition, there are always recommendations on making sure that when staff is hired, appropriate safeguards (using that term outside of the context of HIPAA) are in place to make sure criminals are not hired. For example, hiring an employee who has already been convicted of assisting or committing identity theft should not be hired by a covered entity. This creates too much risk and creates a higher than necessary risk profile.	We also recommend that employees receive yearly security training covering HIPAA, HITECH, and other related regulations and best practices.
Isolating healthcare clearinghouse functions	If a healthcare clearinghouse is part of a larger organization, the clearinghouse must implement policies and procedures that protect the ePHI of the clearinghouse from unauthorized access by the larger organization.	Data sharing is important in keeping the cost of healthcare contained. However, if a covered entity is both a payor and a provider, the payor side of the organization can provide only the information necessary to process payment to the payor side of the organization. Data mining with de-identified data is still allowed, though. To resolve this at a technical level, provide a segmented network with the inability to get from the payer side to the provider. Implement database monitoring software that monitors the types of queries to make sure employees are not behaving badly.
Incident response and reporting	Identify and respond to a suspected or known security incident; mitigate, to the extent practicable, harmful effects of security breaches that are known to the covered entity; and document security incidents and their outcomes.	The time of a data security event is not when you should start testing the workflow of an incident response plan. NIST has a tool called the Computer Security Incident Handling found at http://csrc.nist.gov/publications/nistpubs/800-61-rev1/SP800-61rev1.pdf.
Data recovery plan	Establish and implement procedures to create and maintain retrievable, exact copies of ePHI.	Implement tools and/or backup software to comply with this requirement. When possible, virtualize the servers that the application will run on. Next, install a top-tier enterprise backup package. Free tools or the Windows Backup program within the Windows operating system will not support the recovery objectives in most cases. We have found success using NetBackup and eFolder and are looking into Commvault. Backups are not required under HIPAA to be encrypted, but you should do that as a common security practice. Under HITECH, having encrypted backups allows the CE not to report on the theft or lost tapes.

Table 4.2   Required Administrative Safeguards *(continued)*

Safeguard	Specification	Suggestions
Emergency mode operation plan	Establish procedures to enable continuation and protection of critical business processes and the security of ePHI while operating in emergency mode.	Help the business build out an operational plan to comply with this requirement. A critical component is making sure that they have backup data located off-site to restart their business. We recommend having an open PO for hardware in case there is a need to purchase it immediately. Include the location where the office will resume services, maintain communication with patients, and continue to receive payment.
Authorization and/or supervision	Implement procedures for the authorization and/or supervision of workforce members who work with ePHI or in locations where it might be accessed.	Not all employees in the practice need access to ePHI. Have a documented procedure for granting the access and the level of access the employee should have. If possible, base it on their role in the organization. For example, a front-office staff doesn't need access to the patient's medical record, while a nurse doesn't need access to the billing side. Make sure that the covered entity has a process for training the employee on the HIPAA privacy and security prior to their accessing the data.
Termination procedures	Implement procedures for terminating access to ePHI.	Policies should be in place to identify the times when access to ePHI will be terminated for an employee or vendor. Then have a procedure to remove access. Make sure you understand the application's behavior. For some EHR vendors, once the user account is deleted, the accounting information for what they accessed is deleted. We recommend disabling access, not deleting access.

Table 4.3 Addressable Administrative Safeguards

Safeguard	Specification	Suggestions
Workforce clearance procedure	Implement procedures to determine that the access of a workforce member to ePHI is appropriate.	This is a simple safeguard to address. Have a prospective employee agree to have a background check and possibly a credit check if allowed by your state, prior to employment. Make your hiring decision armed with the information of the interview and third-party checks. Talk with your local police departments to find the best agencies for the background checks.
Access authorization	Implement policies and procedures for granting access to ePHI.	Granting access must be controlled and handled typically by a single person in the organization. This gatekeeper will verify that the individual asking for access indeed needs it. We recommend that the account creator receive additional training from the vendor or you on how to best grant access. In some situations, the employee might not need access to the entire components of the nursing, lab, or other module; they simply need access to a single screen in the module.
Access establishment and modification	Implement policies and procedures that—based upon the entity's access authorization policies—establish, document, review, and modify a user's right of access.	Modifying access must be controlled and handled typically by a single person in the organization. In any organization, employees might have the opportunity to change roles. The key here is to remove the prior access that they no longer need to complete their job. If access is not removed from modules they no longer need access to, they will have more rights than necessary to complete their job. We recommend that the account creator receive additional training on how to best modify access.
Security awareness and training	Implement a security awareness and training program for all members of the workforce.	Online training will track progress, test the individual on the content, and keep a log of when the test was last passed by an employee. In addition, look for training that has specific information about local and state regulations. In California we have found a group called Easyi at www.easyi.com to meet those needs. There are others.

Table 4.3   Addressable Administrative Safeguards *(continued)*

Safeguard	Specification	Suggestions
Testing and revision	Implement procedures for periodic testing and revision of a contingency plan.	The reason to have a contingency plan is to be able to use it and successfully recover the necessary systems when necessary. The law gives flexibility in how to do that by allowing each practice to address their own unique needs. Work with the practice to identify how long they can be down, locate a secondary site for continued operations, and find a third party for off-site backup tape storage. Remember that when creating the contingency plan, though there are technical components, this is an organizational document requiring thought about whether employees will continue to receive pay if they cannot show up for work, about the continuation of benefits, and about how to recover the technology as well. Virtualization will speed recovery, and having remote monitoring tools will let you know quickly when a problem arises. With all of this in place, perform period recoveries to confirm that recovery was possible. Make any necessary changes to the documentation based on the dry run. Keep in mind that every upgrade to the system or application might change the recovery procedures. Keep them up-to-date.
Applications and data criticality	Assess the relative criticality of specific applications and data in support of other contingency plan components.	IT professionals need to have an operations book (aka a playbook or runbook) tracking the system location, type, serial numbers, appropriate part numbers, system configuration, support numbers, location of application install disks, recovery information, and anything else you or the practice might find useful. Once the documentation exists, spend time prioritizing the recovery. For example, there is no point in recovering an application that utilizes Active Directory for authentication, prior to recovering Active Directory.

Table 4.3   Addressable Administrative Safeguards *(continued)*

Safeguard	Specification	Suggestions
Standard evaluation	Perform a periodic technical and nontechnical evaluation based initially upon the standard implemented under this rule and subsequently in response to environmental or operation changes affecting the security of ePHI.	Stay informed as the IT professional on changes. We outlined in Chapter 2 a number of societies, blogs, and websites that will keep you abreast of this ever-changing landscape. Look for conferences about the protection of PHI where you can learn best practices for the healthcare industry. You might have to modify the best practices to fit the workflow or needs of the organization. Once you have learned about the changes to the regulations or better tools to secure PHI, develop a plan to implement them in the practices and businesses you support.

Physical Safeguards

The physical safeguards are defined in section 164.310 of the HIPAA legislation. Four standards support the objectives of the physical safeguards: facility access controls, workstation use, workstation security, and device media controls. Only two of the implementation specifications are required.

As a healthcare IT professional, it is important that you assist the covered entities and business associates you support to create and implement policies and procedures to limit physical access to only authorized users for authorized use. Procedures should enforce the written policies, which should identify the workforce members based on job role or title who are authorized physical access. The procedures must support the policies of controlling physical access. The procedures should outline what type of mechanisms, such as biometric door locks, physical guards, alarms, video surveillance, or proximity cards, should be used. Without consideration of these things, implementation specifications of the physical safeguards might not be met because the policies and procedures do not match or work in unison together to meet the implementation specifications.

Facility access control is the first standard of the physical safeguards. Implementation specifications include contingency operations, facility security plan, access control and validation procedures, and maintenance records.

Implementation specification for contingency operations is meant to control access to a location in the event that a disaster occurs and data must be restored. Procedures are set into motion to protect ePHI and the safety of the workforce when a disaster strikes. When addressing this implementation

physical safeguards
To comply with physical safeguards, you must implement policies and procedures that limit physical access to the electronic information systems and the facility or facilities in which they are housed, while ensuring that properly authorized access is allowed.

specification, the site of the covered entity is going to play a big role. In a small, single-site medical practice, the staff necessary to simply start and complete the restore will be necessary. When a large hospital suffers a disaster or emergency event, there might be a need to move daily operations, recover the systems and data to a secondary physical site, and protect staff members as they transport tapes or systems with ePHI; this must all be considered when developing a contingency operations plan.

Questions to Ponder

Are the roles and individuals identified in the contingency operations plan capable of actually accomplishing the recovery? Do the people or roles identified have responsibilities in other areas during a recovery? Does the recovery staff have a method for gaining access to the recovery media (safety box keys, data tapes, access to recovery site, and codes for alarms)? If the recovery location has no power or sporadic power, is there an alternative location?

Next, the facility access control standards have an implementation standard for a facility security plan. These plans must ensure that unauthorized access to the facilities and devices containing ePHI cannot be accessed. Who should have access? That should be defined in a policy based on job role, job title, and other appropriate operational needs. Procedures used to prevent the modifications, tampering, or destruction of physical controls must be in place. Are there asset tags on devices? More technology savvy covered entities might have RFID tags. Utilizing positive ID controls such as identification badges, guest badges, log books, and even visitor escorts might be appropriate depending on the size of the organization. Ultimately, staff plays a critical role in protecting ePHI from escaping. Informing and training staff about their role in protecting ePHI is a critical step in the plan.

Table 4.4 lists the addressable facility access control safeguards. This safeguard has four implementation standards requiring covered entities to implement policies and procedures to limit physical access to its electronic information systems and the facility or facilities where they are housed.

The next implementation specification is access control and validation procedures. A person's physical access to information must be aligned with their role or function within the organization. Role-based access is a typical topic here. For small medical practices, it is much easier to identify the role and responsibilities, while in much larger organizations it is not. Why? Well, in a large organization, a person who needs access and is acting in one capacity in the morning might be taking on a different role in the afternoon. Additionally, access might not be changed as the person moves from one role to another, and thus their access becomes cumulative.

Table 4.4   Facility Access Control Safeguards

Safeguard	Specification	Suggestions
Contingency operations	Establish procedures that allow facility access in support of restoration of lost data under the disaster recovery plan.	In the event of damage to the place of business, you might not be able to gain physical access because of a fire, safety concerns, or a police event. Work with the covered entity to develop a plan for who can grant access to the location, and place on file with the police the information about who can make decisions for the practice. If the data and infrastructure are damaged but not destroyed, make sure the policy points to procedures to recover the data. Remember that the drives from the shuttle Columbia disintegration were recovered by KrollOnTrack. Therefore, the information on a drive in a fire has the possibility of being recovered. You do not want the system being stolen with the information intact from the office. This is yet another reason for full disk encryption. Use the documentation from your IT playbook to accomplish the recovery. We recommend having all documentation for the contingency plan on encrypted USB drives at all of the providers' homes and, if permissible by the practice, at the offices of the IT provider. You would hate to have all the documentation in a binder that had just burned to ashes.
Facility security plan	Implement policies and procedures to safeguard the facility and the equipment therein from unauthorized physical access, tampering, and theft.	Prevent unauthorized access to systems by controlling access. Place systems behind locked doors at a minimum. The point of the policy creation is that the practice has thought through the purpose of the machines. In highly sensitive areas, people have entered by placing themselves in the vending machine. Thieves also disguise themselves as stationary plant engineers (AC, plumbing, and so on) or electricians to gain access. Do not place computers on desks where the rear of the device can be reached from the other side. We have seen USB keystroke loggers installed on computers with these characteristics. We suggest locking down USB ports either by using software or by changing the registry key from 0 to only allow the devices you want connected. The registration key can be found on Microsoft's website at http://support.microsoft.com/kb/555324 or http://support.microsoft.com/kb/823732.

Table 4.4   Facility Access Control Safeguards *(continued)*

Safeguard	Specification	Suggestions
Access control and validation procedures	Implement procedures to control and validate a person's access to facilities based on their role/function, including visitor control and control of access to software programs for testing.	Employees and vendors should be granted access to the areas that have PHI only upon positive identification. Help the practice write this into a policy. As a IT solutions provider, provide your staff with badges so that they can be easily identified. Go to the local office-supply store and spend $25 in supplies to create laminated cards. Have a written log with the date, location, person, reason for the visit, the person the guest is visiting, and check-in and check-out time. The covered entity staff should be told to not allow anyone without proper identification, purpose, and someone escorting the visitor into the secured areas of the business.
Maintenance records	Implement policies and procedure to document repairs and modifications to the physical components of a facility that are related to security.	Maintain records regarding all services, including when a drive was replaced, when the AC was repaired, and so on. Any change affecting the server or application should be documented in the IT playbook for future reference.

To prevent these weaknesses from happening, it is necessary to put controls in place to protect the covered entity. As a health IT professional, you might recommend that employees wear identification badges at all times. Employees who have multiple roles might be required to carry two name badges. You might recommend guests log in and carry a visitor badges. In most cases, you would also recommend that the visitor be escorted anytime they are in a sensitive area of the facility.

Another area of weakness in large organizations when trying to address this implementation specification is to keep the physical access list current. As you can see, without proper employee onboarding and termination procedures, it would be impossible to keep the security lists accurate. Here again, as a health IT professional, you can provide guidance about the necessary policies and procedures to grant and revoke physical access to a facility in a timely manner. For a covered entity utilizing physical door locks with keys, getting the keys back is a must, or it leaves the organization vulnerable to an ePHI breach.

Maintenance records are the last of the implementation specifications for this standard. A covered entity is required to implement policies and procedures to document any work done to repair or modify the facility as it relates to physical security. When a repair is called in to fix a door lock, that repair request and what was done to repair the lock must be documented. The documentation allows for analysis of prior events in case a breach occurs. For example, when a door lock card reader is installed, that must be documented. Since the covered entity doesn't want to be burdened with documenting every possible change, it is important as their IT professional to address what physical items will be documented in policy. Then put procedures in place to meet the requirements of the policy.

The next standard is workstation use, and it requires that the covered entity document the purpose of each workstation and the processes that utilize ePHI on that computer. The reason for this is so that if a workstation is stolen, there is an understanding as to what data is potentially at risk. The type of ePHI being processed and the physical location are important to understand as a covered entity. As a healthcare IT professional, you need to document it if you know a system processes ePHI but it is located in a publicly accessible location. The workstation use standard applies to computers that are not confined to the physical premises of the covered entity. This is one standard that extends to smartphones, employees' home computers, tablet devices, and any workstation that accesses ePHI.

Table 4.5 lists the required workstation use and workstation security safeguards and provides suggestions for compliance.

workstation use
Implement policies and procedures that specify the proper functions to be performed, the manner in which those functions are to be performed, and the physical attributes of the surroundings of a specific workstation or class of workstation that can access ePHI.

Table 4.5   Required Workstation Use and Security Safeguards

Safeguard	Specification	Suggestions
Workstation use	Implement policies and procedures that specify the proper functions to be performed on a specific workstation.	Each workstation type's purpose should be identified. For example, a standard workstation cannot be used to provide diagnostic radiology reading. Exam-room PCs should not be able to get to back-office systems. If necessary, use a label to identify the use of the system.
Workstation security	Implement physical safeguards for all workstations that access ePHI to restricted authorized users.	Secure the systems to the desk, place in a location away from a window to prevent theft from the outside, and/or install video surveillance. We have customers who have had the entire innards of the PC stolen, 19-inch monitors stolen, and full workstations stolen during broad daylight. We also recommend in sensitive areas installing RFI tagging to sound an alarm if a device leaves a perimeter.

Real World Scenario

Throne for a King

Given ADA laws, a number of medical practices are having to build rather large restrooms to comply with the legislation. To better utilize the rooms, some healthcare practices are utilizing the space as a data closet. (The term *closet* is used loosely.)

We have seen servers supporting the entire business located in a restroom. Without a doubt there are risks associated with placing equipment in an area so accessible. Water damage is another concern. Employees or patients using the space could also steal data without the theft being immediately recognized. To deter theft of data in one particular case, we installed a data rack to house the servers.

Table 4.6 lists the device and media control safeguards. Covered entities are required to implement policies and procedures that govern the receipt and removal of hardware with electronic protected health information into and out of a facility and the movement of these items within the facility.

Table 4.6   Required and Addressable Device and Media Control Safeguards

Safeguard (Type)	Specification	Suggestions
Media disposal (required)	Disposal of any electronic form of media (CD, DVD, tape, disk, diskette, and so on) in a method that makes it unreadable.	Use processes identified in the NIST special publication 800-88 (http://csrc.nist.gov/publications/nistpubs/800-88/NISTSP800-88_rev1.pdf). We send everything through a demagnetizer and run seven low-level formats. Tools found on the Ultimate Boot CD, http://ultimatebootcd.com, include Derik's Boot and Nuke, which formats to DoD standards.

Table 4.6   Required and Addressable Device and Media Control
Safeguards *(continued)*

Safeguard (Type)	Specification	Suggestions
Media reuse (required)	Implement procedures for removing ePHI from electronic media before the media is made available for reuse.	Our stance is that no media should ever be reused. We destroy everything. It saves the free blocks on the media from ever being recovered.
Accountability (addressable)	Maintain a record of the movements of hardware and electronic media and any person responsible for them.	Just as logs are kept for people accessing that areas where ePHI is located, media that has ePHI has to be tracked in a similar method. If you cannot prove that the drive containing ePHI was destroyed, then you cannot prove that you were not the source of the identity theft or other data breach.
Data backup and storage (addressable)	Create a retrievable, exact copy of electronic protect health information when needed before moving equipment.	We feel that this is addressed in other areas of the legislation. By building the business continuity plan, you need to have ways to validate that the plan can work. Second to backing up the data is actually testing that the backup media can be used to do the recover.

With the rise of better remote access technologies, a number of covered entities are choosing to allow remote access only and in some cases internal access to ePHI through terminal server or virtual desktop technologies only. These technologies allow users to get their work done without the data ever leaving the network. Regardless of where the workstation is or how it is connected, the data stays within the confines of the corporate data center. As a healthcare IT professional, it is important for you to understand how desktop virtualization works and the underpinnings of Terminal Services (aka Windows Remote Desktop Services) as this technology is used to deliver either the entire application to the providers and staff, or at a minimum, used to deliver the application on a mobile device. This technology is a game-changer, although we could argue that it is simply a return to the old days of terminal emulators.

Just as important to knowing which computers access ePHI, the covered entity should document which ones do not access ePHI. Having this list helps shorten the time it takes to conduct audits and breach analysis. When the computer doesn't process ePHI, the theft of the device does not need to be reported. However, unless the system was predefined as not containing ePHI, then the computer would have to be assumed to have ePHI. Table 4.7 describes the both the required and addressable access control safeguards and suggestions for compliance measures. To meet the access control standard, there are four implementation specifications.

Table 4.7   Access Control Safeguards

Safeguard (Type)	Specification	Suggestions
Unique user identification (required)	Assign a unique name and/or number for identifying and tracking a user's identity.	Every user must have a unique logon, and the system must be capable of tracking the access within the application. When possible, we suggest exporting the user access information to another server with much tighter security controls.
Emergency access procedure (required)	Establish procedures for obtaining necessary ePHI during an emergency.	It is inevitable that a user will need access to information that they are currently not authorized to view. Many applications have a "break the glass" function where the user is asked whether they are accessing the record in a lawful way. This way, the user cannot come back and say they accidently clicked the celebrity's AIDS test results, for example. Users might also need access in the event of an emergency such as an earthquake. Since most applications behave differently or grant access differently, have a documented process to grant the access. When the application uses Active Directory or another LDAP authentication method, it will be easier to manage the emergency access for large groups of people.

Table 4.7   Access Control Safeguards *(continued)*

Safeguard (Type)	Specification	Suggestions
Automatic logoff (addressable)	Implement electronic procedures that terminate an electronic session after a predetermined time of inactivity.	Depending on the situation, most systems should have a logoff of less than two minutes. The quicker, the better from a security perspective, but the frustration level of the clinical staff increases. Implementing access through proximity card readers such as Xylock can be beneficial. As long as the user is within range, the session stays active. This doesn't work well in situations where two workstations are on opposite sides of the wall. The proximity is just too close. Work with the physicians and clinical staff to identify the appropriate timeout for each location. The longer the timeout, the less secure the data is.
Encryption and decryption (addressable)	Implement a mechanism to encrypt and decrypt ePHI.	Under HITECH, having data breached that is not encrypted opens you and the covered entity up to significant liability to the tune of $1.5 million. Under HIPAA, though, there is no definition of encryption, so it is more difficult to comply with this rule. We suggest looking at the NIST regulations for the best guidance: http://csrc.nist.gov/publications/nistpubs/800-111/SP800-111.pdf.
Audit controls (addressable)	Implement hardware, software, and/or procedural mechanisms that record and examine activity in information systems that contain ePHI.	Use a security information and event management solution such as Nitro Security, www.nitrosecurity.com. There are freeware tools such as Q1-Labs, www.q1labs.com. Splunk, www.splunk.com, is also another tool that can collect data to meet the audit controls. The audit of password changes, changes to group policy, and changes to critical files on the servers are manually intensive without a tool like the ones mentioned. We also recommend utilizing Netwitness, www.netwitness.com, to track access on the network, where the aforementioned tools are best suited for system and application event correlation.
Person or entity authentication (addressable)	Implement procedures to verify that a person or entity seeking access to ePHI is the one claimed.	Work with staff to figure out whether the methods for authentication should be biometric, username and password, token based, or ID badge based. There are many methods to solve this problem. Xyloc, www.xyloc.com, is the vendor we have used for years for proximity card readers. For tokens, many businesses are using SecureID from RSA, www.rsa.com. We also have found success using Phonefactor, www.phonefactor.com, for authentication for web-based applications and VPNs. Phonefactor calls the users phone, and after entering a PIN, the user is authenticated.

Technical Safeguards

The integrity standard requires that covered entities implement policies and procedures to protect ePHI from improper alteration or destruction. Table 4.8 lists both the required and addressable integrity safeguards and the suggested compliance methods. When researching and implementing the applicability of these standards, it is imperative that the covered entity take a holistic view. In many cases, these standards affect how employees gain access to protected health information from their homes, how information is transported between locations, and even the allowed uses of devices.

Table 4.8   Integrity Standard Safeguards

Safeguard (Type)	Specification	Suggestions
Mechanism to authenticate ePHI (required)	Implement an electronic mechanism to corroborate that ePHI has not been altered or destroyed in an unauthorized manner.	Mechanisms to validate data are typically built into the applications containing PHI. They utilize either proprietary or md5 hashes to confirm that the data has not been altered improperly. Other methods include extracting the data to an external database and comparing the data sets.
Transmission security (required)	Implement technical security measures to guard against unauthorized access to electronic protected health information that is being transmitted over an electronic communications network.	All data transmission on the network needs to be secured. Use SSL, TLS, or another method to encrypt the data in motion. For guidance, look at the NIST special publication 800-52 at http://csrc.nist .gov/publications/nistpubs/800-52/SP800-52.pdf. When working with terminal emulators and Telnet clients, make sure that the data going to and from the emulator is encrypted and that SSH is used instead of unencrypted Telnet.
Integrity controls (addressable)	Implement security measures to ensure that electronically transmitted ePHI is not improperly modified without detection until disposed of.	Again, we recommend the validation of data upon receipt. Work with the application vendors to confirm that they verify data integrity from the time it is transmitted and where it is received. Some applications utilize a check digit, while others send hash sequences. The point for the IT professional is that no matter what encryption or integrity controls, they should all add additional CPU, network bandwidth, and memory requirements without negatively impacting system performance.

Real World Scenario ————————————————————————

Security for Security's Sake

We do roughly 75 HIPAA, HITECH, and other security audits annually. There is very little that we haven't seen. When writing about physically securing ePHI, a number of prior findings come to mind that bear notice here.

When auditing a particular data center for a customer, we identified their use of proximity card door locks and biometric door locks as their methods for controlling access to the facility. Still, without a badge or biometric access, we were able to gain entry within three minutes. How? We gained access by removing the screws on the faceplate that held the window in the door. The construction staff placed the head of the screw on the outside of the door, not the inside. After removing the faceplate and glass, we reached in and opened the door.

We also were able to circumvent access to the facility through the biometric device. They had not enabled the tamper alarm, so we were able to unscrew the faceplate of the device without anyone noticing. We then moved the jumper that controlled whether the door lock was latched. By switching the jumper setting, when authorized users did use the biometric device, it actually locked the door. The rest of the time the door was unlocked.

Clearly, the covered entity thought they were protected. They had just forgotten to follow up on the minor details that can cause a major data breach. Remember, it is typically not one bad decision that leads to failure but a series of small compromises. In this case, the policies were correct, but the procedures failed.

Electronic Data Interchange

For centuries information has exchanged hands. Prior to the invention of Gutenberg's printing press in the 1440s, societies communicated using handwritten words. A scribe would write in the native language (or sometimes in code) to transmit information. Caesar used an encryption—aptly named the Caesar cipher—to encrypt messages sent to his military staff. As our civilizations advanced, the printed word was utilized more and more. As populations became more educated and could write in a common language and structure, information sharing and collection started to become commonplace. With the invention and creation of ARPANet in the 1970s (and its sibling the Internet), information could be shared at the click of a button. This had immensely powerful benefits that many organizations latched onto in order to share information between trading partners. Within the healthcare ecosystem, the trading partners include business associates, payers, providers, public health systems, and regulatory bodies.

Information exchanges prior to the widely adopted use of the Internet and clearinghouses were all paper transactions. Even today, some files are transmitted using the postal service or what geeks affectionately call *sneaker net*. File transmittal using these methods is slow, is inaccurate, and can cause data loss.

As a consumer, you probably use a credit card or ATM card to purchase fuel. When the card is swiped, the transaction is sent from the credit card terminal to the processing center. Information is transmitted during the transaction, and the credit card companies and clearinghouses manage which information is stored on the credit card machine. Having this standard framework to work within allows third-party tools to be integrated into the workflow without validating every workflow component separately. A similar transaction framework is used in the healthcare ecosystem.

The Department of Health and Human Services was given the authority to create or adopt the standards necessary to support electronic data interchange (EDI) in healthcare. The administrative simplification subchapter of the HIPAA legislation outlined the need to create a standards-based electronic data interchange infrastructure. Covered entities are required to interchange data with all federal entities utilizing the new standards. Because of the mandate to interact with government entities electronically, nearly all aspects of healthcare comply with the legislation.

HIPAA regulations weren't the only reason to create healthcare data interchange types. DICOM imaging is used to interchange diagnostic imaging data between different computing systems. Health Level 7 (HL7) is another form of EDI. HL7 is used to transfer data between separate healthcare systems.

We will first complete the review of the regulated data transaction sets and code sets. Last, there will be a summary of other common healthcare EDI technologies.

Industry-wide compliance with EDI reduces the cost of doing business. One area of operational expense reduction is the cost of staff (measured both in the number of employees required to process information and the time spent processing each piece of information). Opening and sorting mail is not just expensive; it delays payout for the provider by at least a week. Businesses required to track each interaction with a covered entity or patient could see that the cost to scan paper documentation and then electronically store all those images was prohibitive. Further advantages to EDI surfaced when discussions turned to the amount of revenue lost by payers because of incorrectly applying a higher than necessary payment. All in all, lowering costs across the healthcare continuum was the major reason for adopting HIPAA administration simplification. The lack of a common and shared code was a major obstacle; that's why the largest payer, the U.S. government, intervened.

EDI Transactions and Code Sets

On August 17, 2000, the U.S. Secretary of Health and Human Services adopted the final rule for eight electronic transactions and six code sets. The American National Standards Institute (ANSI) Accredited Standards Committee (ASC) X12N, version 4010, is the actual standard. The electronic transaction sets are for the actual transmission of data. The code sets are part of the information that is sent in the transmission. Imagine having a method for communication, such as grammar, but no common language. The electronic transaction is the framework similar to grammar for the English language. The code sets are the verbs, nouns, and words used to fill the framework to create valuable information. An ICD-9 code might be 078.4 foot and mouth disease (also known as slap cheek disease). Just as languages mature, so do the code sets. The new code set, X12N 5010, which can be used after January 1, 2012, is called ICD-10. Under ICD-10, that same foot and mouth disease would be coded as B08.8.

Adopting new code sets is required periodically. The prior code sets might not reflect the available diseases or treatments a provider might be able to give. Just as Webster's Dictionary periodically adds or removes words based on their frequency of use in America, so will transaction and code sets change to meet current needs. Words such as *Internet*, *intranet*, *email*, and others would not have been used at all when the dictionary was originally released. The latest version of the ICD-9 Diagnosis code set has just 13,000 codes. ICD-10 provides roughly 68,000 codes. For the procedural codes, ICD-9 has 3,000, while the ICD-10-PCS has 87,000.

The following rules apply to the eight electronic transactions and code sets to be used in those transactions.

- ◆ Healthcare Claims X12N 837
- ◆ Eligibility Inquiry and Response X12N 270/271
- ◆ Referral Certification and Authorization X12N 278
- ◆ Healthcare Claim Status and Response X12N 276/277
- ◆ Enrollment and Disenrollment in a Health Plan X12N 834
- ◆ Healthcare Payment and Remittance Advice
- ◆ Premium Payments and Payroll Deduction X12N 820
- ◆ Coordination of Benefits X12N 837

The code sets at the time of this writing are as follows:

◆ International Classification of Diseases, 9th Edition, Clinical modification, Volumes 1 and 2–Diagnosis Codes (to be replaced with ICD-10-CM no later than October 1, 2013)

◆ International Classification of Diseases, 9th Edition, Clinical modification, Volume 3—procedure codes for inpatients (to be replaced with ICD-10-PCS no later than October 1, 2013)

◆ Code on Dental Procedures and Nomenclature—dental procedure coding

◆ Healthcare Financing Administration Common Procedure Coding System—physician and other health services, equipment, supplies, and other items used in providing services

◆ Current Procedural Technology, 4th edition—physician and other health-care services

National Provider Identifier and National Health Plan Identifier

In the past, health plans would assign a unique identification number for each health provider. In some cases, the payer even required a different identifier for each location. Providers spent an enormous amount of money and often had to resubmit claims because the provider IDs were unique to each payer. The *national provider identifier* (NPI) is a unique ID for each provider but is not generated by a health plan; it is created by the government for use by not only the provider but all health plans and clearinghouses. An NPI is a 10-digit number with a validating check digit at the end. No information about the provider is included in the NPI. Doing so would have created an administrative burden for both providers and payers as physicians became specialists or changed how they practice medicine, either privately or in a hospital setting. To receive an NPI, the physician applies online at https://nppes.cms.hhs.gov.

As the indicator for a provider, this piece of data is used in many of the transactions. Providers may use their NPI to identify themselves in any federally regulated electronic or paper data interchange. Pharmacies use the NPI to help automate the creation of patient prescription labels. Payers require the use of the NPI to reduce the cost of handling the payment transaction. The NPI can be used to identify the treating physician in any medical record exchange. The NPI endures over the life of the physician—no matter what type of medicine is practiced, there is no expiration data attached to an NPI. In only the most rare cases of identity theft will new NPIs be issued.

Now that the providers have a national ID, there is a press to have a national health plan identifier. In section 1173(b) of the Social Security Act (42 USC 1320d), the law calls for the creation of a unique health plan identifier. The final rule must be in place no later than October 1, 2012. The rule initially would only affect plans as defined by HIPAA, although initial guidance would allow for non-HIPAA covered health plans (such as workers' compensation, auto insurers, and others) to receive an NHPI. Since many payers have multiple business lines, a request by the American Association of Healthcare Administrative Management (AAHAM) group recommended that the identifier have certain identifiable characteristics. Unlike the NPI where there is no specialty or other practice information included in the identifier, the AAHAM has asked that payers be allowed to identify the type of plan, the network used by the provider to reach the payer, the payer/provider relationship for referrals, authorization, and other expectations at the time of patient registration. AAHAM further recommended that repricers have their own unique ID.

Under the current systems, a patient's insurance card typically provides the subscriber ID, patient and/or subscriber name, the primary provider name, and copay information. To reduce the number of provider calls that are necessary to get information regarding services allowed under the subscriber's insurance, an NHPI could allow for more granular identification of the entity providing the coverage at the payer.

Identifiers are just the beginning of the types of structured data required to reduce the financial burden on the payers and providers. The HIPAA administrative simplification subchapter requires more. Once a payer can be identified, providers also need a way to confirm coverage, support the billing workflow, and improve information about insurance eligibility. To meet those and a variety of other needs, the secretary spent time identifying the transaction and code sets required to reduce costs.

Transaction Sets

Given the uniqueness of each of the types of transaction sets, let's cover them separately. As they are covered, the more ubiquitous the electronic transactions and codes set become, the easier data interchange will become. But before we get into more detail, let's define a few of the terms that will be mentioned periodically throughout the chapter.

Patient Event   A patient event is the service or group of services associated with a single episode of care (visit or stay).

Data Element   Data that comprises the patient demographics, service date, facility location, and other similar information is known as a data element.

Code Set   A code set contains the numerical representation of the medical procedure or diagnosis code.

Data Content   Data content is the combination of the code set and data elements.

Transaction   The effort of exchanging EDI between two covered entities is known as a transaction.

To best understand how the different transaction code sets work from beginning to end, take a look at the workflow illustrated in Figure 4.2.

Figure 4.2   Transaction Codes in the Workflow

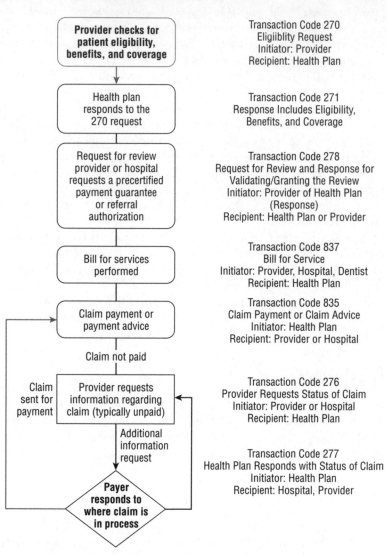

X12 Transaction Set subcommittee N was established to handle insurance transactions. As part of the Electronic Data Interchange group designated to define the transaction sets for the insurance industry, a subset of the X12N is specifically for the transaction set required by the healthcare industry.

Prior to implementing any data interchange technology, the two "trading partners" should come to an agreement on the data sets that will be traded. Partners who are trading should utilize implementation guides as generated by the X12N subcommittees so that each partner knows their responsibilities for compliance. Systems that do not stray from the standard are able to be implemented and maintained more easily. When a similar transaction must occur with another partner, there should be no changes necessary outside of adding the new partner. Partners should be forewarned about changes to any of the data elements, additions to the data segments, and the use of any values not compliant with the established schema.

The ANSI X12N syntax is built on a framework of loops, segments, and data elements. Each data element is a variable-length string of data. Most data elements have a minimum value and a maximum value. The length of the data element value is significantly larger than what was previously possible with older data interchange models. Each segment is made of data elements. The loops are just like loops in programming. They allow categories of segments to be processed within one data interchange. The X12 standards body calls this a hierarchical level (HL). With the proper coding of any HL segment, providers can code many patient visits into a single transaction. When breaking an HL segment in this way, the segment is reported to have a parent-child relationship. Each child has the appropriate data elements organized in the proper segments.

Transactions can be set up to utilize batch or real-time transactions. Batching is utilized typically when data is exchanged.

Each X12N transaction conforms to a very strict format that ensures the integrity of the data. The integrity of the data is also the genesis of a number of efficiencies. One such efficiency is the ability of a multiprovider practice to submit transactions for all of the providers in the group.

Figure 4.3 shows how the HL, segments, and data elements work together in an X12N transaction.

Figure 4.3 Hierarchy Levels, Segments, and Data Elements in an X12N Transaction

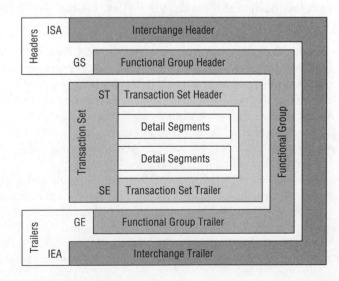

Code Sets

A common language is important. The transaction sets are just like grammar, in that they provide the necessary structure to interpret what is being communicated. For example, ice cream is the best dessert. That sentence should have correct grammar. Here's another example: Dessert best is ice cream. We hope there is a mutual understanding that the prior sentence is incorrect. Because the structure was not correct, then the meaning could not imparted on the other party in a meaningful way. Having a common framework and a common language allow the conversation to happen with a mutual understanding. The International Classification of Diseases version 9 and version 10 accomplish that for a portion of the diseases identified by the World Health Organization.

Code sets are the actual words used within the transaction sets. Reusing the previous example, if someone said, "Eis es muy bien," they might have a hard time understanding that the word *Eis* is German for ice cream, while *es muy bien* is Spanish for it is very good. To prevent any language problems, the secretary of HHS decided that the ICD-9, CPT v.4, CDT, HCPCS, and the NDC are the code sets to be used in data exchange.

So you can begin to understand how the code sets are used, we need to discuss their purpose. The ICD-9 Diagnosis is used first. Without a diagnosis, the provider will not know the best-known next course of action. Clearly, not all ailments are identified during the office visits, nor is the right diagnosis provided each time. The provider makes an educated guess as to the ailment and then continues with the procedures. Here is where the procedure codes such as ICD-9 Procedures, CPT, CDT, and HCPCS come into play. Then depending on the diagnosis, a medication might be dispensed.

International Classification of Diseases, 9th Edition, Clinical Modification, Volumes 1 and 2 ICD-9 CM

The International Classification of Diseases, 9th Edition, Clinical Modification, is a statistical classification system. The three-, four-, or five-number classification system arranges diseases and injuries into groups based on a predefined criteria such as poisoning, skin and subcutaneous tissue, and many more. The codes are revised periodically by the World Health Organization (WHO), which is a working group within the United Nations. Updates to the WHO classifications are also done by Health and Human Services, though they are published by Center for Medicare and Medicaid Services.

ICD-9 was developed to handle the classification of morbidity and mortality information caused by particular diseases. As the classification system matured and more classifications were identified, the medical records departments started utilizing the system to assist in identifying the actual disease or injury a patient has.

Though the ICD classification system has been published under different names since the early 1900s, the U.S. Public Health department had a need to start indexing the mortality and morbidity rates within the U.S. hospital system. They investigated a number of classification systems, and by 1968 the AHA and U.S. Department of Health settled on the use of the ICD classification system. As important as a common language to communicate, the ICD codes are important for showing particular causes of mortality and morbidity.

When the Medicare Catastrophic Act of 1998 passed, it regulated how healthcare professionals could communicate with CMS and HHS. To receive reimbursement for services, the medical billing staff had to use the ICD-9 CM coding framework. Failure to comply could increase time for reimbursement or failure to pay at all. Providers that already utilized electronic coding and billing were already sending claims electronically, so they did not fall under this part of the act. Having the provider electronically enter the diagnosis prevented the insurance company from having to type in the diagnosis. Without the diagnosis, the payer wouldn't send a reimbursement check.

Since April 1, 1989, all reimbursement transactions with Medicare have occurred using the ICD-9 CM code set.

To facilitate the payment and to reduce fraud, a common set of definitions that a technical support person must understand is listed in Table 4.9.

Table 4.9 ICD-9 CM Code Set Terms

Term	Definition
Acute (chief complaint)	The condition that is the primary reason for the visit.
Aftercare	A prior planned encounter for things such as removing stitches or a cast.
Cause	The reason for a condition.
Chronic	A condition that occurs over an extended period of time such as diabetes or hypertension.
Concurrent	The treating of the same patient by more than one provider at the same time for different conditions.
Diagnosis	A description of the reason for a service, clinical procedure, or encounter.
Down coding	Reducing the code that was sent in to the payer for reimbursement, because the diagnosis doesn't correlate to the procedure code being billed for.
Primary code	The ICD-9 CM code defined for the acute encounter.
Residual	Long-term conditions that are the result of a prior acute injury, condition, or disease, such as phantom pain because of the loss of a limb.
Secondary	The other ICD-9 CM codes that indicate other conditions that the patient has other than the acute code.
Sequencing	The submittal of the ICD-9 CM codes in the proper order.
V-codes	ICD-9 CM codes for encounters other than illness or injury. The V codes include immunizations (vaccinations), contact with communicable diseases, and infections with drug resistant micro-organisms.

When submitting a claim electronically, it is required that the appropriate diagnosis codes are entered. The acute diagnosis should be listed. This chief complaint will be the "parent" of all the "child" codes that are used later. If for any reason a preexisting condition is causing the acute symptoms, the prior condition should be documented as well. Following the selection of the primary reason for the encounter, a specific ICD-9 CM code should be coded to the highest specificity. If there is a five-digit code and only a four-digit code is sent, the payer will typically send it back.

Included in the claim submission are the other secondary codes, or V-codes. When a physician requests a lab test, this is the service that is listed. If a finding or diagnosis comes back before submittal of the claim, then the diagnosis should be listed second. When the primary is just a visit for a shot or other identified "therapeutic" encounters, it is necessary to submit the V-code as the first ICD-9 CM code.

The penalties for noncompliance to the ICD-9 CM formats are severe. At a minimum, the claims are rejected and sent back. This delays payment. Too many rejected claims can result in post-payment review of prior payments. If the provider refuses to provide proper ICD-9 CM codes, they are subject to a fine of up to $2,000 per claim. Continued noncompliance can result in the provider being kicked out of the Medicare program for a maximum of five years. Other insurance providers have their own penalties, so review their contracts carefully.

International Classification of Diseases, 9th Edition, Clinical modification, Volume 3 Procedure

ICD-9 Procedure codes are for acute-care facilities and the procedures that they complete. These codes are not to be used by providers in non-operating-room scenarios. The procedures cover vascular, digestive, and other operating room procedures. Insurance providers will not cover procedure codes from the ICD-9 CM Procedure volume billed by doctors who are not associated with a hospital or if the place of service is not a hospital.

Many procedures in hospitals have procedural code sets that will encompass many of the actual codes necessary for the completion of a particular procedure. This prevents coding errors as well as allows for the quick ramping up of coders for the facility. Coding staff must be aware of the uniqueness of the types of procedures done within the hospital setting.

One of the happiest places on Earth is a hospital—really, a hospital that is facilitating the birth of a child is the happiest place on Earth for the parents and family. The codes for a child birth are also one of the most complicated. Why? There are two people involved in the procedure. Some of the billing must be associated with the baby, while the others are associated with the mother. ICD-9 procedure codes for a baby delivery also have three- and four-digit codes. For example, 72.51 is the procedure code for a partial breech extraction with forceps to an aftercoming head. Applying the code to the right patient is important for proper payment.

Now that the coding for hospital settings is complete, coverage outside the hospital is the next step. Ever had a tooth extracted? Well, if you have, we hope the next step won't be as bad.

Code on Dental Procedures and Nomenclature CDT-2

Accurate extraction of a problem tooth is important, and for the health of the dental office, the accurate coding of the dental visit is important. The Code on Dental Procedures and Nomenclature (CPT) is the set of codes used by the American Dental Association. Providing a consistent format and codes for procedures allows for the dental practices to submit billing transactions quickly and accurately.

Unlike ICD-9 CM Procedure codes, these codes are reviewed every odd year. Though requests for updates can be sent in for inclusion at any time, these requests aren't reviewed or agreed upon until at the Code Revision Committee meetings. When HIPAA took effect, the law required that all transactions submitted for reimbursement utilize the CDT-2 codes.

The codes are three or four characters. For example, 150 is a comprehensive oral evaluation. A resin-based composite crown is a D2390. Periodontitis, dentists specializing in TMJ, and even standard dentists utilize the procedural codes.

Healthcare Financing Administration Common Procedure Coding System (HCPCS)

Nearly every year 5 billion claims are processed by the insurers in the United States. Medicare and Medicaid are at the heart of a number of these payments. To support the timely processing of the claims, the Center for Medicare and Medicaid Services created the code set. The code set is actually broken up into two different levels. Level I, which is discussed in greater detail next, is the Current Procedural Terminology. The CPT code set, though, is maintained by the American Medical Association.

CPT codes are incomplete when it comes to the supplies necessary to run a hospital, a nursing facility, or even a standard medical practice. Level II of the HCPCS codes is meant to be used for the supplies, services, and products used when delivering the services required to complete the procedure. For example, there is no CPT code for an ambulance ride. However, hospitals do bill for that service, and it comes out of the HCPCS level II code set. Durable medical equipment, prosthetics, orthotics, and supplies are all included when not used inside a physician's practice. The HCPCS is comprised of a single letter with an additional four digits for the service or product received.

Level III is also known as the local set. Certain locals might utilize different equipment, which is why specialized local codes are needed. Though the level III codes are a recent phenomenon, they are still better than utilizing a code such as "other." The local codes can also be modified more frequently on behalf of the local community. The same level of localization is not possible with the other levels.

Current Procedural Terminology, 4th Edition (CPT 4)

Common Procedural Terminology is a code set that combines a unique code with a particular type of procedure. Each code is assigned to nearly every conceivable type of task, service, or procedure that a provider might render when seeing a patient. Because the procedure codes tell the story of what treatment the patient received, this data is critical for continuity of care. As the National Health Information network grows, the CPT codes will be one of the many code sets required to give a doctor anywhere in the patient continuum of care the right information to make the best educated diagnosis for the current conditions the patient is being seen for and to avoid adverse conditions.

Given the number of types of services that a physician can deliver, the AMA has given criteria that must be met before a procedure or service is assigned a CPT code:

◆ The service or procedure has received approval from the FDA for the specific use of devices or drugs.

◆ The service is provided by "many" physicians across the United States. The AMA doesn't define *many*.

◆ The clinical efficacy of the procedure or services is well-established and documented in U.S.-based, peer-reviewed literature.

◆ The procedure is not a technical splinter of another already defined procedure.

◆ It is not utilized to report extraordinary circumstances related to an already identified and coded procedure or service.

Every year the CPT codes are updated on a case-by-case basis. The code structure, though, has not changed in more than a decade.

CPT codes are at the heart of a medical practice. The collection of data is critical to the financial health of the practice. There are a number of predetermined steps that a physician and practices go through when delivery patient care.

First, the acute problem, also known as the presenting problem, must be categorized into one of five separate categories. *Minimal* is the type of problem categorized as a problem that doesn't require the assistance of a physician, though the physician of course saw the patient; *self-limited* is a transient problem or a problem with a well-defined treatment or pattern. Think of a common cold. It is transient in nature; *low severity* is a condition that if not remediated will have a low probability of killing the patient and full recovery without reduced functionality is expected; *moderate severity* is a problem where there is a medium probability of death without treatment or increased probability of prolonged reduction in facilities; and *high severity* is a condition that has a high risk of killing the patient or high probability of prolonged or permanent functional impairment.

Next, a review of past history is done. This is when the nurse and then physician reviews prior history. Questions are asked about prior surgeries, allergies, current medication list, and immunizations. The list is not exhaustive; providing such a list without the context of the type of provider rendering the services is too broad in scope to cover.

Social history is covered. Used more frequently now to determine the mental state of a patient, a thorough social history review can reveal the actual cause of an illness. Some investigative questions about the use of drugs, how a marriage is going, employment status, and even living arrangements can be all telling. When a patient becomes disengaged because of lack of employment or maybe a recent financial setback, a doctor can use this information to understand the problems the patient is presenting with.

Typically the nurse will do an exam called the *system review*. This is a functional review of the basic bodily functions. It is like a pilot checking the control surfaces of an airplane prior to taking off. Questions regarding recent fevers, weight loss or gain, and the respiratory, neurological, gastrointestinal, and other areas are all probed. Providing accurate information is in the best interest of the patient here. Sometimes we have witnessed patients answer questions regarding respiratory or psychiatric questions differently for the nurse while giving the doctor the truth. Clearly in these examples there is a higher trust level with the doctor than the nurse.

Determining how to code the visit in terms of time is also known as the evaluation and service section of the CPT codes. A doctor cannot list extended visits for 50 patients in a day because there is a minimum time required to make the extended visit chargeable. The AMA has provided guidelines to properly code the encounter regarding time. Basically, the key is to understand how much time was spent reviewing the previous items with the patient and then diagnosing the symptoms.

Physicians typically use a SOAP method during the visit. The format is used to facilitate communication among all entities providing care for the patient, including the patient. In settings where the patient has a chronic illness, the SOAP document is the game plan for the next period of time.

◆ The *S* in SOAP stands for subjective. Questions are asked of the patient to understand what is wrong. The patient may discuss a pain they are feeling, where it hurts, how long it has been occurring, and if the symptoms are causing a drop in the quality of life. The physician's role is to play a private investigator during this time. Asking probing questions will lead the doctor to the right answer.

◆ Following the *S* in SOAP is the *O*. Oh my, the *O* stands for objective observation. Observation can be defined as what the physician is seeing or what labs have produced. Without an objective review of the available data, the physician can make the wrong diagnosis and proceed with the wrong procedures. When necessary, because of a lack of actionable data, the physician might send the patient out for more labs or another diagnostic image depending on the presenting problem.

◆ The *A*, or assessment, culminates in a diagnosis. The diagnosis is based on the subjective data the patient has presented with and the objective data that either the doctor has collected or that lab results have presented. Early on in highly complex diagnosis, the physician might have a number of assessments that are becoming more granular in nature. An initial assessment can result in the proper care plan being created. Other times it might take more than one visit.

◆ Lastly, *P* is the plan. The plan is the treatment or next steps required to get healthier or have lab work done to understand objectively the root cause. During a visit with a pediatrician, the doctor asked a member of the family to have blood work done. Shortly after seeing the results, the pediatrician called and asked that we go to the local trauma center ASAP. After months of more granular blood work and specialist visits, the actual root cause was uncovered. Clearly, that wasn't the plan the doctor initially had for the family member, but it is what resulted from the lab work.

When the physician concludes the visit, they select the amount of time spent. The guidelines from the AMA ask that the provider determine the extent of the examination based on medical complexity, length of history obtained, and comprehensiveness of the examination. When studying the medical practice, following a doctor around for a day and then seeing how they coded visits will provide you with the necessary perspective in understanding how the extent of the office visit is selected.

The other codes within the CPT code set are much easier to determine. They apply to specific procedures. As newer CPT codes are added, even more granularity is available.

National Drug Codes for Pharmacy

Medication is necessary for a number of the ailments facing Americans today. Just as the ICD and CPT codes facilitated a common language of terms, the NDC was developed to have a common language for the types of medications available today. An IT professional must be able to understand how the drug databases will be interfaced with the different modules within the EHR and other clinical applications that use the NDC data. HL7 interfaces are built between each system to query and respond to the database. Placing the system on the same network as the applications needing the data will keep the information in the event of a routing problem. Higher transactions through the interface engine will require increases in system requirements. You might have to increase the amount of memory, CPU speed, number of CPU cores, a minimum gigabit NIC, and higher speed disk. When the interface for the NDC goes down, medication and prescription orders must be placed manually, slowing down patient care.

The format for the data interchange is NCD, which is organized under 10 identifiers:

- Drug trade name
- NDC number—10-digit number in 3 segments
- Dosage form (liquid, gel, solid, and so on)
- Routes of administration (mouth, shot, drop)
- Active ingredients
- Strength
- Units
- Package size and type
- Major drug class
- FDA-approved application number

The HIPAA-identified transaction and code sets are the ones identified in the law, but there are more supportive interface technologies to make transmitting data easier. There are too many to cover them all, so we have chosen the top two other methods for data sharing that are most commonly used. The first is the Digital Imaging and Communications (DICOM) image format. This image format is utilized across many diagnostic imaging systems. The format is so flexible that more diagnostic systems such as cardiology and others are utilizing the format for the purpose of interoperability. Second is HL7, which is a method for interchanging information across systems. The prior code and transaction sets were for the purpose of payment, eligibility verification, and other purposes, but not for sharing patient data across an enterprise. HL7 is meant to interface the different clinical applications found in a healthcare environment.

DICOM

The DICOM imaging format is the standard for diagnostic imaging in radiology and cardiology. Previously focused on radiology, the DICOM format has recently been implemented across a number of image-capturing systems. Retina and cataract imaging are just a few examples of the many imaging care systems that now use DICOM. Created in 1993, the standard allows for storing, displaying, processing, retrieving, and printing diagnostic images. The standard has evolved to include structured documents.

DICOM imaging allows for transmitting images from one modality to another. A modality is the device that is used to capture the image, such as an X-ray machine. Still too many hospitals print images of their patients. This it too costly over the long run. Images have to be tracked, stored, and moved from one site to another. Those hospitals still utilizing fill must also keep a radiologist on-call for after-hours reading of the film. Images such as mammography must be kept for 40 years.

Given the variance in modality vendors, the utilization of a proprietary format by each vendor would exponentially increase support costs. MR scanner, X-ray, CT scanner, mammography, and film digitizers are all examples of the types of imaging capture systems that can communicate together when a DICOM is used.

With an open framework, information can be communicated more quickly, and diagnostic readings can happen more quickly. Physicians can also view the images with their patient inside the exam room without each room having an image light box. When patients also request same-day appointments, there is no reason to worry about the availability of the images because it is available through the Picture Archiving System.

The benefits of using the DICOM format are huge. Physicians can see a boost in productivity because there is no need to fumble for the information (note that network speed and bandwidth must work flawlessly).

Since the genesis of DICOM, the standard has continued to evolve. Currently, the standard is set up to support network communications, offline support, the syntax and semantics of information available for exchange, a standard file format and directory structure, and how conformance to a particular DICOM standard is claimed by the vendor.

To understand how DICOM actual works, it is best to look at how a network stack works. At the top of the stack is the medical imaging application. Within the imaging application, there are different object definition, structures, and encoding that occurs. The output of the encoding is twofold. On one side, there is a message that must be exchanged. On the flip side there is a need to have a standard file format.

The DICOM message exchange as defined by the DICOM Upper Layer Service Boundary has three components. The first is the DICOM upper layer. The optional security layers are added to support HIPAA and HITECH. The last layer is the TCP/IP transport layer.

Health Level 7

So, why the seven? The seven is the level in the ISO networking model that the interface engine and methodology runs at. The key differentiator is that a number of interface systems want to run at a level lower than the application layer. However, the approach that the health level standards organization took was the best one. By not creating another protocol at the lower ISO network stack, they could focus on data exchange of health information instead of worrying about operating system upgrade life cycle, IP version 6, and the many operating system variants.

So, what does HL7 do for the healthcare community? It allows different data systems to communicate with each other. The communication occurs first from a transaction that happens in the originating system. For example, a patient is admitted into a hospital. The patient demographics are transferred from the admissions stem into the hospital clinical care application. Without the interface, the information in the different clinical care system would have to be rekeyed. Once the information is sent out as an HL7 message to the receiving system, the receiving system responds by translating that information into an actionable event in the application. The patient's information is now available for the clinical staff to take action on. The right doses, based on age or weight, for medication are already available to the pharmacy staff dispensing the medication. Once the patient is discharged from the hospital, a discharge message is sent to the billing system along with all the patient charges. Again, if HL7 were not available, each interface would have to be manually programmed and maintained. One-off interfaces not using the standard HL7 messaging format increase costs and the time to test, troubleshoot, and maintain.

Terms to Know

HIPAA	privacy rule
administrative safeguards	physical safeguards
technology safeguards	operational safeguards
required implementation specification	addressable implementation specification
administrative simplification	national provider ID
Electronic Data Interchange	transaction sets
HL7	national drug codes
X12N	D.0

Review Questions

1. What electronic data interchange protocol or technology is used when transmitting admissions and discharges?

   A. DICOM

   B. HL7

   C. EMR

   D. X12N

2. HIPAA was meant to reduce fraud and the administrative costs of providing healthcare. What percentage of healthcare coverage did the feds determine is wasted?

   A. 31 percent

   B. 11 percent

   C. None

   D. 35 percent

3. Workstation use belongs to which safeguard group?

   A. Operations

   B. Administrative

   C. Physical

   D. Technology

4. What government entity oversees medical privacy complaints?

   A. ORC

   B. CMS

   C. FDA

   D. OCR

5. What type of encryption must be used to comply with HIPAA?

   A. AES

   B. MD5

   C. SHA-1

   D. None listed

6. Notices of privacy are required for which covered entities?

   A. Business associates

   B. Medical practices

   C. Hospitals

   D. B and C

   E. All of the above

7. A covered entity must have which one of the following identified as part of the administrative safeguards?

   A. Privacy officer

   B. Security officer

   C. HIPAA officer

   D. HITECH officer

8. True or false? A workstation must be automatically logged off after 10 minutes.

   A. True

   B. False

9. To track providers nationally, what identifier is used?

   A. Federal tax ID

   B. Social Security number

   C. NPI

   D. NID

10. The administrative simplification portion of the HIPAA Act requires the use of code and transaction sets. Which is not part of a code or transaction set?

    A. D.0

    B. ICD-9

    C. CPT

    D. HL7

Chapter 5

HITECH Regulations

The Health Information Technology for Economic and Clinical Health (HITECH) Act was enacted as part of the American Recovery and Reinvestment Act (ARRA) of 2009. The part we will cover in this chapter addresses the privacy and security of patient data, business associate agreement changes, and more. Remember that each subtitle within HITECH can be a financial windfall for you and your business. Pay attention, though, because the penalties for noncompliance have increased to $1.5 million—and jail time. Significantly, changes in the penalties associated with losing protected health information (PHI) increase the likelihood of IT professionals spending time in jail for HITECH violations. As with HIPAA, reducing the liability and vulnerability footprint in the long run reduces the costs of running the business.

In This Chapter
- HITECH background
- Business associates
- Breach notification
- Penalties
- Accounting of disclosures
- Minimum necessary for information access
- Marketing and sale of PHI
- How HITECH affects different CE scenarios
- Nation Health Information Network
- Personal health records

HITECH Background

A recent study by the Kaiser Family Foundation concluded that the amount of money spent on delivering healthcare in the United States can be expected to increase to $4.1 trillion by 2016, an amount equal to nearly 20 percent of all spending today. Currently, the average American spends 18 percent of their income on healthcare coverage. Further, the demand for services will continue to increase because 45 percent of Americans suffer from at least one chronic disease. (The chronically ill account for more than 75 percent of all healthcare spending.) American colleges cannot produce enough doctors to keep up with the demand for care. With this much at stake, having a consolidated view of the patient is important and, based on the U.S. military's experience, can result in lower costs. The U.S. military operates one of the world's largest electronic medical record (EMR) systems and has reaped a number of cost benefits, improved patient outcomes, and reduced medication errors.

As mentioned, the *Health Information Technology for Economic and Clinical Health (HITECH)* Act was born out of the much broader American Recovery and Reinvestment Act (ARRA) of 2009. Based on the success of the military's EMR, Congress and the U.S. President agreed to allocate some of those funds to reduce healthcare costs and improve patient care through the use of technology. The idea is that easy access to patient information for second opinions, radiology image reading, lab results, and coordination of care improves not only patient care but also the overall efficiency of the healthcare system. By adopting an electronic health record (EHR) system, the government believes Medicare and Medicaid costs can be better contained in the future. People in Washington felt that the only way to accomplish this on a meaningful scale was to install EHRs broadly. To increase the abysmally low adoption rate, they instituted programs to fund a portion of the EHR deployment, with incentives ranging from $44,000 to $65,000.

The government further recognized that providing financial resources wasn't going to be enough to increase the adoption rate—or increase consumer confidence in having their information available electronically. Clearly, if some of the largest banks are unable to protect their data, how can a small practice protect sensitive medical data? To counter those concerns, HITECH applied the HIPAA privacy and security rules to all covered entities (CEs) and their business associates (BAs). The HITECH Act created new privacy statutes, *breach notification* laws, disclosure restrictions, and controls on the marketing and sale of PHI. HITECH also established a minimum data set for use when transmitting patient information in the course of patient care. Noncompliance with HITECH and security *breaches* carry new penalties that top out at $1,500,000 and jail time. (Later in this chapter we will provide guidance how to reduce your exposure to the fines as well as time away from your family.) You should be aware that a subset of those medical practices not participating in the ARRA funding reimbursement are under the false assumption that they do not have to comply with the new HITECH privacy and security legislation because they are not seeking the incentive funds. Under HITECH, the definitions of a CE and BA remain the same as under HIPAA (section 160.103 of Title 45 of the federal regulations). All CEs and BAs must comply.

IT Group Gives Themselves High Marks

Healthcare breaches continue to increase. In the 2009 ITRC Breach Stats Report, healthcare breaches account for 66 percent of all breaches. For example, a recent data breach of a Northern California healthcare insurance company lost more than 1.9 million records, including the personal information of their members, employees, and providers, including names, Social Security numbers, and/or financial information. In 2009, an industry preparedness for HITEDH study was conducted by ID Experts. The research found that 41 percent of the business units had experienced a data breach. When the IT departments were asked, only 22 percent indicated that a breach had occurred. These findings are scary, because it means the folks who should be watching the perimeter, the data, and the systems have a false sense of security. Privacy and security are critical to the success of EHR deployments in the United States.

Source: 2009 HIMSS Analytics Report: Evaluating HITECH's Impact on Healthcare Privacy and Security sponsored by ID Experts

With government regulations, it is always best to review the original law and treat it as the source of truth. The information we present in this chapter is based on our experience and understanding of the law. You can find the original text at the following Health and Human Services (HHS) site:

www.hhs.gov/ocr/privacy/hipaa/understanding/coveredentities/hitechact.pdf

We recommend you return to the HHS website at least monthly because it is required to release guidance on how to meet HITECH privacy and security requirements.

Let's dive in before you are scared away by the consequences of a security breach.

Business Associates

HIPAA required CEs to address the security and privacy of ePHI. After HIPAA and the advancements in networking, a number of CEs were able to outsource portions of their business. This would not have been as easily accomplished without the administrative simplification standards under HIPAA.

Real World Scenario

Outsourced Imaging

NightHawk Radiology Services' national business relationships with hospitals and clinics is a prime example of technology permitting outsourcing. To reduce the burden of having radiology staff on-call 24/7, hospitals and other clinics started outsourcing radiology services to NightHawk. Prior to HITECH, when a CE created a business relationship with NightHawk, the agreements typically required NightHawk to adhere to HIPAA. No national law required NightHawk's compliance. If NightHawk breached its contractual obligations, it was liable only to the CE; it was not subject to direct oversight or penalties by HHS. Beginning on February 17, 2010, HITECH increased the stakes for compliance by directly regulating BAs.

As a result of the changes to privacy and security under HITECH, BAs are subject to the breach notification rules and the HIPAA privacy and security safeguards that require the use of technical, physical, and administrative measures to ensure the confidentiality of electronic PHI. Meeting these requirements is important because if a BA runs afoul of its new obligations under the privacy or security rule, it can be penalized directly by HHS and other enforcement agencies.

TIP

Understanding the requirements of the security rule (what types of safeguards are acceptable and how the safeguards should be implemented) will be a challenge for many BAs. To help information technology professionals complete HITECH and HIPAA audits, the National Institute of Standards and Technology (NIST) is currently producing a tool called the HIPAA Security Rule Toolkit. The tool covers HITECH and HIPAA and is meant to help entities identify gaps. When the tool is released, review it for inclusion in your own toolkit. Given NIST's track record of useful security information, we can't wait to get our hands on it.

BA agreements with CEs must include HITECH provisions. If you currently provide technology in a healthcare setting that exposes you or your business, make sure you consult with an attorney to create airtight agreements with the CEs you do business with. A breach is expensive, and you do not want to be left paying for all of the costs of a possible breach. Take the precautions to amend your agreements if you have them. Do not wait until after a breach to negotiate indemnification. There are still IT solution providers that provide network monitoring and systems support that do not believe they are required to comply with HIPAA. It is our opinion that anyone who has an even remote possibility of accessing ePHI is a BA. We base that on the following provision in HIPAA's definition of a BA:

> *(ii) Provides, other than in the capacity of a member of the workforce of such covered entity, legal, actuarial, accounting, consulting, data aggregation (as defined in § 164.501 of this subchapter), management, administrative, accreditation, or financial services to or for such covered entity...*

Because we provide consulting services, management, and system administrative tasks to covered entities, we believe we must comply with HITECH. Speak with your attorney to confirm your liability.

Real World Scenario

Business Associates Unaware of New Requirements

BAs lag behind the rest of the healthcare industry when it comes to privacy and security law as found in the HITECH Act. In a recent study, 30 percent were not even aware that the HIPAA laws now applied to their business. We are not sure whether that is because the BAs are typically smaller businesses with training issues, whether there's a complacency problem, or whether they don't have enough staff to keep up-to-date. Healthcare providers are, however, ready to throw them under the bus if the breach happens with the business associate's data. This is why, as an IT professional, there is enough work in just HITECH and HIPAA audits to keep a business busy forever. Eighty-five percent of the hospitals surveyed indicated that they will take actions to protect the patient data held by their business associates. Fifty percent stated that a breach will most likely end in the termination of their contract with the BA.

Source: 2009 HIMSS Analytics Report: Evaluating HITECH's Impact on Healthcare Privacy and Security sponsored by ID Experts

Breach Notification

HIPAA had no provisions for breach notification, and that was seen as a weakness. Some security professionals confused state legislation, such as California's SB 1386, which does require notification of a breach of protected data (which is more than just protected health information). HITECH, however, closes the gap in legislative oversight and now includes breach notification requirements for unsecured PHI.

TIP

If the data is secured using an approved method as defined by the HHS, there is no requirement to report the breach. Review www.hhs.gov/ocr/privacy/ hipaa/administrative/breachnotificationrule/brinstruction.html **for more guidance.**

unsecured PHI

PHI that is not secured through the use of a technology or methodology specified by the secretary in the guidance is required to issue a breach notification to the affected individuals within 60 days.

Under HITECH, breaches are segmented based on the size of the breach. The delimiter is 500. No matter the size of the breach or how the affected folks are notified, a breach notification must go out to those affected. The notification must include the elements found in Table 5.1.

Table 5.1   Elements of a HITECH Breach Notification

Element	Description
Circumstances	A brief description of what happened, including the date of the breach and the date of discovery.
Data lost	A description of the types of unsecured protected health information compromised (Social Security number, date of birth, name, address, and so on).
Personal response	Steps the affected individuals should take to protect themselves from potential harm.
CE's response	What the CE is doing in response to the breach to mitigate losses, reduce the likelihood of its recurrence, and how the matter is being investigated.
Who to contact	Provide contact information (email, phone, address) for the CE who will address the issue for affected individuals to communicate with. (Make sure this number is answered. It is not the affected individual's fault that the breach occurred.)

The notification, no matter the format, must be sent out without undue delay and not more than 60 calendar days from the time of the breach. All breaches no matter the size must be reported to the secretary of HHS. The website that provides specific instructions for notifications is located here:

www.hhs.gov/ocr/privacy/hipaa/administrative/breachnotificationrule/ brinstruction.html.

You can find more information about breaches in general here:

www.hhs.gov/ocr/privacy/hipaa/administrative/breachnoti"cationrule/ index.html.

Breaches that involve information about 500 or fewer individuals must be reported on a yearly basis. If the breach affects more than 500 people, the notification must also be published in a major newspaper, on television, or in a radio broadcast in the geographic area where the affected population lives.

As with any law, there are some exceptions. The first exception applies to the unintentional access or use of PHI by a workforce member (business associate, employee, contractor, and so on), acting under the authority of the covered entity or business associate, such as when an IT person remotes onto a computer to share the screen with a nurse. There may be unintentional sharing of information in the course of the technician's work. The second exception applies when there is an inadvertent disclosure of PHI at a covered entity or business associate from one authorized person who is allowed to view and access PHI to another authorized person who is authorized to view and access PHI. This covers the inadvertent slipping of information when staff members communicate. There are, however, scenarios that are cropping up where patients had a picture taken with their doctor, who then posts it online within their social network. As an IT professional, make sure that the business you are working in has policies that meet the needs of the patient and business.

The last breach exception applies when the covered entity or business associate in good faith believes that the individual who accesses the information is not able to retain the information. We are not sure how this exemption works, and the feds do not define good faith, but your attorney should be able to advise you.

breach
A breach is defined as an impermissible use or disclosure under the privacy rule that compromises the security or privacy of the protected health information such that the use or disclosure poses a significant risk of financial, reputational, or other harm to the affected individual.

Real World Scenario

Monitoring Employee Behavior

Hospitals are investing in HIPAA privacy and security awareness training to make sure employees understand their responsibility to protect patient data. However, we have seen that after the training, there is a gap, and hospitals vary in the way they measure compliance with policies described in the training.

When we are asked to handle a security assessment, we spend time asking the staff questions about HIPAA privacy and security to see whether the training was effective. When we did one HIPAA security walk-through recently, we found that one out of eight employees still didn't know what HIPAA was. Roughly five out of eight employees could not adequately explain the purpose of HIPAA regulations and policies. Clearly, some type of monitoring was needed to ensure compliance.

Security software vendors have built systems to detect inappropriate access. One such system actually looks at patient demographic information and compares staff access to the patient record based on the proximity of staff residences to the care location. Access to a record by a staff member not involved in that patient's direct care is flagged.

To receive the ARRA incentive dollars, an EMR must be able to report on every access to a particular patient's record. Since EMR vendors will not survive unless they meet all of the application requirements and receive certification, they have invested heavily in developing logging capabilities. One caveat is that security teams might now be inundated with security breach flags, so it is critical to make sure to reduce the number of false positives.

NOTE

With all the data that is available to steal, companies are now investing heavily in encryption technologies.

Real World Scenario

Risk Assessments Don't Equal Security

To prevent data breaches, organizations are spending millions of dollars to have risk assessments done yearly. The question is, how much action is taken after the risk assessment to mitigate the risks that are uncovered? (There is always the risk of a data breach, especially since humans are involved.) In a study by ID Experts, 31 percent of hospitals reported breaches, even though 91 percent had conducted a risk assessment in the past 12 months. All of those hospitals had taken action to remediate the risk assessment findings. On top of the risk assessment, the businesses had conducted employee training, and 81 percent had deployed data encryption.

Source: 2009 HIMSS Analytics Report: Evaluating HITECH's Impact on Healthcare Privacy and Security sponsored by ID Experts

Penalties

The penalties under HITECH are much higher than under HIPAA—from $25,000 to $1,500,000—and there are required fines for willful neglect. State attorneys general now have the power to file a civil action against a covered entity or business associate in the event of a data breach. The head of the California Department of Public Health has been quoted as saying that the state will use the fines collected as a way to pay for public health programs. In addition to the penalties levied by the federal government and states, it is time that the covered entity or business associate look at fiscal penalties for employees who fail to comply with privacy policies. With internal incidents of breaches on the rise, it is clear that there needs to be some personal responsibility by employees. Covered entities (and now business associates) who have weak breach policies will end up being hurt the most financially. Some of their policies do not include the terms "up to and including the loss of employment." This lack of punishment demonstrates a culture of not taking information breaches seriously.

Human resources must partner with the security and privacy programs of the CE or BA to manage every angle of the privacy and security of patient information. This includes prohibiting employees from posting pictures or statuses of patients on online social networking sites. A simple status update like "I saw <insert celebrity name here> today while working at the hospital" is a breach. The employee might feel they are within their rights to share their day, but any release of information about a patient shared by anyone but the patient can create issues for the business. The American Health Information Management Association breaks breaches into four categories, as described in Table 5.2.

Table 5.2   American Health Information Management Breach Categories

Breach Category	Description
Category 1	Unintentional disclosure that was caused by carelessness, poor judgment, a lack of training, or a lack of knowledge.
Category 2	A deliberate disclosure of information in an unauthorized manor. There is no known redisclosure of the information. The employee knew of the policy protecting the information and was sufficiently trained.
Category 3	A deliberate disclosure of information that was unauthorized, and there was redisclosure of the information. The employee had appropriate training and understood that they were breaching the policy.
Category 4	A deliberate disclosure of information that was unauthorized and used for malice or for financial gain. The employee understood the policy.

Accounting of Disclosures

Under the HITECH Act, a patient has the right to a complete accounting of the practice's disclosure of their protected health information that has been released through the EHR/EMR. The law, however, does not address disclosures for internal use. Under HIPAA, a covered entity was required to account for all nonroutine disclosures (disclosures not related to treatment, payment, or healthcare operations). Under HITECH, a covered entity that utilizes an EHR must account for all disclosures including those of their business associates (or provide contact information for their BA) no matter the reason for the disclosure. A patient has the right to ask for this information for a maximum of three years, depending on when the EHR went live. For example, a patient can't ask for an account of the past three years of disclosure if the system has been in place only for a year. However, the patient must be able to get a full accounting for the time the system has been in place.

Disclosures are different from breaches. A disclosure is the controlled release of information to an entity that needs the PHI for the continued care of the patient, for treatment, marketing, payment, and other healthcare operations. A breach is the noncontrolled release of protect information. The timeline for complying with the statute varies depending on the EHR and when it was purchased. If the covered entity purchased the EHR after January 1, 2009, they must comply by January 1, 2011. Of course, an eligible professional can implement an EHR after the January 1, 2011, date. They would not be required to report on the disclosure of information prior to the implementation of the EHR. Those who already had an EHR prior to January 1, 2009, have until January 1, 2014, to comply with the disclosure law.

Minimum Necessary

In most cases, when a patient is transferred from one clinical care setting to another, either too much or too little information is shared between the facilities. Doctors either have to create the information they are looking for or proceed with the care without the information. When too much information is given, then the new care facility now has more data to protect from breach. Hence, the feds came up with the notion of *minimum necessary*. Although the definition isn't finalized, consider the working definition to be "the minimum amount of protected health information to complete the task at hand."

When talking about minimum necessary, the default under HITECH is considered *de-identified data* under HIPAA. This limited data set is typically useless outside of public health or other research departments. To get a glimpse at what is considered minimum necessary, you can review the *Continuity of Care Document (CCD)* specification (`http://wiki.hl7.org/index.php?title=Product_CCD`). This document transfers the critical components necessary to continue treatment from one organization to another. CCDs include demographics, healthcare coverage (this isn't globally required), a problems list, allergies, drug allergies, medications, and recent procedures. Many EHR systems have the capability to produce a CCD in electronic or paper format.

NOTE

Again, the definition is not yet finalized, so our discussion of minimum necessary is our best guess.

---

disclosure

A disclosure is defined as releasing, transferring, providing access to, or divulging in any other manner information outside the entity holding the information.

CCD specification

An XML-based markup standard intended to specify the encoding, structure, and semantics of a patient summary clinical document for exchange.

Marketing and Sale of PHI

HITECH added provisions to require authorization from individuals before disclosing their protected health information for payment. For the use of PHI to be considered *PHI marketing* or a *PHI sale* under the HITECH Act, the covered entity must be paid for the data by a third party. This communication is not allowed without prior authorization from the patient. There are certain exclusions. First is when the communication is for the purposes of treatment. Second is when the communication is for refilling medications *and* the payment to the CE is considered reasonable. A reasonable payment is considered to simply reflect the cost of preparation and transmission of the data.

How HITECH Affects Different CE Scenarios

HITECH has far-reaching effects. Though the penalties are the same no matter the size of the business, the way that various sized practices conduct business presents different challenges to prevent being subject to fines. Table 5.3 lists the implications for Dr. Multisite and his small allergy practice, for Yourtown Pediatrics and its midsized multiphysician practice, and for Central State Community Hospital and Clinics' large practice.

Table 5.3   HITECH Implications for Various Practices

HITECH Implication	Dr. Multisite (small)	Yourtown Pediatrics (medium)	Central State Community Hospital and Clinics (large)
PHI	About 4,000 records must be protected.	Approximately 40,000 records must be protected.	1 million or more records to protect.
Preventing breaches	Secure laptops and all PCs in remote offices using full drive encryption. Verify that the SaaS utilizes SSL or TLS to transfer data between sites. Put device tracking on all devices. Provide computer-based security and privacy training to staff.	Secure all laptops with full drive encryption. Implement centralized access directory to facilitate access control. Verify data on servers is encrypted. No matter the protocol used for the application to communicate with the client, validate the channel is secured. Add device tracking to the most vulnerable devices. Provide computer-based or facilitator-led security and privacy training for staff.	Secure all mobile devices with full device encryption. Create the ability to remotely wipe the mobile device. Encrypt all data on servers. Encrypt tape backups. Secure the communication channels used by applications containing PHI. Have a secured data center. Provide computer-based and facilitator-led instruction on privacy and security.

Table 5.3   HITECH Implications for Various Practices *(continued)*

HITECH Implication	Dr. Multisite (small)	Yourtown Pediatrics (medium)	Central State Community Hospital and Clinics (large)
Business associates	Typically very few BAs. Add HITECH language to BA contract. Hire a third party to perform BA audit.	Typically a dozen or so BAs. Add HITECH language to BA contract. Hire a third party to perform BA audit.	Typically a few dozen BAs. Add HITECH language to BA contract. Outsource BA audit or have internal staff complete the audit.
Breach notification	Won't have financial resources to provide credit monitoring to patients. Change contract with SaaS provider to include monitoring for patients. Damaging to reputation, though typically not fatal.	Protect PHI by implementing the NIST guidelines. Hold mock breach incidents. More damage control necessary because of size. Increased damage to their brand.	Protect PHI by implementing NIST guidelines. Conduct incident responses. Include provisions for credit and identity monitoring. Because of the hospital being part of the government, there is no brand damage.
Accounting of disclosures	Must provide the accounting once live on an EHR.	Must provide once live on an EHR.	If already live with an EHR, must provide accounting by January 1, 2014. If implementing an EHR after January 1, 2009, then must produce reports when asked.
Minimum necessary	Typically sends information regarding referrals to primary care doctor. Information received is typically in paper format.	Must share information with other physicians in the continuity of the patients care.	Important to understand what is important in the care of the patient. Define minimum necessary in policy if possible.
Marketing and sale of PHI	Ask for permission. Not typically a large amount of revenue for physician.	Ask for permission. Can be an integral part of revenue, especially for companies targeting pediatrics.	Ask for permission. Integral part of fundraising. Marketing for medications can reduce the cost of medicine delivery.

National Health Information Network

The *National Health Information Network (NHIN)* system is based on the HITECH/ARRA requirement to provide better exchange of patient information no matter where in the nation the patient is seen. It will enable better patient outcomes because of the vast clinical information available for research and will greatly reduce the cost of care per patient because of the reduction in medication errors, adverse drug reactions, and repetitive lab work and studies. One recent outcome of the NHIN is the Direct Project, which facilitates data interchange between medical entities. The module most widely used is the one for exchanging emails securely between medical facilities. You can find more information at www.directproject.org, and you can view the full scope of the NHIN at the HHS website:

```
http://healthit.hhs.gov/portal/server.pt?open=512&objID=1142&parentname
=CommunityPage&parentid=4&mode=2
```

A number of smaller *health information exchanges (HIEs)* are being created or are already in existence. These exchanges are typically regional in nature, such as a data exchange within a single state. Typically, it is easier to mandate an HIE at a state or local level than at the federal level. Eventually, these local health information exchanges will most likely feed the larger NHIN. In the local area where we live, there is a health information exchange that allows the local hospitals to see patient information for patients in their care. The security of the data continues to be a challenge given the number of entities involved, and the privacy of patients is a concern. The success of the HIE will not be known for awhile because each HIE operates under different guidelines and procedures. The implementation barriers for an HIE are vast. California got stuck and eventually disbanded the group set up to create the privacy and security standards. Until the legal uncertainties are resolved, there will be minimal adoption. Exchanging information is complex. Most organizations have difficulty exchanging data internally, much less externally. Network tunnels must stay up, the data must be validated, and the privacy and security must be maintained no matter the location of the information.

NHIN

A set of standards, services, and policies as defined by the U.S. Department Health and Human Services for the secure exchange of health information across the Internet.

Real World Scenario

Immunization Registry

A local government entity created its own immunization registry in 2002. The registry is used to track vaccines administered to all residents of their county. De-identified data also is sent to public health officials, because they are looking for trends in the data. To reduce and streamline ongoing costs, the public health department decided to migrate their data to a state-run system. The team doing the data extract found that the data at the state had a number of duplicate entries. When working with patient data such as immunizations, it is important to have clean data so that immunizations are not administered multiple times. Given that, under the current system for funding medical care, patients are not necessarily honest about their identities when they present themselves for treatment, the data corruption will be a long-term problem. However, in systems that can do verification based on Social Security numbers (SSNs), medical record numbers (MRNs), and other data such as phone number or address, the accuracy will increase.

Personal Health Records

A *personal health record (PHR)* is considered a non-HIPAA covered entity. However, these entities store individual health information, which means that a PHR could be a specific breach target. When a breach occurs at a PHR site (whether detected by the PHR or by a consumer), both the Federal Trade Commission (FTC) and the individual whose unsecured data was breached must be notified. Should the FTC be confronted with a consumer complaint that has not been addressed by a PHR, the FTC informs the PHR and attempts to resolve the issue. The law encompasses the providers of services to the PHR, just like HITECH extends HIPAA compliance to the BA. A data center, network provider, and others fall into this service provider's provision. It is unclear whether the FTC rule preempts state or local laws. You can read the FTC breach notification rule for electronic health information in its entirety at www.ftc.gov/opa/2009/08/hbn.shtm. Standard FTC notification forms and additional information about the rule are available from the Bureau of Consumer Protection's Business Center at www.ftc.gov/healthbreach.

Terms to Know

Continuity of Care Document (CCD)	breach
breach notification	personal health record (PHR)
PHI marketing	PHI sale
minimum necessary	de-identified data
National Health Information Network (NHIN)	health information exchange (HIE)
Health Information Technology for Economic and Clinical Health (HITECH)	

Review Questions

1. How many individual records must be breached before being required to immediately (within 60 days) report the breach to the HHS secretary?

   A. 10

   B. 50

   C. 500

   D. 100

2. What is the minimum number of individuals who must be affected by a breach of PHI before reporting it to the HHS secretary on a yearly basis?

   A. 1

   B. 10

   C. 100

   D. 500

3. When reporting a breach, fewer than 10 of the affected people do not have current contact information. What must be done to reach those individuals?

   A. Set up a call-in number.

   B. Publish a toll-free number on the corporate website.

   C. Place a notice of the breach on the website.

   D. Place a notice at the location of the breach.

4. When a breach affects 500 or more individuals, which of the following is not required?

   A. Notifying the affected individual

   B. Submitting breach data to the HHS secretary

   C. Broadcasting information regarding the breach via local media outlets

   D. Offering credit monitoring services

5. What is the new civil penalty for the negligent breach of PHI?

   A. $25,000

   B. $250,000

   C. $1,500,000

   D. $2,500,000

6. Are business associates required to comply with the HITECH rules?

    A. Yes

    B. No

7. Are business associates required to comply with HIPAA?

    A. Yes

    B. No

8. When selling PHI, what is required?

    A. The consent of the covered entity selling the information

    B. The consent of the provider to release the information

    C. The consent of the individual whose PHI is being sold

    D. The consent of the individual and the covered entity

9. When selling PHI, what is the maximum payment allowed?

    A. $1,500,000

    B. $2,500,000

    C. No limit

    D. Payment considered reasonable for the amount of effort expended

Chapter 6

ARRA Funding

This chapter provides a high-level overview of the American Recovery and Reinvestment Act (ARRA) of 2009 that is fueling the $27.3 billion investment in healthcare IT and covers the steps necessary to meet meaningful use of that technology. Meeting the promise of the capabilities of health information exchange will not be possible without well-trained IT professionals and technology vendors. Eligible providers (EPs) can receive $44,000 in Medicare incentive funds and $63,500 in incentives for Medicaid—but only if there are IT professionals who understand their business well enough to effectively deploy the EHR. To receive full funding, physicians must have a system installed and meet meaningful use by October 1, 2012. That $27.3 billion is just the tip of the iceberg in terms of spending. We are seeing a trend of nearly $2 in EP investment for every dollar of federal incentive.

ARRA Background

In 2009, the federal government created the American Recovery and Reinvestment Act. This act included a number of financial earmarks. Some of the reinvestment money was to be spent on producing energy, implementing solar cell technologies, fixing potholes, and creating incentive for doctors to use electronic health records (EHRs). The Centers for Medicare and Medicaid Services (CMS, a U.S. federal agency) was asked to publish a set of rules for certifying an EHR package (certification criteria), defining the metrics to be used for meeting *meaningful use*, and using both to improve the quality of care. The dates for meeting meaningful use and reimbursement were set by the ARRA law.

To meet meaningful use, the first step is to make sure the system being used is certified. The Health and Human Services (HHS) was required to develop the criteria for certification. DHHS contains a business unit called the Office of the National Coordinator (ONC), which was charged with developing the criteria. The testing and certification bodies are known as ONC-Authorized Testing and Certification Bodies (ONC-ATCB).

> **AARA**
> The American Recovery and Reinvestment Act provides incentives for providers to use EHRs.

> **NOTE**
> **Because of the possibility that the certification bodies will change, please review the ONC website at** http://healthit.hhs.gov/portal/server .pt?open=512&mode=2&objID=3120. **You can find the current list of certified health IT products at** http://onc-chpl.force.com/ehrcert.

> **ONC-ATCB**
> The Office of the National Coordinator, a business unit of the U.S. Department Health and Human Services, established authorized testing and certification bodies called ONC-ATCB.

ONC was also charged with defining the criteria for meeting meaningful use. Because of the quick ramp-up of the technology, ONC understood that for the first year of receiving reimbursements there would be a need for self-attestation on some of the objectives. The final rule accounts for the change in how reporting is done.

The definitions that follow are the basis for meeting the reporting requirements for EHR incentive payments:

> **Qualified Electronic Health Record** A *qualified electronic health record* is defined as electronic health-related information about an individual that includes patient demographics, has the capacity to provide clinical decision support (CDS), enables *computer physician order entry (CPOE)*, enables the capture of structured data, and enables and is capable of exchanging electronic personal health information (ePHI) with other sources such as the National Health Information Network (NHIN).

> **Certified Electronic Health Record Technology** *Certified electronic health record technology* is a combination of EHR modules where each module meets the requirements included in the definition of a qualified EHR and has been tested and certified in accordance to the criteria set forth by the ONC-ATCB.

There, of course, have been other incentive programs for healthcare providers in the past, and we expect there to be more. Prior to ARRA, there was the Medicare Improvements for Patients and Providers Act (MIPPA) of 2008. This act included provisions for compensating providers that electronically sent prescriptions for fulfillment. Also known as *eprescribing (eRx)* incentive pay, a provider that received payment under MIPPA cannot receive incentive payments under ARRA. However, if the eligible professional is participating the Medicaid *EHR incentive program*, they are eligible. Although the funding comes from the feds, the programs are managed by the states.

Eligible professionals who are participating in the *Medicare Physician Quality Reporting Initiative (PQRI)* are eligible to receive the EHR incentive dollars. Medicare Electronic Health Record Demonstration and Medicare Care Management Performance Demonstration (MCMP) participants are eligible as well. The MCMP demo funding ends prior to the availability of the EHR funding.

EHR Adoption

Federal stimulus is a driving force behind installing EHR systems nationally. According to a study published in the February 2009 *New England Journal of Medicine*, there was only a 4 percent EHR adoption rate among physicians. More recent studies show a higher adoption rate approaching 50 percent, although not all of these are certified EHR systems. The EHR adoption rate should increase over the next few years since, on July 28, 2010, the secretary of CMS published the final rules for meeting the meaningful use requirements under the ARRA incentive program. You can find the initial set of standards, implementation specifications, and certification criteria at http://edocket .access.gpo.gov/2010/pdf/2010-17210.pdf.

A number of challenges must be addressed prior to calling the funding of EHRs a success. The idea that the necessary components will magically fall into place is naïve. CMS has commented that the availability of an EHR system does not mean the system is being utilized. Without proper training, education, and up-front involvement, the successful launch of an EMR will be hindered. Also, each year that the meaningful use rules change, the EHR system must be recertified.

Meaningful use is best described as a framework defined by the federal government. When Congress and the U.S. President established meaningful use, they included three pillars. The first pillar requires the use of a certified EHR system in a meaningful way. The second pillar requires utilizing the EHR technology to improve the quality of care. The last pillar requires that EPs actually use the structured data (as defined by the EHR criteria) to submit information on quality measures to certain agencies. Because of the length of time necessary to test and deploy an EHR on a large scale, hospitals have some leeway when

MIPPA vs. ARRA
A provider that received payment under MIPPA cannot receive incentive payments under ARRA. Those participating in Medicaid EHR incentive programs are eligible, however, because those programs are managed through the states.

it comes to compliance with the meaningful use requirements in their first year of deployment. Under the reimbursement rules, a Medicaid provider that is "demonstrating progress towards integration of EHRs into their routine health care practices to improve patient safety, care, and outcomes" can start receiving reimbursement (page 44504 of the Federal Register). Since the rules for Medicaid reimbursement vary from state to state, verify with the local regional extension center to confirm that the statement holds true for the customers you serve.

The Final Rule for Meaningful Use Stage 1 includes a core set of objective with a pairing of a measurement which must be reported on. Stage 2 and 3 requirements for meaningful use at the time of the printing of this book have not been completed. Most notably, the working group, HITSP, that is helping to guide Stage 2 requirements has actually recommended a one-year delay in implementation requirements. The working group is concerned that EHR vendors and the medical communities are saturated with changes to workflow and programming requirements, coupled with a shortage of qualified staff; meeting the current timeline would be harmful and impractical.

The meaningful use objectives and the approved method for measuring compliance against the objective are broken into 15 core objectives for an EP and a shorter menu set they must select 5 out of 10 compliance items. Funding for hospitals is slightly different with just 14 core objectives and 5 out of 10 menu option or Chinese menu objectives. We will address hospitals later in the chapter. You might hear, when working in the industry, the menu set referred to as the Chinese menu option. The idea behind the new Chinese menu option is that it allows reporting on criteria critical for your organization. The remaining five must be reported when complying with Stage 2 meaningful use. Some eligible professionals might not be able to report from even five objectives on the menu set. The law includes exclusions and identifies who can be excluded and from which objective. As a healthcare IT professional, make sure you spend time with your clients or employers to review which items of the menu set apply and which ones you might need to ask for an exclusion. Once an exclusion is granted, one less report is required to be submitted to meet meaningful use. (We'll cover these in greater detail later in this chapter.) In addition to the 20 objectives that must be reported on to meet meaningful use, the EP must also report on six *clinical quality measures (CQMs)*, specifically, three from a required core set and three from a menu of 38 CQMs.

Funding for Eligible Professionals

eligible professional
An eligible professional is classified for Medicare as a doctor of medicine (MD), a doctor of osteopathy (DO), a dentist or dental surgeon (DDS or DMD), a podiatrist (DPM), a doctor optometry (OD), or a doctor of chiropractic (DC).

Under the *ARRA funding* law, there are two funding programs. Any EP can be reimbursed either under Medicare or under Medicaid. It is critical to understand that an EP cannot apply for both Medicare and Medicaid reimbursement. Before a practice chooses an incentive program, it must understand the reimbursement structure and under which program it will receive the higher payout. (For some specialists, ARRA funding will not play a role at all. There are reimbursements for eprescribing for physicians who do not have a large enough panel of Medicare or Medicaid patients.) Eligible physicians are allowed to change from Medicare to Medicaid or vice versa only once. So, as an IT professional, make sure the proper staff has spent the appropriate amount of time selecting the right incentive program.

Under the Medicare reimbursement structure, an eligible physician will be reimbursed by calculating 75 percent of the total yearly allowed charges. To receive the full incentive payment from Medicare, at least 30 percent of the EP's patient encounters must be with Medicare patients. The reimbursement will be up to the capped reimbursement amount based on the EHR incentive schedule. These allowable charges are the amounts that Medicare pays the physician under the Part B program. Only the professional services rendered by the EP are counted for reimbursement. Medicare also has reimbursements called *technical components* that are not part of the calculation.

technical components
The technical components are the equipment used for testing and the technician who is performing the test.

professional components
The professional components are the fees for interpreting the results of the test.

For example, in 2012, a physician who bills $100,000 for services covered under Medicare would receive the maximum reimbursement of $18,000 dollars if an EHR is installed and the practice meets meaningful use by the deadline. If a physician bills only $10,000 in Medicare services, that physician would receive only $7,500 dollars in stimulus funds. Table 6.1 lists the EHR stimulus funding timetable.

Table 6.1   EHR Stimulus Funding Timetable

First Demon-strated Use	2011	2012	2013	2014	2015	2016	Total
2011	$18,000	$12,000	$8,000	$4,000	$2,000	$0	$44,000
2012	$0	$18,000	$12,000	$8,000	$4,000	$2,000	$44,000
2013	$0	$0	$15,000	$12,000	$8,000	$4,000	$39,000
2014	$0	$0	$0	$12,000	$8,000	$4,000	$24,000
Beyond	$0	$0	$0	$0	$0	$0	$0

For those medical practices that have not deployed an EHR package that meets meaningful use, Medicare reduces reimbursement to the practice by 1 percent per year up to a total of 97 percent. If the EHR adoption rate doesn't hit 75 percent nationwide, the secretary of Health and Human Services (HHS) can reduce reimbursement by a total of 5 percent.

When an EP selects to be reimbursed under ARRA through Medicaid, the provider's Medicaid patient load must be at least 30 percent of their total patient load. The only exception is for pediatricians, who are required only a 20 percent Medicaid workload. The 30 percent of the patient workload requirement must have been met for at least a continuous 90-day period in the calendar year being reported for incentives. Since some services might not be allowed under Medicaid, the regulation allows for an encounter to be treated as a Medicaid encounter if any part of the encounter is reimbursed by Medicaid.

The eligible base for Medicaid also was expanded to include Medicare eligible physicians, certified midwives, nurse practitioners, and physician assistants (PAs) practicing in a federally qualified health center (FQHC) or rural health center (RHC) that is led by a PA. (Many rural clinics do not have physicians, and thus a PA runs the environment.)

Physicians might also ask you whether the payment is in a single lump sum or will trickle in over the year. Once CMS has validated that the EP has met the meaningful use requirements, the EP is eligible to receive reimbursement. The payments are made once the first provider has reached the maximum reimbursement amount or after the calendar year ends.

Another question that you will be asked as an IT professional in the healthcare vertical is whether all physicians must go live on the EHR system at the same time. Some medical practices have physicians retiring, so they may not want to participate because their retirement conflicts with the installation dates. In all practicality, most physician offices with fewer than five doctors go with a big-bang approach and migrate all participating physicians to the system on the same day. The larger the practice, the more challenging the issues they'll face when selecting the right reimbursement structure. Provide guidance and explain the benefits. At the end of the day, it is their decision to purchase a system. In practices where a few doctors hold out, we have found a benefit analysis—provided by an IT professional and delivered by a colleague who advocates deploying an EHR—is an effective tool. Remember that the complexities of having two workflows for staff defeats many of the efficiencies gained by deploying an EHR.

Funding and Eligibility for Hospitals

Since physicians (those who provide 90 percent or more of their services in a hospital) could not receive funding, there was a perceived misappropriation of funds if the hospital was not eligible for incentive payments for completing EHR deployments. Eligible hospitals incentives are initially based on the initial amount, the Medicare share, the transition factor, and a discharge-related amount. The base amount for the EHR reimbursement is $2 million. Added to this initial payment is a discharge-related amount. The discharge amount is calculated based on the number of actual discharges. No discharge amounts are added for fewer than 1,149 discharges. A maximum of 23,000 discharges are eligible for reimbursement. Each discharge within the 1,149 to 23,000 discharge range receives a $200 payout. The total reimbursement would be $2 million plus a maximum discharge payment of $4.37 million.

The funding under the Medicare hospital reimbursement structure is complex. (The CMS provides the formulas on pages 44459 and 44460 of the Federal Register.) Critical-access hospitals are under different rules, so the previous formulas do not apply. In addition, Medicare and Medicaid incentives are available for hospitals, but we are not CPAs or hospital CFOs, and we suspect the same is true with you. Please make sure you leave the complex financial number-crunching to the professionals. We provide these numbers only for reference.

Medicaid Incentives

The Medicaid EHR incentive program is offered to states and territories. Eligible acute-care hospitals and children's hospitals that actively participate in the incentive program can receive reimbursement payments of up to $63,750 over a six-year period. These years do not have to be consecutive. The hospital must begin receiving payments by 2016, and the last payment must be received in 2021. In terms of the incentive program, an acute-care hospital is defined as having an average patient length of stay of 25 days or less, and with a CMS certification number (CCN), that falls between 0001–0879 or 1300–1399.

Since Medicaid reimbursement comes from the individual states, there are no set penalty adjustments for providers that do not adopt EHR technologies. Additionally, states might impose additional requirements to receive funding. To make sure funding is paid and the adoption rate continues to grow, the CMS recommends that regional extension centers be responsible for marketing and promoting EHR adoption. States will have access to a centralized system that will allow them to securely verify whether payments under the Medicare program have been made to a particular provider.

Medicare Reimbursement Database

The database that will be published by CMS will be a significant target for hackers. If providers were intentionally removed by hackers, they could receive double payment. On the other hand, if someone really disliked a particular EP and illicitly added the provider to the database, even though the EP never received reimbursement, different problems present themselves. As IT professionals, we are not yet sure how to handle issues that might arise with the database. If the federal government allows the states only to view the information, then we suspect that EPs will demand a reporting method (much like credit reporting) and a process for querying and correcting inaccuracies.

CMS has defined other rules for eligible providers under the Medicaid incentives. These incentives require that eligible physicians over a continuous 90-day period have a patient load from Medicaid of 30 percent in all but two cases: pediatricians are required only to have a 20 percent *Medicaid patient volume*, and acute-care hospitals need only 10 percent to qualify.

Starting in 2017, hospitals cannot receive payment under Medicaid. Also, states may not reimburse a hospital more than 50 percent of their aggregate incentive payment amount in a single year or 90 percent in two consecutive years.

Meaningful Use: Stage 1

As stated earlier, meaningful use has 15 *core objectives* for EPs and 14 core objectives for hospitals; both hospitals and EPs have 10 *menu set objectives*. All of the core objectives must be met, and information must be reported for 5 of the 10 menu set objectives. In addition, CQMs must be reported. You can find the clinical quality measures at https://www.cms.gov/QualityMeasures/03_ElectronicSpecifications.asp.

To demonstrate meaningful use, hospitals must be able to report on all 15 measurements in the *CQM core set*. Hospitals must also be able to report on one of the following:

◆ Immunization data

◆ Reportable lab results

◆ Syndromic surveillance data

EPs must be able to report on at least three of the measurements in the CQM core set, as well as three additional measures.

Core Objective Set for Hospitals

The meaningful use core objective set for hospitals includes requirements for recording demographic information; information about medications, drug-to-drug interactions, and drug allergies; known problems being experienced by the patient; current conditions, including height, weight, smoking status, and the like; and at least one clinical decision support rule. For 2011, a hospital must provide aggregate numerator, denominator, and exclusions through attestation. For 2012, hospitals must electronically submit clinical quality measures. Submission through a portal is the only mechanism that is feasible and practical for 2012. This rule applies only to patients whose records are maintained using a certified EHR.

Demographics   More than 50 percent of all unique patients admitted to the hospital as inpatients or to the emergency department (ED) must have demographics recorded as structured data. This includes preferred language, gender, race, ethnicity, date of birth, date, and preliminary cause of death in the event of mortality in the hospital. (This does not have to be the cause of death included on the death certificate.) No exclusion is available for this objective; however, the hospital is not obliged to record the information if the patient declines to give it or if an element is contrary to state law.

Race and ethnicity codes should follow the current federal standards found at www.house.gov/OMB/inforeg_statpolicy/#dr.

Medications   More than 30 percent of unique patients with at least one medication in their medication list admitted to the hospital inpatient department or ED have at least one medication order entered using CPOE. This applies only to patients whose medical records are maintained using certified EHR. Any licensed healthcare professional can enter orders using CPOE.

Another core set is drug-to-drug and drug allergy interaction. The hospital must have this functionality enabled for the entire reporting period.

More than 80 percent of all unique patient admitted to the hospital inpatient department or ED have at least one entry or an indication that no problems are known for the patient recorded as structured data.

More than 80 percent of all unique patients admitted to the hospitals inpatient department or ED have at least one entry or an indication that no active medicines are known and thus recorded as structured data. To meet the structured data, the information about the medication should be made available without having to look into an order.

More than 80 percent of all patients admitted to the hospital's inpatient department or ED have at least one entry or an indication to the contrary that the patient has no known medication allergies recorded as structured data.

Current Condition   For more than 50 percent of all unique patients age two and older admitted to the inpatient department or ED, height, weight, and blood pressure are recorded as structured data. This applies only to patients whose records are in a certified EHR. Height self-reporting is allowed.

More than 50 percent of all unique patients 13 years old and older admitted to the hospital's inpatient department or ED have smoking status recorded as structured data. This applies only to patients whose records are kept electronically. There is an exclusion if the hospital admits no one 13 or older like in a children's hospital. ONC has adopted the following data: current daily smoker, current some-day smoker, former smoker, never smoked, smoker, status unknown, and unknown if ever smoked. The frequency of updating this is up to the provider.

Clinical Decision Support Rules   To meet meaningful use, a hospital must implement at least one clinical decision support rule. The hospital is fortunate in this case because there are a plethora of possible CDS rules to use. The best decision on CDS reporting is to make sure that the CDS rule chosen will have the greatest impact.

Information Request Response Time   More than 50 percent of all patients of the inpatient department or ED who request an electronic copy of their health information are provided it within three business days. This objective applies only to patient information kept in a certified EHR. Only information kept electronically must be given. The number of patients served includes only the patients requesting information prior to the closing of the fourth day prior to the close of the reporting period. The provider can withhold certain information.

Electronic Discharge Instructions   An electronic copy of the discharge instructions are provided to more than 50 percent of all inpatients who are discharged from a hospital's inpatient department or ED who request an electronic copy. This is not applicable if no patients make the request. Discharge instruction or instructions on how to access them electronically should be furnished at the time of discharge.

Certified EHR Technology Capacity Testing   Perform at least one test of certified EHR technology with the capacity to exchange key clinical information (discharge summary, procedures, problem list, medication list, medication allergies, diagnostic test results). The test must involve the actual submission of information to another provider of care with distinct certified EHR technology or other system capable of receiving the information. Dummy information is permissible.

Security Risk Analysis   Conduct or review a security risk analysis and implement security updates as necessary to correct identified security deficiencies as part of its risk management process.

Menu Set for Hospitals

Information must be reported for five of the 10 meaningful use *menu set objectives* by each hospital seeking reimbursement.

Drug Formularies   Enable the functionality and have access to at least the OMB internal or external drug formulary for the entire reporting period.

Advanced Directive Status   More than 50 percent of all unique patients who are 65 years old or older and are admitted to the hospital's inpatient department have an indication of an advanced directive status recorded. This item applies only to patients whose records are maintained using the certified EHR. If the hospital doesn't serve older patients, there is an exclusion.

Clinical Lab Results   More than 40 percent of all clinical lab results ordered by an authorized provider of the hospital's patients admitted to its inpatient department or ED during the reporting period whose results are either positive or negative or numerical format are incorporated into the certified EHR technology as structure data.

This item applies only to patients whose records are maintained using certified EHR. Hospitals may count all structured data in numerator, not just data received via electronic exchange. Hospitals are not required to receive the transmittal or receive the information electronically. Structured data that is not fully dependent on an established standard within the certified EHR technology merely requires the system to be able to identify the data as providing specific information commonly accomplished by creating fixed fields.

Specific Condition Reports   Generate at least one report listing patients of the hospital with a specific condition. This applies only to patients whose records are maintained using certified EHR; this report does not need to be submitted.

Education Resources   More than 10 percent of all unique patients admitted to the hospital's inpatient department or ED are provided patient-specific education resources. This includes using the EHR technology to identify the education resources and providing those resources to the patient.

Transition of Care Medication Reconciliation   The receiving hospital performs medication reconciliation for more than 50 percent of the transitions of care in which the patient is admitted to the hospital's inpatient department or ED. This item applies only to patients whose records are maintained using certified EHR. The denominator is the number of transitions of care during the reporting period for which the hospital was the recipient of the transition. Medication reconciliation is the process of identifying the most accurate list of all medications that the patient is taking including name dosage frequency and route by comparing the medical record to an external list of medications obtained from a patient hospital or other provider.

Transition of Care Summary of Care Records   The hospital that transitions or refers their patient to another care setting provides a summary of care record for more than 50 percent of transitions of care and referrals. This applies only to EHR patients. The transition of care is defined as the movement from one setting of care (for example: hospital, ambulatory, primary-care practice, specialty-care practice, long-term care, home health, and rehabilitation facility) to another. The EHR must generate the summary of care.

Immunization Data Submission Testing   The hospital must perform at least one test of the certified EHR technology's capacity to submit electronic data to immunization. It requires registries and follow-up submission if the test is successful. The exception is if no immunizations were administered. Dummy information is permissible. If the test fails, it does comply. If it is successful, the hospital should continue to submit.

Public Health Agency Reporting   The hospital has performed at least one test of the certified EHR technology's capacity to provide electronic submission of reportable lab results to public health agencies and follow-up submission if the test is successful. Exclusion is possible if the public health agency can't receive the data.

It performed at least one test of the certified EHR technology's capacity to provide electronic syndromic surveillance data to public health agencies and follow-up submission if the test is successful.

Clinical Quality Measures for Hospitals

In addition, there are 15 core set CQMs available for selection. Participating hospitals must be able to generate reports for all of these:

- Anticoagulation overlap therapy
- Emergency department throughput–admitted patients: median time from ED arrival to ED departure for admitted patients
- Emergency department throughput–admitted patients: admission decision time to ED departure time for admitted patients
- Incidence of potentially preventable Venus thromboembolism (VTE)
- Intensive care unit VTE prophylaxis
- Ischemic (decrease in blood supply caused by an obstruction or constriction of the blood vessel) stroke: discharge on antithrombotics
- Ischemic stroke: anticoagulation for A-fib/flutter
- Ischemic stroke: thrombolytic therapy for patients arriving within two hours of symptom onset
- Ischemic or hemorrhagic stroke, antithrombotic therapy by day 2
- Ischemic stroke: discharge on statins
- Ischemic or hemorrhagic stroke: stroke education
- Ischemic or hemorrhagic stroke: rehabilitation assessment
- Platelet monitoring on unfractionated heparin
- VTE prophylaxis within 24 hours of arrival
- VTE discharge instructions

Core Set for Objectives Eligible Professional

Medications   More than 30 percent of all unique patients with at least one medication must have their medication order entered electronically. The only exclusion is for providers who prescribe less than 100 prescriptions during the EHR reporting period.

Implement drug-drug and drug-allergy interaction checks. There are no exclusions for this objective.

EPs must generate and transmit permissible prescriptions electronically for more than 40 percent of all permissible prescriptions written. An EP who writes fewer than 100 prescriptions is exempt from this requirement.

An active medication list must be maintained in a certified EHR for more than 80 percent of all unique patients by the EP. There is no exclusion.

80 percent of an eligible professional's patients must have an allergy list maintained. If the patient has no known allergies, this fact must be documented as well. There is no exclusion.

Demographics   More than 50 percent of all unique patients seen by the EP must have demographics recorded as structured data. This includes preferred language, gender, race, ethnicity, date of birth. No exclusion is available for this objective.

Race and ethnicity codes should follow the current federal standards found at www.house.gov/OMB/inforeg_statpolicy/#dr.

Current Condition   Eligible professionals must maintain an up-to-date problem list of all current and active diagnoses for 80 percent of all unique patients seen by the EP. If no problem list or active diagnoses are available for a patient, then that must be noted in the EHR. There is no exclusion for this measure.

The vital signs (height, weight, blood pressure, BMI, and display of growth charts for children 2-20) of a patient must be recorded. EPs are required to measure these vital signs across 50 percent of the unique patients age 2 and older. Any EP who doesn't see patients 2 or older, or believes that the three vital signs of height, weight, and blood pressure of their patients have no relevance in their scope of practice.

More than 50 percent of all unique patients 13 years old and older seen by an EP must have smoking status recorded as structured data. This applies only to patients whose records are kept electronically. There is an exclusion for an EP who doesn't see patients 13 years or older.

Clinical Decision Support Rules and Quality Measures   Implement at least one clinical decision support rule relevant to the specialty, or high clinical priority and the capability to track the compliance with the rule. There is no exclusion for this measure.

Report ambulatory clinical quality measures to CMS in a manner specified by the CMS. There is no exclusion. The clinical quality measures are defined later in the chapter, and can be found at http://www.cms.gov/QualityMeasures/03_ElectronicSpecifications.asp#TopOfPage

Information Request Response Time   Provide patients with an electronic copy of their health information including diagnostic test results, problem list, medication lists, and medication allergies upon request. The information must be provided within three business days to 50 percent to the patients who request the information. The only exclusion is for providers who have not received the request by any patient.

Electronic Discharge Instructions   An electronic copy of the discharge instructions are provided to more than 50 percent of all inpatients who are discharged from a hospital's inpatient department or ED who request an electronic copy. This is not applicable if no patients make the request. Discharge instruction or instructions on how to access them electronically should be furnished at the time of discharge.

Certified EHR Technology Information Exchange Testing   Perform at least one test of certified EHR technology with the capacity to exchange key clinical information (discharge summary, procedures, problem list, medication list, medication allergies, diagnostic test results). The test must involve the actual submission of information to another provider of care with distinct certified EHR technology or other system capable of receiving the information. Dummy information is permissible.

Security Risk Analysis   The objective is to protect electronic health information created or maintained by the EHR technology through the appropriate technical capabilities. This risk assessment and security review must be completed in accordance with the requirements outlined by 45 CFR 164.308(a)(1). There is no exclusion.

Menu Set for Eligible Professionals

Information must be reported for five of the 10 meaningful use *menu set objectives* by each Eligible Professional seeking reimbursement.

Drug Formularies   Enable the functionality and have access to at least the one internal or external drug formulary for the entire reporting period. An EP who writes less than 100 prescriptions is not required to comply.

Generate Patient Lists by Condition   Generate at least one report listing patients of the EP with a specific condition to use for quality improvement, reduction of disparities, research or outreach. There is no exclusion.

Clinical Lab Results   More than 40 percent of all clinical lab results ordered by an EP during the reporting period whose results are either positive or negative or numerical format are incorporated into the certified EHR technology as structure data. An EP who does not order lab test which result in a positive/negative or numeric format during the EHR reporting period.

Clinical Summaries and Education Resources   Clinical summaries are provided to patients for more than 50 percent of all office visits within three business days if the patient's data is kept electronically. An office visit is defined as any billable visit that includes concurrent care or transfer of care visits, consultant visits, and prolonged physician service without direct face-to-face patient contact.

The EP must use certified EHR technology to identify patient-specific education resources and provide those resources to more than 10 percent of al unique patients seen. There is no exclusion.

Patient Electronic Access   Provide patients with timely electronic access to their health information (including lab results, problem list, medication lists, and allergies) within four business days of the data being available to the eligible professional. Compliance with the measure requires that at least 10 percent of all patients seen by the EP who ask for electronic access to their health information subject to the EP's discretion to withhold certain information.

Patient Reminders   Send patients, if the have chosen to opt in, a reminder for preventive or follow-up care. The EP must do this for more than twenty percent of all patients 65 years or older, or 5 years old or younger during the EHR reporting period. An EP who does not have patients within this age range is excluded from this measure.

Medication Reconciliation   The EP who receives a patient from another care setting, provider, or believes an encounter is relevant should perform medication reconciliation for more than 50 percent of the transitions of care.

Immunization Registries Data Submission   The EP must have tested at least once, the submission of electronic data to immunization registries or immunization information systems and the actual submission must comply with applicable law and practice. If the test is successful, then a follow-up submission is required. EPs who do not administer immunizations during the reporting period or have no immunization registry to send the data to are exempt from this objective.

Syndromic Surveillance Data   At least one test submitting electronic syndromic surveillance data to a public health agency in accordance to applicable law, must be done by the EP. If successful, a follow-up submission is required. The EP who does not collect any reportable syndromic information is not required to submit the data.

Eligible Provider Clinical Quality Measures

EPs must report on three measures from the *CQM core set* (substituting from the *CQM alternate core set* where necessary) and three additional measures. (You can download a copy of the *Eligible Professional Clinical Quality Measure* from www.cms.gov/QualityMeasures/03_ElectronicSpecifications .asp.) The CQM alternative core set measures exist just in case one of the measurements in the core set has zero as a value. They must pick three additional measures from a menu of 44 measures. If reporting zero values for any of these measures, the EP must attest that zero is the value expected. For the core CQMs, the EP must select one for another measurement to report. Ambulatory clinical quality measures are to be submitted through attestation in 2011. In 2011, all CQM must be submitted electronically.

Proposed Meaningful Use Objectives: Stage 2 and Stage 3

At the time of this writing, Stage 2 and Stage 3 of the meaningful use objectives have not been finalized. The HITPC developed a preliminary set of recommendations designed to solicit feedback. Table 6.2 summarizes the proposed rule contained in the "Request for Comments Regarding Meaningful Use Stage 2." The HITPC voted 12-5 to recommend a delay until 2014 to meet meaningful use Stage 2. You can find this document at http://healthit.hhs.gov/media/ faca/MU_RFC%20_2011-01-12_final.pdf.

Table 6.2   Meaningful Use Stage 2 and Stage 3 Summary

Stage 1 Final Rule	Proposed Stage 2	Proposed Stage 3	HITPC Comments
CPOE for medication, 30% of unique patients (EP/EH).	CPOE 60% for at least one lab and/or medication. Doesn't have to be transmitted electronically.	Same as Stage 2 but 80%.	None.
Drug-to-drug/drug-allergy interaction checks (EP/EH).	Employ drug-to-drug interaction checking and drug allergy checking on appropriate evidence-based interactions.	Employ drug-to-drug interaction checking, drug age checking, drug dose checking, drug lab checking, and drug condition checking on appropriate evidence-based interactions.	Reporting of drug interaction checks to be defined by quality measures group.

Table 6.2   Meaningful Use Stage 2 and Stage 3 Summary *(continued)*

Stage 1 Final Rule	Proposed Stage 2	Proposed Stage 3	HITPC Comments
Eprescribing by EP for 40% of orders (EP).	50% of orders.	80% of orders.	If pharmacy cannot receive order electronically, automatically fax it.
Record demographics (EP/EH): 50%.	80% of patients have demographics recorded and can use them to produce stratified quality reports.	90% of patients have demographics recorded and can use them to produce stratified quality reports.	None.
Report clinical quality metrics (EP/EH).	Continue as per quality measures workgroup and CMS.	Continue as per quality measures workgroup and CMS.	In December 2010, a quality measures workgroup issued a request for comments.
Maintain problem list (EP/EH): 80%.	Continue Stage 1.	80% problem lists are up-to-date.	Expect to drive list to be up-to-date by making it part of patient visit summary and care plans.
Maintain active medication list (EP/EH): 80%.	Continue Stage 1.	80% medication lists are up-to-date.	Expect to drive list to be up-to-date via medication reconciliation.
Maintain active medication allergy list (EP/EH): 80%.	Continue Stage 1.	80% medication allergy lists are up-to-date.	Expect to drive the list to be up-to-date by making it part of the visit summary.
Record vital signs, weight, blood pressure, BMI, and growth chart for 2 to 20 year olds (EP/EH): 50%.	80% of unique patients have vital signs recorded.	Same as Stage 2.	None.
Record smoking status (EP/EH): 50%.	80% of unique patients have smoking status recorded.	90% of unique patients have smoking status recorded.	None.

Table 6.2   Meaningful Use Stage 2 and Stage 3 Summary *(continued)*

Stage 1 Final Rule	Proposed Stage 2	Proposed Stage 3	HITPC Comments
Implement one clinical decision support rule (EP/EH).	Use CDS to improve performance on high-priority health condition. Establish CDS attributes for purposes of certification. 1) authenticated, 2) credible, evidence-based, 3) patient context-sensitive 4) Invokes relevant knowledge, 5) timely 6) efficient workflow, 7) integrated with EHR, 8) presented to the appropriate party who can take action.	Same as Stage 2.	None.
Implement drug formulary checks.	Move to core set.	80% of medication orders are checked against relevant formularies.	None.
Record evidence of advanced directives for eligible hospitals: 50%.	Make advanced directives a core requirement. For EP and HE: 50% compliance for those unique patients 65 years or older.	Same as Stage 2 but 90% compliance.	Potential issues include the following: state statues, challenges in outpatient settings, age, privacy, specialist, needs to be accessible and certifiable, needs to define a standard.
Incorporate labs as structured data: 40%.	Move current measure to core.	90% of lab results electronically entered by EHR and stored as structured data.	None.
Generate patient lists with specific conditions.	Make core requirement. Generate patient lists for multiple patient-specific parameters.	Patient lists are used to manage patients for high-priority conditions.	None.
Send patient reminders: 20%.	Make core requirement.	20% of active patients who prefer to receive reminders electronically for follow-up or preventative care.	How should "active patient" be defined?
None.	30% of visits have at least one electronic EP note.	90% of visits have at least one electronic EP note.	Can be scanned, narrative, structures, and so on.

Table 6.2   Meaningful Use Stage 2 and Stage 3 Summary *(continued)*

Stage 1 Final Rule	Proposed Stage 2	Proposed Stage 3	HITPC Comments
None.	30% of EH patient days have at least one electronic note by a physician, NP, or PA.	80% of EH patient days have at least one electronic note by a physician, NP, or PA.	Can be canned, narrative, structured data, and so on.
None.	30% of EH medication orders automatically tracked via electronic medication administration recording.	80% of EH inpatient medication orders are automatically tracked via electronic medication administration recording.	None.
Provide electronic copy of health information upon request (50%) (EP/EH).	Continue Stage 1.	90% of patients have timely access to a copy of health information from EHR, upon request.	Applies only to data already in EHR.
Provide electronic copy of discharge instructions (EH): 50%.	Electronic discharge instructions for hospitals are offered to at least 80% of patients.	Electronic discharge instructions for hospitals are offered to at least 90% of patients in their primary language.	Electronic discharge instructions should include a statement regarding the patient's condition, discharge medication, activities and diet, follow-up appointments, pending tests that require a follow-up, referrals, and schedule tests.
EHR-enabled patient specific educational resources: 10%.	Continue Stage 1.	20% offered patient-specific educational resources online in the common primary languages.	
None.	80% of patients offered the ability to view and download via a web-based portal within 36 hours of discharge (EH). Data is in human-readable and structured forms.	Same as Stage 2.	Inpatient summaries include the following: hospitalization admit and discharge date and location, reason for hospitalization, providers, problem list, medication lists, medication allergies, procedures, immunizations, advanced directives, smoking status vital signs at discharge, care transitions summary and plan.

Table 6.2   Meaningful Use Stage 2 and Stage 3 Summary *(continued)*

Stage 1 Final Rule	Proposed Stage 2	Proposed Stage 3	HITPC Comments
Provide clinical summaries for each office visit (EP): 50%.	Patients have the ability to view and download relevant clinical encounter information within 24 hours of the encounter. Future summaries of that encounter should include tests within four days of becoming available. Data is available in human-readable and structured forms (HITSC to define).	Same as Stage 2.	
Provide timely electronic access: 10% (EP).	Patients have the ability to view and download on demand relevant information contained in the longitudinal record, which has been updated within four days of the information being available. Patient should be able to filter by date, encounter, and so on. Extract in human- or computer-readable form.	Same as Stage 2.	The following data elements should be included: encounter dates, locations, reasons for encounters, providers, problem list, medication list, medication allergies, procedures, immunizations, vital signs, diagnostic test results, clinical instructions, orders, longitudinal care plan, gender, race, ethnicity, date of birth, preferred language, advance directives, smoking status.
	EPs: 20% of patients use a web-based portal to access encounter information.	EPs: 30% of patients use web portal.	None.
New.	EPs: online secure patient messaging is in use.	Same as Stage 2.	
	Record preferred patient communication method for 20% of patients.	Record 80% of communication preference.	How will the communication method be delineated? Will text messaging be part of the method?

Table 6.2   Meaningful Use Stage 2 and Stage 3 Summary *(continued)*

Stage 1 Final Rule	Proposed Stage 2	Proposed Stage 3	HITPC Comments
None.	None.	Offer electronic self-management tools to patients with high-priority health conditions.	What is necessary at Stage 2 to meet this goal?
None.	None.	EHRs have capability to exchange data with public health records (PHR).	Seeking comments on how to accomplish this.
None.	None.	Patients offered capability to report experience of care measures online.	What is necessary at Stage 2 to meet this goal?
None.	None.	Offer ability to upload and incorporate patient-generated data.	What is necessary at Stage 2 to meet this goal?
Perform test of *health information exchange (HIE)*.	Connect to at least three external providers in "primary referral network" but outside the same EHR system *or* establish an ongoing bidirectional connection to at least one HIE.	Connect to at least 30% of external providers or establish an ongoing bidirectional connection to at least one health information exchange.	Successful HIE will require the development and use of infrastructure like entity-level provider directories.
Perform medication reconciliation on care transitions by receiving partner: 50%.	Medication reconciliation for at least 80% of care transitions by receiving partner.	Medication reconciliation conducted at 90% of care transitions by receiving provider.	None.
Provide summary of care record for transitions of care: 50%.	Move to a core requirement.	Summary of care provided electronically for 80% of transitions and referrals.	None.
None.	List of care team members including the PCP for 10% of patients in EHR.	List of care team members including PC available for 50% of patients via electronic exchange.	None.
None.	Record a longitudinal care plan for 20% of patients with high-priority health conditions.	Longitudinal care plan available for electronic exchange for 50% of patients with high-priority health conditions.	What elements should be included in a longitudinal care plan including care team members, diagnoses, medications, allergies, goals of care, and other elements?

Table 6.2   Meaningful Use Stage 2 and Stage 3 Summary *(continued)*

Stage 1 Final Rule	Proposed Stage 2	Proposed Stage 3	HITPC Comments
Submit immunization data.	EH and EP: Mandatory test. Some immunizations are submitted on an ongoing basis to Immunization Information System, if accepted and as required by law.	EH and EP: Mandatory test. Some immunizations are submitted on an ongoing basis to Immunization Information System, if accepted and as required by law. During well-child/ adult visits, providers review IIS records via their EHR.	Stage 2 implies at least some data is submitted to IIS. EH and EP may choose not, for example, to send data through IIS to different states in Stage 2. The goal is to eventually review the IIS-generated recommendation.
Submit reportable lab data.	EH: Move Stage 1 to core. EP: Lab reporting menu. For RPs. ensure that reportable lab results and conditions are submitted to public health agencies either directly or their performing labs.	Mandatory test. EH: Submit reportable lab results and reportable conditions if accepted and as required by law. Include complete contact information in 30% of EH reports. EP: Ensure that reportable lab results and reportable condition are submitted to public health agencies either directly or through performing labs.	None.
Submit syndromic surveillance data.	Move to core.	Mandatory test. Submit if accepted.	
None.	None.	Public health button for EH and EP. Submit if acceptable. EHR can receive and present public health alerts or follow-up requests.	We are seeking comment on what steps will be needed in Stage 2 to achieve the Stage 3 objective.

Table 6.2   Meaningful Use Stage 2 and Stage 3 Summary *(continued)*

Stage 1 Final Rule	Proposed Stage 2	Proposed Stage 3	HITPC Comments
None.	None.	Patient-generated data submitted to public health agencies.	We are seeking comment on what steps will be needed in Stage 2 to achieve the Stage 3 objective.
Conduct security review analysis and correct deficiencies.			Additional privacy and security objectives are under consideration via the HIT Policy Committee's Privacy and Security Tiger Team.

Some of the suggested objectives are going to be a challenge to implement. Having patients enter data into a public health system will require advanced data analytics to make sure appropriate information is submitted. Doctors' EHRs will also have to be managed and secured differently than they are now if the objective of allowing patients to load information about other treatments is approved in the final Stage 3 objectives. There are a number of issues with allowing patients to load information. For instance, if patients upload very large files and the EHR is not set to control the size of the data upload, the EP's network connection could become saturated, causing denial-of-service attacks. If the system allows large files, the disk drives could be burdened with too much data. Also, what will the privacy and security requirements be for patient data if it is intercepted in transit because the patient used an insecure protocol, computer, or connection to transfer the information?

Terms to Know

ARRA funding

core objectives

clinical quality measures (CQMs)

CQM alternate core set

EHR incentive program

National Health Information Network (NHIN)

eprescribing (eRx)

qualified electronic health record technology

professional components

Medicare Electronic Health Record Demonstration and Medicare Care Management Performance Demonstration (MCMP)

meaningful use

menu set objectives

CQM core set

Medicaid patient volume

health information exchange (HIE)

computer physician order entry (CPOE)

qualified electronic health record

Medicare Physician Quality Reporting Initiative (PQRI)

technical components

Review Questions

1. In Stage 1 of meaningful use, how many objectives must be met by an EP?

   A. 20

   B. 24

   C. 25

   D. 27

2. How many Stage 1 objectives must be met by an EH?

   A. 21

   B. 23

   C. 24

   D. 26

3. For an EP who has a number of locations but has access to the EHR at only some of the sites, what is the minimum amount of encounters that must be recorded in the EHR?

   A. 50 percent

   B. 60 percent

   C. 75 percent

   D. 100 percent

4. How many CQMs are available in the additional set for EPs?

   A. 25

   B. 35

   C. 37

   D. 38

5. What is the last day for an EP to start using a certified EHR to meet meaningful use and receive full Medicare Incentive pay?

   A. October 1, 2012

   B. October 3, 2012

   C. January 1, 2013

   D. January 1, 2012

6. What is the last year that eligible hospitals can receive EHR reimbursement under Medicaid reimbursement?

    A. 2015

    B. 2017

    C. 2020

    D. 2021

7. What percentage of unique patients seen by the EP or admitted to a CAH or EH must maintain an active medication list that has been entered as structured data?

    A. 30 percent

    B. 50 percent

    C. 70 percent

    D. 80 percent

8. Is a security assessment required to receive EHR incentive reimbursement?

    A. Yes

    B. No

9. A requirement to meet Stage 1 meaningful use is to transmit data electronically with another facility or public health system. Is the transmission required to be successful to meet meaningful use?

    A. Yes

    B. No

10. What is the percentage of Medicare patients that a pediatrician must see to receive full reimbursement of ARRA stimulus funds?

    A. 10 percent

    B. 20 percent

    C. 25 percent

    D. 30 percent

Chapter 7

PCI and Other Regulations

In the previous chapters, we spent a great deal of time reviewing the regulations that have a direct impact on healthcare and the way the industry does business and employs IT. In this chapter, we will explore additional regulations that impact the healthcare community, including payment card industry group standards and regulations at the federal and state levels that apply to protecting personally identifiable information. Nearly all medical service providers rely on debit and credit cards as methods of payment for services rendered. The Payment Card Industry Data Security Standard (*PCI-DSS*) is the overlying security standard that governs how data is stored, transmitted, and used by companies that accept credit and debit transactions. At the federal government level, the Sarbanes–Oxley (*SOX*) Act of 2002 and the Federal Trade Commission red flags rule were put in place to provide oversight and accountability and to limit the use and sharing of medical information.

State regulations are also part of the mix when talking about protecting personally identifiable information. Personally identifiable information protection is at the forefront in regulations such as *Massachusetts 201 CMR 17.0*, which set the standard for safeguarding personal data both electronically and on paper. This far-sweeping regulation is on par with the stringent requirements found in *California's SB 1386*. Each of the 50 states has its own regulations and laws protecting personally identifiable information; we will discuss the most complex of those regulations. With these regulations, it is important to recognize that the protected information relates not only to the delivery of medical services but also includes individual addresses, names, and other information. Be sure to research and understand the requirements in the states you serve.

PCI-DSS

The Payment Card Industry Security Standards Council was formed in 2006 by a number of the international payment card companies, including American Express, Discover Financial Services, MasterCard Worldwide, Visa, and JCB International. As part of the council, each of these leading financial transaction companies agreed to use PCI-DSS as the technical foundation of requirements for their worldwide security compliance programs. The PCI standards are mandatory for any businesses that acquire, collect, process, and/or store credit card information. Businesses are classified by the number of credit card transactions they process in any given year and have increasingly complex compliance requirements as the number of transactions increases. Table 7.1 lists the credit card transaction criteria for each merchant level.

Table 7.1 PCI Business Classifications and PCI-DSS Compliance Requirements

Merchant level	Transaction criteria	Requirements for PCI-DDS compliance
Level 1	Any business handling more than 6 million transactions a year	Complete an annual on-site PCI Data Security Assessment and complete a quarterly network security scan.
Level 2	Merchants processing 1 million to 6 million transactions	Complete a quarterly network security scan. Submit an annual PCI self-assessment questionnaire and complete a quarterly network security scan.
Level 3	Merchants processing 20,000 to 1 million e-transactions	Complete a quarterly network security scan. Submit an annual PCI self-assessment questionnaire and complete a quarterly network security scan.
Level 4	Merchants processing fewer than 20,000 ecommerce transactions and all other merchants processing up to 1 million transactions	Complete a quarterly network security scan. Submit an annual PCI self-assessment questionnaire and complete a quarterly network security scan.

PCI recommends that Level 1 merchants use a *qualified security assessor (QSA)* to complete their required annual data security assessment reports. Level 1, Level 2, and Level 3 merchants also must complete quarterly automated tests where an *approved scanning vendor (ASV)* attacks the merchant's publicly accessible external IP address to check for vulnerabilities. Once the test is completed, a report must be sent to the payment companies that acquire the transaction.

In addition to the technical security standards, the PCI Security Standards Council certifies companies to act as auditors, vulnerability scanners, and the like. QSA companies must be certified by the PCI Security Standards Council and have employees who are certified annually as QSAs. To view an active list of certified QSAs, you can visit https://www.pcisecuritystandards.org/approved_companies_providers/qsa_companies.php.

QSA Companies

Only 266 companies worldwide are certified as QSAs. Companies that attain the QSA must go through a rigorous certification process in order to achieve the certification and are required to revalidate the certification annually. Additionally, the individual QSA employed by the certified company must renew their certification annually.

Approved Scanning Vendors

ASVs are organizations that perform vulnerability scans that validate the target company's compliance against PCI-DSS standards. As of this writing, there are more than 130 approved ASVs.

Payment Application Standards

The PCI security standards include data security standards, payment application data security standards (PA-DSS), and PIN transaction security requirements. PA-DSS standards are different from the PCI-DSS standards. Adherence to the payment application standards is determined by the payment brands, not the council. PA-DSS applies to software vendors that develop applications that store, transmit, or process payment cardholder data as part of an application that is sold, licensed, or distributed to other companies. It is important to understand that any application that handles credit card transactions from any of the major brands must have the PA-DSS certification. If the application has not passed such validation, the application may be storing more information than is necessary.

PCI-DSS Control Domains and Requirements

The core of the PCI-DSS is a group of principles and accompanying requirements, around which the specific elements of the DSS are organized. PCI-DSS consists of 12 requirements grouped into 6 control domains, as described in Table 7.2.

The PCI Security Standards Council recommends many steps to meet the requirements listed in Table 7.2. The Description column lists examples of compliance items and is not an exhaustive list of how to comply with the standard. A number of these PCI-DSS requirements are also covered in the HITECH and HIPAA regulations. Any healthcare organization not in compliance with these standards risks having their capability of handling credit card transactions revoked and therefore losing an important revenue stream. The PCI Security Council has done an exceptional job in reducing the number of breaches. Its guidance is reasonable for the industries they serve; however, some regulations are not as well thought out.

Table 7.2   PCI-DSS Control Groups and Requirements

Control Domain	Requirement	Description
Build and maintain a secure network.	Requirement 1: Install and maintain a firewall configuration.	1.1 Establish firewall and router configuration standards that have change control mechanisms in place. The configuration must identify all connections that permit access to cardholder data, and all firewall rules will be reviewed twice a year.
		1.2 Build a configuration that restricts all traffic from untrusted networks except for those protocols for cardholder data environment.
		1.3 Prohibit direct Internet access between the Internet and the cardholder data environment.
		1.4 Install firewall software on any mobile or employee-owned computer with direct connectivity to the Internet and the organization's network.
	Requirement 2: Change the vendor-supplied passwords.	2.1 Change all vendor-supplied passwords *prior* to installing on the network.
		2.2 Develop configuration minimums for all system components that address all known security vulnerabilities. Update standards and minimums as appropriate.
		2.3 Encrypt all nonconsole admin access using strong cryptography.
		2.4 Shared hosting providers must protect each entity's hosted environment.
Protect cardholder data.	Requirement 3: Protect stored cardholder data.	3.1 Only store what is required to run the business. When possible, store nothing.

Table 7.2   PCI-DSS Control Groups and Requirements *(continued)*

Control Domain	Requirement	Description
		3.2 Do not store authentication data after authorization occurs no matter if the data is encrypted.
		3.3 When displaying the PAN, mask it.
		3.4 Render PAN unreadable anywhere it is stored.
		3.5 Protect any keys used for encryption of cardholder data from disclosure and misuse.
		3.6 Implement appropriate controls for encryption key management.
	Requirement 4: Encrypt transmission of cardholder data when sent across open and public networks.	4.1 Use SSL/TLS, SSH, or IPSec to safeguard cardholder information when transmitting on open networks.
		4.2 Cellular networks based on GSM and GPRS require encryption as the packets do not have the capability of encrypting the traffic.
Maintain a vulnerability management program.	Requirement 5: Maintain a vulnerability management program.	5.1 Deploy antivirus to all computers connected to the network that can be impacted by malicious software. These must be able to detect, remove, and protect against other malicious software such as Trojans, spyware, malware, and adware.
		5.2 Configure antivirus and anti-malware to generate centrally managed logs.
	Requirement 6: Develop and maintain secure systems and applications.	6.1 Patch computer systems regularly. This includes the customary Microsoft Patch Tuesday, Adobe patches, and other vendors.
		6.2 Develop a method for identifying and assess newly found vulnerabilities. The Department of Homeland Security keeps a vulnerability database at http://web.nvd.nist.gov/view/vuln/search. At this website, you can also sign up to receive weekly vulnerability update emails.

Table 7.2 PCI-DSS Control Groups and Requirements *(continued)*

Control Domain	Requirement	Description
		6.3 Develop applications based on industry best practice and with security thought-out throughout the entire software development life cycle.
		6.4 Ensure all public-facing sites and applications are protected from well-known attacks. Perform vulnerability reviews at least annually or install a web application firewall.
Implement strong access control measures.	Requirement 7: Implement strong access control measures.	7.1 Limit access to system components and cardholder data to only those employees who need access.
		7.2 Establish an access control system for system components with multiple users that restricts access to cardholder data on a need-to-know basis.
	Requirement 8: Assign a unique ID to each person with computer access.	8.1 All users must have a unique ID to allow them to access system components or cardholder data.
		8.2 Implement two-factor authentication for remote access by employees.
		8.3 All passwords in storage and transmission must be unreadable.
		8.4 Users must authenticate to the system by using something known, something they have, or something they are.
	Requirement 9: Restrict physical access to cardholder data.	9.1 Limit access to facilities that process cardholder data.
		9.2 Physically secure all media, such as backup media, USB, floppy disks, and hard drives, to name just a few.
		9.3 Classify media to allow appropriate controls.
		9.4 Destroy media after it is no longer needed or used.
		9.5 Maintain a visitor log and have methods to distinguish between the employees, visitors, and contractors.

Table 7.2 PCI-DSS Control Groups and Requirements *(continued)*

Control Domain	Requirement	Description
Regularly monitor and test networks.	Requirement 10: Track and monitor access to the network.	10.1 Establish a process to link an access event to individual users. 10.2 Created automated audit trails for reconstructing security events and access events to cardholder data. 10.3 Use synchronized time servers so that logging of all events can be correlated. 10.4 Secure audit trails so that they cannot be altered. 10.5 Retain audit trail history for a year.
	Requirement 11: Regularly test security systems and processes.	11.1 Test for the presence of rogue wireless access points. 11.2 Run internal and external vulnerability scanning against the network. 11.3 Perform penetration testing annually against the network and applications in the cardholder environment. 11.4 Deploy file integrity monitoring tools.
Maintain an information security policy.	Requirement 12: Maintain an information security policy.	12.1 Establish, publish, and maintain a security policy that addresses all PCI-DSS requirements. 12.2 Develop daily, monthly, quarterly, and annual security procedures to meet PCI-DSS requirements. 12.3 Assign responsibilities to appropriate staff. 12.4 Implement a formal security awareness program.

By now your head might be spinning from the regulations. There are even more that follow this segment. Let's look at the applicability of the regulations based on our case scenarios. Table 7.3 lists the regulation focus and items of concern for small practices, like our fictional Dr. Multisite.

Table 7.3   Applying PCI Regulations to Small Practices

PCI Regulation Focus	Items of Concern
Requirement 1	Establish firewall configs for the practice. Install firewall software on all mobile platforms. Use swipe-only technology for payments that will not keep data stored locally.
Requirement 2	Change all passwords prior to install.
Requirement 3	Store nothing related to the credit card transaction.
Requirement 4	Use SSL or IPSec when transmitting cardholder data. This should be the function of the merchant services vendor.
Requirement 5	Outsource vulnerability scanning to a third party. As a smaller entity, ask the merchant services vendor if they have an assessment vendor. These typically cost $75 to $1,000 to do for an office this size.
Requirement 6	Work with the practice to deploy managed services to protect their computers. Especially when they are mobile, keeping them patched is an important step in keeping a secure network.
Requirement 7	Limit access to the credit card readers to only the necessary minimum.
Requirement 8	This is already handled because of HIPAA and HITECH.
Requirement 9	Secure the credit card reader when not in use.
Requirement 10	By using the managed platform tool and installing Wireshark or NetWitness, monitor the network flow. Look for signs of data going to suspicious locations such as Russia, China, and Nigeria.
Requirement 11	Use a tool such as Nmap to search for open ports, vulnerabilities, and the like.
Requirement 12	Maintain a security policy. If helping the doctor, work with legal counsel prior to submitting it for final approval.

Table 7.4 lists the regulation focus and items of concern for midsize practices, like our fictional Middleton Pediatrics.

Table 7.4   Applying PCI Regulations to Midsize Practices

PCI Regulations Focus	Items of Concern
Requirement 1	Establish firewall configs for the provider. The card reader we see most frequently in medical practices is connected over a phone line, so the onus of securing the data in transit is on the vendor. There are no segmentation of network requirements. Install firewall software on all mobile platforms. Use swipe-only technology for payments that does not keep data stored locally.
Requirement 2	Change all vendor supplied passwords prior to install. Encrypt all nonconsole access using SSL or Secure Socket Host.
Requirement 3	Store nothing related to the credit card transaction.
Requirement 4	Use SSL or IPSec when transmitting cardholder data. This should be the function of the merchant services vendor.
Requirement 5	Outsource vulnerability scanning to the IT provider, or as the IT provider, have the vulnerability scanning as part of the managed services package. Reach out to the credit card processor to see whether they have free or low-cost assessment tools. Centrally manage antivirus and anti-malware logs.
Requirement 6	Work with the practice to deploy patch management services to protect their computers. Develop a way to assess the risk of newly discovered vulnerabilities against what is deployed at the practice. Use a web hosting provider when possible.
Requirement 7	Limit access to the credit card readers to only the necessary minimum.
Requirement 8	Assigning a unique ID is already handled because of HIPAA and HITECH.

Table 7.4   Applying PCI Regulations to Midsize Practices *(continued)*

PCI Regulations Focus	Items of Concern
Requirement 9	Secure the credit card reader when not in use.
Requirement 10	By using the managed platform tool and installing Wireshark or NetWitness, monitor the network flow. Look for signs of data going to suspicious locations such as Russia, China, and Nigeria.
	Implement Active Directory and synchronized time servers so events can be correlated.
	Secure the audit trail from alteration by using encryption and tracking the hash codes.
	Complete a vulnerability assessment yearly.
Requirement 11	Use a tool such as Nmap to search for open ports, vulnerabilities, and the like.
	For a practice this size, use Tripwire to monitor for improperly changed system files.
Requirement 12	Maintain a security policy. If helping the doctor, work with legal counsel prior to submitting it for final approval.
	Assign staff to the security role as appropriate.
	Train staff through a formal awareness program.

North Community Hospitals and Clinics has a credit card transaction system embedded into a payment application. Because it is using a third party to handle the transactions but the data does flow across the network, its PCI-DSS compliance will be significantly different from the other two providers. Table 7.5 lists the regulation focus and items of concern for hospitals and large practices.

Table 7.5   Applying PCI Regulations to Hospitals and Large Practices

PCI Regulations Focus	Items of Concern
Requirement 1	Establish firewall configs for the provider.
	Segment the network used to process credit card information from the entity's network. Use virtual local area networks or firewalls.
	Prohibit direct access between the card transaction system and the Internet.
	Install firewall software on all mobile platforms.

Table 7.5   Applying PCI Regulations to Hospitals and Large Practices *(continued)*

PCI Regulations Focus	Items of Concern
Requirement 2	Change all vendor-supplied passwords prior to install.
	Encrypt all non-console access using SSL or Secure Socket Host.
Requirement 3	Store only what is required for the transaction and nothing else.
	Confirm that the system doesn't store data after the credit card transaction.
	Confirm that the primary account number is masked in all screens.
Requirement 4	Use SSL or IPSec when transmitting cardholder data. This should be the function of the merchant services vendor.
	Cellular is used in remote locations, so verify that the customer is not using GSM or GPRS.
Requirement 5	Implement an in-house tool for automated vulnerability scanning.
	Reach out to the credit card processor to see whether they have free or low-cost assessment tools.
	Centrally manage antivirus and anti-malware logs.
	Install firewalls on all remote devices.
Requirement 6	Work with the hospital to deploy patch management to protect their computers.
	Have documented project plans that include security at the forefront of the software development life cycle.
	Using a Microsoft management suite, LANDesk, or others for path management.
	Develop a way to assess the risk of newly discovered vulnerabilities against what is deployed at the practice.
	Use a web hosting provider when possible.
Requirement 7	Limit access to the credit card processing servers to only the minimum necessary.
	Work with the operations team to limit access to a select few.

Table 7.5 Applying PCI Regulations to Hospitals and Large Practices *(continued)*

PCI Regulations Focus	Items of Concern
Requirement 8	Assigning a unique ID is already handled because of HIPAA and HITECH.
Requirement 9	Use door locks to limit access to the facility's credit card information processing.
	Physically secure all media including backups in locked cabinets with limited access.
	Destroy all media after it is no longer in use.
	Retain and secure audit trails of system and server access for a year.
	Secure the audit trail from alteration by using encryption and tracking the hash codes.
	Implement and deploy a tool that validates file integrity.
Requirement 10	By using the managed platform tool and installing Wireshark or NetWitness, monitor the network flow. Look for signs of data going to suspicious locations such as Russia, China, and Nigeria.
	Implement Active Directory and synchronized time servers so events can be correlated.
	Complete a vulnerability assessment yearly.
Requirement 11	Use a tool such as Nmap to search for open ports, vulnerabilities, and the like.
	For a hospital this size, we have also used Foundstone and Retina vulnerability scanners. Though they cost about $75,000, they are worth every penny.
	Perform or hire a company to provide a vulnerability assessment.
Requirement 12	Maintain a security policy. If helping the doctor, work with legal counsel prior to submitting it for final approval.
	Assign staff to the security role as appropriate.
	Train staff through a formal awareness program.

Massachusetts 201 CMR 17.0

In an effort to reduce the amount of identity theft affecting the citizens of Massachusetts, their state government passed the far-reaching 201 CMR 17.0 law, which not only impacts the citizens of Massachusetts but impacts any company doing business with its citizens. Originally set to go into effect on January 1, 2009, the state legislature delayed implementing the law because of the economic ramifications, which were considered far too great for businesses that were suffering in the worst economic downturn our country has seen since the Great Depression. The law went into effect on March 1, 2010.

The purpose of 201 CMR 17.0 is to establish minimum standards that must be in met in the safeguarding of personal information in both electronic and paper form. The confidentiality and security of customer information must be secured in a manner that is consistent with industry standards, protected against threats caused by vulnerabilities, and protected against unauthorized access to or the use of customer information that will result in harm or inconvenience of the customer. In only four pages of legislation, the business landscape changed for anyone doing business in Massachusetts. Similarly, the regulation regarding the security portion of HIPAA is just seven pages. Full industries have been spawned from HIPAA, PCI-DSS, and legislation such as 201 CMR 17.0. The Massachusetts Consumer Affairs and Business Regulations cites that anyone conducting commerce must comply with 201 CMR 17.0. You can find the exact verbiage at www.mass.gov/Eoca/docs/idtheft/201CMR17faqs.pdf. Therefore, any business, no matter whether they are based in Massachusetts or out of state, must comply with the law. However, if an out-of-state entity sees a citizen of Massachusetts at a location outside of the state, it is not clear whether the law still applies. We believe that the law applies only to those conducting business in the state, because state laws do not cross state lines. However, that is our interpretation of the law, not an attorney's. So, consult your legal counsel. Let's dive into the legislation to understand what it entails.

Section 17.02

In Section 17.02 of the law, the definitions are listed. It is important to understand the nuances here. A person is identified as any person, corporation, association, partnership, or other legal entity. So, data of an individual must be protected in the same way that a corporation's data is protected. The following definition extracts are taken without any editing from the regulation as published by the State of Massachusetts:

> **Section 17.02: Definitions**
>
> **Breach of security**, *the unauthorized acquisition or unauthorized use of unencrypted data or, encrypted electronic data and the confidential process or key that is capable of compromising the security, confidentiality,*

or integrity of personal information, maintained by a person or agency that creates a substantial risk of identity theft or fraud against a resident of the commonwealth. A good faith but unauthorized acquisition of personal information by a person or agency, or employee or agent thereof, for the lawful purposes of such person or agency, is not a breach of security unless the personal information is used in an unauthorized manner or subject to further unauthorized disclosure.

Encrypted, *the transformation of data into a form in which meaning cannot be assigned without the use of a confidential process or key.*

Owns or licenses, *receives, stores, maintains, processes, or otherwise has access to personal information in connection with the provision of goods or services or in connection with employment.*

Person, *a natural person, corporation, association, partnership or other legal entity, other than an agency, executive office, department, board, commission, bureau, division or authority of the Commonwealth, or any of its branches, or any political subdivision thereof.*

Personal information, *a Massachusetts resident's first name and last name or first initial and last name in combination with any one or more of the following data elements that relate to such resident: (a) Social Security number; (b) driver's license number or state-issued identification card number; or (c) financial account number, or credit or debit card number, with or without any required security code, access code, personal identification number or password, that would permit access to a resident's financial account; provided, however, that "Personal information" shall not include information that is lawfully obtained from publicly available information, or from federal, state or local government records lawfully made available to the general public.*

Record or Records, *any material upon which written, drawn, spoken, visual, or electromagnetic information or images are recorded or preserved, regardless of physical form or characteristics.*

Section 17.03

Section 17.03 is titled "Duty to Protect and Standards for Protecting Personal Information." As we pointed out earlier, the legislation covers all residents of Massachusetts. First, every person who licenses personal information about a Massachusetts resident must develop, implement, and maintain a comprehensive written information security program that contains administrative, technical, and physical safeguards for the data. The security program should be appropriate for the size, scope, and type of business; the number of resources that the business has; the amount of stored data; and the need for the security and confidentiality of both employee and customer data. Items that must be included or addressed in the security program include the following:

◆ Designating at least one employee to maintain the information security program

◆ Providing methods for identifying and assessing internal and external risks to the availability, confidentiality, and integrity of any record containing regulated personal information

Additionally, an employee must be identified to be responsible for evaluating and improving, as appropriate, the current effectiveness of the safeguards in place, including the following:

◆ Providing ongoing security training for any employees, temps, and contractors

◆ Ensuring compliance with policies and procedures

◆ Monitoring implemented methods to detect and prevent security system failures

◆ Creating security policies for employees regarding regulated data storage, access, and transportation

◆ Imposing sanctions for security program violations

◆ Preventing terminated employees from post-employment access to records containing regulated information

Third parties might need to be engaged to deliver security services or meet the compliance and vulnerability assessment needs of this legislation. The employee (or employees) responsible for the security program must take reasonable steps to choose and retain third-party service providers that are capable of maintaining appropriate security measures to protect such personal information. They must require by contract that the third party do the following:

◆ Implement and maintain such appropriate security measures for personal information

◆ Provide reasonable restrictions upon physical access to records containing personal information

◆ Provide regular security monitoring to confirm compliance with the program and ensure that the program meets industry best practices

◆ Upgrade safeguards as necessary to limit risks

◆ Review the security measures annually or when there is a material change in business

The employee in charge of the security program also is responsible for documenting actions taken in response to any incident involving a breach of security, the mandatory post-incident review of events, and the actions taken in response to the post-incident review.

Section 17.04

Section 17.04 is titled "Computer System Security Requirements." Because of the exacting language in this portion of the law, we felt it important to include the exact verbiage:

> **Section 17.04: Computer System Security Requirements**
>
> *Every person that owns or licenses personal information about a resident of the Commonwealth and electronically stores or transmits such information shall include in its written, comprehensive information security program the establishment and maintenance of a security system covering its computers, including any wireless system, that, at a minimum, and to the extent technically feasible, shall have the following elements:*
>
> *(1) Secure user authentication protocols including:*
>
> *(a) control of user IDs and other identifiers;*
>
> *(b) a reasonably secure method of assigning and selecting passwords, or use of unique identifier technologies, such as biometrics or token devices;*
>
> *(c) control of data security passwords to ensure that such passwords are kept in a location and/or format that does not compromise the security of the data they protect;*
>
> *(d) restricting access to active users and active user accounts only; and*
>
> *(e) blocking access to user identification after multiple unsuccessful attempts to gain access or the limitation placed on access for the particular system;*
>
> *(2) Secure access control measures that:*
>
> *(a) restrict access to records and files containing personal information to those who need such information to perform their job duties; and*
>
> *(b) assign unique identifications plus passwords, which are not vendor supplied default passwords, to each person with computer access, that are reasonably designed to maintain the integrity of the security of the access controls;*
>
> *(3) Encryption of all transmitted records and files containing personal information that will travel across public networks, and encryption of all data containing personal information to be transmitted wirelessly.*
>
> *(4) Reasonable monitoring of systems, for unauthorized use of or access to personal information;*
>
> *(5) Encryption of all personal information stored on laptops or other portable devices;*

(6) For files containing personal information on a system that is connected to the Internet, there must be reasonably up-to-date firewall protection and operating system security patches, reasonably designed to maintain the integrity of the personal information.

(7) Reasonably up-to-date versions of system security agent software which must include malware protection and reasonably up-to-date patches and virus definitions, or a version of such software that can still be supported with up-to-date patches and virus definitions, and is set to receive the most current security updates on a regular basis.

(8) Education and training of employees on the proper use of the computer security system and the importance of personal information security.

Massachusetts 201 CMR 17.0 was written to put some teeth into the laws regarding the protection of personal information. Financial penalties include provisions for fines of up to $50,000 for improper disposal and up to $5,000 per violation. Some businesses might be tempted to say, "This would hurt, but it's not the end of the world. Heck, the cost of implementing the security requirements will cost more than the fine." But one of the problems is that the law does not define exactly what constitutes a violation. Is it per case, per person, or per file? Consider the cost of losing an unencrypted laptop containing 2 files with 10,000 records of personal data in each. The total fine could be $50,000 for improper disposal, plus $5,000 for each file, and $5,000 for each record, for a grand total of more than $100 million! We are not aware of an upper limit to the fine. We hope there is one.

Real World Scenario

Technical Feasibility

The computer security provisions of 201 CMR 17.0 applies to all businesses, if they are technically feasible. The standard of technical feasibility takes reasonableness into account, which means if it is technically possible and a reasonable thing to do, the business is expected to implement the appropriate safeguards. For example, most business owners would agree that off-site backups are a good idea. If the backup data contains personal information, it is reasonable to expect that the data should be encrypted in case it is lost or misplaced. Numerous technologies are available to encrypt the data, so it is technically feasible to do this, and many professional IT organizations do encrypt data that is moved off-site. Now, consider the medical practice owner who makes an unencrypted copy of their data to a portable USB drive and takes it home on Friday. This is a very common practice, but it exposes the business owner, who would be subject to fines if the portable drive were ever lost or stolen because it was both reasonable and technically feasible to encrypt the data.

The law also allows for the state attorney general to file suit, and courts could award treble (3×) damages if the violation is found to be willful. On top of this, the individuals whose data was lost can also file suit for actual damages or $25, whichever is greater. All of these costs are in addition to the other costs of a data breach, such as the cost of mailing the letters alerting of the breach, the loss of revenue, and the like. As of this writing, the law has not been tested, so the impact cannot be fully determined. Suffice to say, the potential costs are enough to get someone's attention.

Encourage the practice or hospital to invest in preventative tools such as Foundstone or Retina eEye. These tools can be set up to send alerts and reports every time they are run. They are network intensive, so choose to run them after-hours or in smaller network segments. You don't want to bring down the network while trying to uncover vulnerabilities.

California State Law SB 1386

California was one of the first states to write a law that protects consumer information. The bill was first introduced by State Senator Stephen Peace on February 12, 2002, and was signed into law by Governor Gray Davis on September 25, 2002. The bill reported that in the year 2000 there were 1,932 reports of identity theft. That number reflected a 108 percent increase from 1999. The State Senate felt it appropriate to pass a law protecting consumer data.

Section 1798.92

SB 1386 requires a business to notify any resident of California whose unencrypted personal information was, or is reasonably believed to have been, acquired by an unauthorized person. The following is an extract of section 1798.92 of the California Civil Code:

Section 1798.29 of the California Civil Code is amended to read:

(a) Any agency that owns or licenses computerized data that includes personal information shall disclose any breach of the security of the system following discovery or notification of the breach in the security of the data to any resident of California whose unencrypted personal information was, or is reasonably believed to have been, acquired by an unauthorized person. The disclosure shall be made in the most expedient time possible and without unreasonable delay, consistent with the legitimate needs of law enforcement, as provided in subdivision (c), or any measures necessary to determine the scope of the breach and restore the reasonable integrity of the data system.

(b) Any agency that maintains computerized data that includes personal information that the agency does not own shall notify the owner

or licensee of the information of any breach of the security of the data immediately following discovery, if the personal information was, or is reasonably believed to have been, acquired by an unauthorized person.

(d) For purposes of this section, "breach of the security of the system" means unauthorized acquisition of computerized data that compromises the security, confidentiality, or integrity of personal information maintained by the agency. Good faith acquisition of personal information by an employee or agent of the agency for the purposes of the agency is not a breach of the security of the system, provided that the personal information is not used or subject to further unauthorized disclosure.

(e) For purposes of this section, "personal information" means an individual's first name or first initial and last name in combination with any one or more of the following data elements, when either the name or the data elements are not encrypted:

(1) Social security number.

(2) Driver's license number or California Identification Card number.

(3) Account number, credit or debit card number, in combination with any required security code, access code, or password that would permit access to an individual's financial account.

In the event of a breach, any corporation doing business in California must notify those affected by the data breach. Just like HITECH, the law applies only to unencrypted data. As part of our breach checklist, we always ask the following:

- Does the breached data include that which is protected under 1798.29 (e) 1-3?
- Was the protected data unencrypted?
- Was protected data accessed or acquired by an unauthorized person?

Note that the California law deals directly with the breach of unencrypted data. First, it is imperative that you understand that nowhere does the law list the minimum standards to meet the encryption standards. Second, the definition of *breach* is also very broad.

Enforcing this law requires that a company that has had a California customer's data breached must notify the customer in a timely fashion. If the company determines that the cost of breach notifications is greater than $250,000, they can use other methods (such as local media outlets) to notify customers of the breach. Additionally, if the breach affects half a million customers, the business can notify customers via email, statewide media outlets, or a conspicuous posting of the breach. If the business has its own notification process as part of an information security program, then it is OK for that business to follow their notification process as long as it meets the minimum requirements of the law.

Small, midsize, and large practices, as well as hospitals, must comply with this legislation if they are seeing patients in California. The cost for each is relative to the prevention steps that each chooses to implement and the cost of their response to a breach. Our fictional large practice, North Community, might include the cost of identity theft monitoring as part of the breach, while the much smaller Dr. Multisite wouldn't be able to afford to provide that service. By securing the data based on the HITECH standards, the breached entity is secure in most cases from the state law, which requires the same level of encryption.

Sarbanes–Oxley

During the dot-com days of the 1990s, the reporting of financial data for publicly traded companies came into question. Businesses such as Enron (a publicly traded company with 22,000 employees) were perpetuating fraud and corruption by manipulating and misstating their true financial positions. The fraud at Enron even brought down Arthur Andersen, a large accounting firm. Ultimately, the existing law couldn't protect the folks swindled by the massive fraud at Enron, so legislators created measures to protect future investors. The law is named after U.S. Senator Paul Sarbanes and Representative Michael G. Oxley. These legislative leaders were able to get this law enacted on July 30, 2002. In the Senate, the bill was known as the Public Company Accounting Reform and Investor Protection Act, while in the House, it was known as the Corporate and Auditing Accountability and Responsibility Act. The reason for giving you the bill's true names is to help describe the actual intent of what the industry now refers to as Sarbanes–Oxley (SOX).

SOX was designed to do the following:

◆ Provide a method to improve corporate governance for publicly traded companies larger than $75 million

- Enhance the accuracy of the financial reports
- Improve investor sentiment
- Promote better business practices

SOX drove large businesses to collectively spend billions of dollars in order to comply with the law. Some firms looked at the cost of compliance and chose to spend money researching the fine for noncompliance.

SOX Titles

The SOX Act is broken into 11 sections, and these sections are referred to as *titles*, as described in Table 7.6. Each title deals with a specific area of compliance and has multiple subsections that call out the requirements of that title. Many in the industry believe that compliance with SOX sections 301, 401, 404, 409, and 802 are the most important provisions for companies that must comply with this legislation. Compliance for SOX is mandated for publicly traded companies with revenue greater than $75 million.

Table 7.6   Sarbanes–Oxley Titles and Key Provisions

Sarbanes–Oxley Title	Description	Key Provisions
Title I	Public company accounting oversight board	Section 103: Auditing Quality, Control, Independence Standards Rules. Section 103 requires that the auditing company be independent of the organization. Additionally, the auditor must keep documents used to complete the audit for seven years. This requirement has created a massive amount of data storage and search engine needs.
Title II	Auditor independence	Section 201: Services Outside the Scope of Practice of Auditors. Section 201 is focused on limiting or even prohibiting the types of activities that an auditor can perform. Arthur Anderson, the $9+ billion consulting company that was dispended during the Enron scandal, also had a large IT consulting firm. This section prohibits the auditing company from providing IT services if they are providing financial auditing services.

Table 7.6 Sarbanes–Oxley Titles and Key Provisions *(continued)*

Sarbanes–Oxley Title	Description	Key Provisions
Title III	Corporate responsibility	Section 301: Public Company Oversights Board. The Public Company Accounting Oversights Board was created under Section 301. This independent and competent auditing company is required and held responsible for hiring practices, supervising the independent auditor's activities, and setting the compensation for staff. The company's board of directors must include a member of the firm's audit committee and cannot be part of the daily management of the company. The auditing committee of the company should also include a financial expert, though there are no minimums set under this legislation as to what the definition of a financial expert is.
		Section 302: Corporate Responsibility for Financial Reports. News outlets have clung to Section 302 as a method for cleaning up the financial records of publicly traded companies. Section 302 requires that the CEO and CFO certify the accuracy of the financial records. Additionally, the CEO and CFO must honestly represent the operational condition and financial stability of the business. News outlets hang on to the fact that failure to comply with this section of SOX can result in criminal proceedings for those who falsified the documents.
Title IV	Enhanced financial disclosures	Section 402: Enhanced Conflict of Interest Provisions.

Table 7.6   Sarbanes–Oxley Titles and Key Provisions *(continued)*

Sarbanes–Oxley Title	Description	Key Provisions
		Section 402 prohibits the company from making loans to the company directors or executive management. The CEO of Tyco had criminal charges brought against him because of the massive amount of loans and extra compensation he made. He received $81 million in bonuses, received $14+ million in art, and authorized the payment of a $20 million investment banking fee to a Tyco director. Of course, Dennis Kozlowski wasn't the only CEO taking millions from their respective companies.
Title V	Analyst conflicts of interest	
Title VI	Commission resources and authority	
Title VII	Studies and reports	
Title VIII	Corporate and criminal fraud accountability	
Title IX	White-collar crime penalty enhancements	
Title X	Corporate tax returns	
Title XI	Corporate fraud and accountability	

COSO Framework

The *Committee of Sponsoring Organizations (COSO)* is a private-sector organization that has established a common internal control model that companies can use to assess their control systems. The COSO framework contains five specific areas of control, which include control environment, risk assessment, control activities, information and communications, and monitoring. The COSO framework is an excellent model and can be adapted for use in any size organization to ensure effectiveness and efficiency of operations or to comply with applicable laws and regulations. For more information on COSO, please visit www.coso.org.

In addition, the IT Governance Institute (ITGI) spent time interpreting and digesting the COSO framework from an IT perspective. ITGI has an excellent resource center and is a good source for information regarding SOX compliance. Please visit www.itgi.org for additional information.

Other Provisions

SOX also includes provisions that protect employees who blow the whistle on illegal activities. Criminal penalties are possible for those taking any punitive or employment action against the person or persons who blew the whistle. To protect the organization you work for or represent, it is important that there are internal procedures for dealing with financial and accounting complaints. Some businesses will allow for complaints to be written anonymously.

Publicly traded companies are more heavily regulated than small local medical practices. Through career advancement, you may end up working for a healthcare provider that must comply with these rules. Legislation has a tendency to linger. The last large piece of legislation that affected the financial reporting of publicly traded companies or investment companies happened in 1940. We hope it will be another 70 years before the next massive piece of legislation!

The laws mentioned previously are just the tip of the iceberg. Moving forward, as hospitals and ambulatory-care systems begin to share data, additional laws and requirements will be put in place. In the United States, the creator of the data (such as the hospital or medical practice) is the owner of the data and can share it in a way that was identified in their HIPAA Privacy and Consent form. In nearly all of Europe, the customer actually is the owner of the data.

As a healthcare IT technologist, it is critical to know what laws affect you and the medical business you are serving. Sarbanes–Oxley compliance is a consideration for publicly traded companies with greater than $75 million in revenue. We gave just a little taste of the state laws. We believe, at the time of this writing, these are the most stringent laws. Before providing guidance, make sure you understand the protected information and breach laws that govern the states you operate in.

Real World Scenario

A Northern California Medical Business Seeks State and Federal Compliance Guidance

Dr. B has asked that you and your staff provide guidance on how to comply with just the state and federal regulations. One of the other physicians in the practice is also interested in understanding the business's liability to a data breach. Specifically, is the business at risk for having multiple pieces of legislation instantiating fines for violations, or does one law supersede the others? At a partner meeting with the doctors and practice manager, it is agreed that you will provide the business with guidance on how to meet the state and federal obligations that ride on top of HIPAA and HITECH.

The practice has four physicians, a physician's assistant, four front-office staff members, two nurses, and three back-office billing staff. The practice has an attrition rate of two employees a year. These employees are typically front-office staff. The back-office staff is reaching retirement age, which is a factor that must be considered. After further review with the medical practice, you discover that they have patients who travel from Massachusetts to receive treatment for their neurological problems. Dr. B. is also curious whether his business must comply with the laws that govern the citizens and businesses of the Massachusetts.

As their trusted advisor, what guidance would you provide?

To meet the needs of this practice, it is imperative that you understand the following items:

◆ The financial penalties for noncompliance are cumulative.

◆ Since the services to Massachusetts residents were provided in California, we do not believe you are required to comply with Massachusetts law, but we recommend you seek legal advice, because this may change.

◆ The medical practice needs to have a breach notification policy in place to meet the requirements of SB 1386.

◆ If you keep personal data encrypted, then the requirements for notification are substantially reduced. For example, if a drive is stolen and the data it contains is encrypted, then a breach did not occur per SB 1386.

◆ Employee retention and how the practice handles employee termination should be addressed through a willful or unwillful termination procedure and policy; having a usable policy is imperative to reducing risk.

Terms to Know

PCI-DSS

Massachusetts 201 CMR 17.0

approved scanning vendor (ASV)

Committee of Sponsoring
Organizations (COSO)

SOX

California's SB 1386

qualified security assessor (QSA)

Review Questions

1. How are businesses classified under the PCI-DSS standard?

   A. By brand—Visa, MasterCard, American Express, and so forth

   B. By location—domestic vs. international

   C. Number of credit card transaction in a given year

   D. Total dollar amount of transactions in a given year

2. What merchant level requires an annual on-site PCI Data Security Assessment?

   A. Level I

   B. Level II

   C. Level III

   D. Level IV

3. Which classification of company performs vulnerability scans?

   A. QSA

   B. ASV

   C. PCI-DSS

   D. PA-DSS

4. Which PCI-DSS requirement establishes the need to change the default vendor-supplied password?

   A. Requirement 1

   B. Requirement 5

   C. Requirement 2

   D. Requirement 6

5. Which of the following is *not* a PCI-DSS control domain?

   A. Protect cardholder data

   B. Regularly monitor and test networks

   C. Maintain an information security policy

   D. Management assessment of internal controls

6. According to Massachusetts 201 CMR 17.0, a breach of security occurs when which of the following happens?

   A. Encrypted data is taken off-site for storage

   B. Unencrypted data is accessed by an unauthorized person

   C. Unencrypted data is accessed by an authorized person

   D. Unencrypted data is accessed by an unauthorized person acting in good faith

7. Technical feasibility takes reasonableness into account. Which of the following would be an unreasonable requirement for protecting personally identifiable information?

   A. Encrypt backup data going off-site

   B. Require laptops to have encrypted hard drives

   C. Require screen savers at the front desk

   D. Require every business to have a Certified Information Security Professional on staff

8. Which of the following sections of SOX requires a public oversights board?

   A. Section 301

   B. Section 402

   C. Section 404

   D. Section 103

Chapter 8

Operational Workflow: Front Office

Technology is an integral part of the healthcare delivery process in modern medical practices. The front-office staff uses computers and applications to schedule and track patient appointments; the back-office staff uses the Internet to transmit patient billing and receive payment in the form of electronic fund transfers from the payers. Physicians use email to communicate with patients and rely on the Internet for up-to-date information on trends affecting patient care and safety. With the push to adopt electronic health records, the expanded use of technology within and between medical practices will compel providers to turn to a trusted partner to help them implement and manage a much more complex technical environment.

It is important to understand how the medical practice operates in order to provide the same level of service to the medical practice that they are accustomed to giving to their patients. Medical offices strive for excellence in patient care and safety, and they look to partners to help them in areas that are important to the success of their practice but are not necessarily part of their core competency.

In this chapter, we will explore the ambulatory medical practice front-office workflow from various perspectives, including patient, front-office staff, and back-office staff.

Medical Practice as a Business

front office
The term *front office* is used to describe the medical practice personnel and business processes that come in direct contact with the patient.

The *front-office* workflow begins and ends with the patient. When patients visit a medical practice, they are primarily concerned with their medical treatment, and it is sometimes easy to overlook that the medical practice is a business. Like any well-run business, the medical practice seeks to maximize profitability while providing something of value. Income for the business is derived from the fees the practice charges for its services and the number of patients a practice can see in a given time period (volume). Each provider determines what they will charge for their services based on their specialty, business expenses (payroll, insurance, rent, supplies, and so on), and desired profitability. In many cases, the fees providers charge for their services and the amount the payers (private insurance companies and the state and federal governments) are willing to reimburse are set through prearranged agreements called fee schedules. The fee schedule establishes the maximum allowable fee the payer will reimburse for the services the provider delivers. The fee schedule will be discussed in more detail in Chapter 9, "Operational Workflow: Back Office."

Scheduling

With fee schedules more or less determined, a medical practice's ability to process patients becomes a critical factor in maximizing profitability. Patient volume is driven by the provider's ability to attract and retain patients and how effective they are at moving patients through the various steps that make up the front-office workflow. The effectiveness of the processes influences the number of patients a provider can see in a given time period and directly relates to patient satisfaction.

NOTE

In this chapter, we use the terms *medical practice* and *provider* interchangeably when describing the processes that take place in an ambulatory medical office setting.

Patient scheduling is unique to every medical practice. The scheduling style of the provider is influenced by many factors, such as the quantity and availability of front-office staff, including doctors, nurses, and medical assistants. Patient scheduling may seem like a routine task, but the ability of the provider to execute against the schedule will determine whether the day is considered a success. Consider how a late arrival by a patient or a staff member who calls in sick might impact a full schedule. As the day progresses, the staff gets further behind until what started as a ripple on the schedule turns into a full-fledged tsunami by the end of the day. Patients are unhappy because their schedules are thrown off by an appointment that took longer than expected.

TIP

If you want to avoid delays with your own medical appointments, it is best to have one of the first appointments in the morning or an appointment right after lunch.

Most medical practices utilize some form of computerized scheduling software to help them manage the patient flow. These applications such as a practice management system or an EMR application have a subset of functionality that enables them to schedule patient appointments, manage staff schedules, and keep track of resources such as equipment and examination rooms.

While we are on the subject of scheduling, here are a few thoughts about scheduling office visits. As a VAR, you must be flexible enough to schedule appointments with the provider before they open in the morning, at lunch, or after hours. Medical offices start seeing patients around 9 a.m. The lunch break is usually about two hours in length. This extra time provides the staff with time to finish any late appointments in the morning, have lunch, and, if they need it, have a little extra time to prepare for the afternoon schedule.

If the practice has a problem that requires immediate assistance, service providers should keep the patient schedule in mind and be minimally invasive when performing work that could impact patient schedules.

Resource Tracking

Keeping track of which patient is in which exam room and where the staff needs to go next is very challenging in a busy medical practice. Taking this a step further, the medical practice needs visibility into how the resources are being used in order to maximize their effectiveness. Practice management (PM) and EMR applications are designed with this in mind and help the staff keep track of the availability of exam rooms and other resources that are needed during the patient's visit. The PM and EMR applications show the staff which patient is in an exam room and which staff member is expected to meet the patient. Resources such as specialized rooms or equipment are also tracked in the same manner, and staff can schedule these resources at the time of appointment or check on availability during the patient's visit. Finally, these applications can show historical data that can be used to identify potential bottlenecks or resource contention that would slow the patient flow as they move through the workflow processes.

Medical practice workflow processes vary depending upon a number of factors, including the number of physicians in the practice, their specialties, and the number of support staff assigned to the physician. With that said, there are generic workflow processes that are common to many medical practices, and they can be used to demonstrate how patients move through a medical practice.

Basic Workflow

The basic workflow in a medical practice involves the following steps:

1. Check-in
2. Intake
3. Examination

4. Checkout

5. Claims processing

6. Follow-up

In the following sections, we will break down the front-office workflow steps (shown in Figure 8.1), the interactions between the different players, and the technology used during the execution of these processes.

Figure 8.1   Front-Office Workflow

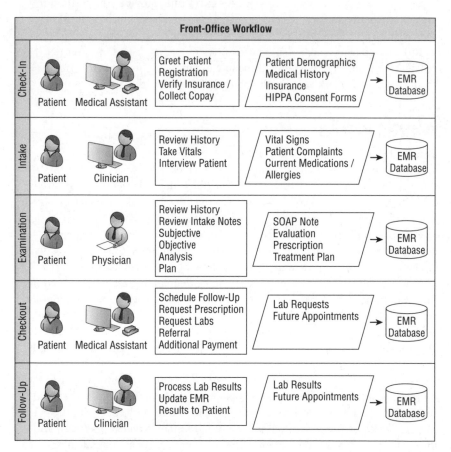

Check-In

The check-in process is the first of two processes that are designed to collect the information needed by the medical staff to assess and treat patients during their visits. The data collected during check-in is used to populate the medical applications, such as the PM, accounting, and EMR systems the front-office staff uses when delivering their services to their patients.

The check-in process begins with the patient and the front-office staff member (usually a medical assistant) assigned to receive and record the information that will be used to verify the patient's identity, health insurance coverage, and medical history. Traditionally, the insurance verification process is performed prior to the initial visit by using the payer's toll-free phone number or a website to confirm the patient's coverage. As EMR adoption increases, verification functionality is built into the application, and coverage can be assessed in real time with a simple click of a mouse. Verifying existing patients requires a valid form of identification and their health insurance card showing the dates of coverage.

The data collected and verified during the check-in process includes the patient demographics, including name, address, phone, gender, and age; medical insurance provider name and account number; family medical history; and any consent forms required by law. HIPPA consent forms are required when protected health information (PHI) will be used or disclosed or the use or disclosure of PHI is necessary to carry out the treatment, payment, or healthcare operations. This patient information is entered into the PM system, EMR system, and accounting applications for use during subsequent processes, including the examination and billing processes.

During the check-in process, the front-office staff may collect and process the insurance copayment. As such, care must be taken to protect credit card data and abide by Federal Trade Commission (FTC) red flag rules that govern the use of payment card information (PCI).

The most common problems associated with the check-in process involve the time it takes to capture and enter the demographic and historical data associated with new patients. There are many opportunities to reduce the check-in time and improve efficiencies in the check-in process. Some providers have installed a scanner to capture an image of the patient's driver's license or insurance card. This information is transferred directly into the practice management or EMR system, reducing the time it takes to input the data and the potential errors associated with manual input. An automated document feed scanner can also improve the time it takes to import a patient's medical history from the forms they fill out on arrival. Kiosks are another way providers improve the check-in process by allowing patients to enter some of their own information, via a terminal, directly into the application, rather than fill out forms and wait for the medical assistant to enter the data. Finally, one of the best ways to improve upon the check-in process, particularly for new patients, is to collect the necessary information before the patient arrives for their first appointment. Patient portals are becoming increasingly popular and allow the patient to register and enter their information in a secure browser session prior to their arrival. In the absence of a portal, blank forms can be faxed or emailed to the patient so that they can have them filled out when they arrive for their appointment.

PHI

Protected health information includes any information about health status, provision of healthcare, or payment of healthcare that can be linked to a specific individual. There are 18 types of PHI identifiers: name, address, phone numbers, fax, email addresses, SSN, medical record number, health plan beneficiary number, certificate/license number, vehicle or device numbers, web URL, IP address number, finger or voice prints, photographic images, dates (such as date of birth, admission dates, and discharge dates), and any other characteristic that could be used to uniquely identify an individual.

FTC red flag rules

The FTC red flag rules require businesses and organizations to implement a written identity theft program to help detect warning signs or red flags of identity theft in their day-to-day operations. A healthcare provider must take steps to protect patient information and payment card information as well.

When the check-in process is complete, the patient is asked to have a seat in the waiting area until they are escorted to an examination room for the intake process.

Intake

meaningful use
The data collected during the intake process is also used as a measurement or indicator to satisfy the meaningful use requirements for payment of ARRA funds toward EMR implementation. The criterion for meaningful use requires recording the patient's vital signs in the EMR application.

In the examination room, the nurse collects specific information about the patient's current health and symptoms. This includes the patient's vital signs (weight, blood pressure, pulse, and respiration), current medications, and allergies. The data is entered into the EMR system using a computer or a tablet PC and is used by the physician during the objective portion of the patient examination.

Increasingly, medical devices that capture results and interface directly with the EMR system are used to improve the intake process. As an example, a device such as a spirometer, which measures the volume of air inspired or expired by the lungs, is connected to a PC, and the patient's data is uploaded into the EMR system, eliminating the need for manual data entry, printing, and scanning. The direct input also reduces the possibility of transcription errors associated with manual data entry.

When the intake process is complete, the patient remains in the exam room and waits for the physician to arrive to perform the examination process.

Examination

SOAP note
This is an EMR system format intended to capture subjective and objective data on the patient's symptoms, the physician's assessment, and the treatment plan.

The examination process varies by medical specialty and even by physicians working in the same specialty within the same office. Even so, there are some basic components of an examination that are captured by the physician and entered into the EMR system by the physician or clinician. Many EMR systems use the SOAP note format to capture the examination results. SOAP is an acronym that stands for the four components of the examination process—subjective, objective, assessment, and plan.

> **Subjective Observations** The subjective component of the examination captures the patient's own description of their symptoms. These observations could include the patient's description of pain or discomfort, presence of nausea or dizziness, a brief history detailing when the problem started, and how the symptoms led the patient to seek medical treatment.
>
> **Objective Observations** The objective component of the examination captures symptoms that that can be measured, seen, felt, heard, or touched. An example of an objective observation might include visible swelling or discoloration caused by a bruise. The patient's vital signs, which were recorded during the intake process, are included as a component of the objective evaluation.

Assessment   The assessment component of the examination is the physician's analysis of the subjective and objective data. In some cases, the diagnosis is clear as in the case of a bone fracture. In other cases, further examination and tests may be needed to determine the diagnosis.

Plan   The plan component addresses the action plan the physician will follow to treat the patient. This may include further tests, a prescription for medication, a referral to a specialist, education, or other treatments.

A wireless network infrastructure and a portable device such as a tablet PC or iPad can improve a physician's productivity by allowing them to remain connected to the EMR system and patient data as they move between exam rooms. In the absence of a portable device, a virtual desktop infrastructure (VDI) can be used instead of a traditional computer in the exam rooms. VDI gives the physician the ability to maintain a personalized connection to the systems they need via a remote desktop session, which is particularly helpful in environments where multiple physicians are using the same examination rooms. The VDI session allows the physician to maintain their own desktop environment from exam room to exam room without having to log in and wait for the operating system to load their individual user profile on each unique computer.

Real World Scenario

Virtual Desktop Infrastructure

In the San Francisco Bay Area, office space is expensive, and many of our clients make full use of their environment. Placing a computer in the exam rooms and staging areas is not practical, because it takes up too much room and gets in the way of the staff effectively performing their tasks. Some of our clients have opted to install a solid-state device about the size of a Rubik's cube called a Pano System by Panologix (www.panologic.com). With the Pano System, they can attach the entire setup (terminal, mouse, keyboard, and Pano device) to the wall and enjoy the same user experience of a traditional computer. What makes this solution unique is the speed with which each staff member's customized environment loads when compared to a traditional roaming profile and the fact that there are no moveable parts at the client side. This means the workstation will outlast a traditional desktop by a couple of years.

When the examination process is complete, the patient's health record is updated, and the patient is returned to the reception area where the front-office staff processes checkout and follow-up activities such as scheduling and referrals.

Sales Cycle

In some cases, there might be a sales cycle in between the exam and the checkout processes. During the sales cycle, the patient is sold on the benefits of a procedure and may be offered payment terms to help offset any costs not covered by insurance. The sales cycle can occur in specialties such as LASIK surgery, cosmetic surgery, and elective dental procedures.

Checkout

At checkout, the front-office staff gives the patient a copy of their evaluation and treatment plan (if the physician has not already done so) and will collect any additional fees for services. If further testing or lab work is required, the front-office staff will order these services as necessary. Finally, they will schedule follow-up appointments using the PM system.

One of the many promises/benefits of the EMR is the ability to share patient data between providers. At checkout time, referrals, lab requests, and prescriptions are processed. Submitting these requests electronically can improve the time it takes to process them and reduce the burden on the front-office staff.

Follow-Up

Follow-up activities include receiving lab and test data and entering those results into the patient's health record. When necessary, the physician or clinician may call the patient to discuss the results and determine the appropriate next steps.

We mentioned patient portals as a method to improve the check-in process, and it bears mentioning again as a method to improve the follow-up processes. The patient portal provides a secure communication platform for patient-physician communication, where the patient can ask questions or in some cases review portions of their medical history at a time that is convenient for them.

Miscellaneous Office Activity

Some activities worth noting fall outside of the normal patient workflow process. These activities may be performed by any member of the provider's staff but generally are managed by the front-office personnel. These activities include the following:

Call Management   Call management activities include routing calls, responding to messages left on the voicemail system, and calling patients to confirm or reschedule appointments.

Patient Questions   Front-office staff are often tasked with responding to patient questions via phone or email.

Logistics   This includes following up on outstanding lab and test results and routing the results to clinicians and physicians as necessary.

Network Infrastructure

All of the processes in the front-office workflow depend upon a secure and reliable network infrastructure. Established medical practices typically started with one or two computers, added a couple more, and finally got to the point where they needed a real server. Along the way, the network was grown organically through purchases made at the local electronics store and pieced together to make everything more or less work.

Starting with the physical cable plant, the network switches, the router, the server, and finally the desktops, the demands of the EMR application expose the weaknesses of the network infrastructure. Processes break down very quickly when staff can't get to the data or the resources they need to effectively process patients. Add to those issues the security regulations we discussed in Chapter 4, "HIPAA Regulations," the administrative safeguards that require written security policies, and the physical and technical safeguards that require secure data transmission and protection against unauthorized access. With an understanding of the regulations, safeguards, and front-office processes and the knowledge that there are potential weaknesses in the underlying network infrastructure, a VAR should have little trouble identifying opportunities.

Patient Impact

Every practice has an established workflow process for managing patient throughput. The practices that have high patient satisfaction and high patient throughput review their processes on an ongoing basis and look for opportunities to improve inefficiencies and remove wasted time and effort. Methods used to review processes include creating a process map to visually identify their workflow and timing the individual steps to identify wasted effort or bottlenecks.

In the process described in Table 8.1, the patient spends equal time waiting and interacting with the medical staff. Optimally, processes should be designed to maximize patient time with their healthcare providers and minimize the amount of time spent waiting. Appointments are often scheduled back to back, and when one step of the patient process is delayed, the delay cascades through other patient interactions in the remaining schedule. Patients scheduled to arrive later in the day might have to wait longer if the lost time cannot be made up.

Table 8.1   Example of Process Map and Time—Existing Patient

Activity	Time Taken
Patient arrives at reception and is greeted	1 minute
Insurance verified and copay collected	3 minutes
Patient waits in waiting room	13 minutes
Nurse takes patient to exam room and collects vitals	5 minutes
Patient waits in exam room	7 minutes
Physician examines patient	8 minutes
Patient checkout—schedule follow-up appointment	3 minutes
Total time	**40 minutes**
Total time with physician or nurse	**13 minutes**
Total time with front office	**7 minutes**
Total time waiting	**20 minutes**

Medical practices review their schedules on a daily and weekly basis to identify potential conflicts and bottlenecks. Even with these reviews, delays occur, and the staff adjusts as best they can to keep everyone on schedule. When delays become systemic or processes break down more frequently than they should, a more in-depth review might be in order to identify the cause and take corrective action.

Is Efficiency Enough?

The HealthBlog is written by Bill Crouse, MD, Microsoft's worldwide health senior director. In his blog post about aligning properly placed incentives, he writes about the way the best health systems connect the patient with the provider. Dr. Crouse continues to write that many hospitals do not consider the patient their customer; they see the provider who referred the patient as their customer. This is an interesting finding because when hospital funding is looked at, more dollars are spent on integrating medical practices for efficiencies than on having patients communicate or receive services electronically with the hospital.

Keys to Successful Processes

The keys to successful processes are written with the medical practice staff in mind. However, they can easily be applied to the VAR and their staff as well.

Staff Education　Every staff member should understand their job function and the role they play in the patient care delivery process. To maximize efficiency, each staff member should be performing the work they are trained for and know the processes for which they are accountable. Having someone perform tasks that they are not familiar with or have not been trained on will introduce delays and errors in the process. When cross-training, it is a good idea to certify that the staff understands the processes before asking them to perform them during an especially busy schedule.

Patient Education　Educating patients on office procedures before they arrive will reduce uncertainty and help avoid unnecessary delays. Also, prepping patients for what comes next in the workflow process will help improve efficiencies.

Process Review　Medical practices review their patient schedules on a daily and weekly basis to identify potential problems. These review processes give the staff an opportunity to make adjustments to the schedule and the process as conditions change. These reviews can help avoid or minimize potential problems.

Measurement　Many medical practices have identified a set of metrics that they use to measure how well their processes are performing. These measurements could be time (amount of time a patient is waiting between processes), volume (total number of patients seen by hour, week, or month), or errors (number of transcription errors).

Technology is an important component of the modern medical practice, and the future technological demands are going to increase as providers move toward the adoption of EMR. This move will not come without some pain; workflow processes will invariably need to change to incorporate the new technology. As a trusted advisor to the medical practice, you have an opportunity to add value in many areas of the provider's business through the application of technology solutions.

In the front-office workflow process, providers need to efficiently and effectively move patients through their practice. Each step in the process is designed to capture and record the patient data the staff requires to provide quality medical care. The EMR system and the practice management systems are updated throughout the process, and the data is input directly into the systems whenever possible. This helps ensure the provider's staff has access to the patient data when and where they need it.

In addition to technology, process improvement techniques can be used to streamline the patient visit and improve patient satisfaction. The keys to successful process improvement are staff and patient education, periodic review, and metrics that provide meaningful data on the effectiveness of the process.

The success of the front-office workflow is a team effort. The medical team of the front office works together to provide quality patient care, while the VAR team helps them implement the technology to streamline and improve their processes.

Terms to Know

front office	protected health information (PHI)
FTC red flag rules	SOAP note

Review Questions

1. In addition to the fees a provider charges, what determines how much money a medical practice brings in?

    A. Patient scheduling

    B. Patient volume

    C. Staff scheduling

    D. Utilization of resources

2. Why is scheduling and resource management important to a medical practice as a business?

    A. Patient satisfaction

    B. Effective process management

    C. Maximize profitability

    D. All of the above

3. During which process are the patient's vital signs recorded?

    A. Intake

    B. Check-in

    C. Examination

    D. Follow-up

4. Which part of the examination process allows the patient to describe their symptoms?

    A. Subjective

    B. Objective

    C. Assessment

    D. Plan

5. At the end of their visit, the patient is scheduled for a follow-up appointment. Which process typically handles this?

    A. Follow-up

    B. Sales cycle

    C. Checkout

    D. Intake

6. What is a process map used for?

    A. Provide direction to the exam room

    B. Determine patient satisfaction

    C. Minimize opportunities for improvement

    D. Visually identify individual workflow and timing

7. Name one key to a successful process.

   A. Timing

   B. Process review

   C. Scheduling

   D. Cross-training

8. Why is it important to measure your processes?

   A. To compare the front office with the back office

   B. To determine who is not pulling their weight

   C. To determine how well your processes are performing

   D. To cross-train your staff

9. Why is it necessary to certify that the staff understands the process when cross-training?

   A. It reduces delays and errors.

   B. It is a violation of HIPAA regulations to have noncertified staff.

   C. Certification maximizes inefficiency.

   D. A certifiable staff member is an asset to any organization.

Chapter 9

Operational Workflow: Back Office

Healthcare is one of the few industries where services are not paid for when they are received. The medical practice provides service to the patient and bills a third-party insurance company to receive payment for the service provided. Cash flow is essential for any business, and managing the flow of money is critical to the viability of a medical practice. The provider's back-office staff is responsible for the administrative functions of the medical practice, including patient billing and accounting. Medical billing is a complex job that demands knowledge of medical codes, forms, procedures, and insurance claim processes. The billing cycle occurs for each patient, and the medical practice could have hundreds of outstanding invoices at any given time. On top of this, you have claims rejections and underpayments, so you can begin to understand what a mind-numbing experience it is trying to stay on top of the back-office processes.

Revenue Management Cycle

One of the keys to learning about any business lies in understanding its revenue stream. This is particularly true of medical practices because the claims, billing, and payment processes are extremely complex (some would argue unnecessarily complex). Accurate and fair reimbursement for services requires diligence from the staff and some help from technology to stay ahead in the game. The use of the term *game* was deliberate because the process connects providers who are seeking the maximum allowable payment for their services with *payers* who are seeking to reimburse only what is covered under their plan, based upon contractual obligations and medical necessity. Even the *patient* gets into the game when the denial and appeal process does not go their way and leaves them with an unexpected out-of-pocket expense. Each player expects to and should receive the maximum value for every dollar they are entitled.

The revenue management cycle includes provider/payer contracts, medical coding and billing, collections, and dispute resolution.

Players in the Game (The Free Dictionary by Farlex)

The Free Dictionary by Farlex (http://thefreedictionary.com) bills itself as the world's most comprehensive dictionary. It's hard to argue that assertion with medical, legal, and financial dictionaries available in 14 languages. The medical dictionary draws upon multiple sources and is an excellent resource that provides authoritative definitions of medical terminology in an easy-to-understand format. The following definitions of *providers, payers*, and *patients* come from Farlex's medical dictionary (http://medical-dictionary .thefreedictionary.com/).

Provider   A hospital, clinic, healthcare professional, or group of healthcare professionals who provide a service to patients.

Payer   In healthcare, generally refers to entities other than the patient that finance or reimburse the cost of health services. In most cases, this term refers to insurance carriers, other third-party payers, or health plan sponsors (employers or unions).

Patient   One who receives medical attention, care, or treatment.

There is considerable debate regarding the appropriate use of the term *patient*. In some institutional settings, it is not used because it is thought to denote a dependent relationship on the part of the person undergoing treatment. The words *client*, *resident*, and at times *guest* can also be used to refer to a person receiving treatment.

Contracts

For a medical practice to process claims and receive payment from an insurance company, it must enter into an agreement in the form of a contract with the payer. In the contract, the provider agrees to accept payment for their services from an insurance company at predefined rates called a *fee schedule*. In addition to the fee schedule, contract terms include language that specifies time frames for the submission of claims, payment terms, and how disputes will be handled.

The contract language is often sufficiently ambiguous as to leave room for interpretation. Typically, any ambiguity is leveraged by the payer, and this is sometimes used to underpay or deny a claim. When this happens, the provider must go through an appeals process, which takes additional time and effort by the back-office staff and further delays payment. In the health IT space, several companies specialize in providing software and services to help providers manage their payer contracts to ensure they are properly reimbursed.

fee schedule
A fee schedule establishes the maximum allowable fee the payer will reimburse for the services the provider delivers.

Medical Coding and Billing

Medical coding and billing are important functions in a medical office. Staff members who specialize in coding are called *medical coders* or *coding specialists*. Medical coders assign a code to each diagnosis and procedure by using an EMR application or some other classification systems software. The diagnostic and procedure codes determine the amount for which healthcare providers will be reimbursed if the patient is covered by Medicare, Medicaid, or other insurance programs using the system. When coding is performed properly, the medical office receives the maximum payment allowed under their agreement. Improper coding can lead to errors in the claims process and money left on the table. In this section, we will explore the transcription process and the standardized medical codes.

Transcription

In the previous chapter, we discussed front-office workflow and the examination process. During the examination processes, the physician updated the patient's medical record by entering the diagnosis and treatment information. At some point during or following the examination, this information was transcribed (translated) into medical codes by someone who understands the services rendered and can match them to a medical code. Medical codes are used to describe diagnoses and treatments, determine costs and reimbursements, and relate one disease or drug to another.

The person responsible for transcribing the patient diagnosis and treatment varies by medical practice. In some cases, it is a coding specialist, and in others, the physician or nurse must make the translation. More commonly, the EMR application is configured to make the selection of the medical code very easy to complete during the examination.

EMR applications have an administrative function that allows a medical practice to update and manage these codes to ensure they are accurate. Most medical practices use a subset of medical codes that are applicable to their specialty and configure the EMR application to make it easy to select the codes that are used most often in the practice.

Medical Codes

Medical codes are standardized to ensure a consistent format and an appropriate level of specificity to accurately describe the diagnosis and treatments (procedures). Here are some common types of codes used in medical practices.

CPT Codes   *Current Procedural Terminology (CPT) codes* were developed by the American Medical Association. These five-digit codes describe every type of service a healthcare provider can deliver to a patient. They are used to make a list of services rendered to the patient, which the provider then submits to the payer for payment. There are approximately 7,800 CPT codes, and in some cases, a two-digit modifier is used to provide a more detailed description of the procedure and enhance the payment for the procedure. CPT codes change periodically as new codes are released and old codes are deleted. It is important for the medical practice to have a process for keeping these codes up to date.

ICD Codes   *International Classification of Diseases (ICD) codes* are maintained nationally by the Center for Disease Control and internationally by the World Health Organization. ICD codes change over time and have a number appended to them. The current version is ICD-9, and there are about 17,000 codes. The next generation is ICD-10, and medical practices are preparing to begin using this version in 2011.

HCPCS Codes   *Healthcare Common Procedural Coding System (HCPCS) codes* are used by Medicare. Level I HCPCS codes are identical to CPT codes. Level II HCPCS codes are used for services provided outside of the medical practices, such as ambulance, medical equipment, or supplies.

DRG Codes   *Diagnostic-Related Group (DRG) codes* were developed by Medicare. DRG codes group patients according to their diagnosis, age, and type of treatment, among other things, to determine what the reimbursement should be. The rationale for this is that patients that fit the same profile will require the same amount of care.

CPT codes

These five-digit codes developed by the AMA describe every type of service a healthcare provider can deliver to a patient.

ICD codes

These five-digit codes developed by the WHO and CDC describe every type of diagnosis a healthcare provider can assign to a patient.

NDC Codes   *National Drug Codes (NDC) codes* are maintained by the Food and Drug Administration. The FDA requires all drug and insulin manufacturers to uniquely identify all of their products using a three-segment code.

CDT Codes   *Code on Dental Procedures and Nomenclature (CDT) codes* are maintained by the American Dental Association (ADA) and are used to describe dental procedures.

ICF Codes   *International Classification of Functioning, Disabilities, and Health (ICF) codes* are maintained by the CDC and are used to describe how functional a disabled patient is in their environment.

DSM-IV-TR Codes   *Diagnostic and Statistical Manual of Mental Disorders, 4th Edition, Text Revision (DSM-IV-TR) codes* were developed by the American Psychiatric Association to describe psychiatric illnesses.

HIPAA and EDI

Electronic data interchange (EDI) transactions have been in use for decades in the financial and retail industries, but the healthcare industry had been slow to adopt any standards that would broadly enable the transmission of healthcare information until it was mandated by the Administrative Simplifications provisions of the Health Insurance Portability and Accountability Act of 1996 (HIPAA Title II). Title II requires that the Department of Health and Human Services (HHS) create standards for the use and dissemination of healthcare data.

EDI X12 Data Format

The EDI X12 data format is the current standard used by the healthcare industry in the United States. There are multiple versions (releases) of this standard, and each release contains a set of message types that "define" the electronic version of a paper-based document, such as an invoice, a purchase order, or a healthcare claim. Each message type has a specific number assigned to it instead of a name. For example, an invoice is an 810, a purchase order is an 850, and a healthcare claim is an 837.

Table 9.1 describes key EDI transactions.

EDI X12
The EDI X12 data format is the current standard used by the healthcare industry in the United States.

Table 9.1   Key EDI Transaction Message Types

Message Type	Description
837	Medical claims with subtypes for professional, institutional, and dental varieties
820	Payroll deducted and other group premium payment for insurance products

Table 9.1 Key EDI Transaction Message Types *(continued)*

Message Type	Description
834	Benefits enrollment and maintenance
835	Electronic remittances
270/271	Eligibility inquiry and response
276/277	Claim status inquiry and response
278	Health services review request and reply

All HIPAA-compliant systems currently use version 4010 of the X12 standard. Testing is currently underway to support the migration to version 5010, which will take effect January 1, 2012.

CMS 5010 and ICD-10 Timeline

ICD-10 codes are scheduled to go into effect on October 1, 2013. All HIPPA transactions performed on or after this date must use ICD-10 codes, or the claim will be rejected. Electronic healthcare transactions switch from using CMS version 4010/4010A1 to 5010 on January 1, 2012. Preparing for the transition to ICD-10 and CMS 5010 will require updates to existing applications and forms, changes to business operations and workflows, internal and external testing, and possibly outside assistance from a third party (VAR or IT consultant) to complete.

ICD-11 is currently being drafted, and the WHO is targeting 2013 to release the first public draft and 2015 for implementation.

Claims Process

Claims processing cost is estimated at $210 billion dollars annually, and it is estimated that medical providers spend up to 14 percent of their revenue on administrative costs related to claims management to ensure the claims are paid accurately. Accuracy is extremely important when processing a claim because any incorrect data will cause the claim to be rejected, which will delay the payment.

The medical billing process, shown in Figure 9.1, begins with a patient visit to a provider and ends when the payer (or patient) remits payment for the services provided. The time it takes to complete this cycle varies, and it can take anywhere from several weeks to several months, with multiple iterations to finalize the transaction. A typical time frame to process a claim is about 45 days.

Figure 9.1   Medical Billing Process

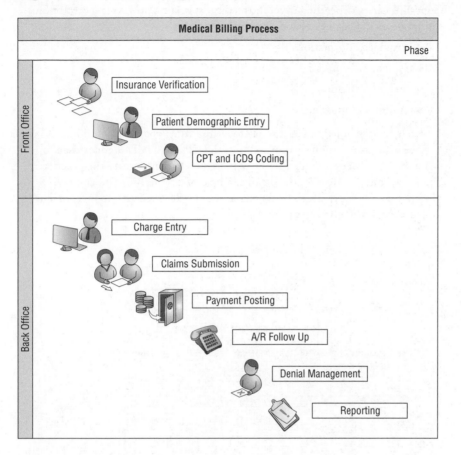

Charge Creation

Charge creation begins with the preparation of what is referred to as a *SuperBill* for each patient. The SuperBill is a form that providers submit to the payers to get reimbursed for their services. In this section, we will look at the charge creation process and the steps involved in processing the transaction between the provider and the payer.

SuperBill

The SuperBill is an itemized statement that the providers use to file the claim with the insurance company. Typically, there is a billing component built into the PM or EMR system that will create the electronic copy (electronic

SuperBill
The SuperBill is an itemized statement that providers use to file a claim with an insurance company.

claim), which is then sent to the clearinghouse for processing. The format of the SuperBill varies depending upon the medical specialty; however, there are four components that will be found on every SuperBill:

- Provider information
- Patient information
- Visit information
- Additional information

Each must be filled out accurately to ensure timely payment.

The visit information section contains the CPT and ICD-9 codes used to identify the services provided to the patient during their visit to the practice. Figure 9.2 and Figure 9.3 provide an example of a SuperBill. You can review the content in greater detail by downloading the file `SuperBill.pdf` from `www.sybex.com/go/healthitjumpstart`.

Figure 9.2 SuperBill Example Page 1

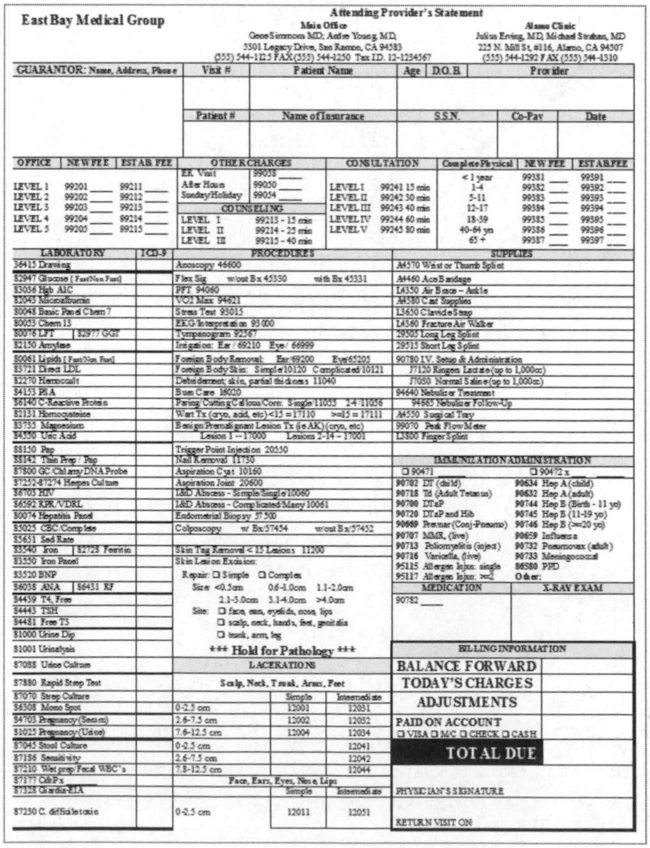

East Bay Medical Group

Attending Provider's Statement

Main Office
Gene Simmons MD; Arfee Young, MD,
5301 Legacy Drive, San Ramon, CA 94583
(555) 544-1125 FAX (555) 544-1250 Tax I.D. 12-1234567

Alamo Clinic
Julius Erving, MD, Michael Strahan, MD
225 N. Mill St, #116, Alamo, CA 94507
(555) 544-1292 FAX (555) 544-1310

GUARANTOR: Name, Address, Phone	Visit #	Patient Name	Age	D.O.B.	Provider
	Patient #	Name of Insurance	S.S.N.	Co-Pay	Date

OFFICE	NEW FEE	ESTAB. FEE
LEVEL 1	99201 ____	99211 ____
LEVEL 2	99202 ____	99212 ____
LEVEL 3	99203 ____	99213 ____
LEVEL 4	99204 ____	99214 ____
LEVEL 5	99205 ____	99215 ____

OTHER CHARGES	
ER Visit	99058 ____
After Hours	99050 ____
Sunday/Holiday	99054 ____
COUNSELING	
LEVEL I	99213 - 15 min
LEVEL II	99214 - 25 min
LEVEL III	99215 - 40 min

CONSULTATION	
LEVEL I	99241 15 min
LEVEL II	99242 30 min
LEVEL III	99243 40 min
LEVEL IV	99244 60 min
LEVEL V	99245 80 min

Complete Physical	NEW FEE	ESTAB. FEE
< 1 year	99381 ___	99391 ___
1-4	99382 ___	99392 ___
5-11	99383 ___	99393 ___
12-17	99384 ___	99394 ___
18-39	99385 ___	99395 ___
40-64 yrs	99386 ___	99396 ___
65 +	99387 ___	99397 ___

LABORATORY	ICD-9
36415 Drawing	
82947 Glucose [Fast/Non Fast]	
83036 Hgb A1C	
82043 Microalbumin	
80048 Basic Panel Chem 7	
80053 Chem 13	
80076 LFT / 82977 GGT	
82150 Amylase	
80061 Lipids [Fast/Non Fast]	
83721 Direct LDL	
82270 Hemoccult	
84153 PSA	
86140 C-Reactive Protein	
82131 Homocysteine	
83735 Magnesium	
84550 Uric Acid	
88150 Pap	
88142 Thin Prep / Pap	
87800 GC/Chlamy DNA Probe	
87252-87274 Herpes Culture	
86703 HIV	
86592 RPR/VDRL	
80074 Hepatitis Panel	
85025 CBC/Complete	
85651 Sed Rate	
83540 Iron / 82728 Ferritin	
83550 Iron Panel	
83520 BNP	
86038 ANA / 86431 RF	
84439 T4, Free	
84443 TSH	
84481 Free T3	
81000 Urine Dip	
81001 Urinalysis	
87088 Urine Culture	
87880 Rapid Strep Test	
87070 Strep Culture	
86308 Mono Spot	
84703 Pregnancy (Serum)	
81025 Pregnancy (Urine)	
87045 Stool Culture	
87186 Sensitivity	
87210 Wet prep/Fecal WBC's	
87177 O&P x ____	
87328 Giardia-EIA	
87230 C. difficile toxin	

PROCEDURES
Anoscopy 46600
Flex Sig w/out Bx 45330 with Bx 45331
PFT 94060
VO2 Max 94621
Stress Test 93015
EKG/Interpretation 93000
Tympanogram 92567
Irrigation: Ear / 69210 Eye / 66999
Foreign Body Removal: Ear/69200 Eye/65205
Foreign Body Skin: Simple/10120 Complicated/10121
Debridement; skin, partial thickness 11040
Burn Care 16020
Paring/Cutting Callous/Corn: Single/11055 2-4/11056
Wart Tx (cryo, acid, etc) <15 = 17110 >=15 = 17111
Benign/Premalignant Lesion Tx (ie AK) (cryo, etc)
Lesion 1 -- 17000 Lesions 2-14 – 17001
Trigger Point Injection 20550
Nail Removal 11730
Aspiration Cyst 10160
Aspiration Joint 20600
I&D Abscess - Simple/Single/10060
I&D Abscess - Complicated/Many 10061
Endometrial Biopsy 57500
Colposcopy w/ Bx/57454 w/out Bx/57452
Skin Tag Removal < 15 Lesions 11200
Skin Lesion Excision:
Repair: ☐ Simple ☐ Complex
Size: <0.5cm 0.6-1.0cm 1.1-2.0cm
2.1-3.0cm 3.1-4.0cm >4.0cm
Site: ☐ face, ears, eyelids, nose, lips
☐ scalp, neck, hands, feet, genitalia
☐ trunk, arm, leg
*** Hold for Pathology ***

LACERATIONS

Scalp, Neck, Trunk, Arms, Feet	Simple	Intermediate
0-2.5 cm	12001	12031
2.6-7.5 cm	12002	12032
7.6-12.5 cm	12004	12034
0-2.5 cm		12041
2.6-7.5 cm		12042
7.8-12.5 cm		12044
Face, Ears, Eyes, Nose, Lips	Simple	Intermediate
0-2.5 cm	12011	12051

SUPPLIES
A4570 Wrist or Thumb Splint
A4460 Ace Bandage
L4350 Air Brace – Ankle
A4580 Cast Supplies
L3650 Clavicle Strap
L4360 Fracture Air Walker
29505 Long Leg Splint
29515 Short Leg Splint
90780 I.V. Setup & Administration
J7120 Ringers Lactate (up to 1,000cc)
J7030 Normal Saline (up to 1,000cc)
94640 Nebulizer Treatment
94665 Nebulizer Follow-Up
A4550 Surgical Tray
99070 Peak Flow Meter
L3800 Finger Splint

IMMUNIZATION ADMINISTRATION
☐ 90471 ____ ☐ 90472 x ____

90702 DT (child)	90634 Hep A (child)
90718 Td (Adult Tetanus)	90632 Hep A (adult)
90700 DTaP	90744 Hep B (Birth - 11 yo)
90720 DTaP and Hib	90745 Hep B (11-19 yo)
90669 Prevnar (Conj-Pneumo)	90746 Hep B (>=20 yo)
90707 MMR, (live)	90659 Influenza
90713 Poliomyelitis (inject)	90732 Pneumovax (adult)
90716 Varicella, (live)	90733 Meningococcal
95115 Allergen Injxn: single	86580 PPD
95117 Allergen Injxn: >=2	Other:

MEDICATION	X-RAY EXAM
90782 ____	

BILLING INFORMATION
BALANCE FORWARD
TODAY'S CHARGES
ADJUSTMENTS
PAID ON ACCOUNT
☐ VISA ☐ M/C ☐ CHECK ☐ CASH
TOTAL DUE
PHYSICIAN'S SIGNATURE
RETURN VISIT ON

Figure 9.3   SuperBill Example Page 2

The electronic claims are combined into batches and are sent to a clearing-house for processing. A batch often contains multiple claims that are destined for different payers.

Clearinghouse

Clearinghouses are best described by painting a picture of the service they provide. For the sake of argument, let's say there are 4 million medical providers and 3,000 insurance carriers spread across all 50 states. Now, keep in mind that each state has its own insurance regulations, and each insurance carrier has its own software infrastructure. Imagine every practice submitting 10 claims per day to five different insurance carriers, and you begin to see the enormity and the complexity of the problem the clearinghouse solves.

clearinghouse
A clearinghouse is an aggregator of information that serves as the middle-man between the medical practice and the insurance company.

A clearinghouse is an aggregator of information (sending and receiving) that serves as the middleman between the medical practice and the insurance company. They accept and sort claims and then convert each claim into a standard EDI format before translating it into the specific EDI format required by the payer and securely transmitting it to the payer for processing.

Clearinghouses process trillions of transactions annually (most of which are handled by software) and provide a valuable service to both the medical provider and the insurance carrier.

For the provider, they do the following:

♦ Provide a single location to manage their claims

♦ Reduce errors by preprocessing prior to submitting the claim, resulting in fewer rejected claims

♦ Shorten payment cycles from weeks to days

♦ Improve staff efficiency

For the payer, they do the following:

♦ Improve the quality of claims

♦ Reduce transaction costs by consolidating number of connection points

♦ Reduce personnel costs associated with processing the claim

When the claim is first presented to the clearinghouse, they perform an initial screen to ensure the required data elements are present. If there are missing elements or the data is incorrect, the claim will not be accepted, and the provider will have to go back and correct the errors before resubmitting the claim. The clean claim is accepted for processing and is converted into the specific format required by the payer. The transactions are again formed into a batch and transmitted to the payer or the payer's clearinghouse where it goes through another review process before being paid.

Payer

When the claims are submitted to the payer, they have a finite time to process the claim. The time frame varies based on the payer contract and state and federal regulations.

EOB and ERA
The explanation of benefits and its electronic counterpart, the electronic remittance advice, are documents that explain what was paid on a patient's behalf.

At the payer, the claim goes through an adjudication process where the claim is reviewed to determine the insurer's responsibility and the medical benefits owed to the subscriber. During this process, the payer also takes into account the patient's co-pay and deductible, provider's fee for services, and contractual obligation. The review process compares the procedure codes with diagnostic codes to make sure they are consistent and provide evidence of medical necessity. Finally, if there are no issues with the claim, the payer issues an *explanation of benefits (EOB)* or an *electronic remittance advice (ERA)* and remits payment to the medical practice.

EOB and ERA

The EOB and ERA (the ERA is an electronic version of the EOB) are important documents. Many insurance companies and medical providers make billing errors. These mistakes can be annoying and, more importantly, could have serious financial implications for the provider and the patient if they are not identified and corrected.

The EOB is a window into the medical billing history, provided by the insurance company; it explains what was paid on the patient's behalf. It should be carefully reviewed to ensure that the amount billed for the service, the amount received, and the diagnostic and procedure codes are correct.

Collections Process

Once the claim has been processed by the payer organization, payment is submitted to the provider. Keeping track of payments and verifying that they have been paid correctly ensures the medical practice gets fully compensated for the services they provide. At any given point in time, the provider could have thousands of dollars "in the system," and they need to know when and how much money is going to come in during the month. As such, the successful medical practice keeps a close watch on the receivables that are outstanding and the timing of the payments.

A/R Management

Accounts receivable (A/R) management is important to the success of any business, but it is especially important to the medical practice where the number of days a claim remains unpaid can quickly go to 45, 60, or 90 if it is not carefully tracked. Medical practices run reports on their A/R balances on a periodic basis and track outstanding balances.

The practice management system or billing system has the ability to produce a variety of reports that show exactly how the practice is performing. With these reports, the practice manager or billing manager can track their financial performance and look for trends that indicate a problem.

Healthcare industry experts suggest tracking A/R balances on a weekly basis, and monitoring claims daily is a best practice that helps the practice improve cash flow. Cash flow is also improved by posting receipts promptly so outstanding balances can be billed and collected from the patient.

Benchmarks and key performance indicators are additional tools that medical practices use to track their financial performance. The following benchmarks are considered best practices and demonstrate target measurements for A/R management:

- ◆ Average number of days revenue in A/R at a maximum of 35 days
- ◆ A/R greater than 90 days less than 20 percent of total A/R

- Credit balances less than 4 percent of total A/R
- Bad debt write-off less than 2 percent of total charges
- Net collection percentage 96 percent or greater

Real World Scenario

A/R Mismanagement

We had a doctor come to us for help with his practice management system; it was fairly old and ran on SCO Unix. The medical practice had a hard drive crash and had not been keeping up with their backups. The practice management system contained all of their billing, which at this particular point in time amounted to more than $400,000 in receivables! Based on the amount of the receivables, it was safe to say that this practice had revenue older than 90 days. Nevertheless, this data was important, and they needed to either recover or re-create it.

The medical practice was small—one doctor and a couple of staff—and re-creating these billing records would have taken months, if not years to complete. Even if they attempted to re-create the records, there was a high probability that they would not be exact, and they were facing a significant hit to their revenue. We managed to recover the system and their billing records. We billed them on a time-and-materials basis, but in retrospect, we probably could have negotiated an outcome-based agreement that took into account the value of the data. At any rate, we gained a new customer and a very happy one at that.

Payments

When a payer has completed processing a claim, they issue a document to the medical practice explaining what was covered and the amount that will be paid. Payments are issued in the form of a check or in some cases can be received directly into the practice's bank account via electronic fund transfer from the payer. Payments must be matched against the original claim to determine whether the claim was paid correctly and that the amount is correct.

In some instances, the amounts will not match because the payer did not pay the entire amount of the claim. A short paid claim can happen for a variety of reasons including dropped procedures, procedures that are bundled and paid against one code instead of two, multiple units ignored, and payment based on the wrong fee schedule. When this happens, the medical practice must rebill the claim in order for it to be paid correctly.

Payer contracts have provisions for an appeal process if the rebilled claim remains unpaid. The billing manager must determine whether the amount is worth their time and effort to go through the appeals process or whether they will pass the difference onto the patient. In all cases, the billing manager will take note of the explanation on the claim so that future transactions will not be affected.

Dispute Resolution

In some cases, claims are "short paid" or rejected based upon the payer's adjudication process. In every contract, there is a dispute resolution process outline that details the process for handling disputed claims.

Claims Rejection

Industry experts claim that up to 30 percent of claims are rejected on first submittal. Common causes of claims rejection are as follows:

◆ Incorrect patient demographic (name, age, date of birth are wrong)

◆ Errors in provider data

◆ Incorrect insurance ID

◆ Incorrect, missing, or invalid CPT and ICD codes

◆ Treatment code does not match diagnosis code

◆ Lack of preauthorization

◆ Incorrect place of service code

◆ No referring provider ID

Real World Scenario

Check and Double-Check: One Author's Experience with Claims Processing

Every time a patient record is edited, there is an opportunity to introduce an error that might prevent a claim from being processed. A simple transposition of two numbers is enough to cause a claim to be rejected. Even if the record is not edited, there might be errors. For example, one of the authors recently went in to have his teeth cleaned. When the front-desk person asked him if there were any changes to the insurance, he said no. Now, he gets his dental insurance through his wife's employer, and unbeknownst to him, their new dental plan took effect that very day. He knew that it was going to change, but he didn't know when. When the claim was presented to the payer, he was no longer covered, and the claim had to be resubmitted to a different payer. The point is that rejected claims cause more work for everyone and slow down the payment to the provider.

Most, if not all, of these are preventable; clearinghouses and practice management software catch the obvious errors such as missing or invalid information, but the best way to prevent a claim from being rejected is to make sure the data is clean at every opportunity. Patient data should be checked and verified by the front desk when the patient arrives, and the procedure codes should be verified before sending.

Appeals Process

Medical practices lose money every day because of partially paid, delayed, or denied claims that go unnoticed and unchallenged by the billing staff. To successfully challenge a claim, the provider must have the proper processes in place and understand the payer contracts and payment policies.

The keys to the appeals process are auditing and documentation. The auditing function works best when this role is a primary responsibility of a specific employee, because it requires continuity and attention to detail. Armed with the proper documentation, including the payer contract, the fee schedule, the aged accounts receivable report, and the explanation of benefits report, the billing manager can identify which claims have not been paid, the reason a claim was denied, and whether it was denied incorrectly based upon the agreed-upon terms.

When tracking the claims and the appeals, it is helpful to have a follow-up log that identifies unpaid claims, the insurer's reason for denial, and the outcome of collection efforts. This log can also be used as a source for identifying patterns in the payer's denials and as a teaching tool to correct errors made in the front-office and coding processes. Lastly, the log is an important source document when writing and supporting the appeals letter to the payer.

When an appeal becomes necessary, most payers require documentation to support the medical practices position in a dispute. The documentation requirements vary depending upon the payer and the reason for the denial. When writing the appeal letter, it is best to be specific and to the point. Appeal letters should be reviewed and signed by the attending physician whenever practical.

Third-Party Billing

As a practice grows, billing becomes more difficult to manage. Some providers choose to outsource their billing operations to a third party, who for a fee will manage the billing process. Practice size notwithstanding, there are many advantages to this approach, including more efficient billing cycles, reduced denials, lower operating costs, and improved reimbursements from the provider.

Typically, providers scan their insurance carrier and diagnosis information and upload (transmit) it to a third party. The third-party biller generates the claim, submits the claim to the payer, tracks the payment, bills the patient, reports, and performs any follow-up necessary to ensure the claim is processed correctly.

Third-party billing services charges are based upon percentage-based pricing or flat-fee pricing. In percentage-based pricing, the billing service usually charges between 4 percent to 8 percent of one of the following items:

- Actual collections
- Gross claims submitted by the service
- Total collections for the practice

Fixed-fee pricing models charge $1 to $2 per claim for basic claim submission and generation and $3 to $4 more per claim for additional follow-up services.

The cost of follow-up services should not be underestimated because studies have shown that medical practices that perform their own in-house billing function spend up to 14 percent of overall revenues on the billing and collections process when you factor in employee costs, training, overhead from business operations, and fees charged by collection agents when the bill goes unpaid.

There are many advantages to using an outsourced billing service:

- Reduced operational costs: Payroll, technology investment, and training costs are significantly reduced or eliminated.
- Better cash flow: Faster claim processing leads to improved revenue stream.
- Reduced billing costs: Clearinghouse fees are eliminated.

One of the biggest advantages is that the third-party service has the ability to spot patterns or trends because of their relationships with multiple providers and multiple payers. This knowledge generally improves the quality of the billing process (reduced denials) and increases the amount collected over time.

The disadvantages of outsourcing the billing function are as follows:

- Data security: Critical data is exposed to a third party, and that could expose the medical practice if the data is mishandled.
- Control: The provider has less control over the application and has to abide by the terms and conditions agreed upon with the third party.
- Costs: Costs for extra services that are not included in the base agreement could offset the savings from outsourcing.

When considering a third-party billing solution, providers need to be comfortable with the trade-offs (control vs. cost), and they need to make sure that the data transfer processes are HIPAA compliant and secure.

Third-Party Billing Considerations

In discussing third-party billing with one of our clients, we gained some valuable insight into the trade-offs between in-house and external billing. The billing process for this client is handled by one full-time and one part-time professional, or the equivalent of 1.5 full-time employees (FTEs). The cost of outsourcing was approximately 6 percent of revenues, and that happened to be more than the cost of the 1.5 FTE. Even so, the practice manager stated that it would have to be significantly cheaper for her to consider such a change, and even then, she might not do it because of the loss of control over the process. The entire staff felt very strongly about having direct access to the EOB, and that if removed from the internal workings of the practice, the third party could miss or misinterpret what really happened during the patient visit, which they believed would offset any potential savings.

From a VAR perspective, this example demonstrates that sometimes there are other considerations when deciding on a particular solution or path, and that what appears to be a good solution may in fact be counterproductive to the business operation.

Terms to Know

fee schedule	CPT codes
ICD codes	SuperBill
clearinghouse	EOB
ERA	

Review Questions

1. Name two components of the revenue management cycle.

   A. Contracts and billing

   B. Intake and checkout

   C. EOB and ERA

   D. ICD-9 and ICD-10

2. What is the payment agreement between the provider and the payer called?

   A. Claim

   B. EOB

   C. Billing code

   D. Fee schedule

3. When is the medical code typically entered into the patient's record?

   A. Intake process

   B. Examination process

   C. Billing process

   D. Checkout process

4. Which medical code describes the type of service rendered to the patient?

   A. CPT codes

   B. ICD-9 codes

   C. ICD-10 codes

   D. NDC codes

5. What do the simplification provisions of HIPAA require HHS to do?

   A. Enable the transmission of healthcare information

   B. Enter the diagnostic and treatment information into the patient's record

   C. Create standards for the use and dissemination of healthcare data

   D. Pay providers for their services

6. What is a SuperBill?

   A. The bill presented by the bartender after a particularly long week at the office

   B. An itemized statement that the providers use to file the claim with the insurance company

C. A law enacted by the ruling majority in the House of Representatives

D. A window into your medical billing history, provided by the insurance company, which explains what was paid on the patient's behalf

7. What is the purpose of the clearinghouse?

A. Create and submit the SuperBill

B. Determine the medical benefits owed to the subscriber

C. Collect payment for services rendered

D. Accept, translate, and submit the claim for payment

8. What is an explanation of benefits form used for?

A. To track the A/R and A/P balance statements

B. To challenge a disputed claim

C. To document the amount paid on an insurance claim

D. To collect payment from the payer

9. Which of the following is an advantage of using a third-party billing service?

A. Improve efficiency of billing operations

B. Reduce denied claims

C. Reduce operating costs

D. All the above

10. As a percentage of revenue, what percent of the medical practice overall revenues typically are related to billing and collections?

A. 14 percent

B. 5 percent

C. 25 percent

D. 7 percent

Chapter 10

Operational Workflow: Nursing

In the previous chapters, we explained the front-office and back-office workflows from the perspective of processing a patient and subsequently billing for the services rendered. In this chapter, we will cover how technology impacts patient care from the nursing operational perspective.

Nursing is an age-old profession whose basic processes have remained unchanged for many years. With the adoption of EHRs, though, these processes have changed to adapt to the use of technology. To understand the operational workflow, you need to understand the basic processes of nursing.

Nursing Process

The *nursing process* was first described by Ida Jean Orlando in 1958 based upon observations she made of nurses in action. She witnessed both good nursing and bad nursing, and her observations led her to three conclusions:

◆ The patient must be the central character.

◆ Nursing care needs to be directed at improving outcomes for a patient.

◆ The nursing process is an essential part of the nursing care plan.

The nursing process consists of five steps designed to help patients improve their health and assist physicians in treating patients. The five steps are identified by using the acronym *ADPIE*, which stands for assessment, diagnosis, planning, implementation, and evaluation.

The nursing process is an organized sequence of problem-solving steps that are used to identify and manage the health problems of a client.

ADPIE
ADPIE is the acronym that describes the five steps of the nursing process: assessment, diagnosis, planning, implementation, and evaluation.

Elements of the Nursing Process

In the following sections, we will break down the nursing process and discuss the individual steps in more detail. Figure 10.1 shows the nursing process, including the assessment, diagnosis, planning, implementation, and evaluation.

Figure 10.1   The Nursing Process

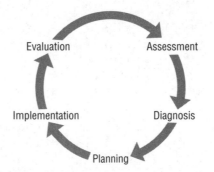

Assessment

The assessment phase answers the question "What is happening?" (the actual problem) or "What could happen?" (the potential problem). This is a two-part process consisting of data collection and data analysis. Assessment involves taking a patient's vital signs, listening to their comments and questions about their current health status, and observing their reactions and interactions with others. During this phase, the nurse collects subjective and objective data via the following:

◆ Client interview

◆ Physical examination

◆ Health history (including dietary data)

◆ Family history/report

◆ Diagnostic data

◆ Observation

Nursing assessments provide the starting point for determining nursing diagnoses.

Diagnosis

The nursing diagnosis is the nurse's clinical judgment about the client's response to actual or potential health conditions or needs. The diagnosis reflects not only whether the patient is in pain but also whether pain has caused other problems such as anxiety, poor nutrition, and conflict within the family or whether it has the potential to cause complications. The accuracy of the nursing diagnosis is validated when a nurse is able to clearly identify and link to the defining characteristics, related factors, or risk factors found within the patient's assessment. The diagnosis is the basis for the nurse's care plan.

Planning

In the planning phase, the nurse works with the patient to address each of the problems identified in the diagnosis phase. When there are multiple diagnoses, the nurse must prioritize which one will receive the most attention, based upon their severity and potential to cause more harm to the patient. The plan must set measureable and achievable short-term and long-term goals for the patient.

Implementation

Implementation involves setting the plan in motion and applying the skills needed to implement the nursing orders. To ensure the continuity of care, the plan must be written and shared with all healthcare personnel caring for the client. The major tasks include reassessing the patient, validating the accuracy of the care plan, carrying out nurses' orders, documenting care and results on a patient's chart, and so forth.

Evaluation

Both the patient's status and the effectiveness of the nursing care must be continuously evaluated, and the care plan must be modified as needed. Evaluation involves not only analyzing the success (or failure) of the current goals and interventions but also examining the need for adjustments and changes. The evaluation process incorporates all input from the entire healthcare team, including the patient. Evaluation leads back to assessment, and the whole process begins again.

Operational Workflow

The basic workflow steps were discussed in Chapter 8, "Operational Workflow: Front Office." There, we described how patients move through the process of receiving care from an outpatient medical provider. These steps included check-in, intake, examination, checkout, claims processing, and follow-up.

You can think of the nursing operational workflow as a series of tasks that accomplish a defined step of an activity in the clinical care of patients, as shown in Figure 10.2.

Figure 10.2   Activities, Steps, and Tasks in Nursing Operational Workflow

Taking a top-down view of the process gives us activities based on steps accomplished by performing specific tasks. Activities can be categorized as administrative, clinical, and post-clinical processes. These activities and processes develop into routines, which are different for every office and based upon the needs and cultural styles of the practice.

Patterns of fundamental clinical routines are the by-product of years—even decades—of personal work and experience.

Real World Scenario

A Tale of Two Nurses

Cultures vary from practice to practice, just as individual nursing styles vary from nurse to nurse within the same practice and when performing the same activities. For example, in one of the practices we support, a patient evaluation goes something like this: after the patient is checked in, the nurse takes the patient to the evaluation room, collects their vital signs, interviews them to determine the reason for their visit, and enters the data into the EHR system. Let's examine this process from the vantage point of two nurses working in the office. For their privacy (and our safety), we will identify them as Nurse M and Nurse L.

Nurse M is the head nurse. She performs her patient evaluations and workups in a methodical, step-by-step manner. Prior to escorting the patient to the exam room, she reviews their charts and the reason for their visit. When she takes a patient to the examination room, she starts with the blood pressure, followed by the temperature, and then the pulse, carefully recording the results in the EHR after each test. When the vital signs data is recorded, she moves on to discuss the reason for their visit and documents that. Next, she discusses their current medication, allergies, and when they last took any antihistamines. Finally, she discusses any change in medications and completes her chart.

Nurse L performs these same basic functions, although not in the same order. Nurse L does not review the patient chart ahead of the examination. Instead, she uses the chart to prompt her questions during the interview. When Nurse L seats her patient in the examination room, she begins the interview and continues as she checks the patient's vital signs, committing each answer to memory. At the end of the encounter, Nurse L sits down and documents the results in the EHR.

The practice's EHR is configured to keep staff members on a screen until all the required patient data for that screen is entered. This process was natural for Nurse M because when the practice was using the paper records, she methodically updated the patient's charts as she collected the data. Nurse L, on the other hand, found that the requirement to update the current pages in the EHR before moving to the next screen interrupted her rhythm and rapport with the patients, so she waited until the end of the examination to record her findings. At the end of both examinations, the necessary data was collected, and the patient results were documented. However, each nurse took a path that was comfortable, and both achieved the expected results.

The moral of this story is that there may be many paths—each has its own advantages, and each arrives at the destination. In this example, the nurses used workstations to enter their data, but even a laptop or portable device would not have helped in this situation. The limiting factor was the way in which the EHR was configured. The practice wanted to follow the same format as the paper records, and they wanted to make sure that the records were accurate, so they required the fields to be filled out before going to the next screen. If you work like Nurse M, this is not a problem. On the other hand, if you work like Nurse L, there are limited options to accommodate your professional style.

Continues

From a technical prospective, it is possible to change the application configuration and not enforce the mandatory field entry for everyone. The risk in implementing this change would be possible claims rejections for missing data. Most EHR applications allow for customized templates that support alternate workflows. In this case, the EHR application did not offer this functionality. Customizing the application would have been too cost-prohibitive.

Administrative

The administrative activities occur during the preexamination room steps that identify the patient and prepare them for the clinical activities to follow. These steps are performed during check-in when the patient is registered and the medical record is retrieved. Specific tasks performed during these steps include registering, retrieving the medical record, and updating the patient information. Data collected during administrative activities includes patient identity, health insurance records, and demographic information. During the administrative activities, the nurse is typically prepping the exam room and reviewing the patient records. Technical needs during this stage include access to the EHR system and verification that any clinical equipment that interfaces with the EHR is working as well. Common issues during the administrative activities involve login and authentication.

A nurse in a busy office could see up to 20 patients per day, and HIPAA security requirements dictate that access to PHI be restricted to authorized personnel. Authorization in the form of a login takes time, and if the login process takes two or three minutes, this time can add up over the course of the day. Some practices solve this problem by issuing tablets to the nurses, while others use Terminal Services that allows quick connections to existing sessions.

Following the administrative activities, the patient is transferred to the clinical activities processes.

administrative data
Data collected during administrative activities includes patient identity, health insurance records, and demographic information.

Clinical

Clinical activities occur while the patient is in the examination room by applying elements of the nursing process identified in the previous sections. During the intake process, the nurse begins by collecting specific information about the patient including vital signs, current health issues, and symptoms. The data collected comes from a variety of sources, including the nurse's observations, interviews, and examination. The data is recorded and documented in the patient's health record. As we mentioned in the previous chapters, a medical practice needs to quickly move patients through the examination process. Most EMR applications are configurable and can be modified to present the most common choices for any particular field. There are also third-party applications, such as ShortKeys, which integrate with the OS and present as much text as you have associated with that short key. For example, a short key for a common procedure could be represented in as few as two characters, and the software would present the entire text in whatever application you are currently working in.

You can learn more about ShortKeys text replacement software for Windows at www.shortkeys.com.

Following the data-gathering steps, the nurse synthesizes the data and provides this information to the physician. Using this information, the physician performs their own examination and analysis that, ideally, leads to a diagnosis and plan for treatment. If the physician requires additional information, they might order additional tests, order lab work, or refer the patient to a specialist.

With an established diagnosis, the physician and the nurse develop a care plan to meet the goals established for the patient. For example, a patient with an infection might require antibiotics to treat the infection. The goal in this example is to rid the patient of the infection, and the treatment plan might be a regimen of taking the antibiotics orally twice a day for two weeks.

Treatment plans are always developed in consultation with the patient or their guardian. Once the treatment plan is documented, it becomes a permanent part of the patient's records and needs to be communicated to everyone involved in treating the patient to ensure a continuity of care.

Post-clinical

The post-clinical activities occur following the examination process and involve evaluating the success (or failure) of the treatment plan. During the evaluation, the steps might include reviewing the test results to determine whether the diagnosis was correct, contacting the patient to determine the patient's response to treatment, and scheduling additional labs or procedures as required.

As with all steps and activities in the nursing process (Figure 10.3), critical thinking is vital to the successful treatment of the patient. Nursing professionals need to recognize health problems, anticipate complications, and initiate actions to ensure appropriate and timely treatments. This involves decision making and reasoning in order to digest the data and make an accurate assessment of the patient's health issue.

Decision making and reasoning are only part of the equation. Fundamentally, nurses must also have a knowledge foundation from which they make their decisions. This knowledge comes from a variety of sources, including training, experience, advice from peers, and research.

TIP

clinical data
Clinical data includes vital signs; current health issues and symptoms; orders for tests, lab work, or specialist referrals; diagnoses; and treatment plans.

post-clinical data
Post-clinical data is collected following the examination and is used to evaluate the success (or failure) of the treatment plan.

Figure 10.3   Nursing Workflow

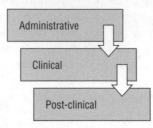

Evidence-Based Practice

Evidence-based practice (EBP), evidence-based medicine (EBM), and empirically supported treatment (EST) are all terms that describe a growing trend in healthcare that applies a scientific decision-based approach to patient care. The ultimate goal of EBP is to shift healthcare decisions, choices, and action to a higher, more scientific level.

The adoption of technology in the medical practice has been a key factor in the development and promotion of EBP. Conceptually, EBP is depicted in Figure 10.4 by using a triangle to show the relationship between data, information, and knowledge to represent the value proposition of EBP to the nurse and ultimately to the medical practice. At the base of the triangle is data, which is a collection of facts such as a patient's vital signs, current medications, symptoms, and the like, which may or may not be interesting when reviewed individually. Collectively, these facts tell a story or otherwise provide meaning in the context of the patient's condition, which in turn provides information to the nurse and the physician that they will use in their diagnosis and treatment plans. The collection of information provides the foundation for the practice to make better and more informed decisions regarding the patient's care.

Figure 10.4   EBP

In theory, clinical decision making based upon EBP requires research into the effectiveness of healthcare interventions based upon controlled trials and observational studies. In practice, nursing clinical decision-making is based upon their professional know-how and experience.

Nurses use a variety of sources to facilitate their use of evidence. These sources include their nursing training, personal experience, advice from colleagues, research studies, and medical journals. Online tools are available to nurses from within the EHR system or via a web browser. For instance, nurses can now electronically link to several (or all) information systems that influence their practice, including electronic health records, medical knowledge bases, prescription drug interaction data, and clinical decision support systems.

Health Information Exchanges

We introduced the concept of data exchanges in Chapter 1. The *Health Information Exchange (HIE)* refers to the process of interoperable and reliable electronic sharing of health-related data in a manner that protects the confidentiality, privacy, and security of the information. HIE systems provide secure access to clinical data shared within a community for the purposes of providing safer, more timely, and efficient patient care.

In a self-contained network, such as those linking hospitals to affiliated practices, HIE systems enable physicians and clinicians to quickly and easily share patient data for the purpose of continuity of care among multiple providers. This helps reduce duplicate testing, time spent tracking down missing patient data, manual processing (scanning, faxing, and printing) of documents, and costs associated with the delivery (mail, FedEx, and courier) of patient charts and test results. Studies have shown that a single clinician office spends more than $17,000 per year on traditional methods of exchanging patient information.

In an integrated network, defined data types and standards such as HL-7 and X.12 are used to share de-identified data on local, regional, and national levels to support research, public health, emergency response, and quality improvements in patient care.

Connectivity between the EHR and the HIE systems does not come without cost. Interfaces must be defined and configured. Depending upon the number and type of interfaces, the cost of HIE connectivity could eclipse the potential savings over the traditional methods of exchanging patient information. EHR vendors and HIE systems recognize this and continue to work together to come up with ways to make EHR and HIE integration easier and affordable.

evidence-based practice
Various definitions of evidence-based practice (EBP) have emerged in literature, but the most commonly used definition is "The conscientious, explicit, and judicious use of the current best evidence in making decisions about the care of individual patients" (Sackett, Rosenberg, Gray, Hayes, & Richardson, 1996).

HIE
HIE systems provide secure access to clinical data shared within a community for the purposes of providing safer, more timely, and efficient patient care.

> ### HIMSS State HIT Dashboard
>
> HIMSS has put together a dashboard that links to healthcare information technology initiatives on a state-by-state basis. With a click of the mouse, you can drill down on your state to find out about HIE resources, regional extension centers, state resources, and local HIMSS chapters. The dashboard is available at www.himss.org/statedashboard/.

Nursing Technology Implementation

Technology is dramatically altering the ways in which medical professionals diagnose, treat, care for, and manage patients. Nurses play a central role in the adoption and overall success of many HIT projects.

 Real World Scenario

Nursing Goes Live with EMR Without Major Issues

A large hospital system in Georgia was going live with the EMR system. Since patient care was the top priority from executive management, they needed a way to install an EMR system without negatively impacting the patients or nursing staff. Management took a long hard look at the employee makeup and planned accordingly. The IT team attached to the project knew that training was going to be critical. The staff had a typical tenure of 20+ years and limited exposure to computers, and some were looking to retire if the project failed. A smaller group of staff were younger than 40 and had greater exposure to computers and technology; many were admired because of the ease with which they used technology. The team capitalized on that admiration and recruited nursing champions who were comfortable with technology and respected in their units to be on the implementation team. The chief nursing officer (CNO) was also younger and came from a clinic that had recently migrated to an EMR system. As staff retired, staff members who were familiar with technology were hired to replace them. This bottom-up replacement philosophy worked. One project manager for the EMR deployment stated, "A key factor of success on this project was the hiring of younger whippersnappers." When further probed, the key factor was the employee's exposure to computers, not their age.

The IT team tackled the project in earnest. First, they found the right nursing team to support them. The nurses had enough years of work at the hospital to understand the workflow but had no ingrained fear of computers. They spent a great deal of energy on putting only the necessary check boxes, free text, and imported data on the screen. They found that too much data on a screen detracted from patient care; it was considered clutter.

Continues

The IT team worked with the nursing staff to set up a lab that included the actual equipment used for patient care, the new equipment necessary to integrate with the EMR, and the actual application running. Nurses who needed one-on-one training could schedule time in the lab for personalized training. The IT team worked with the nurses to modify the workflow as approved change requests came in.

Training for the nurses was mandated within six weeks of going live. Each nurse was required to attend 16 hours of training. The training sessions were held in a computer lab and limited to 12 nurses. Each was led by the subject-matter experts, with staff from the EMR vendor there to answer any question the team couldn't address. At launch, subject-matter experts were on site at each facility. They were backed up by a command center of roughly 60 people focused on resolving issues.

Overall, the project went off without a significant hitch. As a team, the nurses, IT staff, and executives knew that moving to an EMR wasn't going to be an easy transition for staff unless it was done right. They committed the resources to do it right, and they were successful. The EMR deployment was successful because the nurses' needs were addressed by assembling the right implementation team, providing expert personalized training using real equipment and real applications, and holding out helping hands during the launch.

Systems Implementation

Technology specialists are experts in their field of practice, and they understand the mechanics of how their technology works. Nurses are experts in the field of nursing, and they understand the dynamics of patient care. It is equally important for nurses to understand a new technology as it is for technical specialists to understand how their systems are used in the context of delivering patient care.

The introduction of new technology into the nursing process must involve the nurses in every phase of the implementation in order to be successful. This seems obvious, but studies have shown that up to 30 percent of failed HIT projects are caused by lack of involvement and buy-in from the users of the system. Similar studies have also shown that nurses will and do adopt new technology when they are given the opportunity to provide input into the planning and implementation processes and have had a chance to confirm that the changes to their processes are effective.

Recognizing that each provider's workflow pattern is unique also ensures the successful adoption of new technology. Technology specialists often bring a one-size-fits-all approach without taking the time to understand the nuances of how the technology fits (or doesn't fit) into the culture and workflow of a specific provider.

Finally, successful implementation requires the appropriate resources to support the implementation. Again, this might seem obvious, but we have seen many instances where HIT projects become an additional responsibility of a nurse, and it almost always interferes with their primary responsibilities. When this happens, there is resistance—nurses generally do not resist technology; they resist adding more to their current workload and any interference with patient care.

Considerations

Based on our experience, a mid-career nurse has had little, if any, formal training in the use of computers and technology. Most of their technical knowledge has been developed organically and absorbed through the use of the practice management system, billing system, or other browser-based tools while on the job. The modern medical practice requires a new skill set that incorporates technology in addition to the basic nursing skills. Nursing schools recognized that and began incorporating technology in their curriculum in the early 1990s by incorporating PowerPoint presentations instead of overhead projectors and adopting the use of email as a communication medium.

In the past 10 years, the work setting for nurses has undergone a rapid technological change. For these mid-career nurses, their career began using paper records, then moved to electronic scheduling, billing, and practice management systems. The unavoidable truth is that the use of technology in the medical practice is no longer optional. These same nurses are now being asked to embrace EHR and interconnected systems in order to improve workflow, patient outcomes, and quality of patient care. Most of these nurses will agree wholeheartedly with the concepts tied to improving patient care, yet they might resist the implementation and adoption for reasons stated and unstated.

For example, the nurse might say, "Technology is not always a panacea, and technology solutions that require too much effort get in the way of patient care" or "Patient care comes first, and we won't allow technology to get in the way."

When you begin to examine these statements, consider that it is not uncommon for physicians and administrative personnel, such as a practice manager, to drive the selection process for new technology. In areas that impact their processes, nurses want and need to be part of decision-making process. The problem is that their technical skills are not always up to par. (This could be the reason for their exclusion.) It is, perhaps, not right, but it is worth noting that when it comes to successful implementations of technology that involves nurses and their workflow, a nurse can make or break an HIT project.

Technology/systems implementation is a peculiar thing, and your interpretation often depends upon your particular viewpoint. On one hand, technology can be viewed as up-to-date or leading edge and the very best in patient care. On the other hand, technology can be viewed as bureaucratic overhead that gets in the way. Nursing resistance can kill an IT project; it is essential that technology providers help nurses (technical and nontechnical) see the value that new technology can bring to their jobs and to the quality of patient care, no matter what their frame of reference might be.

Nursing Technology Innovations

New technologies have the potential to improve the environment for nurses by improving their efficiency and effectiveness, which in turn allows them to devote more of their time and expertise to caring for patients.

Enhancing Nursing Care Delivery

Several technologies can increase efficiency and improve patient outcomes. Here we look at examples of technology that increase efficiency, increase effectiveness, reduce potential errors, and improve the overall outcomes for patients. The following sections are not by any means exhaustive but will provide some insight into the potential for enhancing patient care.

Wireless

Wireless technologies have become critical to an efficient nursing workflow. They facilitate quick access to other staff members and patient data without ever leaving the point of care.

Quick access to staff is critical in clinical settings such as a birthing unit, mental/behavioral health ward, or emergency department. Since the staff is mobile, technology must be employed to meet the staffing and rapid response needs of the organization. Paging is one method for accessing clinical staff. A nurse or other staff member will send a page to the attending physician or clinical staff member needed at the time. Some advantages of using pagers are that they are usually simple to use, almost always are powered by just a single AA battery, and are made to take a significant amount of abuse. You should be aware that we are seeing fewer two-way pagers. We bring that up because one of the significant challenges with a pager is that it is a one-way communication device. There is no positive confirmation that the message was received. Using pagers also requires phone companies to invest in the infrastructure required to make sure the pager works within a hospital or clinic setting. For example, one of our clients doesn't have digital or analog cell reception in about 30 percent of their building. Since they could cannot force the phone company to invest in the technology required to support pagers, it was simply not cost-effective to pay $250,000 in build-out for a $10 per month device for 30 physicians.

Wireless technology in support of clinical information systems has proven to be invaluable in improving patient care by enabling access to patient data at the point of care. Devices such as touchpads, tablets, and virtual desktops are replacing computers on wheels (COWs) and stationary nursing workstations. Wireless-enabled devices improve the speed, efficiency, and safety of traditional healthcare delivery.

Wireless communication devices, such as VoIP handsets and communication badges, offer vast improvements over the traditional pagers and centralized telephone services used in hospital settings. Nurses now carry telephones with them and can make and receive calls without having to go back to the central nursing station. Studies suggest that nurses were able to reclaim an average of 58 minutes per shift by not having to stop what they were doing in order to go find a phone or answer a call.

Communication badges work similarly to wireless phones but have the added advantages of hands-free operation and speech recognition. Other wireless-enabled applications include messaging, event management, and workflow communications. Wearable mobile communication devices are becoming more pervasive. The market leader here is Vocera. Its mobile communication badge uses the standard 802.11a/b/g/n wireless spectrum. The low-end badge includes two microphones; the first is located near the top of the unit, and the second microphone is located on the side. The microphone on the side captures ambient noise, which is pulled out of the voice signal sent back to the communication station so that the wearer's voice can be clearly understood. The advantage of a system such as Vocera is that it can be deployed using the existing wireless infrastructure. If additional infrastructure investments are necessary to deploy the system, the funding to support the initiative will usually come out of the IT department. The deployment is not dependent upon outside investments by a Telco provider. Also, Vocera has developed a voice recognition capability to make sure that if the device is stolen, an unknown voice cannot control the device. This voice printing capability can be valuable when controlling access to the device, so medication and other treatment orders aren't carried out without proper authentication.

NOTE

Some IT folk have experienced difficulties with the badges during security audits. They were dinged because the badge speaker allowed anyone in the vicinity of the transmission recipient to hear the conversation, and thus, they were not considered secure. There was no way for staff initiating a communication to know where the recipient was or who else might be listening. Headset models can alleviate those concerns, but they are uncomfortable, and the connecting wires can become tangled in equipment. The small size, ease of operation, and reliable communication offered by these light-weight badges, however, override concerns, and they continue to be popular.

Before deploying the technology, there must be a robust wireless infrastructure. A heat map tool allows you to document what the signal strength will be. From there, try different frequencies. Depending on the location, 11 to 14 channels are available. Get a heat map for each. Once the heat map per frequency is created, it is time to see which frequency will be best for deployment. A robust environment will have wireless spectrum frequency management tools that will alert staff when a new wireless access point is transmitting on the same channel.

Having this information empowers you as the IT professional to track down the rogue wireless access point. With the advent of mobile hotspots, tracking down these rogue devices will become more important over time. When wireless access points are transmitting on the same frequency, there will be less bandwidth available on that frequency. Lower bandwidth can mean less reliability and dropped communications.

Real World Scenario

Nurses in Motion

In a recent healthcare roundtable discussion with a VAR, we had the opportunity to listen to a presentation from a product manager at Research in Motion (RIM), the makers of the BlackBerry phone. The presentation focused on the use of BlackBerry smartphones by the nursing staff at the University of Pittsburg Medical Center (UPMC). Using SmartRoom technology (www.smartroomsolutions.com), nurses receive real-time data from EMRs, including allergies, vital signs, test results, and medications that are due, directly on the phone. The My Rooms application presents nurses with a list of their patients and a list of all the nurses working the same shift and allows the nurse to receive a doctor's orders without being tied to a computer. The information shown on the screen is tailored to the needs of the specific worker. For example, a host who delivers meal trays will see only dietary orders and allergy information. A transporter will receive instructions about where to pick up a patient and where to take them. Doctors will see different information than nurses. The software also helps determine which tasks should be completed in which order to most effectively and safely care for the patients.

The beauty of this application is that it is deployed using the BlackBerry Enterprise Server (BES). Why is this important? Each BlackBerry has access to PHI and could become a security risk if they are lost or stolen. The BES allows you to control the phone and immediately shut it down if it can't be accounted for. The product manager continued to explain that UPMC is working on an integration with its PBX using a unified communications solution from Cisco. When the integration is complete, the BlackBerry devices will not require cellular activation, and costs to deploy these devices will drop dramatically.

The SmartRoom technology and BlackBerry smartphone combination is just one example of technology used to improve patient care delivery by nurses. This technology also has the potential to make its way to smaller environments and eventually to the ambulatory medical practice.

Electronic Medication Order Fulfillment

Medication errors occur all too frequently in hospitals. Recent studies suggest that there are 400,000 preventable adverse drug events annually—at a cost of up to $3.5 billion. Patient medication order and delivery is a complex process that involves professionals from multiple disciplines, including nurses, physicians, pharmacists, and pharmacy technicians. Errors and adverse events can easily be made at any step, especially during administration by the nurses.

Software called *electronic medication administration (eMAR)* with barcoding helps prevent errors and improve patient safety by providing information about the drugs, such as when it was last administered and when it needs to be given again. Most importantly, the information is presented in a legible format without the need for transcription.

A scanner quickly identifies and verifies the five rights checklist—the right patient, the right drug, the right time, the right dose, and the right route—by scanning the barcodes on the medication and the patient's wrist identification band. The ability to perform this verification each time medication is administered reduces errors and increases patient safety.

Other technologies that reduce medication errors are eprescribing and the robotic dispensing of medication. The practice of eprescribing involves the electronic transmittal of prescriptions from the physician to the pharmacy. Robotic medication dispensing machines use suction cups attached to electronic arms to grab medication packets and scan them to ensure accuracy. After verifying the correct barcode, the robot places the dose into an envelope marked for a specific patient. Medication reconciliation and electronic fulfillment increase patient safety and provide better continuity of care by reducing errors associated with medication administration.

Workflow Management

Lack of coordination can cause slowdowns in one area that lead to roadblocks in other areas. One cause for this is difficulty in locating information. For example, if a nurse is waiting on lab results before starting medication, the nurse needs to either call the lab or log in to the clinical information system to see whether the results have been posted. Depending upon where the nurse needs to go to access the information, the delay could slow or halt the current processes while the data is being retrieved.

Workflow management systems collect data from multiple sources and integrate the data into a single easy-to-read display that can provide real-time information about patient status, including wait times, lab results, outstanding orders, and other care metrics and alerts. The display can also show utilization metrics that might allow resources to be redeployed to where they are needed most. The benefits of a workflow management system include near real-time access to patient information that is presented in an easy-to-digest format. Streamlined patient flows and quicker access to information result in more nursing time devoted to patient care.

Electronic Clinical Documentation

Nurses spend a great deal of time filling out forms and documenting patient care. Studies suggest that for every hour nurses spend on patient care, they spend 30 minutes to an hour on paperwork. Manual documentation is time-consuming and

eMAR
Electronic medication administration (eMAR) software employs barcodes to link information about drugs (dose and route), the last administration to a patient, and the next scheduled administration.

often incomplete or illegible. Retrieving information from paper charts and notes is time-consuming and error-prone.

Ideally, nurses capture patient data at the point of care, and there is no delay in the availability of the most up-to-date patient information. Examples of electronic clinical documentation include standard templates for assessment plans that include information already captured and input from biomedical devices that integrate with the EHR.

The benefits of electronic clinical documentation include improved data sharing and task management support. Nurses with the ability to use an electronic device at the point of care show, on average, a 24 percent increase in productivity. The increases in productivity notwithstanding, there are additional benefits, including improved accuracy and completeness of nursing documentation.

Do You Have an App for That?

As handheld devices become more prevalent in healthcare, the availability of applications is increasing exponentially. One such application is Nursing Central from Unbound Medicine (www.unboundmedicine.com/).

Unbound Medicine was founded by a physician who recognized the difficulty of accessing the wealth of available medical knowledge and resources where it is needed most—at the point of care. With this in mind, Unbound Medicine developed a series of applications and a subscription model to deliver mobile and web-based products through an end-to-end digital publishing platform.

The Nursing Central suite, which is compatible with most mobile devices, includes *Davis's Drug Guide*, *Diseases and Disorders*, *Taber's Cyclopedic Medical Dictionary*, selected MEDLINE journals, and *Davis's Laboratory and Diagnostic Tests*.

Unbound Medicine leverages its content and delivery platform to provide clinicians with immediate, authoritative, and accurate answers where and when they are needed.

Terms to Know

nursing process

evidence-based practice (EBP)

electronic medication administration (eMAR)

ADPIE

Health Information Exchange (HIE)

Review Questions

1. Which of the following is not an element of the nursing process?

   A. Assessment

   B. Plan

   C. Implementation

   D. Follow-up

2. What is an example of an administrative activity in the nursing workflow?

   A. Registering a patient

   B. Recording a patient's vital signs

   C. Interviewing

   D. Ordering lab tests

3. The goal of evidence-based practice is to do what?

   A. Prove the nurse has made the right diagnosis

   B. Shift healthcare decisions to more scientific level

   C. Recognize health problems, anticipate complications, and initiate actions

   D. Determine the patient's response to treatment

4. What is the Health Information Exchange?

   A. A subcomponent of an EHR system

   B. A network of public and private medical providers

   C. The delivery of patient data via FedEx

   D. The process of interoperable and reliable electronic sharing of health-related data

5. Which of the following is not a reason to participate in an HIE?

   A. Enable physicians and clinicians to quickly and easily share patient data

   B. Reduce time spent tracking down patient data

   C. Increase the costs associated with manual delivery of patient data

   D. Reduce office expenses

6. What percentage of all HIT projects fail because of lack of involvement and buy-in from users of the system?

   A. 90

   B. 45

   C. 30

   D. 15

7. Which of the follow helps ensure a successful systems implementation?

  A. A one-size-fits-all approach

  B. Exclusion of key stakeholders from the process

  C. Technical specialists understanding how their systems will be used in the context of patient care

  D. Unlimited budget

8. Nursing resistance is _____.

  A. An unavoidable part of any technology project

  B. Their attempt to bring back the paper office

  C. Never a consideration when selecting technology that will impact their ability to provide quality patient care

  D. Avoidable if they are treated fairly and included in projects that impact their job

9. Why is it important to get buy-in from the nurses when it comes to implementing technical solutions?

  A. The adoption rate of the solution is much higher

  B. Nurses can provide valuable insight into the problems and the process

  C. Nurses are key decision makers and influence the purchase

  D. All of the above

10. Nurses with access to electronic devices at the point of care show an average productivity increase of _____ percent?

  A. 12

  B. 24

  C. 50

  D. 75

Chapter 11

Operational Workflow: Clinician

In previous chapters, we discussed the basic workflow of the front-office, back-office, and nursing processes. The clinician is central character around which all of those processes revolve. The clinician exerts a great deal of control over everything that goes on around them and ultimately is responsible for the safety and well-being of the patients under their care. In this chapter, we will look at the challenges of delivering patient care from the clinician's perspective.

Challenges

Issues that impact the clinician operational workflow tend to affect the entire practice, and when we uncover complications, we find issues that impact the business as a whole. You might say that the practice revolves around the clinicians, but perhaps a better visual metaphor would be something like electrons (office staff) moving around the nucleus of an atom (clinicians), as shown in Figure 11.1.

Figure 11.1   Clinician's world

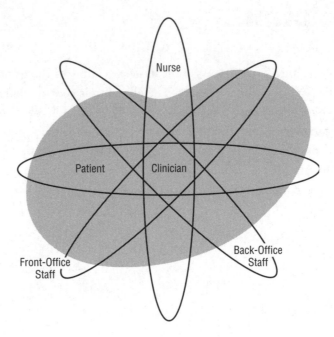

Staffing

Staffing expenses represent one of the largest, if not *the* largest, expense to the medical practice. The challenges surrounding staffing are multidimensional and can impact the practice in a variety of ways. In a medical practice, the administrative staff turnover rate can be as high as 20 percent annually. The reason for this is that these positions, while critical to the daily operation of the practice, have a certain degree of monotony and do not pay as much as the positions that require a college degree. Turnover adds expense (replacement costs and training) and reduced efficiency while the new staff member gets up to speed learning their responsibilities. Additionally, the likelihood of an error causing other problems increases.

The retention of the clinical workforce is ongoing concern, as well. Patient load, patient mix, working hours, and professional development are factors that help determine the clinician's overall sense of happiness and well-being. Turnover at the clinical workforce level impacts the number of patients that can be seen, and that has a direct impact on the bottom line of the practice. Recruiting costs are higher, and the time it takes to find a replacement is much longer than with other staff. Emphasis is placed on making sure that the needs of the clinical workforce are continually being met. The right mix of skills and personalities is also an important consideration for a harmonious and productive work environment. Medical office staff work very closely with one another, and the wrong combination is a productivity killer for the practice.

Preparation

The revenue for the medical practice is driven by the number of patients that the clinician can see in a day, and the amount of time that the clinician can spend with each patient is limited. Preparation is extremely important to efficient patient flow, and many practices go through a review of their patient schedule on a daily and weekly basis to ensure that they understand the patients and their needs. For example, senior patients take longer to get ready for exams, so efficient practices schedule appropriately and allow for additional time in the examination room. Clinicians get input from all staff and particularly the nurses, who understand the type of patients that require more time. Consider that if every patient takes an extra 10 minutes to process, the clinician will be 90 minutes behind after 9 patients. Clinicians need to be realistic about what can get done in a 15- to 20-minute time slot and budget their time accordingly.

Communication

Effective communication is important in any work environment, and this is especially true in a medical practice, where miscommunication can have serious consequences for the patient and the clinician. Communication in healthcare is not limited to the physician–patient relationship. Oral and written communication concerning a patient's status and health are routinely exchanged between the clinician, the nurse, payers, laboratories, and other specialists. Patient information is passed via telephone, email, fax, consultation notes, laboratory reports, and the like; there are ample opportunities for an error to occur. Miscommunication is sometimes the result of efforts by the medical practice to comply with HIPPA regulations designed to protect patient information. In removing personally identifiable data, the likelihood of mixing up patient information has actually increased. Studies also suggest that although the number of miscommunications related to patient care might be low, the severity of error could be quite high and even fatal. Any number of technical solutions can help reduce miscommunication, and each depends upon the environment and situation. Be aware of these challenges and look for opportunities to correct issues as they come up.

Listening skills are just as important in the communication process as oral and written communication. Careful listening might uncover clues regarding a patient's condition that indicate a need to gather more information. Observation of nonverbal communication also plays an important role in clinician–patient communications. A head nod from a patient who is Asian might mean something totally different from the same action coming from someone with a different cultural background. The head nod might be an indication that the patient is trying to be polite and is not necessarily a sign that they understand and agree. Effective and timely communication between the functional components of the process is essential for smooth workflow and is one of the best ways to ensure the highest-quality patient care while preventing malpractice and mistakes.

Workflow

EHR adoption and new technologies have introduced a transitional phase in many medical practices. Clinicians age 40 and older understand the need to move in the direction of EHR, and they see the value in using these tools, but they did not grow up using a keyboard to perform day-to-day tasks. Using a keyboard has significantly slowed down their ability to process the patients they see. As a result, some clinicians have compensated for this by continuing to use dictation devices and paper and pen to record their notes and instructions. At the end of the day, they go back and enter the data into the EHR when they are not crunched for time. This behavior has resulted in some very difficult decisions for the clinician and their practice. Faced with a slower response time in processing patients, clinicians either have reduced the number of patients they see in a day or have kept patient levels the same and work an additional one to two hours each night catching up on their data entry. Even the clinicians who choose to see fewer patients find themselves working more hours, and this has resulted in a decrease in revenue for the practice and a dramatic decrease in the quality of life for the clinician. Compounding the problem of slower patient processing is the difficulty in managing patient scheduling when the patient arrives late for an appointment. Despite the staff's best efforts in preparing for the patient's arrival and the reduced patient schedule, a late arrival throws all of this preparation out the window. What begins as a 5- to 10-minute delay can turn into an hour or more by the end of the day.

Organizations that benefit the most from the use of EHR technology (payers, Medicaid, and Medicare) are systematically working to reduce the amount of reimbursement payments to the clinicians for their work. When you factor in the patient reduction because of adoption, with the decreasing revenues from payment reduction, clinicians can't afford to hire someone to help with the data input, and they can't afford to see fewer patients. Often, their only option is to work additional hours. Clinicians refer to this as the new economics of medicine.

Technology

The use of technology (or misuse, depending upon your point of view) needs to be understood from the clinician's point of view. Like the nurses, there is an overriding view that EHR should not interfere with the doctor–patient relationship. When you consider the examination process and the limited amount of time the clinician has with the patient (15 to 20 minutes), spending an excessive amount of time (excessive in the clinician's view is 50 percent or more) navigating and using the EHR system seems to lend credence to the interference claim.

Adapting to the technology is not the only difficulty in using the EHR system. The configuration of the application and the underlying technical stack used to deploy the EHR system are also factors. EHR applications rarely support the existing clinician's workflow without some form of customization. This is especially true of specialists who must adapt their workflow to the application because there are no configurations or individual modules that support their particular specialty. Without the ability to configure the EHR interfaces so relevant fields are available quickly or to configure EHR to match the needs of the specialist with their patients, there will less than full adoption, and the EHR system will not be used to its full advantage.

The underlying technical stack refers to the combination of hardware, software, and LAN/WAN infrastructure used to deliver the EHR to the clinician. Unforeseen errors such as an unexplained slowdown of the application or disconnects introduce delays in the workflow process and inhibit the use of the EHR system.

Real World Scenario

Wireless Access Issues

One of our clients has five locations and 11 doctors. They selected an EMR package from a local independent physicians association (IPA) because the monthly cost was significantly lower than purchasing a system and running it on their own. In our opinion, the IPA selected a hosting organization that wasn't prepared to handle the workload of the physician groups coming on. As the trusted IT provider, we were put in a number of very sensitive situations that required delicate handling and owning the right tools.

The technology selected by the IPA for the wireless deployment created a lot of challenges in delivering effective wireless coverage throughout the office. The practice had more than 15 tablet PCs connected to a single access point, and the access point was not placed in an optimal location within the practice. Additionally, the IPA controlled the supporting T-1 circuits because of the business associate

Continues

agreements they signed with the practice. When application usability issues surfaced in some of the exam rooms, staff members reported that the lack of access to the network caused workflow issues. At one point, they actually shut down one exam room because they could not get a consistent connection to access the EHR system. There was a lot of finger pointing, and no one was certain whether a hardware issue, a software issue, or a network issue that was the source of the problem. We chose to look at the wireless connection problems. To help diagnosis the problem, we purchased an AirPcap NX series wireless packet capture device called the Cascade Pilot from CACE Technologies (now Riverbed Technology) that offered network analysis, visualization tools, and reporting tools. This product is a version of the packet sniffer called Wireshark on steroids. Coupled together, the technology allowed us to see signal strength in particular locations, see whether there was a particular chatty network card, and even find out whether there was a chatty network segment.

What we found was very interesting. First, there was a system monitoring tool installed that was scanning the network segments every five seconds. Though not saturating the network, it was unnecessary scanning. Next, the access point was located inside a filing cabinet (not the ideal situation to reach through the number of walls to get to the furthest exam room), and the power output on the wireless access point was only 50 percent. The company that set it up didn't want the wireless to leak to the parking lot. Clearly, they didn't consider the ramifications of the reduced signal strength on the legitimate wireless operations within the practice. Lastly, we found that the wireless channel that was selected was in conflict with the other multiple wireless access points in the same facility. In the 2.4GHz range, wireless channels operate much like television channels, and each access point broadcasts on a specific channel. In a densely populated office environment, wireless access point broadcasts often overlap, causing interference and degradation of network performance. Switching the access point to a new, nonoverlapping channel (channels 1, 6, and 11 are nonoverlapping) also helped.

We were able to take our findings to the medical practice and show them what needed to be done. We worked with the IPA to fix those issues and helped train IPA staff on securing, troubleshooting, and doing the analysis necessary to uncover the root of the problem.

Needs of the Clinician

The clinician has many needs when it comes to optimizing the use of technology in support of their workflow process. On a professional level, there are things that will help them be more productive and will improve patient care. Technically, the clinician needs help with recommendations, implementation, configurations, and support from the team that they can trust and rely on given what is at stake. Personally, they need understanding, in so much as most clinicians are businesspeople who are trying to remain profitable, despite the added burden of debt and high business costs.

A clinician's needs vary by specialty and differ even in practices within the same specialty. The following are needs we have uncovered based upon our client mix.

Professional Needs

As we discuss the professional needs of the clinician, keep in mind that the solutions discussed here were collected in discussions with clients and represent wishes as much as they represent needs that will help clinicians be more efficient in using technology to perform their clinical duties. In some cases, the solution exists and is within reach, while in other cases the needs represent a desire or direction that is not yet available.

EHR-Integrated Dictation   EHR-integrated dictation is a technology need that is mentioned frequently, and a number of companies are working to address this need. Applications currently exist that allow dictation into an iPhone or Android-based phone that take the spoken word and transcribe it into text that can be emailed and copied into the patient record. Direct dictation into the EHR application is not currently available or, if it is available, is not sufficiently vetted to enable widespread adoption.

Imaging and Laboratory Data Access   Clinicians also want to have access to imaging and lab data from within the EHR application. The current issue is that not all EHR applications have HL7 interfaces or a way to easily import and present external data. Many systems offer a workaround in the form of linking to an external data source, but that requires context shifting between the applications, which makes it harder for the clinician to compare the current data in the EHR with the external data.

Customization   Some EHR applications require all of the users to behave in the same way when using the system, which does not take into account the unique differences between the practices or between physicians in a practice. Clinicians want the ability to customize the EHR application such that it can be adapted for each of the physicians in a practice.

Tracked Changes   In a shared environment where multiple practices within a physicians group use the same application and share access to the patient record, clinicians want the ability to track changes to the patient information. In one instance, our client reported that front-office staff in other practices caused more work for their practice when they scanned patient data to the wrong location, deleted data, or made a mistake when entering data. Our client subsequently had to correct the errors after their billing processes failed and their claims were rejected.

Business Needs

Business needs involve recognizing that clinicians are also business people with some of the same issues that you have in your everyday life. When approaching a clinician for a project that requires a significant investment, VARs might be tempted to believe that with ARRA funding and a thriving practice, financing an EHR system or other technical projects will not be a problem. Unfortunately, this is the exception rather than the rule. Here are some data points worth considering. The average clinician has a credit rating of approximately 718, which is the same as the average American and is good but not great. When they come out of school, clinicians are carrying about $250,000 in student loan debt, and most of their medical equipment is leased. When you factor in office expense, staff salaries, malpractice insurance, and other costs of doing business, the clinician needs a revenue stream of about $400,000 per year just to break even. Recognizing and understanding the clinician's financial concerns goes a long way when discussing projects that require them to come up with a significant amount of money. Partnering with solution providers that offer financing options is another way to improve your chances of winning a project. Also, it would be wise to consider (when it comes to setting your sights on the ARRA incentives for EHR implementation) that statistics have shown that the bulk of the improvement benefits associated with EHR implementation goes to everyone but the physician. Finally, understand that clinicians are trying to manage the same life-work trade-offs that we all are. Any projects or technologies that can be shown to improve the balance between work and life will be well received, especially if you can show them how to pay for it.

Technical Needs

The technical needs of the clinician are driven by their need for implementation and support of business and clinical systems. When we ask potential clients what they are looking for in an IT provider, the answer is almost always the same: availability when there is a problem. This is a reasonable request and one that most VARs would say is achievable. So, why is it that this statement keeps coming up? One reason is that there are multiple companies in the technology value chain. You have the IT vendor that services the hardware and networking infrastructure that supports the EHR application delivery. Then there is the software vendor that is responsible for the functionality of the application, and in some cases, you have an intermediary support organization from the IPA that oversees the use and implementation of the EHR system within their environment. With multiple vendors and support organizations involved, it becomes very easy to blame the other guy. The constant playback of the issue between the vendors and the lack of understanding of the system as a whole is one of the clinician's biggest frustrations.

From the clinicians' perspective, they have a problem that is impacting their ability to care for patients. They don't really care who is responsible for the issue—they just want it fixed in the shortest amount of time possible. Clinicians struggle when their systems do not work as required, and in a multi-vendor environment, it is important that all parties recognize that it requires a team approach to problem resolution. As one physician put it, we are all in this together. Clinicians understand that the IT vendor is only one piece of the puzzle, yet they are in a position where they need to rely on someone to own the problem and drive its resolution.

As a technology partner with the clinician and the other vendors, it is sometimes necessary to provide supporting data that helps narrow down the cause of the problem or have the ability to definitively show that the problem is not within your control or responsibility in order to keep the troubleshooting process moving toward a resolution.

Point-of-Care Devices

As EHR technologies continue to advance patient care, clinicians are beginning to realize the value in having access to patient information at the *point of care (POC)*. Clinicians' need for information anytime, anywhere is absolutely essential to the quality of care they provide. Point-of-care devices (such as a laptop, tablet, or smartphone) are the tools clinicians use to access patient information when and where they need it. Physicians are not unique in their expectations for technology. They want all technology to be as robust as the FDA-approved technologies that they have been using for decades. However, they also want to be able to use the latest and greatest tablet or smartphone device to access patient information. The physicians we work with are notorious for bringing their most recent technology purchase into the office and expecting that it will just work. Sometimes we have to tell them that, although their new device is very cool, it will not work in their environment without a lot of expensive changes.

Warranties

So, the sky is the limit in terms of the types of devices that can be deployed. Before we jump into the devices, we need to cover the way different companies warranty their devices.

> **Business-Grade Products** When a physician chooses a consumer-grade product, that product may not have the 24/7 support that a typically more expensive business-grade device would have. Physicians want to receive timely support to fix their broken devices. The support they need might not be available for consumer-grade products.
>
> **24/7, NDB, and Field Support** For tablets or other clinical devices, it is important to get 24/7 next business day (NDB) support. For certain devices, you might also recommend a four-hour response. Certain manufacturers do not have a field tech organization. In those cases, the device must be shipped to the manufacturer. This causes a three- to five-day outage for the physician. If the device vendor doesn't have on-site service, make sure you purchase a spare device or become an OEM-certified repair center. This allows you to do the repairs without voiding warranties.
>
> **No Warranty** We have run into situations where a doctor purchased devices without a warranty from a previous vendor. When the device broke a year later, it was not covered. They ended up having to buy a

replacement system. The up-front $300 warranty would have served that client well. Instead, they were forced to buy another $2,000 device.

Pro Services Pro services are offered by the major vendors. Apple has ProCare, which allows your technician to jump ahead of the line and get immediate service; it costs just $100 a year for this privilege. Dell and HP have Pro or business support lines that allow access to North American call centers. The expectation here is that you have better resources to resolve the technical issue. Having access to the pro support enables you, as a health IT professional, to provide better service to the clinician.

Durability and Usability Issues

Gaining access to the EMR is typically the sole goal of the compute platform for the office staff. However, for the clinician, their compute platform (tablet, laptop, or desktop) becomes their primary platform. They take their device home, to conferences, on vacation—name a place, and chances are a physician's compute platform has been there. Therefore, it is critical that it is built to withstand the beating it is going to take. To get an idea of the difference between a consumer-grade and business-grade product, head to your local technology shop and pick up any laptop. Open the laptop and hold it on one of the front corners, and if the body of the laptop flexes, the device will not withstand the daily abuse it will experience in the hands of a clinician. When looking at a business-class laptop or tablet, you will see that there is no flexing of the case. This is important because each time the chassis flexes, the parts attached to the motherboard can work themselves free. The challenge is that the parts only partially disconnect typically and thus cause frustrating intermittent issues.

Tablets have been all the rage within the healthcare market, but we don't recommend them. In our experience, the convertible tablets are used as laptops, not as tablets. Tablets have the smaller screens, and many physicians find that their eyes are strained, and they become fatigued more easily during the day. Tablets also require a lot of pecking at the screen; few have accurate typing screens.

Since the tablet screen sizes are typically smaller than 12 inches, we are seeing more physicians adopting the use of laptops. The human body wasn't developed to hold a laptop for extended periods of time. So, part of the discussion you need to have with the clinician is the use of carts that will support the device as the doctor moves from room to room. Another solution is wall-mounted screens with a laptop dock, keyboard, and mouse. For now, we are recommending the use of ultralight devices with greater than six hours of battery life that run either Mac OS X or Windows 7. The power management within these devices has improved the length that the physician can stay disconnected from the power cord.

Clinicians are also adopting mobile tablets with 10-inch screens or smaller. Here, the clinician isn't using this platform for daily access to the EHR. They are using these platforms to connect remotely to a virtual desktop, terminal server, or their personal desktop. These devices are typically connected via WiFi or 3G. Typically, they do not have a remote screen-sharing tool, so they are more complex to support. To meet the support demands, we have found that by having at least one of the devices from each of the major OS vendors, we can stumble our way to a resolution. The Android has a different interface for each device; however, the major settings are located in the settings folder. The Apple-based product interfaces are similar, so having an iPad, iPod touch, or iPhone often will suffice.

Another option is to use computers located within the exam room. There are many considerations when deploying exam-room computers. First, the location of the device is critical in how the doctors interact with the customer. If the device is on a swing arm and placed between the physician and the exam bed, then the physician will have to look around the screen to interact with the patient. This should be avoided when possible, because this is where technology physically interferes with patient and doctor interactions. Next, the noise generated by fans and hard drives can also present problems. Thin clients are an option for exam rooms where noise is a problem. These devices are used just like a normal PC but have no fans, hard drives, and other components making noise. The size of the device is also important. The larger the device, the harder it is to mount and work around. Remember that exam rooms and other clinical areas must be cleaned, and typically a mop is used. This means water could get on the system and damage it. Finally, think ahead to servicing the unit. If you mount the device on the wall, make sure that the case can be opened without having to unmount it from the wall.

So, when working with clinicians, do the following:

- Take the time to understand how they will access the EHR.

- Make sure that portable devices are light enough to hold, or provide a cart to support the device.

- Do not skimp on wireless technologies. Having a robust wireless infrastructure is the backbone of the devices deployed. A wireless access point that costs less than $200 is not robust enough to be in production.

Implementing the Right Technology

Physicians have embraced technological advances in medicine throughout the years. They readily adopted the technology required to replace a heart valve, ultrasound for monitoring blood flow, and imaging technology that gives a slice-by-slice image of the human body. What they are adverse to adopting is technology that disrupts workflow or kills their patients. Practicing medicine is a scientific art. It is not meant to cause more harm than good. Unfortunately, many physicians, especially the older ones, have admitted the following to us: They do not like interacting with technology during the patient visit. They believe it distracts them from the care of their patient. What IT professionals need to be thinking in response is that technology distracts when the wrong technologies are deployed. To get the best fit between the provider and the technology, it is necessary to observe their existing processes and how they use paper in their current workflow. Without understanding that, you will never understand how they perceive they will be using a computer in the future.

Real World Scenario

Three Families in an Airport

Recently at a restaurant in the Orlando airport, I (Patrick) observed three different families.

The first family was consumed by technologically and seemingly disconnected from each other. Two kids and two adults were sitting at the table waiting for their meal to come. One child had a portable game system; the other had an MP3 player going. The father was pecking away frantically at his tablet device. (Given the length of time he was pecking, he was writing either a dissertation or an email message.) The mother was on her smartphone talking under her breath. The family was distracted by technology. They could no longer sit at the table and have a meaningful conversation. The table was just a place to refuel the body—not the family unit.

The second family was an older couple. Raised from his lap was the local newspaper. He was not able to see his female companion without dropping the newspaper a good eight inches. She sat there reading a novel. As I thought about this couple, I wondered if over the years they had talked too much, talked too little, or just simply had nothing say to each other.

The third family was poring over maps of the theme parks they had visited. Each of the three children engaged in the conversation about rides they enjoyed, which ones they would have gone on again, and which ones they should have skipped. Their parents were engaged in the conversation as well. I could see their worn faces, but I knew they had something special at that table. They had memories that would last a lifetime.

So, why do I bring up these three families? Well, it is how I see doctors and how they perceive the world. They are afraid that the technology used to meet the government mandates will put them behind a computer device doing data entry for proper Medicare billing rather than enhancing actual patient care. Physicians don't incur massive debt loads to become glorified data entry specialists.

On the other hand, too much paper can drive the same wedge between doctor and patient, just as it did between the elderly couple. Fishing for information in a paper or novel takes time; flipping page by page through records causes longer visits, and the abnormal test results can fail to percolate to the top. You have to read the whole story before you understand what is being shared. This complicates and lengthens the delivery of healthcare.

In my opinion, the last family had it figured out. They used paper to show which rides were the most fun. They shared their experiences with each other openly, and the mother documented this using her camera. As a family unit, this group knew what was important and what wasn't. The doctors want the same results as the last family. They want technology to be used to document the events but not to interrupt the sharing that occurs in the patient visit.

The next thing that doctors are looking for is an IT professional who does not disrupt the organization. What disrupts a clinical organization? Well, one of them is the way technicians are dressed. Don't be the technician who shows up in a T-shirt with a silhouette of a naked woman. If you are not dressed appropriately to be in a professional setting, it doesn't matter how bright or competent you are. You become a disruption.

Another disruption for physicians is an IT staff that is not available to handle urgent issues. Take note: as the IT professional, you do not get to decide what is urgent and what is not. Most likely, you did not attend years of medical school, so you cannot know the difference between an urgent and a nonurgent issue. When a physician calls, make sure that the issue is clearly defined so that a resolution can be found quickly. You must also understand that working times can make or break your relationship with the physician. The clinician gets paid by the number of visits and procedures done. Taking down the network during the middle of the day will not make you friends. Most offices open at 9 a.m. and work through 12:30 p.m. They return to the office at 2 p.m. and work until 6:30 p.m. With those typical time frames, your least disruptive work will happen before 9 a.m., between 12:30 p.m. and 2 p.m., and after 6:30 p.m. Take the time to talk with the physician to find out the best time to do the work. Physicians do not like surprises, especially ones that cause disruptions to patient flow.

Remote Access

Trying to find time to participate in the lives of their families, doctors are looking for ways to work outside of the office. In the past, the physician would load a pilot's briefcase full of medical records, throw them in the trunk, and head home to work on the files after the family had gone to bed. This practice caused a great deal of operational workflow issues within the practice. Consider the patient being seen by a physician one day. The physician runs out of time to dictate the visit, so the chart goes into their briefcase and out to the car. Something happens to the patient overnight, and they need to be seen the following morning. The patient is seen by another doctor who, of course, is unable to find the chart. Time is spent searching the first doctor's desk, but nothing is found. The office staff manages to locate the doctor, who is stuck in traffic and will not be in an office to fax over the chart for another 45 minutes. You might think this is abnormal, but practices with multiple offices, paper charts, and multiple physicians face this issue every day. The staff is overburdened with tracking paper charts, and having to track the information down to a physician's car is even more work. Remote access to charts and other records kept electronically resolves the issue.

Remote access to the scheduling system can also provide a great benefit. When physicians are unable to access their most up-to-date schedules, they can end up at the wrong location. In the San Francisco Bay Area, where we live, going to the wrong location can actually cause a two-hour delay in seeing patients, even though the offices are just a few miles apart.

For a certain class of physicians, remote access means a completely different thing. It is less about work-life balance and more about their workflow. Certain specialists (such as orthopedic, nephrology, gastrointestinal, and others) spend a good deal of their day in an outpatient surgery center or hospital; the other part of their day is spent in the office. They need to be able to view patient information about a procedure and see the patient record from a variety of locations. With remote access, they can view information about medication allergies, recent lab results, and other important details, assuming the data is in the system.

In addition to supporting work-life balance, a number of physicians are connecting from their smartphones or tablets the same way that they connect remotely from their PC or Mac. A properly constructed remote access setup allows the physician to connect to their EHR and other internal systems, no matter what digital device they are connecting from. An overly complex and restrictive remote setup actually causes more frustration for the physician.

Real World Scenario

Remote Access Blues

A large medical system we worked on had a remote access system that was so restrictive that many physicians and their IT staff did anything they could to avoid using it. The system was based on an SSL VPN platform and was configured to use self-signed certificates. Unfortunately, the certificates were email encrypted and couldn't be forwarded to an outside email address. At that time, the business didn't have remote access to email, so users had to use a USB flash drive, copy the certificate, and take it home. Once the certificate was installed, they had to log onto a separate certificate server to get the actual certificate used to be authenticated against the VPN. These overly complex installations steps prevented users from embracing remote technology. The method for granting access was so complicated that it drove employees to install tools like GoToMyPC to circumvent the VPN. Some even reverted to the old method of using a token-based IKE-VPN, which placed the computer they were connecting from on the corporate network. Every virus or piece of malware on the connecting computer now had a way to infiltrate the corporate network.

We suggested, and ultimately deployed, a phone-based authentication tool. The system, after authenticating a username and password, would call the user back and ask for an authentication PIN. Once the proper PIN was entered, they would be granted access to the VPN and their files. This method was used to deploy nearly 100 accounts in less than two days and allowed remote access by a variety of users who were involved in fighting a pandemic flu outbreak. The doctors, the IT team, and others found this methodology so useful that they are now using it to authenticate all of their remotely accessible applications.

Ultimately the physician, radiologist, and other clinicians want access to their data anytime, anywhere, and from anything. Deploying the right set of infrastructure systems, such as VMware, Citrix, terminal servers, file shares, and SSL VPNs, can enable this technology. One of the benefits of having a remote desktop or terminal server environment is that the user gains access to the necessary information without that information ever leaving the network. Only the bits related to the screen changes are sent, never the actual files. This definitely improves their risk and vulnerability posture as it relates to HIPAA, HITECH, and other government regulations.

Continuing Education

Although the chapter is about technology and workflow, we felt it would be unjust if we didn't write a little bit about continuing education credits. In California, physicians need to complete 50 hours of continuing education units every two years in order to maintain their medical license and stay current on new developments that affect them professionally. (The requirements vary from state to state.) In addition to the required professional development courses, many physicians find it desirable to stay up-to-date on the latest changes in healthcare laws and technology innovations. VARs are discovering that one way to help clinicians on the technology front is to reach out to them and invite them to a seminar or a "lunch-and-learn" session hosted by their company. This is a great way to showcase your ability to help them solve a business need or to introduce them to a new technology that can improve some aspect of one of their processes. Hosting an event is also a good way to leverage partner relationships for a joint marketing opportunity. Joint marketing events can add credibility to your company while offsetting costs associated with hosting the event. Many vendors that specialize in healthcare or have a healthcare vertical, such as Microsoft and Cisco, have set aside marketing funds to support these types of events. We recommend that you contact your vendors to learn more about their joint marketing programs.

Regional Extension Center

Recognizing the enormity of the effort to establish the use of EHR in medical practices and to accelerate the adoption of EHR, the authors of the HITECH Act authorized and funded the creation of a health information technology extension program. That program created a national *Health Information Technology Research Center (HITRC)* and *regional extension centers (RECs)*. The RECs are located across the country and play a critical role in advancing the use of EHR systems. The goal of the REC is to provide assistance to some 100,000 healthcare providers in their efforts to establish and meaningfully use EHR in their practices.

There are currently 62 regional centers serving a defined demographic area. In rural and sparsely populated areas, the closest REC might be in an adjoining state. The RECs offer a variety of services, including technical assistance, guidance, and information on best practices on the use of EHRs in a medical practice. These regional centers also host workshops and seminars on topics such as meaningful use, privacy and security, vendor selection, and workforce development. Although the regional centers are funded with government grants, some charge a nominal membership fee to help offset some of their expenses. The California Health Information Partnership & Services Organization charges an annual fee of $150 per physician or a maximum of $750 for practices with fewer than 10 physicians. Practices with more than 11 physicians pay $1,500 annually per site or a max of $3,000 annually per organization.

The regional centers are supported by *local extension centers (LECs)* that bring health IT experience to the local communities. The role of the LEC is to coordinate REC services in the local community with the help of service partners and vendor partners. Service partners are individuals, consulting firms, and companies that have been approved by the REC to contract with the LEC and clinical providers to assist with the EHR adoption process. Vendor partners are the companies that provide either the EHR software or the technology that connects to the EHR system. The RECs work on the behalf of their membership to negotiate favorable pricing and terms from the vendor partners.

TIP

To find out whether you or your company can qualify as a service partner in your local region, go to http://healthit.hhs.gov/portal/server.pt/community/hit_extension_program/1495/home/17174 **and enter your zip code. Once you find the nearest REC, go to their website to learn what the requirements are for becoming a service partner. This is also an excellent place to find out what is going on with health IT in your area.**

Terms to Know

Point-of-care (POC)	regional extension centers (RECs)
Health Information Technology Research Center (HITRC)	local extension centers (LECs)

Review Questions

1. What are the common reasons for administrative staff turnover in a medical practice?

   A. Working hours

   B. Monotony and low pay

   C. The uniforms they are forced to wear

   D. Administrative staff members feel they can do things better than the clinician

2. How do medical practices compensate for patients who take longer getting ready for an exam?

   A. Come in early and stay late

   B. Ask the slower patients to hurry up

   C. Review the patient list and adjust the schedule

   D. Medical practices rarely compensate for slower patients

3. Which of these is *not* a component of good communication between the clinician and their patients and staff?

   A. Clearly documented notes and orders

   B. Acute listening skills

   C. Detailed observations of nonverbal communication

   D. The ability to read minds and know what the other party wants

4. To compensate for their slower than average typing skills, clinicians have _____.

   A. Increased the number of patients they see in a day

   B. Decreased the number of patients they see in a day

   C. Asked the administrative staff to fill in on examinations

   D. Replaced the keyboard with a newer wireless model

5. Which of the following is *not* a clinician need that was identified in this chapter?

   A. Professional needs

   B. Business needs

   C. Vacation needs

   D. Technical needs

6. When helping a clinician choose a point-of-care compute platform, what factors should you consider?

   A. The availability of 24/7 support

   B. Next business day replacement

   C. The size of the screen

   D. All of the above

7. Remote access to the EHR for the clinician should _____.

   A. Never be attempted

   B. Be easy and secure

   C. Require approval from the HIPAA auditor

   D. Be ultrasecure and unusable

8. The primary goal for the RECs is to _____.

   A. Educate physicians and help them use EHR in their practice

   B. Educate the public about the importance of EHR

   C. Educate colleges and universities about the importance of EHR

   D. Educate software developers on the best practices for deploying EHR

9. Whose role is it to coordinate REC services locally?

   A. HITRC

   B. Service partners

   C. Vendor partners

   D. LEC

10. Which of the following is not a consideration when selecting a point-of-care device?

   A. Warranty

   B. Durability

   C. Color

   D. Usability

Chapter 12

Clinical Applications

Clinical applications are the heart of a physician's business. The needs for each specialty are unique. Allergists use radiology and spirometers to analyze a patient's condition, while cardiologists use EKG machines to help diagnose a patient. In the following pages, we will discuss the myriad of systems found in an ambulatory or hospital setting and how each system impacts network and server decisions—and your job as an IT professional.

Physicians now have access to more diagnostic equipment than in any other time in history. The availability of the equipment can sometimes muddy the water when searching for a diagnosis. To provide structure to the barrage of information, systems have been built to interpret the information and present it to the physician in a meaningful way. The sections that follow are not exhaustive, though we feel this chapter does justice to the most commonly used systems that rely on networks, servers, and workstations in a healthcare environment.

In This Chapter

- ◆ Maternal and infant care systems
- ◆ Radiology imaging systems
- ◆ Picture archiving and Communications system
- ◆ Encounter forms
- ◆ Prescription labels
- ◆ Patient eligibility
- ◆ Third-party databases for drugs
- ◆ Third-party databases for toxicology
- ◆ Laboratory systems
- ◆ Disease registries
- ◆ Emergency department systems
- ◆ Cardiology systems
- ◆ Clinical decision support systems
- ◆ Pharmacy system

Maternal and Infant Care Systems

We will start of this chapter discussing the *maternal and infant systems* that are used in the maternity wards of a hospital.

Maternal and fetal monitors capture blood pressure, the heart rate of the mother, and the heart rate of the fetus and can also monitor the temperature of the mother. In the case of a mother with twins, there are independent audio controls to monitor each fetus, which allows the heart rates to be heard simultaneously. Additional functionality can include the monitoring of fetal movement. The mother is given a remote clicker that allows her to indicate when she feels the baby move. In older hospitals, all of this information is collected on a continuous strip of paper. In more advanced hospitals, the labor monitoring systems and pediatric carts send information to a centralized reporting system. The systems are also integrated with the admit, discharge, and transfer tools so that the monitoring systems update the demographics of the patients automatically or with reduced data input by nursing staff. Audible and visual cues are available in the system to improve the response rate and provide the appropriate information at the right time.

Mobility in the labor and delivery units can be important as well. Some vendors have telemetry systems that can send heart rate and other vital information while the mother is walking around the labor unit. To do this, the systems utilize the FCC-allocated frequency band called *Wireless Medical Telemetry Service (WMTS)*. The wireless telemetry device communicates to the bedside monitoring station. As an IT professional, it is critical to understand that wireless interference can cause these expensive devices to become useless—or at least less functional. Additionally, if there are no spare units, it is critical to provide an immediate response to any requests for help from the labor unit. When Patrick's wife was having the couple's second child, they were actually put in a spillover room. The room was underequipped and used antiquated paper printouts that caused a spike in the nursing workload, and without the electronic updates, the nurses actually forgot about them.

Pediatric carts are used in the maternity wards to care for newborns, and in nearly all cases, those who are born prematurely are placed in incubators. To help the children grow without exposure to airborne illnesses or exposure to viruses, incubators have complex airflow systems, vitals monitoring, and heaters to regulate temperatures. In addition, the beds typically have network connectivity to send vitals to medical record systems, clinical support systems, and the nursing stations. In some cases, even moving the premature child from one cart to another causes sudden drops in temperature, so some vendors have self-contained units that can move from cart to cart with enough battery capacity to maintain the required temperature.

We run into two common incubator systems, the GE Care Plus Giraffe OmniBed and Drager's Isolette neonatal unit. The units from Drager use an RS-232 port to send the vitals, heat, humidity, and other information to a central workstation monitored by the nursing staff. The Giraffe OmniBed has an embedded X-ray cassette tray. Once the image is captured, it is sent to be scanned into the radiology system.

Radiology Information Systems

Radiology departments in hospitals and stand-alone radiology centers have to manage their workflow and the images created. A *radiology information system (RIS)* complements another system we will write about later called a *picture archiving and communications system (PACS)*. The PACS handles the images, while the RIS handles the workflow.

Radiology departments must prepare two bills for their services. They must code for the technical components of the services provided, and they must bill for professional services separately. The RIS splits the charges as necessary to allow for the best billing. With external billing systems, an RIS is required to send the study information outbound via *HL7*. Without the outbound HL7 interface, no billing would go out. When the RIS is configured in a stand-alone mode, the system will handle the billing components.

An RIS also schedules patients, as well as the entire treatment package. Some radiology modalities require taking medication or fluids within a specific time frame of the images being taken. If the time frames aren't kept, then the patient has to be rescheduled. Advanced functionality can include interfaces to a telephone system that calls patients to confirm appointments.

The dictation integration also is important in an RIS. Depending on the modality, once the study is underway, the radiologist can dictate what they are seeing. Images such as X-rays are simply dictated once the image is ready to be viewed. Either the system allows direct dictation or it allows for dictation that is then transcribed into the patient's chart. Once the radiologist signs off on the transcription, the radiology study is considered complete.

Since not all studies are generated at the location where the current imaging study is taking place, most RISs allow for image scanning. Scanned images can be imported as *Digital Imaging and Communications in Medicine (DICOM) standard* images and later transmitted to a PACS. Most RISs will allow off-site physicians to request appointments, view appointments, and view signed radiology reports. Be aware that it can be a bit of a challenge if the RIS employs Java or ActiveX controls that require administrator rights to install. Once able to reach the image, the doctor can then view it, show the patient if necessary, and attach notes for the radiologist to review if needed.

In most cases, the RIS is based on what the main clinical application is for the hospital or physician office. For example, if the hospital selected Epic for its EMR, ambulatory care, and acute care, the hospital would also deploy Epic's Radiant RIS product. Having the same RIS vendor as the vendor for the clinical applications is typically easier to support, reduces the number of interfaces

HL7
Health Level Seven International (HL7) is the global authority on standards for the interoperability of health information technology.

modality
A modality describes the type of imaging system being used. The modality could be an X-ray, CT scan, or other system.

between systems, and increases the amount of data such as demographics and prior exams that can be viewed in the RIS.

Some hospitals, though there are fewer selecting to do this, are choosing to use a different vendor from their clinical applications. When this is the route chosen, the RIS vendor is typically the same vendor as the PACS. PACS vendors inherently have an RIS to support their application. To prevent a loss of revenue, they continue to bundle their RIS with as many PACS sales as possible. As an IT professional, be cautioned that when the RIS is from a different vendor than the clinical applications, there will be a number of interfaces for patient demographics, diagnostic reports, study criteria, and other data that must be sent in and out of both systems. Increasing the number of interfaces increases the amount of work necessary to test upgrades, increases the complexity of troubleshooting, and nearly always reduces the amount of information available to the radiologist.

The top products in the RIS market are GE Centricity RIS, Synapse RIS from Fuji, and Impax RIS from Agfa. Just like the EHR market, there are many more vendors, but most have very small segments of the market. When looking for a vendor in this category, verify that the workflow will support the workflow of the radiology technicians and the radiologists. Most of these systems can integrate through HL7 or a proprietary tool to connect to the phone system. The radiology system will call the patients reminding them of their appointments. As an IT professional, if this functionality is not already in use, suggest it. In one case alone, we witnessed no-show rates drop by 72 percent. Reducing the number of no-shows enables better utilization of the millions of dollars in equipment investment. Ultimately, the facility will make more money as well.

Interfaces are not the only concern when working with RIS products. As an IT professional, make sure that the system is built for fault tolerance. When the system goes offline and the modalities do not have their workflow for the day, the department must do everything manually. This increases the workload of the department, increases errors because of the manual entry of data, and increases the workload on the PACS administrator to fix studies assigned to the wrong patient. Redundancy must include more than one data circuit to the modalities and to the clinical systems.

Picture Archiving and Communications System

DICOM
Digital Imaging and Communications in Medicine (DICOM) is the industry standard for distributing and viewing any kind of medical image regardless of the origin.

There is little use for an RIS unless there are radiology images of patients to view. That is where the PACS becomes part of the workflow. A radiologist sees the next patient for the exam when the images show up on the PACS workstation. Some PACSs are part of a full RIS suite of applications, while others rely on an HL7 feed from the scheduling and the admission, discharge, and transfer (ADT) system. When the next patient is present and situated, the radiologist works on doing the examination. Depending on the type of the exam, it could be a short burst of X-rays, or it could an MRI study, which normally takes 30 minutes. During the study, the PACS is constantly gathering images and correlating them to that particular patient. When the study is done, the entire group of images is available for the radiologist to review.

Radiologists are some of the highest paid staff in a hospital, and having them on call can be expensive. Many hospitals outsource their after-hours radiology imaging reading to third parties. Without a PACS to remotely view the image and connect that image to an individual patient, outsourcing the department to off-site staff would be very difficult. To make sure each captured image is attached to the right patient, during the study process the image is encoded with information regarding the demographics, medical record number, and location of the study. This information is attached to the image in a format known as DICOM. The DICOM format, as discussed in Chapter 4, "HIPAA Regulations," is a standard utilized by most medical devices to capture images for later use. However, not all modalities are DICOM-capable.

If the imaging system is old, it might not be able to send out the image in DICOM format. To allow the image to be sent in the right format, some systems have image scanners that convert the physical film into a DICOM image. Another method is to connect the modalities to DICOM converters, which will electronically capture the image, tag it with the appropriate information, and send it down to the PACS for archiving. In most cases, modalities still have the capability to print images.

Printing film is a last-resort response for when the PACS is down. In this case, the image is still captured by the modality and can be re-sent when the PACS is live. Patients also might request a printed film to take to their treating physician. When this happens, the entity doing the printing of the film should have the patient sign a release. The release form should include language that the patient is responsible for the safekeeping of the film and that the entity releasing the fill is not liable for any disclosure caused by the patient losing the film.

You should be aware that there are security concerns whenever film is printed. Be sure the system does the following:

- Prevents disclosure of the image
- Tracks who saw the image
- Destroys the image when it is no longer needed

More and more frequently, the imaging sites (hospitals, medical offices, or imaging centers) allow secure remote access to the PACS. The system is accessed via a web portal in nearly 100 percent of the sites we have worked with. After authenticating (we have yet to see an imaging center use two-factor authentication), the doctor is presented with a web page where they can search for their patient. These systems can be compromised if the IT department has not secured the web server and the network. When working on behalf of an imaging location to install a PACS, there are a few things an IT professional should take into consideration. First, verify that the web server is hardened based on vendor recommendations and the appropriate National Institute of Standards and Technology (NIST) document 800–44 at http://csrc.nist.gov/publications/nistpubs/800–44-ver2/SP800–44v2.pdf.

Second, spend time hardening the server to the NIST guidelines found at http://csrc.nist.gov/publications/nistpubs/800–123/SP800–123.pdf. This guide is a general checklist for the technology, staffing, and operational needs necessary to secure a server environment. Remember that most systems are breached from the inside, so be very careful who has administrative rights to the server. Also, as a standard practice, give each administrator their own logon account separate from each other and separate from their normal domain user account.

Third, if you are helping the customer select the PACS, take the time to understand how the external practices will access it. Check to see whether there are browser restrictions. With the proliferation of Macintosh computers, which no longer have Internet Explorer (IE) installed, a PACS that can only use IE to view images is typically not the best selection. Some PACS vendors, such as Agfa, employ a Java client to access the application. The challenge with Java is that some functions are release dependent. The end user might have to install multiple versions of Java, depending on the applications the user has. One click of a Java update button can break the PACS application. Many of the larger PACS vendors are upgrading their systems to support browser-independent access. Agfa just released its Xero PACS access server to address compatibility issues it was having with prior releases.

Next, be extra careful about the selection of hardware. We have found that buying hardware that exceeds the specs by 50 percent allows a longer life span for the servers used to process the imaging and demographic data. Also, when modalities are upgraded, the fidelity of the image and the image size typically increases. By planning ahead for the eventual additional or replacement modalities, you reduce the amount of server-side work required to install and turn up the modality. Swapping out a server because it needs, for example, just 20 percent more CPU to support the modality is a costly upgrade. The downtime necessary to swap out the unit in the data center and the additional testing are just not worth the added cost. Purchase the initial hardware with the long view in mind.

Lastly, bandwidth can be the single biggest bottleneck in a PACS. Some images are hundreds of megabytes in size. When data is sent from the modality to the PACS and there isn't enough bandwidth, the images are queued. This delays the reading and processing of the image by the radiologist. A gigabit network is a minimum requirement for this application. When the PACS is used across many WAN links, pay special attention to the site-to-site connections. Use a metropolitan link (MPLS, Metro Ethernet, or other high-speed connectivity) or other externally facing network link that allows bandwidth increases on demand without additional configuration on the on-premise devices. Having the flexibility to increase bandwidth at will reduces the amount of administrative time spent upgrading circuits as more PACS stations are deployed at remote locations or as additional modalities are installed.

Encounter Forms

Prior to electronic records, eligible professionals typically would document their treatment of a patient in two ways. Both are terribly inefficient. First, the physician would chart the upcoming visit. The chart would include information about services to be rendered. The physician must write the notes, the biller must pull the notes to validate the coding, and the insurance company may dispute the charges if they were not properly documented. At the end of a visit, the physician would then document the visit, either by handwriting information within the chart or by filling out a sheet called an *encounter form*. Depending on the type of practice management software used, the encounter form could be preprinted with the patient's information, or worst case, the nurse or front-office staff would have to write or type it. (You can see examples of encounter forms at www.ehrmentor.com.)

With encounter forms attached to the patient's chart, the physician would simply document each service provided to the patient by filling in the circle next to the service. Essentially, it was like taking a Scantron exam. This is more efficient than writing notes, but that, too, is fraught with errors. The encounter form is actually scanned in using a Scantron-like system. However, misread CPT codes result in inaccurate billing and typically reduced pay. The encounter form is still alive and well in physician and hospital settings, because it reduces the amount of time it takes to get paid.

Real World Scenario

Anybody Got a LaserJet III?

When printing forms from older practice management systems, be careful about the printer selection. Some of the old server operating systems do not support the latest printing protocols such as PCL 6. Therefore, if PCL 6 is the only printer language the "new" printer understands, the server will not be able to successfully send the print job. At one client, we actually had to find an old LaserJet III so that they could continue printing encounter forms.

Typically, printing has very little impact on the network or practice management server. However, when the printer is not working, the practice or hospital sees a hit to productivity. We have found that having a local printer resource comes in handy when we are not able to find a replacement printer. Not wanting to become printer repair experts, we used the expertise of a local business that has been fixing printers for decades. What takes this shop just 15 minutes to diagnose and repair would take us more time and expense than the printer is worth.

Prescription Labels

Recent patient safety legislation in California SB 292 requires that all medication dispensed bear a *prescription label* that includes a description of the pill or capsule. As patients grow older and have more medications to counteract or fight chronic illnesses, they need an easier way to identify their medication. In a number of cases, patients confused medications and were harmed by an incorrect dosage. The description now must include the following:

◆ Color

◆ Shape

◆ Scoring

◆ Markings

◆ Brand or generic name

◆ Strength

◆ National drug code (NDC)

◆ Delivery type (capsule, pill, liquid)

(Refer to state or local regulations to confirm whether the customers you work with are obligated to meet these or similar requirements.) Given the size of the market, most pharmacy systems now are capable of printing the information required by California SB 292 from within the application. However, before those capabilities were commonly available, one of our larger hospital installs had to code their own pharmacy label system to meet the deadline for implementation. Although ultimately phased out as the pharmacy system was upgraded to support the legislation, the three weeks of programming by the hospital staff supported the business needs for nearly 18 months as the pharmacy vendor made their changes.

Prescription medication labels require special printers and label stock. When working with a pharmacy system, only use devices that the vendor recommends. We have found that we have far fewer problems with getting the labels to print properly when we use the prescription system's preferred vendor. Yes, it does come at a premium, but it is worth the expense, given the instant drop in productivity by the pharmacy staff when they are unable to print.

Patient Eligibility

There are many reasons to look at eligibility systems in the healthcare ecosystem, but in a private-practice office, the two most commonly seen are drug formulary and remaining benefit amount checks. Medicare, Medicaid, and private payers have thousands of prescription formularies. Physicians who are treating patients with chronic illnesses either have the nurse pull up the eligibility information or handle the lookup themselves. In most cases we see, the doctor will look up the formulary so that the right generic or brand medication is dispensed. Sending a patient to a pharmacy to get a medication not on the formulary creates operational nightmares. When a patient is prescribed a particular medication and arrives at the pharmacy to find out their medication is not covered, a slurry of phones calls (and sometimes name-calling) occurs. First come the phone calls to the nurse at the provider's office. They can work with the physician to change the medication, or the nurse can state the medication is the only option for the patient. In some cases, the nurse sends a request for authorization to approve the nonformulary drug. Certain types of medication like a bee-sting kit (we know from personal experience) costs $150. After a formulary approval, the kit cost $20.

Other eligibility factors come into play with dentists. They constantly review benefits for their patients so that they can do as much work on the teeth as possible. Teeth are one area that patients are willing to skip in order to keep their medical expenditures low. With dental benefits typically pegged at $2,000 per year, checking to confirm benefits and the amount remaining on their eligibility is critical for the practice. Never does a doctor's office want to surprise a patient with an unexpected bill.

Patient eligibility systems come in multiple forms. There can be thousands of different prescription medication formularies. While monitoring a patient exam, we documented nearly 13 minutes of time spent just looking up the drugs the patient's insurance allowed. When we asked the physician why it took so long, he mentioned that there were simply too many formularies and that certain covered medications wouldn't work for the type of patient he was seeing. You should also be aware that formularies change without notice. A medication listed as covered when the prescription was written might no longer be eligible for coverage by the time the patient arrives at the pharmacy to fill the order. For chronically ill patients with limited insurance, medication costs can be a real burden, so physicians spend valuable time looking up coverage. For formulary lookups, most insurance companies have an online portal to access the information. The one for Medicare is at http://plancompare.medicare.gov/pfdn/FormularyFinder/DrugSearch.

Third-Party Databases for Drugs

To reduce medication errors, increase patient survivability, and reduce the cost of patient care after an adverse reaction to a medication, companies have created drug databases to provide real-time information for physicians, pharmacists, nurses, and even the electronic medical record system. These databases have information on the 100,000-plus medications on the market. In most cases, the database has an image attached to each drug so that the clinician or pharmacists can verify it has the right shape, markings, and coloring. Keep in mind that these databases contain information about the compounds used to make medications, over-the-counter drugs, and prescription medications—both brand and generic. With the number of changes happening to formularies, new medications on the market, and medications being pulled from the market, this creates a massive database.

When implementing an EHR, the vendor will either supply a drug database or ask the practice or hospital to license one. The license is a critical component because EHR systems do not have the appropriate information about drug-to-drug interactions. Some EHR systems also pull in the images from the drug database so that a doctor can identify medication a patient brought in.

The drug databases link to the internal clinical application, so, as the IT professional, it is important to find out which drug databases are supported by the clinical application vendor. The two that we use most often are Medispan and First Data Bank (FDB) www.firstdatabank.com. Medispan, www.medi-span.com, is increasing its market share. This drug interaction database is what pharmacists use to keep track of changes to medications, dosages, costs, and adverse reactions. Both accomplish the same tasks with their database, though we are sure their marketing folks will disagree.

Third-Party Databases for Toxicology

As an engineer, you will run into toxicology databases when working with public health departments, hospitals, and certain outpatient facilities. Toxicology has generated a large set of databases focusing on different aspects of the hazards and risks associated with toxic substances. Health and Human Services maintains a list of 20-plus different databases where you can find toxicology information. They point to the databases and the appropriate information. Toxicology databases can help uncover unique symptoms that occur when patients have been exposed to certain toxic materials. The databases include information on treatment plans for various exposures levels.

People can be exposed to toxins through many different paths. Radiology exposure is becoming a hot topic and cause for concern. Too much exposure, and it becomes toxic to the patient. Exposure to the toxin doesn't have to be something malicious. One benefit of using an EHR system when caring for patients receiving extensive radiology treatments is that their exposure to radiation can be better tracked across all care settings. As an IT professional implementing an EHR system, you can help save a life.

Aspirin and other medications in high dosages are also toxic. That's why a database is needed that has the documented research as to the exposure limits, best course of treatment, and other clinical information in support of the patient. The federal government has a database known as TOXNET (`http:// toxnet.nlm.nih.gov`). Nearly all forms of toxicology can be researched here, such as plant exposure, chemical exposure, and medication exposure. Most systems we have seen use TOXNET as the basis of their data.

Real World Scenario

Child Toxin

One night, Patrick was assisting a hospital during a labor dispute. This meant he was working in medical records, ER, and other places, as necessary. A father presented his young son who drank fluid out of a tiki lamp. As a father of two, Patrick was really concerned for the parents and their son. He went back into the ER after registering them and asked a nurse to see the child. The child was admitted immediately but was not treated as expected. You might wonder why, as did Patrick. Well, although the fluid in the tiki lamp was toxic, the toxicology database indicated that the treatment was typically to have the patient swallow charcoal to absorb the toxin and simply allow it to pass through the system. Luckily, the parents had not given the child ipecac syrup (an over-the-counter medication that induces vomiting)—vomiting could have caused additional burning of the esophagus. Ultimately, the attending physician let the child rest and pass the tiki fluid without incident. Without easy access to the toxicology database, the outcome could have been much different.

Laboratory Systems

Laboratory information systems (LISs) or *laboratory management systems (LMSs)*—not to be confused with learning management systems—are hardware and software systems that manage the entire workflow of a medical laboratory setting. Most lab systems have scheduling, data management, interfaces for the lab equipment, and workflow management capabilities. All of them must have auditing capabilities to ensure that samples are handled appropriately and for access to lab results for HIPAA compliance.

Ambulatory-care sites typically do not provide their own lab infrastructure. They send patients to a laboratory services provider in the area. Like hospitals, these providers have integrated systems that allow specimens and the results of the lab work to be tracked. Once the lab work is complete, the provider sends the results via fax or allows access to a web portal. In certain cases, labs will call the physician to notify them of an extreme case that needs to be addressed immediately. Physicians often can choose the way they would like to receive the information.

When the patient arrives to donate the sample or the specimen kit is sent home, labels on the container allow the sample to be tracked. The labels typically include a barcode that allows the lab technician to enter the patient demographic information once and then use the barcode to track the progress of the sample. Timely tracking is important because some samples have a short time before they become useless. Lab equipment integration allows many of the devices to report findings electronically. The information is immediately stored by the system. If there are variances in the samples, the discrepancies are caught quickly. If the patient is still available, the technician might return to collect more samples.

Once the information is collected from the lab equipment, it must be sent to the appropriate personnel. The patient might get the results, the referring physician will definitely get the results, and possibly public health organizations will be informed if the sample was associated with a public health hazard, such as an *E. coli* outbreak.

When an LIS is deployed at a lab-only facility, you will typically find scheduling modules, inventory management systems, and time tracking. This allows the business to know when to increase staff, what services to cut, and how to keep the operations running as smoothly as possible.

Once all the information is collected and sent to the appropriate recipients, the business has a decision to make. Some delete the data after the lawful requirement for keeping it is met. Others keep the data and parse it to find root causes for an outbreak, commonalities between patients and their ailments, or common factors in chronic illness.

To meet customer demands, many IT professionals are being asked to build large data warehouses for this information. A large dataset requires a lot of technical input. Is SQL, MySQL, Oracle, or another system the best database for the application? How many CPUs will the database need to complete the calculations in a timely fashion? Will the dataset require more RAM or more disk I/O? For databases that cannot keep a large amount of the data in RAM, it is more important to have higher disk I/O than memory. Without proper configuration, the data would simply be too difficult to extract and be less meaningful.

Disease Registries

Public health departments have a number of disease registries that are used to track diseases within the communities. A wide range of factors come into play when determining how diseases are managed. Disease management is so varied that there is now considered to be such a disparity in disease care that it is a federal target for funding. Programs to reduce health disparities are popping up around the United States.

Where do disease registries collect their information? It's mainly from registries that track diseases within individual communities. Disease registries are being deployed because clinicians are finding that the more information they have about the particular triggers for a disease, the better they can treat that disease. Having better outcomes means a healthier population, which reduces the costs of healthcare. The diabetes registry is probably the number-one registry that we run into. Another commonly accessed registry is a registry for asthma. Registries are becoming more common in the behavioral health specialties. These include registries for depression and other psychological illnesses.

Take the registry one step further, and there are disease management systems. These systems most often are found in healthcare companies. As a business, if you can help the patient manage their disease, you lower the cost of their care and thus have either increased profits or lower premiums. Patients who are less symptomatic with their disease are more mobile, and mobility is typically an indicator of health and quality of life.

Emergency Department Systems

Hospitals are adopting electronic triage systems to increase the survivability of their patients. In the past, these systems were paper-based and typically tagged on (physically attached to) the patient. In our training with the Community Emergency Response Team (CERT), we were even given briefings on how to quickly triage a situation. There were only three tests: breathing, pulse, and how alert the subject is. Triage systems in a emergency department (ED) are much more complex. Typically, the *ED triage system* accepts patients and triages them based on the type of symptoms presented. The symptoms are input into the system, and a possible cause is defined. However, if the patient presents themselves with a gunshot wound, there is little time to use the triage system.

Once the priority of the patient is determined, they either return to the waiting room or are transferred to a bed. Once on the bed, the information collected in the ED system is constantly updated, similar to an EMR. Once the patient is admitted, the information is sent to the inpatient system. The information is typically sent using HL7 transactions.

Most IT professionals will not be at the beginning of the deployments, since hospitals have typically been running ER applications for quite some time. We, as IT professionals, can add extreme value in the way the data regarding room status and triage information is displayed on the large screens in the nursing area. These status boards help the operation work efficiently. Computers on wheels (COWs) are used in most ER departments to interact with the ED system. To support COWs, wireless will need to be deployed to best utilize these devices. All of these devices and hardware support the required workflow for the ED.

Cardiology Systems

Systems within the cardiology area are data intensive and require integration across the entire spectrum of business and clinical applications. Prior to starting a case, the cardiology system pulls admission-related information from the ADT system at the hospital or outpatient facility. Once imported into the system, the demographic information is attached to the case that the cardiologist will be working. The demographics of the patient are confirmed. During the procedure, the cardio system sends images to the PACS. The images can be read by a cardiologist or radiologist depending on the procedure. Cardio waveform capture stations and electrophysiology capture equipment integrate with fluoroscopy and other images that are captured and referenced during the procedure. Images from the PACSs are typically imported so that they can be viewed at one location during the procedure. Finally, the images captured during the cardio lab workup are dictated by the physician and placed in the patient's record.

Each of the cardio-related systems plays a critical role in the care of patients. In many cases, however, these systems end up in the wrong hands when initially deployed. For example, one hospital system's EKG system was installed in the office of the manager of the cardiology department. As a result, the system was not maintained, backed up regularly, or identified for routine scheduled maintenance (out of sight, out of mind...). Without proper care, these systems cannot process the data necessary to give doctors the information needed to make informed decisions.

To best support cardio-related applications, it is often necessary to first hunt them down. Look for cardio, vascular, diagnostic imaging, and even medical records management systems that are deployed throughout the facilities. This is true for even the smallest medical offices, where a doctor might use a tool that is critical to the practice's success, but only the doctor using the tool is aware of its existence. We suggest using tools such as Nmap to query the network to find what servers are out there. Not every application will be identifiable via a network scan, though many will be. Once the systems are identified, work with each department to place the server in the most appropriate area. Typically, that involves migrating the server to the data center in a hospital setting or to the data closet in smaller practices. From there, work with the vendor to identify daily, weekly, monthly, quarterly, and yearly tasks that must be done to keep the system operating optimally. Document the tasks and assign them to the appropriate team. Then, periodically audit the tasks to ensure that they are being completed.

Clinical Decision Support Systems

Clinical decision support systems (CDSSs) are now required to meet HITECH meaningful use for Stage 1. However, these systems have played a role in healthcare for a number of decades. They pair a significant collection of clinical knowledge with the vast amounts of data being collected while providing health-care services. Information has been collected across the continuum of care from disease investigation, long-term care, and clinical diagnosis. These systems are constantly getting better as they provide better case-level advice to clinicians.

CDSSs can be classified into a few categories. Decision support is where the CDSS is used to provide a treatment plan, a diagnosis, and condition/symptom-specific guidance. Operational efficiencies focus on reducing redundant tests, reducing medication errors, possibly changing treatment plans, and reducing unnecessary lab work.

When a decision support system is developed to support the uncovering of complex patterns, the value of the data becomes actionable. Here, researchers work on developing better protocols. Health systems follow up with patients regarding preventative care. Protocols for care and treatment are developed to reduce health disparities. Without the business intelligence working against the large data sets, better outcomes would be harder to come by.

Lastly, CDSS logic can improve the administrative aspects of the medical facility. The systems can be configured to track and report procedures that are not profitable. One system we work with stopped doing hip replacements. They did only six to seven a year, and to keep the surgeon on the staff, they had to pay a competitive salary. Dropping that single procedure saved $1.7 million in yearly operational costs. Hard facts were extracted from the different business and clinical application databases to support changes in what the hospital delivered.

Crystal Reports and SQL Report Services are the two most common business intelligence applications we run into. Certain EHR systems, especially for the larger hospitals, might have their own database tool. For Epic, data is extracted using a multilayered system called Clarity, which pulls information for the Cache database and inputs the information into a SQL or Oracle database.

Pharmacy Systems

Pharmacy systems come in all shapes and sizes. Inpatient, outpatient, and out-sourced systems each solve a unique problem in a particular care setting. An inpatient system is developed and delivered based on the patients not moving much and standard medications dispensed by nurses on each floor. Outpatient systems handle much higher volumes where drug-to-drug interactions can be harder to catch, because not all medication prescribed to a patient is filled at the same pharmacy. An outpatient pharmacy service is also billed differently than inpatient. The medication is not associated with a stay; it is associated with a formulary and copay.

Inpatient pharmacy systems are used to deliver medication at the point of care. The dispensing systems are connected via a network to a pharmacy (Rx) management system. The medication cabinets, which can house hundreds of different medications, are typically running on a Microsoft Windows operating system. The order entry system sends data to the pharmacy information system (Rx IS), which, in turn, sends the order to the medication cabinet where the patient is located. The medication can then be chosen by logging into the cabinet. Then, the nurse will select the patient from a pick list and, if necessary, select the appropriate medication when more than one is present in the list. The nurse in most cases will pull all of the medication ordered for a particular patient for the dispensing time frame. Once the patient and medication are selected, there are LED lights that flash, directing the eyes of the nurse to the right drawer or cabinet shelf. The nurse pulls the prescribed amount and closes the drawer or closet door. A disposal box is provided on the side of the cabinets for use when medication is refused by a patient. Refused medication can be reused if it is sealed; it cannot be reused if it is unpackaged. When morphine and other narcotics are refused, they must be returned to a locked disposal cabinet.

Outpatient pharmacy systems are very different. Here, the medication is dispensed in higher volumes across a broader spectrum of clients. Often, outpatient pharmacies are integrated into an EMR system at the health center or physicians group serving the patient. The insurance is checked by the pharmacy or by the health center/physicians group for formulary coverage. If the medication is a brand name not covered under the formulary, the Rx system will notify the pharmacy tech. If the generic medication is on the formulary and meets the treatment needs as outlined by the physician, then the pharmacy tech distributes the generic medication.

A unique scenario is an outsourced medication service provided to a local municipality. After an order is placed in the computerized physician order entry (CPOE) system and the patient is located in any of the three facilities where the service is provided, the order for the medication is sent to a queuing system that submits the order for fulfillment. The order ends up at a medication-dispensing robot that acts as a medication package machine. A strip of plastic packets is filled with the daily medication required for the patient; medication packets are dispensed three times a day. To track patients who are outside the hospital, an ADT interface was created to track where the patient was. Sending medication to the wrong site reduces quality of care and increases operational costs. To reduce dispensing errors, each packet is labeled with the patient name, medical record number, medication name, dosage, form of the medication (liquid, gel, capsule, tablet), and time to dispense (morning, noon, evening, or bed time).

Each one of the systems is important in the proper care of patients. The better the integration, the more simplistic their use, and the better the care we will all receive as patients. As IT professionals, we must honor the fact that we are helping the doctors deliver better care.

Terms to Know

radiology imaging system (RIS)

encounter form

maternal and infant systems

drug, toxicology, disease, and laboratory databases

laboratory information system (LIS)

emergency department (ED) triage system

admission, discharge, transfer (ADT)

Digital Imaging and Communications in Medicine (DICOM) standard

disease registries

prescription label

patient eligibility

picture archiving and communications system (PACS)

laboratory management system (LMS)

clinical decision support system (CDSS)

Health Level Seven International (HL7)

Wireless Medical Telemetry Service (WMTS)

Review Questions

1. A pharmacy dispensing system uses what protocol to communicate orders?

   A. HL7

   B. x12N

   C. x12H

   D. 5010

2. True or false: An RIS captures images from the radiology modalities.

   A. True

   B. False

3. When running a search to look up the harmful effects of a cleaning detergent, what database would you be connected to?

   A. Disease management database

   B. Laboratory database

   C. Toxicology database

   D. Modality database

4. Radiologists store images in which system?

   A. RIMS

   B. PACS

   C. APCS

   D. .NET

5. Cardiologists use which type of system to attach their findings to patient images?

   A. Radiology imaging system

   B. Radiology archiving system

   C. Picture archiving and communication system

   D. HL7 interface systems

6. What California law requires medication bottles to have better descriptions?

   A. 299

   B. 1386

   C. 292

   D. 1368

7. Which is not a right of the patient who is receiving medication?

    A. Right route

    B. Right size

    C. Right person

    D. Right medication

8. Pharmacy systems use data code set for identifying medications?

    A. HL7

    B. X12N

    C. DICOM

    D. D.0

9. Encounter forms are used for what part of the clinical workflow?

    A. Patient discharge summary

    B. Nurse documentation

    C. Clinical notes

    D. Document services rendered

10. When working with a toxicology database, what is the government database that the data is pulled from?

    A. http://toxicology.hhs.gov

    B. http://toxnet.nlm.nih.gov

    C. http://toxnet.nih.gov

    D. http://toxicology.nlm.nih.gov

Chapter 13

Administrative Applications

Every medical practice has one or more administrative applications that are critical to the success of the business. These applications do not necessarily include clinical data; however, the line separating the clinical and administrative functions is becoming increasingly hard to discern. In this chapter, we will look at the applications that support the business/administrative functions of the medical practice, including the practice management, accounting, payroll, and other systems used on a daily basis in support of the business. Some of the business challenges faced by healthcare providers are similar to other businesses, while others are unique to the healthcare industry. Challenges such as accessing multiple systems and managing the associated accounts are not unique to healthcare. However, the added complexity of federal and state regulations puts an interesting twist on some challenges, such as the use of email in a medical practice. Finally, we will look at tools and technologies that impact workflow and enhance operational efficiency.

Practice Management System

The practice management system (PMS) is arguably the most important application in the medical practice because it is used to manage the day-to-day operations of the practice. As you learned in the workflow chapters, the PMS is used to capture patient demographics, schedule appointments, maintain lists of insurance payers, perform billing tasks, and generate reports.

Performance

Medical office staff spend the majority of their time interacting with this application, and the performance of this application has a great deal to do with how quickly the practice can move patients through their appointments. Performance is influenced by a number of factors including the number of users, the hardware configuration, the network topology, and the actual software design.

Software designers design, build, and test their applications on very powerful computers connected to very fast LANs. In many cases, the connectivity and network configuration at the medical practice are not fully considered when the developers are building the features and functionality of the application. The software designers tend to focus on graphical presentation and often add images that serve no useful purpose other than making the application more visually appealing. When medical office staff members need to access the application remotely, they get very frustrated when they have to sit and watch a background image being repainted on the application before they can access or update the data.

When deploying any technology in a medical practice, it is wise to consider how it will be used and where it will be accessed. If you are using remote desktop, for example, turning off some features (such as the desktop background and animation) and reducing the display colors will go a long way toward improving the performance over a remote connection. Medical staffers are willing to make the trade-off between visually appealing and faster-performing applications.

PMS and HIPAA Compliance

HIPAA has been around long enough that it is unlikely that you will find any PMS application that does not have features to support HIPAA compliance. HIPAA compliance is not something you do once and forget about. It is a continuous and evolving process that must be reviewed and maintained to ensure continued compliance by the provider. It requires software vendors to update their applications to support the future regulations.

On January 16, 2009, HHS published two final rules to adopt updated HIPAA standards. In one rule, HHS adopted X12N version 5010 and the National Council of Prescription Drugs Program (NCPDP) Version D.0 for HIPAA transactions. NCPDP creates and promotes data interchange standards for the pharmacy services sector of the healthcare industry. These standards must be in place by January 1, 2012, for large providers and by January 1, 2013, for smaller providers. PMS applications must be updated and tested prior to implementation. Under the second rule, HHS modified the standard medical data code sets for coding diagnoses and inpatient hospital procedures by concurrently adopting the International Classification of Diseases, 10th Revision (ICD-10) code sets. The ICD-10 code sets replace the existing ICD-9 codes and are designed to provide a greater level of detail to the coding and classification of procedures. The ICD-10 code set must be fully implemented by October 1, 2013, for all covered entities. Both of these impending changes will be considered major releases by their respective software vendors and will require testing prior to implementation.

HIPAA-Compliant Software

The term *HIPAA compliant* is thrown around so much that it is tempting to believe that software applications can actually be HIPAA compliant. The truth is that there is no such thing as HIPAA-compliant software or any software that will magically make the medical practice HIPAA compliant. It is the medical practice itself that must be HIPAA compliant, and they achieve that by implementing policies and procedures that support best practices for protecting patient data. The best practices can be achieved by looking for software that supports the following features and functionalities:

Audit   HIPAA guidelines require organizations to keep an audit log of who did what. It is important that software applications are able to track which person accessed which record, on what date, and whether the record was viewed, updated, or deleted.

Role-Based Security   HIPAA specifies that each user should see only the minimum amount of data necessary to perform their job. Role-based security provides a mechanism to grant access to the specific data and records that are necessary to perform an employee's job.

Messaging   Email is ubiquitous to business these days, but it is not a secure way to send patient data unless the message and the data are encrypted. A number of encryption technologies are available for email; however, a more secure method to handle the transfer of patient data is to exchange it within the application itself via a built-in messaging system.

Electronic Data Formats   From the outset, HIPAA designated a specific code set and transaction specifications to enable the standardized transmission of billing data. At this stage of the HIPAA regulations' adoption and evolution, it is unlikely that any software package designed for the healthcare vertical would not support these standards.

PMS and EHR

In the medical practice, the decision to migrate to an electronic health record (EHR) is fueled by financial incentives and advances in information technology. As medical practices move toward EHR, they have several choices to make, and one of them is whether to keep their existing PMS application and integrate it with the new EHR or whether to migrate the data into the new EHR and run everything from one application. The integration of the EHR and PMS software is considered one of the most challenging aspects of the medical practice management software implementation. Interoperability between the EHR and the PMS requires a standards-based application interface and data formats that enable the mapping of data and functions between the applications. The scope of interoperability can range from a total absence of interoperability to custom-built interfaces that support the import and export of transactions to fully automated data and workflow integration. The barriers to successful interoperability can include incompatible and proprietary interfaces that require significant programming (technical barrier), financial disincentives in the form of additional software costs (financial barrier), and the lack of vendor support for interoperability failures (service-level barriers).

Given the level of effort and the cost involved with a meaningful integration of the PMS and the EHR, some medical practices are opting for a single EHR application with integrated PMS features that support scheduling, billing, reporting, and, to an increasing level, core accounts receivable (A/R), accounts payable (A/P), and general ledger (GL) features found in stand-alone packages such as QuickBooks and Peachtree. Moving to the EHR from a PMS requires a data conversion process between the two applications. At its most basic level, electronic data conversion between two systems is a multistep process involving exporting the data from the old system, matching data types where possible (or converting data types where it is not), and importing data into the new system.

Real World Scenario

Four-Step Process

The following is an example of the steps necessary to transfer data from the PMS application to the EHR application.

Step 1: Data Export   The source vendor should be able to provide a mechanism to export data in a universal format (CSV or XML). The export process must be done on multiple tables from the source system, and the primary data to be exported includes patient demographic, insurance,

Continues

---

referring physicians, charges, and payments. Depending upon the level of effort involved in the export, it is not uncommon to focus solely on the patient demographic data and build smaller data sets such as insurance, payer, and referring physicians over time as you update the patient records during their visit.

Step 2: Schema Crosswalk   The schema crosswalk is an exercise where data elements from the source schema are matched to their equivalent type in the destination schema. More simply, the exercise shows people where to put the data from the PMS into the EHR. For example, a PMS may identify a parental relationship as a text field with valid data entries of mother or father, while the EHR system may refer to the same data as a numeric field with valid data entries of 1 or 2. Where fields do not match (for example, alphabetic source data and numeric destination data), the data needs to be converted to the proper format.

Step 3: Data Type Conversion   Sometimes vendors have different data types, and often one vendor will allow characters and numbers in a field where the other vendor will not. When this happens, the data needs to be converted from one type to another, and special programs must be written to perform the conversion. If you are managing this process for your client, make sure all conversion costs are identified up front so there are no surprises.

Step 4: Data Import   The final step in the migration process is the data import. As a rule of thumb, it is best to test the import in small batches to be sure that it is coming over as expected. Once the data is imported, it should be thoroughly tested before signing off on the acceptance of the converted data.

Once the decision has been made to transfer data from a PMS to an EHR system, the question of what data to transfer and how to transfer the data needs to be addressed. One of the first questions that needs to be answered is whether the data can be imaged or whether it should remain separate and searchable. The answer of course is—it depends. If the data is primarily going to be viewed only and there is no need to search the data, then an image file might be appropriate. However, if a search is required to use the data, then there may be justification for the additional time and expense of the data conversion. The typical scenario is a hybrid approach that converts a limited amount of data, such as patient demographics, and the rest is imported as images.

Accounting Applications

The medical accounting software market is somewhat fragmented with multiple vendors offering solutions suitable to the healthcare market. Traditional accounting applications, such as Peachtree or QuickBooks, are suitable for small practices that need to track business expenses, but they do not offer much in support of medical billing and managing the payment processes. Larger accounting applications, such as Microsoft Dynamics GP (formerly Great Plains), Sage Mas90, or JD Edwards, are suitable for the larger practices, and, to varying degrees, they offer integration support via HL7 standards or have support for EDI transactions. All of the accounting applications have a core functionality, such as G/L, A/P, and A/R.

With a few exceptions, the majority of patient billing functions are handled outside of the practice's accounting software solution. PMS and EHR systems offer partial accounting solutions, such as billing and claims management, to give the practice the ability to manage the entire patient encounter from one application. The growing trend is to provide more core accounting functionality in the PMS and EHR applications to eliminate the need for integration or manual processes to move the data between the medical and accounting applications.

The integrated accounting solutions offer advanced management features for the billing and collections processes, including ticklers or notifications to follow up on claims that were submitted and not paid, automatic generation of letters to payers challenging a claim rejection, or letters to patients requesting payment, and automatic report generation of key financial metrics.

Reporting is a key component of accounting applications, and the medical practices rely on reports to manage their business operations. Most medical practices run accounts receivable aging reports (30 day, 60 day, and 90+) and days sales outstanding (DSO) as a key metrics to determine how well they are managing the billing and payment processes.

Payroll Systems

Healthcare is a business that has to meet the needs of the patients on an around-the-clock basis, which often entails employees working rotating shifts that include nights and weekends. To compensate employees for their willingness to work varied shifts, medical practices come up with complex payroll schemes that include pay adjustments based upon shift, location, and department. To address the unique demands of healthcare organizations, payroll systems need to be able to deal with complex pay structures, including shift differentials, varying pay rates, employees working in multiple departments and positions, and overtime rate calculations. In addition to complex pay structures, the payroll system might provide workforce management and time and attendance.

Workforce Management

In larger clinical settings such as hospitals, administrators and management need to ensure that they have the right people in the right place at the right time to assure they have proper coverage. In some cases, the coverage is mandated by nurse-to-patient ratios; in others, it is based upon current or predicted demand. *Workforce management* solutions help the healthcare providers manage the balance between quality patient care and the cost-effective use of healthcare staff. These solutions offer visibility into where staff are deployed at any given time and interface with patient admission systems to provide demand-led scheduling based upon projected need.

Hospitals are moving toward on-demand coverage to control their labor costs. In an on-demand model, the hospital adds staff based upon expected patient load and required staff skills. For example, in a maternity ward, staffing demand can be unpredictable. If the patient level unexpectedly grows, additional resources can be brought in to meet the additional needs from an outside agency. Medical staffing companies manage a pool of skilled nurses that can be brought in with just a few hours' notice. Analytics in the workforce management solutions provides a real-time view into which areas are approaching trouble in critical areas such as cost, overtime, productivity, scheduling, and absences.

Time and Attendance Systems

In environments where there are multiple pay structures, shifts, and pay rates, keeping track of employee hours is a challenge. A *time and attendance system (TAS)* helps medical practices manage payroll automatically and easily. There are a few unique characteristics of staffing and scheduling in healthcare that will affect a TAS. In larger healthcare environments, the TAS solution might need to support floating shifts and shift bidding (for those hospitals that allow preference votes), compliance with nurse–patient ratios, compliance with labor rules (Family Medical Leave Act and Fair Labor Standards Act), and compliance with the resident 80-hour workweek. The TAS also might need to support paid-time-off tracking and overtime for staff.

There are a number of device options and methods for time collection, including badge readers, web-enabled applications, biometric devices, and bar code scanners. From an IT perspective, it doesn't really matter which of these technologies is deployed, because they are all effective. What does matter is that these collection devices accurately capture and record the time worked and are appropriate for the environment.

TAS systems have built-in reporting capabilities that help the practice manage employee-related expenses. The reports capture utilization and track hours worked, overtime and vacation, and paid time off, to name a few. Finally, with an interface to the payroll system, the TAS data can be transferred electronically to eliminate the need for manual payroll data entry.

Single Sign-On

Secure access to patient data across multiple systems is a big challenge in healthcare, and managing multiple login credentials is one of the biggest headaches for physicians. Physicians understand the need to protect patient data and will readily embrace authentication and identification solutions that are easy to use and don't impede care delivery. On the other hand, if the solutions are not easy to use, they will most certainly impact care delivery, and physicians will find any number of ways to circumvent the authentication and identification controls.

Workflow

Tactically, authentication and identification solutions are workflow issues. Workflows vary depending upon the medical specialty, the task at hand, and the patient's current condition. What may be an acceptable authentication solution in one environment might be totally unacceptable in another, so it is best to consider the entire workflow and perhaps multiple authentication technologies when looking at a solution. Although there are many authentication technologies on the market today, the effective solutions must address these key problems:

Speed   Security that introduces delays, such as logging off one application in order to access another, will not be accepted in the medical practice. Technology that streamlines access will be welcomed with open arms.

Security   Medical practices need authentication that cannot be circumvented or compromised.

Adaptability   The authentication technology must be suitable for the environment. For example, a fingerprint reader would not be suitable in a sterile environment that requires latex gloves.

Compliance   Authentication technologies must adhere to regulatory requirements to ensure the privacy and security of the applications and data.

Authentication Technologies

When it comes to authentication and identification, there a multitude of technology choices—and each one has its merits and shortcomings. In this section, we will examine a few technologies that either have or are finding their way into the medical practice:

Active Directory/LDAP   Microsoft introduced its Small Business Server (SBS) in 2002 as an integrated solution for small businesses that provided authentication, email, and collaboration services at an affordable price. Most medical practices have SBS or are running a Microsoft Server that provides authentication services via Active Directory. Active Directory-aware applications fetch a Kerberos-based ticket that is associated with the user's login credentials to grant access to the system without the need for additional authentication. Using Active Directory as the sole authentication method is risky because of the negative impact from stolen or misused credentials and the potential loss of availability of the server, which would prevent access to the application.

Biometric   Biometric authentication is the verification of a user's identity by means of a physiological trait such as a fingerprint or retinal scan or a behavioral characteristic such as a voice pattern. From a usability and security perspective, the fingerprint is an effective basis of authentication in many healthcare environments. It is unique to an individual, there is nothing to remember, and it is quite fast. The identification hash of the user's fingerprint is computed from the scan and is compared to the numerical hash of the fingerprint stored on file during the enrollment process. From an IT perspective, biometric fingerprint authentication does have some limitations that should be considered. The initial enrollment should involve the scanning of multiple fingers. This is because not all fingers will reliably image when the user subsequently attempts to authenticate. Injury, humidity, and other factors can also affect the reliability of subsequent scans. Fingerprint scans can have a false reject rate of up to 20 percent, and in a fast-paced healthcare environment, this could lead to frustration and rejection of the technology.

Proximity Cards   Active proximity technology uses a low-power radio signal from a battery-powered card that is worn by each user. Workstations are equipped with an antenna that detects the arrival and departure of each user's card. The system identifies the user who then simply enters a password to access the workstation. If multiple authorized users are in proximity to the same workstation, the list of detected users is presented, and the staff member picks his or her identifier and enters the associated password. If the workstation is currently in use, the signal is ignored until the active user logs out. The logout is one of the benefits of active proximity technology. The system monitors the immediate area around the workstation (the range is configurable) for the continued presence of the radio signal from the user's card. When the user leaves the area, the workstation can be locked, or the user can be logged off.

Like biometrics, there are also some limitations to proximity technology. The lower-power RF signal is very sensitive, and each individual user needs to be tuned with respect to where they wear the proximity badge. The distance between wearing the badge on a lanyard around the neck vs. wearing it on the belt could be enough to impact the reliability of the detection process. Also, the placement of the antenna is critical to the detection process. If the antenna is moved, the signal strength is impacted, and the effective range might change, which would cause an inconsistent experience for the user.

As with all authentication strategies, multiple factors increase the effectiveness of the solution. Something you have (a fingerprint) combined with something you know (a password) provides a stronger solution.

Email

Email is the most widely used Internet application in the world. In healthcare, email is a commonly used tool that supports a variety of business transactions during the course of daily operations. In this section, we will look at the HIPAA regulations that affect email in a regulated healthcare environment.

HIPAA Compliance

HIPAA is the defining authority on how healthcare providers handle patient-related information. Under HIPAA, the use of email to exchange PHI is not prohibited, and the sections of HIPAA that relate to email security are covered in the Privacy Rule and the Security Rule.

The specific standards affecting email systems can be found in the Technical Safeguards section of the HIPAA Security Rule. These standards are described in Table 13.1.

Table 13.1   Technical Safeguards for Email Systems

Safeguard	Description
Access controls	A covered entity must implement technical policies and procedures limiting access to systems containing electronic protected health information (ePHI) only to personnel with sufficient access rights.
Audit controls	A covered entity must implement software that record and examine activity in information systems that contain or use ePHI.
Integrity	A covered entity must implement policies and procedures to protect ePHI from improper alteration or destruction.
Person or entity authentication	A covered entity must implement procedures to verify that a person or entity seeking access to ePHI is the one claimed.
Transmission security	A covered entity must implement technical security measures to guard against unauthorized access to ePHI that is being transmitted over an electronic communications network.

Depending upon who you ask, there are multiple approaches to email security. Vendors that specialize in email security products will tell you that you need to scan inbound and outbound email for PHI, that you need to authenticate both the sender and the receiver, that you need to request read receipts to make sure that the message was delivered to the right person (audit), and that all email must be encrypted (transmission security) in order to achieve HIPAA compliance. On the other end of the spectrum are those who believe that they can get by with plain-text email provided that they have a business associate agreement in place that specifies they will appropriately safeguard the protected health information they receive or create on behalf of the covered entity.

So, which is it? Technically, both are correct; however, the answer lies in another question: how big do you want your liability to be? Sending a plaintext email over an unencrypted link, even with a business associate agreement in place, is the equivalent to sending a postcard through the U.S. postal service. If the email (postcard) is intercepted and read and there are damages, it could prove very costly for the practice.

There are third-party companies that provide email security services at a reasonable price. One such company is Proofpoint (www.proofpoint.com), which offers an in-house or hosted solution that is affordable and effective.

Real World Scenario

Email Encryption with Proofpoint

One of our clients asked us to help them improve their email security posture, because they were beginning to rely more heavily on email in their daily communications with patients and labs. After consultation, we came up with the following requirements:

Security   The solution must support at least 128-bit encryption.

Ease of Use   The solution must not require a steep learning curve or require the staff to perform extra steps in order to send an email.

Configurable   The solution must be able to adapt to changes in the data and be able to adjust to data that does not need to be protected.

Affordability   The cost must be reasonable.

After reviewing several solutions, we came up with a solution from Proofpoint.

Proofpoint is a best-of-breed email security provider that offers appliance- and cloud-based email security services. It is a flexible solution that allows a healthcare provider to encrypt based upon a rules set. The rules engine can be configured to scan for PHI in the form of demographic data, medical ID numbers, keywords, or procedure codes and apply encryption based upon the data included in the message.

Email is sent to Proofpoint via mail exchange (MX) DNS records using a cryptographic protocol such as Transport Layer Security (TLS). The email passes through the provider's preconfigured rules engine. If PHI is discovered, the message is quarantined, and another message is sent to the recipient with an embedded HTML link. The recipient then clicks the link and is directed to Proofpoint's secure website to retrieve the message. If they already have an account, they log in; if not, they can create an account in a couple of minutes. Once they have registered, email is automatically sent directly to them in the future.

Continues

Replies to emails sent through the Proofpoint solution are directed back through the rules engine courtesy of the MX record. Proofpoint also scans inbound messages for viruses, malware, and phishing attempts and blocks these messages from making it into the recipient's inbox.

Proofpoint is a very effective solution and, given the potential liability associated with exposing PHI, is a very reasonable and affordable solution for healthcare providers and covered entities. We implemented the Proofpoint solution for our client, and they have been very happy with the results. Beginning with patient IDs and demographic data, we configured the rules engine to encrypt only the messages containing PHI. Over time, we have had to adjust the rules because some messages were quarantined unnecessarily, but the end result continues to be very effective. Their email is now secure, and there were no adverse impacts on their productivity.

Reasonable and Appropriate Security

The Privacy Rule allows healthcare providers to communicate electronically, such as through email, provided they apply reasonable and appropriate safeguards in doing so. HIPAA requires that covered entities have in place appropriate administrative, technical, and physical safeguards for protected health information (PHI). As you learned in Chapter 4, "HIPAA Regulations," there is no one-size-fits-all, and the definition of the terms appropriate and reasonable are left up to the covered entity to determine what that means in their environment.

You also learned that, specifically, the medical practices must ensure that email messages containing PHI are secured even when sending over unencrypted links, verified (both sender and receiver are known), and authenticated and that they are stored securely in the mail server's file system.

Email Encryption

Email encryption does not have to be a burden or a huge expense for the provider. Large healthcare entities might have the resources to manage a Public Key Infrastructure (PKI) and all that it entails (registering, certifying, and validating keys, as well as the support infrastructure necessary to manage the keys); however, this type of infrastructure is well beyond the capabilities of most healthcare providers. The solution for smaller providers is to outsource the encryption to a third party. Email encryption via a third party is relatively painless and can be almost transparent to the staff. Outsourcing email encryption involves sending the messages using TLS encryption to a third party. The third party then scans the message for sensitive data and, based upon a set of preconfigured rules, applies encryption to protect the data contained in the message. Not all messages will require encryption, so when selecting a third party to perform this function, here are the features worth considering:

Customizable Rules   Scanning email and encrypting the contents is an adaptive technology that needs to have the ability to be reconfigured based upon the makeup of the data. For example, one provider might use a 10-digit account number to identify a patient. The first 9 digits are the actual patient number, and the 10th digit could be a checksum that when applied to the patient number validates it. Coincidently, telephone numbers also use 10 digits, and without the ability to provide some intelligence in the email scan, the phone number might be mistaken for a patient number, which could result in the email being quarantined.

Monitoring and Reporting   The effectiveness (or ineffectiveness) of the encryption technology needs to be reviewed periodically to ensure it is meeting the needs of the provider. If too many emails are being quarantined, then it might be necessary to educate the staff or adjust the rules if there are false positives.

Account Revocation   The third-party solution should allow the revocation of an account to prevent account holders from sending email if they are no longer authorized. Further, the third party should allow for the revocation by expiring a key for a particular message.

Retention Considerations

Email messages in a healthcare environment, especially those messages that are used to document and discuss patient treatments, become part of the patient's record and are bound by the retention requirements established in federal and state regulations. The preservation period for medical records varies. Medicare and Medicaid stipulate a retention period of at least five years, while HIPAA requires that PHI must be kept at least six years or two years after the patient's death. The federal False Claims Act allows claims to be brought up seven years after the incident. State laws vary, so it is important to know what laws apply in your particular state.

Email messages (as well as other documents) should be covered in the medical practice's records retention policy. Given that there are a multitude of state and federal regulations to abide by, there is no one-size-fits-all approach. When designing a policy with your clients, here are some general considerations and approaches:

- The records retention policy needs to clearly specify what is kept.
- It also needs to specify what is kept for 6 years, 7 years, or 10 years.
- The policy also needs to identify how you are keeping the records (scanned, paper, and so on) and how you destroy records that are no longer needed.

Other considerations include where you store these records, how they are organized, how they are designated for destruction, who can approve the destruction, and so forth.

These are just a few of the considerations for records retention. The takeaway from this is that email messages must be included in records retention policies and that there needs to be a policy in place that is reasonable for the medical practice.

Hosted vs. Local Solutions

As access to the Internet becomes faster and more reliable and as always-on connectivity becomes the norm, the growth of applications using a hosted delivery model continues to expand. Many small medical practices have embraced the software-as-a-service (SaaS) delivery models as a compelling alternative to traditional in-house solutions because they do not have the resources (time, space, or budget) to maintain the hardware and software required to run an EHR application on-site.

Benefits of Hosted Solutions

Using a hosted application has many benefits, including reduced costs, maintenance, and administration. With a hosted implementation, the application service providers (ASPs) are responsible for the hardware and software, while the medical practice is responsible only for the Internet connection. This is a big advantage for the smaller practices where they get access to hardware configurations (clustered, highly redundant) and software (feature rich and best of class) solutions that, in a traditional in-house installation, might be out of their reach in terms of affordability and manageability. Upgrades, security, backups, and access are all the responsibility of the ASP vendor. Licensing, in many cases, is based upon the number of users the practice needs, which makes it very easy to manage growth and predict future costs based on the number of employees who need access. Space is also at a premium in the smaller practices, and the ASP model reduces the need to have space dedicated to servers and backup equipment that is usually associated with an in-house deployment.

Concerns for Using an ASP

Reliable high-speed Internet access is widely available in most areas. However, in areas where the reliability and speed are insufficient, the ASP model might not be the best choice for a medical practice. Imagine losing connectivity to the EHR system when the doctor brings a patient into the exam room and needs to review the patient's history to determine the treatment options. ASP vendors have recognized the importance of Internet connectivity and are beginning to introduce the synchronization of patient data to a local computer to remove the Internet connection as a single point of failure for the system. With synchronization, the practice schedule and the scheduled patient records are downloaded to a local computer at the beginning of the day. If Internet connectivity is interrupted, the patients can still be seen, and the schedule will not be delayed.

Security is another area of concern for hosted delivery solutions, and given the penalties associated with the disclosure of PHI, it is a justifiable concern. ASPs routinely use encryption to ensure the patient data is protected between the practice and the hosted application. A good hosting provider will have the tools and processes in place to ensure that their customer's data is not available or released to anyone who is not legally entitled to see it.

Finally, the last area of concern in a hosted environment is control. The medical practice must give up a certain amount of control over the application in a hosted environment. Customizations to the software that change the underlying schema are not allowed. Instead, most ASPs will allow for configuration changes, such a renaming a field or adding a flexible field, as long as it does not change the underlying schema.

Certifications

When deciding to implement a hosted solution, one of the quickest and most effective ways to ensure that the ASP has the proper processes and procedures in place to ensure that the application and the underlying data are secure is to look for independent third-party certifications. One such certification is the Statement on Auditing Standards (SAS) N0.70 Type II report. The *SAS70 Type II* report is an independent auditors report attesting that the ASP's controls surrounding physical security, computer management, environmental security, backup and recovery, change management, human resources, and disaster recovery are sufficient and sound. An SAS70 Type II report is very good indication that the ASP has its act together and can support the application delivery in a consistent manner.

Servers

Server placement in an ambulatory medical practice is always interesting. Medical practices make the best use of their limited space, and when it comes to finding a place for the server and networking equipment, any open space will do. It is not uncommon to find servers under desks, in closets, or on a shelf.

When servers are placed in an open area, there is increased risk that patient data will be affected. At medical practices where physical access to the server is available, the biggest risk to patient data comes from someone accidently unplugging or shutting down the server. That is not to say that risks of someone accessing the hard drive or logging on to the console are not there, but in our highly connected world, the chance of a malicious person taking advantage of a server that is physically accessible appears to be less than someone taking advantage of a server that is vulnerable to remote security threats.

Unauthorized server access is mitigated by the use of firewalls, data shares, access lists, security rights, and secure passwords, to name a few methods. In a healthcare environment, the biggest threat to patient data comes from viruses, Trojans, and other malware unwittingly downloaded by a staff member. Social engineering techniques and web-based threats have evolved to the point where even the most diligent user can be fooled, especially if the message containing the threat is delivered from a trusted source via email, Facebook, YouTube, or what appears to be a known site that the user frequently visits.

Productivity Applications

A number of additional applications are used in the medical practice that can be described as productivity applications that legitimately support the office tasks needed to provide quality patient care. Each medical practice has its own set of applications and tools such as Microsoft Office, web browsers, patient education applications, and training applications that they will tell you they cannot live without. Medical practices with loosely defined policies also have a class of applications that we refer to as unproductive applications. Examples of these applications include Facebook, YouTube, personal email, and MySpace, to name a few. Threats from these applications should not be underestimated. In addition to degrading employee performance, these applications pose a security threat to the practice and to the PHI contained within the legitimate applications. Even with strong policies, it is difficult to police employee behavior, especially in remote office environments where staff members work without the benefit of direct supervision. One way to mitigate this risk is to manage what they can do with the Internet connection with a product such as *OpenDNS*.

OpenDNS

OpenDNS is an Internet-based service that provides an alternative to using the ISP DNS servers and provides additional web security and content filtering for home, school, and businesses. Like standard Domain Name System (DNS), OpenDNS helps translate IP addresses into more a user-friendly name context. The service is configurable and allows filtering based upon content, domain blocking, phishing filters, and typo correction. There are 57 categories of content available for filtering, including adult, social networking, video streaming, and P2P file sharing.

Continues

The OpenDNS membership community helps categorize websites with an effort called Domain Tagging, in which members review a website and submit tags based upon the preconfigured categories. OpenDNS also offers preconfigured levels of filtering (low, medium, high) and will allow you to set up custom filtering based upon the needs of your organization. The advantage to OpenDNS is that it not only provides content filtering but also can block phishing, botnet, and malware from getting onto your network. Additionally, OpenDNS offers the ability to block adware (which can sometimes come with spyware) via web content filtering.

The basic version of OpenDNS is free. The deluxe version offers additional whitelist/blacklist options for a nominal annual fee of $9.95. Finally, the Enterprise version offers enhanced malware protection and delegated administration for remote sites. Setting up OpenDNS is very straightforward and takes but a matter of minutes from the time you register. All that is required is a valid email address and a public network address.

Payer Portals

Verifying patient eligibility, tracking claims issues, processing paperwork for prior authorization, and managing hundreds of payer remittance and patient bills consume a large amount of the staff's time every month and represent a significant cost to the medical practice. It has been reported that billing- and insurance-related functions consume as much 14 percent of the practice's revenue, or more than $85,000 per full-time equivalent physician. On the other side of the equation, payers have reduced their costs by taking advantage of technology and moving the traditional phone-, paper-, and fax-based functions online in the form of a website or *payer portal*.

Payer-supported websites are some of the most frequently used applications in the medical practice. They provide access to a wide variety of functions that are critical to the practice's daily operations. These sites are used to track patient eligibility and benefits verifications; claims management; payment management; and referrals, notifications, and preauthorizations. However, there are more than 380 insurance companies in the United States, and although an individual medical practice might use a fraction of these payers, the number of websites (and associated log-on credentials) becomes difficult for the office staff to manage. Payers also figured out that providing individual websites didn't make sense, so many have joined the growing trend and become part of a multipayer portal.

Multipayer portals give access to multiple payer information and processes from a single sign-on through a web browser. These sites reduce costs both for the payer (by not having to maintain their own site) and for the provider (by streamlining access and enabling insurance and billing transactions across several payers from a single interface). Although there are cost savings for the medical practice, there are also challenges to accessing these sites from their computers. Computers are very unforgiving when it comes to the underlying technology needed to access payer websites and multipayer portals. In some cases, these sites will support only a limited number of browsers. All sites support Internet Explorer, and fewer sites offer support for other browsers such as Firefox, Safari, and Google's Chrome. Browser settings are also common sources of difficulty. JavaScript, ActiveX, .NET, cookies, and browser add-ons all have the ability to impact the end user experience, and in some cases, the settings might be incompatible between sites. Another area of incompatibility could come from the version of Java installed on the computer. We have seen instances where a newer version of Java is required for a website and the upgrade broke another unrelated application.

For some of our clients, Internet access is synonymous with access to these websites. We have received phone calls from clients stating the Internet is down because they could not get to a particular site. In troubleshooting these errors, we might discover that the Internet is indeed working; another issue, such as DNS resolution, is impacting the connectivity.

Lastly, the printing experience varies between these websites. Some sites offer very robust printing options, while others are lacking. Websites that have it figured out allow the staff to print the specific data they need, while the sites that don't might present you with a four-page document when all the data you needed was on a single page.

Phone Systems

Internet Protocol-Private Branch Exchange (IP-PBX) has been around for quite some time and has become so integrated in workflows that it is almost impossible to remember what it was like before it came along. Take customer service applications, for example. When you call your cable provider, you press a couple of numbers on a touchtone phone and are automatically routed to the next available support person who can handle your particular issue. When you get to a live person, they have your account information displayed on their computer screen courtesy of a database lookup using your phone number as the search key. The cable company has access to all the information associated with your account, including your service plan, financial status, and current status of your service, including known issues from their support system that could impact your service. Wouldn't it be great if calls to your healthcare provider were equally efficient?

Phone systems are increasingly becoming integrated into the workflow of the medical practices through integration with the EHR and PMS applications. Currently, many of the integrated applications and use cases are primarily deployed in larger environments such as hospitals and are centered on messaging to smartphones and other devices. There are ways the IP-PBX could be used in smaller practices, but thus far the IP-PBXs and EHR/PMS applications have really not integrated their technologies to leverage their respective capabilities.

As the adoption rate of EHR grows, here are some of the automated features that will extend the capabilities of the office staff through their IP-PBX. Note that the data exposed by the EHR continues to be based on a staff member's defined role in the EHR system.

Patient Screen Pops   This technology is heavily used in call centers and is just now making its way into healthcare. When a call comes in, the attendant's station recognizes the caller ID and automatically brings up the patient demographic data that shows appointments and encounter summaries.

Appointment Reminders   Missed appointments can cost the medical practice money, especially when the practice uses contract help based on the expected workload. Some healthcare providers use automated appointment reminders to let patients know they have an upcoming appointment and to give them the opportunity to cancel or change the appointment using a telephone keypad.

On-Call Forwarding   Call forwarding in an IP-PBX is standard technology, and phones can be configured to route calls based upon time of day or job function. In healthcare, this is used to route calls to the on-call physician and when the physician is out of the office. An interesting twist on this technology would enable pertinent patient data to accompany the call when the physician is out of the office. This would be very useful for an on-call situation and would necessitate the use of smartphone technology. As of this writing, we are not aware of any IP-PBX/EHR combination that has this technology, but we're sure it will not be long before it is available.

Prescription Refills   Some healthcare providers have an automated refill system that allows patients to request prescription refills over the phone. On the backend, the system checks their medical record and prompts the patient to select the appropriate prescription.

Faxing   Many medical practices still use faxing as a means to exchange patient data, and IP-PBXs have very robust faxing capabilities. EHR integration to enable the faxing of patient records is probably one of the simpler technology implementations.

Financial Counseling   When calling to schedule an appointment, patients with outstanding balances can be automatically rerouted to the credit and collections group based upon their caller ID in order to give them an opportunity to take care of their bill prior to scheduling additional appointments.

The applications discussed in this chapter are used by medical staff to perform their daily tasks, and they are important to the successful operation of the business. There might be other applications that you will run across when you engage a medical practice; however, the challenges and issues will likely be similar.

Terms to Know

time and attendance system (TAS)	workforce management
SAS70 Type II	OpenDNS
payer portal	

Review Questions

1. Why is it important to understand how applications are used in a health-care environment?

   A. So that you know how much to bill the client

   B. To ensure the technology used to support the application is appropriate

   C. To know who to call for help when it breaks

   D. To ensure that you as the vendor can provide the best possible patient care

2. When is it necessary to test applications in a healthcare environment?

   A. When a major version release is provided by the application vendor

   B. When integrating the data of two or more applications

   C. When making changes to the data base schema

   D. All of the above

3. HIPAA-compliant software _____.

   A. Does not exist

   B. Ensures the healthcare provider is compliant with federal regulations

   C. Is required for all healthcare providers

   D. Provides peace of mind for the physicians and practice managers

4. Which of the following is a key metric for measuring the billing processes?

   A. Employee time and expense

   B. Patient throughput

   C. Days sales outstanding

   D. Accounts payables aging

5. Workforce management is _____.

   A. used as a disciplinary tool when necessary

   B. the practice of making sure you have the right people in the right place at the right time

   C. necessary only for large healthcare organizations

   D. having a buddy clock in for you when you are running late

6. Single sign-on refers to _____.

   A. accessing multiple data sources across multiple systems using multiple user IDs

   B. accessing multiple data sources on a single system using multiple IDs

   C. accessing multiple data sources across multiple systems using a single ID

   D. accessing multiple data sources across multiple systems by an unmarried person

7. Which of the following technologies are not used in authentication technologies?

   A. Active Directory

   B. LDAP

   C. Biometrics

   D. HL7

8. HIPPA regulations specify that patient medical records have a retention period of _____.

   A. Six years or two years after the patient's death

   B. Seven years

   C. Five years

   D. Forever

9. Which of the following is an advantage to using a hosted solution?

   A. Reduces the need to have space dedicated to servers and backup equipment

   B. Gives access to hardware and software that might not be affordable otherwise

   C. Upgrades, security, backups, and access are all the responsibility of the ASP vendor

   D. All of the above

10. What type of certification should you look for from an ASP?

    A. HIPAA compliant

    B. SAS 70 type II

    C. MS-ASP

    D. CPHIMS

11. Which of the following is the best place to put a server?

    A. Under a desk in a locked room

    B. In a rack in the handicapped bathroom

    C. In a rack in a locked room dedicated to IT equipment

    D. Servers? We don't need no stinking servers!

12. Multipayer portals serve what function?

    A. Speed up collections of DSO of less than 90 days

    B. Increase physician angst by requiring multiple log-on credentials

    C. Provide access to multiple payer information and processes from a single sign-on

    D. Reduce costs associated with the delivery of PMS and EHR applications

Chapter 14

Tying It All Together with Technology

Determining the size of a medical practice will drive a number of decisions later when deploying the EHR. Take the time to uncover the challenges the practice is facing. Spend time knowing where the hardware for the server and network are going. Remember that without a proper project plan, deploying the EHR will be fraught with more challenges than necessary. Technologies such as Terminal Services and single sign-on can be used to improve the use and security of the EHR. And with all these moving parts, sometimes you will get caught up in the work and forget to take care of yourself, so we'll cover what has worked for us. This chapter culminates with an operational checklist for deploying an EHR. Use it as a base and build onto it as necessary for each deployment.

Sizing a Practice

When heading into a project in the business, it is important to understand what size of medical practice you will be working with. We have used three case studies to show the different challenges faced by small, medium, and large practices. Even with that knowledge, when you walk into a practice, you will need decision-making tools to determine how to best help that practice.

When sizing a practice, it is important to look at a number of factors, including the number of physicians, staffing levels, internal lab work, internal imaging services, number of sites, and billing needs (see Table 14.1).

Table 14.1   Factors in Sizing a Practice

Measurement	Reason
Number of eligible professionals (EPs)	Knowing the number of physicians helps in pricing your solutions and understanding the complexity of the installation.
	The more physicians there are, the more likely there will be a committee decision on the purchase of any technology or services.
	The greater the number of EPs, the greater number of egos.
Number of staff	Physicians typically have at least three staff members each.
Number of clinical staff	Training costs increase with the number of clinical staff.
	Familiarity with computers is often an issue with clinical staff.
Number of back office staff	The number of back-office staff also factors into the training costs and is an indication of the size of the billing and claims functions.
Number of patients seen in the past three years	Typically, doctors do not want to transfer the paper charts for patients who have not been seen in the past three years into the EHR. Assessing the current patient count will help you determine the scope of the data that will be migrated. Verify that three years is the appropriate marker for a particular practice.

Table 14.1   Factors in Sizing a Practice *(continued)*

Measurement	Reason
Number of locations	The number of locations impacts the following: VPN connectivity Staff movement Chart access, update, and security issues Doctor scheduling Patient notification of office closures
Specialty	The specialty often defines interconnects between clinical equipment and the EMR, can narrow the EHR selection, and can define the type of meaningful use that applies to the practice.
Current practice management software (PM)	If the PM is written in a proprietary format, language, or system, there might not be a way to integrate data from the old system into the new PM or EHR. The best way to gauge the complexity is to see whether the EHR vendor has done the data extraction before or see whether the data is stored in a relational database. If you are only deploying an EHR, remember that it is critical to get data from EHR to PM. You will need to verify compatibility. Please note that practice management systems are not certified under HITECH. Only EHR systems are certified. Most practice management packages comply with HIPAA data interchange formats.

To correctly size the practice, you will also need to inventory the existing hardware, as described in Table 14.2. Without knowledge of the existing hardware in terms of age, type, function, location, bandwidth, capacity, and the like, it will be impossible to accurately determine the needs for the new system or adequately secure it.

Table 14.2   Existing Hardware Inventory

Hardware	Information
Current servers	Age Type Location if there is more than one site

Table 14.2   Existing Hardware Inventory *(continued)*

Hardware	Information
Current wireless	Age Type Location (closet, exam room, server room, and so on)
Current workstations	Age Type Function (radiology station, retinal scanner, standard PC, and so on) Location if there is more than one site
I/O devices	Age Type Function Location (nurses' station, Dr. Jones office, and so on)

The sections that follow provide more detail.

Network

The network is at the heart of the operation. It is to the EHR system like nerves are to the human body. Therefore, if there are any kinks in the network system, there can be delays in the system's operation. Imagine your brain sending a signal to move your index finger, but your toe moves. You might want to see a chiropractor or neurologist to figure out why there are issues with your body's signaling system. When it comes to networks, you become the doctor, and it becomes your job to find (and iron out) the kinks.

Hubs and Switches

When you go into a practice or hospital, it is important to understand what networking equipment is in place. When the network utilizes hubs, remember that every packet sent is broadcast to all ports on the system. So if a doctor is reading an image file, that file is actually seen by all systems attached to the hub. This allows systems attached to the network to view all the data packets—and thus the image—even though they might not have the rights to do so. A switch network is more secure and faster. When you find switches within the practice, it shows that they have made relatively recent technology purchases. (As recently as 2009, we found and replaced a ThickNet network running Windows 3.11.) Switches move packets from a single port to another port on the switch. This prevents unsavory people from sniffing the network traffic. Switches also provide more throughput, increasing the capabilities of the local network to move information.

For healthcare installations, make sure the switches you use have capabilities that improve troubleshooting and management. First, the switch should be managed. A managed interface allows a network engineer to log in remotely to troubleshoot a networking issue. Without the remote management function, your business will require additional resources to support the medical practice. Being able to log in without showing up allows you to increase profits. The switch also must support Simple Network Management Protocol (SNMP) and NetFlow. SNMP enables the network monitoring/management system to periodically poll the device to confirm functionality. More advanced SNMP implementations allow the monitoring system to see port utilization, to view system load, and even to download configurations. NetFlow is a protocol originally developed by Cisco to send the actual data packets from the network interface card (NIC) to a NetFlow data collector. The NetFlow collector arms an engineer with additional information to track down the source of a problem when a fault or slowdown occurs. A new Cisco collector protocol, Internet Protocol Flow Information eXport (IPFIX), is on the horizon. Although it is not yet broadly supported, it is worth investigating.

Bandwidth Capacity

Baselining the current network will reduce or remove completely all of the guesswork regarding current network capacity. Without knowing the current capacity, you might get to the end of an installation just to find out that there is not enough capacity. Finding that the network is too slow is indicative of poor planning. Finding the load on the internal network might be a challenge if the switches cannot be managed. When the switches are managed, NetFlow data can be pulled off and provide you with insight into what is really happening on the circuit. If you are lucky, SNMP will give you the data.

When you are looking at the capacity of the internal Internet connection, you can use online tools such as www.dsltools.com to see the current capacity on the line. However, the tool represents only a snapshot in time, not the average bandwidth consumption over a time period. We have found that having a network monitoring tool that we are familiar with in our toolkit is the best method. If you cannot afford a monitoring tool, contact the provider to understand what the network capacity of the circuit really is. Remember, if you are testing the capacity on any network (cable, wireless, DSL, and the like), make sure you have collected enough data points to accurately measure the capacity, especially at the expected high-use periods for the practice. When a hosted application is deployed, the connection to the Internet is critical. Verify that the vendor for the network connection has deployed a business-class managed circuit. Just like proactively managing the customer's network, you should demand the same level of monitoring from the vendor.

When upgrading to a business-class circuit, make sure the cutover occurs after patient hours. In instances where the circuit is being installed but it is not a hot cutover situation, test the circuit for at least 72 hours to make sure the circuit was provisioned properly. When upgrading an existing circuit, choose the least disruptive time with the greatest downtime window. We have experienced long outages caused by bandwidth being increased on an optical circuit and incorrectly bringing the network down for more than a day.

Access Points and Cabling

Now that you have an idea about the tools to use and the importance of data connectivity from a capacity standpoint, it is as critical to understand where the network will be accessed from inside the practice. Walk the office and practice floor with the practice's manager to find out where the network connections will go. Also, if feasible, run two network drops to each location. This can save the practice money in the long run. (We have had connections eaten by rats before.)

When selecting the type of network cable, make sure to select the type capable of handling the network load. At a minimum, install Cat5e—or better yet, Cat6. Although copper has gotten extremely expensive, do not skimp on the cable type. When a network must be upgraded to support gigabit connections and the cabling is unable to support it, the practice will be out a huge amount of money, and your reputation will suffer.

Lastly, prepare a wireless layout. There are tools to identify the best locations for access points (APs). Consult your preferred AP provider to see whether they have a tool. If they do not, then purchase an extra AP, and place it in multiple areas to identify the best location for it. Generate a heat map by walking the facility for every location the wireless access point has been placed. Identify other wireless networks and which channel they are transmitting on. In high-density medical buildings, wireless frequencies bleed from office to office. This creates a lot of frequency utilization. Selecting the wrong frequency bands will make the wireless experience for the medical practice painful. Spend the time up front to generate the radio frequency (RF) study to reduce the frustrations after launch. If necessary, talk to the other practices in the facility and have them change to other frequencies. In most cases, they will be happy because the channel overlap will not occur and their wireless experience will improve.

Security

Wireless networks increase the exposure of the business. They should be hardened as best as possible. Read the NIST guide we mentioned earlier for more information on how to do that. Although it is not specific to any brand, the guide will give you information about what to look for in the model of AP you use. Wireless Protected Access (WPA) version 2 with *802.1x* authentication is about the best any practice is likely to deploy. Remember that it should be just as hard to break into the wireless network as it is to break into the building and gain physical access. Security comes at a cost. Any network without 802.1x authentication using AES encryption based on certificates can be breached. However, deploying an 802.1x system is costly. However, so is a $1.5 million fine. Pay special attention to scenarios where the cost of the fine plus the damage to the brand would be more than the cost of deploying an 802.1x authentication system.

If you are deploying wireless access for the patients, make sure there are methods to control access. Limit the DHCP lease times to less than two hours to prevent the DHCP pool from running out of IP addresses to lease. If the wireless system doesn't have built-in filtering capabilities, have the practice subscribe to OpenDNS. This cloud-based DNS service is used by large and small companies alike. It filters websites based on content and prevents inappropriate content from being displayed. More information about OpenDNS subscriptions is available from www.opendns.com.

Next, take the time to identify vulnerability points in the network drops. These can be as simple as network drops that are connected in the data closet but have nothing connected at the far side. Data closets shared by multiple providers can increase the vulnerabilities, depending on who controls access. Uncover any unsecured areas where hubs or switches have been placed because of the lack of network drops. Other vulnerabilities are unseen. Firewalls misconfigured to allow SNMP traps without authentication expose the device to be probed for vulnerabilities.

802.1x
802.1x is an IEEE standard for authenticated network access to wired Ethernet networks and wireless *802.11* networks.

Monitoring

As a provider of technical services, it is critical to have every device on the network monitored. Every network point that is not monitored is a point of failure that your team will never see until it does fail. Reactive responses to network problems are many times more costly to the practice since the downed network switch, router, or access point must be tracked down manually. Knowing where the issue is before arriving to fix it reduces the downtime typically to the length of time it takes to dispatch a technician.

Table 14.3 is the checklist we use when walking a medical practice to determine the network configuration for an EMR.

Table 14.3   Walk-through Checklist for Network Configuration

Task	Additional Thoughts
Location of drops	Are they high or low? Is there easy access? Find out where patient care will occur.
Identify the number of jacks	Find out how many ports are needed at minimum and how many are preferred. Find out where the wireless ports are being dropped.

Table 14.3   Walk-through Checklist for Network Configuration *(continued)*

Task	Additional Thoughts
Longest cable run length	Is the longest cable run under the 100 meter limitation?
Wireless access point locations	Are the APs using Power over Ethernet (PoE)? Is the location visible to the naked eye for easier troubleshooting?
SNMP configuration	Use v3, which is secure. What SNMP traps are most important for the practice?
Potential network vulnerabilities	Locate any APs that are bleeding into the parking lot. Note any physical access controls and vulnerabilities.
A need for wireless filtering	Do you need to protect the innocent from seeing content they shouldn't? Reduce the liability exposure to the medical practice.
Protocol used for wireless authentication	WPA2 is the minimum. Include 802.1x, if possible.
Location of data closet	Is it shared? Is it in a restroom or other unsecured, high-traffic area?

Servers

Now that the network infrastructure has been identified, it is time to identify the server hardware currently available at the practice and determine where the new (and possibly the old) equipment will be located. Consider the following:

Server Placement   First, when deploying multiple servers to handle the load, look to see whether the current location can support a four-post rack or a server cabinet. A cabinet, of course, is better because physical access to the system can be controlled. If a two-post rack must be deployed, then make sure the server rails ordered are the right type. Getting on-site with the wrong rails can delay the project a few days while waiting for the correct ones to ship.

Environment Controls   Having a separate AC unit for the space is ideal. That way, the temperature can be maintained no matter how the staff heats or cools their environment. Individual units can be expensive to operate, so the practice can choose to run an AC vent to the location and cut a vent in the bottom of the door.

Electrical Needs   The new EMR system might require additional outlets, depending on the draw. We always recommend sizing a UPS based upon 150 percent of the actual anticipated load. This provides room for growth. Most UPSs require a different electrical plug. Make sure the UPS will connect to the plug being ordered. Also, consult the electrician installing the line on how many phases the UPS is expecting. Some are single-phase, while the larger units are three-phase. Most commercial UPSs have the capability to manage it remotely. Invest in the module that allows remote monitoring. In our own data center, we once had a UPS go out, though we aren't sure how long it was out given that we heard the alarm only when we came to the office.

Selecting the Server Type

The type of server being purchased will be highly dependent on the EMR selected. Always spec for higher requirements than the minimum specifications provided by the EMR vendor. When upgrades occur in the future, they will almost always require additional resources. These resources are cheaper to purchase now than later.

We recommend the following configurations as a foundation no matter what EMR is being deployed:

Root Drive   First, have a server with a RAID 1 volume for the root drive. Build out the entire drive for the OS. We have never understood why folks would break a single RAID volume into two. That never makes sense since it is the same drive spindles being used. We recommend having the hypervisor on this volume. The volume can also hold the ISOs used for building systems.

Data Volume   The data volume should be RAID 5 at a minimum. This provides speed and the necessary redundancy if a drive fails. RAID 6 is becoming more common as a way to protect data as the parity bits are spread across two drives. Having two drives fail is highly uncommon. RAID 10 and RAID 50 can also increase the speed of the data volumes used by the guest operating systems running on the hypervisor. Review the hypervisor best-practice guide to determine which RAID configuration is best for the situation.

Hot Standby   No matter the RAID type chosen, make sure that there is a hot standby on the RAID controller. The hot standby will allow the system to automatically add the drive to the RAID group while a replacement drive is selected. Another RAID controller feature is the battery backup write cache. Having the write cache backed up with battery increases disk writes, thus improving performance.

SATA or SAS   Drive types are always a source of banter around the water cooler. With SATA quality improving, many resellers are choosing to use SATA instead of SAS drives. Our recommendation is to buy the drives that the customer can afford based on the data being placed on the drives.

Hypervisor   Next on the list for configuration is a hypervisor. No matter which one is selected, it will provide you and your customer with better recovery capabilities. We utilize all three of the hypervisors on the market with our customers. When the server hardware is made into a hypervisor, upgrading the individual guest operating systems is made easier because of the snapshot capabilities in all of the top vendors. If something goes horribly wrong, the guest operating system can be recovered quickly without having to recover from tape. Also, having the EMR host as a VM allows for the system to be backed up and recovered to a separate server or system quickly. This flexibility increases your customer's uptime and again shows that you should be their trusted IT provider.

SaaS Platform   The previous points are moot if the customer is going to use a hosted platform. However, the SaaS platform should have the previous as minimum requirements as well. Most providers already do these all and much more. Some, however, are skimping on the hypervisor. Clearly, you cannot change every part of their implementation, but you should provide feedback to the medical practice if you are concerned about how the SaaS data center or application is configured. At a minimum, make sure that the provider has completed an SAS 70 audit. The SAS 70 audit confirms compliance by the business of their own operating procedures and policies for data center operations, security, application recovery, and data center monitoring.

Security Configuration   Once the system has been purchased, you must secure it. Spend time with the NIST special publications that identify steps to secure a server. For Windows- and Unix-based systems, there are step-by-step configuration guides. Do understand that if you use every one of the recommendations, the server may become useless. Take the time to understand what each configuration does. Making configuration changes willy-nilly will cause system management problems. These documents are periodically updated, so if it has been a few months since you retrieved your copy, go back to the NIST site and download the latest copy.

Guest Operating System   Once the hypervisor is operational, it is now time to carve out a guest operating system. When configuring the system, use the configuration guidelines from the vendor as the basis for your configuration. If there are discrepancies between the guidelines and the way you believe the guest operating system should be configured, then have an open and candid conversation with the vendor. It is much easier to have those conversations up front than when trying to troubleshoot performance issues.

Disk Image   Once the system is built, take the time to image the initial clean guest. Use this as a template for future deployments or when having to revert from scratch. Taking the image once the application is installed is another milestone. Typically this is not converted into a template. Once the application is installed, take snapshots of the guest system. The snapshots will reduce the time to recover the system. We also recommend recovering the guest image to another system to prove that the image is good. This is simpler if the storage is shared among the systems.

Remote Monitoring

Remote monitoring enables your team to respond proactively to system issues. SMART, a predictive disk failure algorithm, is used by many of the drive manufacturers. This predictive code can help prevent application outages by replacing the drive prior to a complete failure. However, if the system isn't being monitored, the technology and effort put into developing SMART doesn't make you any smarter.

One of the common questions we receive is about what system parameters should be monitored. We recommend at a minimum the items listed in Table 14.4.

Table 14.4   Minimum Monitored System Parameters

Hypervisor	System
CPU utilized	CPU utilized
Memory utilized	Memory utilization
I/O reads and writes	Disk I/O reads and writes
Network utilization	Network utilization
Free disk	Free disk
OS level	OS level
SNMP traps	Application performance WMI or SNMP specialized traps

---

Real World Scenario

The Melting Server

The items listed in Table 14.4 include just the basic monitoring that must occur to keep your client's server running optimally and provide historical trends for reporting. The trending information can help you troubleshoot problems that might occur only at certain times. For example, in one non-EMR deployment we worked with, the systems consistently shut off at 3 p.m. daily. We investigated and

Continues

found that the AC unit in the server room was on the local electrical grid, which had a power-saving feature that shut down high-consumption products when there was not enough electricity in the grid. The server would overheat and shut down before it could melt. We quickly moved the AC unit to a different circuit.

You can set a number of alerts for the systems you monitor. For example, an alert could trip when system activity or system logon errors reach a certain threshold. When the system log file is filling up with bad logon entries, the system could be under attack. It could just as easily be that an administrator used their domain credentials for a service. Then after the password changed, the service was constantly trying to restart. Always consider your client's behavior and needs when setting alerts, and always investigate when an alert triggers.

SAN Environments

In some environments, you may deploy technology that requires a storage area network (SAN). The SAN can bring a level of comfort when a hypervisor is being used in conjunction with a separate file server, domain controllers, and other systems needing the high reliability. When selecting a SAN, you must choose between using Fibre Channel, iSCSI, or FCoE. When selecting Fibre Channel, you must deploy a separate fabric for the disk traffic to ride upon. Having a separate fabric can be extremely useful when working with high-bandwidth applications. Advancements in the iSCSI and FCoE protocols have improved their capabilities and I/O response times on the IP networks that are deployed in most of the practices you will serve.

In medical practices with fewer than 10 doctors and no internal lab or imaging department, you will most likely not deploy a SAN. The systems are just too cost-prohibitive. However, the price becomes very attractive when deploying more than just an EMR. The cost of the SAN can be spread across the multiple projects.

Backup Architecture

Lastly is the backup architecture. The type of server and hypervisor and whether the data is on a SAN will determine the best way to back up data. If a SAN is deployed, then back up the data on the drives directly from the SAN. This will reduce backup windows and reduce the amount of time required for recovery. When a SAN is not used, then the system can be backed up utilizing a local tape drive and software or using a disk target. We recommend using a separate appliance for the backups. When using tape, there is a lot more handholding that must occur. Plus, if the target is a disk drive, deduplication tools can be used to decrease the amount of data required to be backed up. We have seen data deduplicated across an enterprise to the tune of 93 percent.

Table 14.5 contains the checklist we use when assessing the server component of the EMR deployment.

Table 14.5   Server Component Assessment Checklist

Tasks	Additional Thoughts
Server room space	Is there enough?
	How many posts?
	Can a cabinet be used?
	What kind of rails are needed (round or square holes)?
	Is there a multisystem IP KVM switch that allows more than one server to be connected to the same keyboard, monitor, and mouse?
Environmentals	Is there AC?
	Is there proper electrical?
	Is there a UPS?
	Is there a vent in the door?
Server configuration	Which hypervisor is best for this deployment?
	What RAID configuration will best serve the practice?
	Which guest OS is best for this deployment?
	Is a backup battery unit available?
Monitoring	See Table 14.4.
Backup	Will the system be backed up to tape or disk?
	Will the backup data be stored on-site or off-site?
	Will the data be sent to the cloud once it is backed up?

Workstations

Workstations and portable computers are in the next area that must be addressed when assessing the needs of a medical practice. Depending on the selection, the practice might need to purchase more servers to support the implementation.

Conventional Systems   Walk the office, the exam rooms, and any other space where the staff suggests a system will be used or placed. Most offices already have desktop workstations in place for front- and back-office staff. If possible, grab the service tag or serial number. Later confirm what the configuration is, whether the system is under warranty, and whether the system will be used with the new EMR. Continue walking the facility. Pay special attention to the exam rooms or other tight quarters. The exam rooms might not have enough space to have a wall-mounted computer. For those situations, look at deploying a computer built into the monitor. Vendors are now building PCoE, Citrix ICA, and Windows embedded into touchscreen monitors. When space is a constraint, look at having the electrical and network jacks at the same height and location as the unit that is being placed.

Specialized Systems Next look for any specialized systems. These might be spirometry machine, imaging systems, lab equipment, or even retinal scanners. These devices will most likely be connected to the same physical network at minimum. Some might have disk shares on the local file share. Some of these devices aren't owned by the practice. They are leased, so support is provided by a separate company. Work with the support group from the vendor to connect the device to the network and/or EHR. Remember that some of these devices might still be running older versions of operating systems that cannot connect to a domain controller. These same systems typically cannot be remotely monitored because agents aren't available for their platform. Understand this limitation prior to committing to remotely monitoring the device.

Tablets and Portable Devices Last, but definitely not least, most eligible professionals (EPs) will use a tablet or portable device. These devices will require robust wireless connectivity and be ruggedized. We replace keyboards constantly on certain brands of laptops because they simply weren't meant for daily use. Have a few sample types for the EPs to use for a day or two. These machines must have a minimum battery life of four hours, preferably six. The more battery, however, the heavier the machines are. When the machines are too heavy, the doctors complain of arm strain, wrist issues, and fatigue. Manufacturers are listening because a few new laptops on the market include batteries that are less than four pounds and last seven hours. These machines are much lighter and in most cases are just as powerful as the more common laptop. The challenge is that they are made for the mass consumer market, so 24/7 support with next-day on-site support is not available. If you choose to use these consumer products, you might want to invest in a spare for times you might need to swap the unit while the other is being repaired.

Consumer Devices The healthcare market is no different from many others when it comes to members of the workforce expecting that their consumer device can be enabled with typically secure data from the enterprise. Only business policies will enable or disallow this behavior of bringing your own computer (BYOC). The staff costs soar when enabling these technologies. We personally spend at least an hour a week working on a CIO's tablet or laptop because they fail to communicate because of some odd error (though it is never the same error).

Compute Power To enable small form-factor PCs protocols and programs such as PCoE, Citrix, VMware View, and other virtual desktop infrastructure (VDI) technologies, the data center compute power must increase. For these VDI technologies, you will have to deploy server, disk, and network infrastructure support. You will have to decide whether a blade server or whether pizza-box servers are the way to go. Next, decide whether a SAN architecture is best to serve up the desktops.

Take the time to define the right workstation architecture. Remember, if you do not have a plan, you will not succeed. There are a number of moving parts. If you are uncertain about the types of workstations that will work, visit a few hospitals, local medical practices, and your local system distributor. We recently presented at a distributor that had gone to the expense of providing an entire hospital room, a physician's office, and a radiology imaging station for testing.

Table 14.6 provides a basis of our workstation reviews at a medical practice.

Table 14.6   Workstation Assessment Checklist

Tasks	Additional Thoughts
Current number of machines	Determine system configuration. How many systems can be used with new EHR and PM system? How will data be transferred? Will applications need to be upgraded?
System location	Will there be power, a network, and room?
Best device for EP	Look at the best solution for EP based on use, the longest schedule without a break, and familiarization with the OS.
VDI	Is a VDI worth deploying?
Management	What is the best way to manage the devices? Define the power settings. Develop a plan for rebuilding or replacing each system. Build time to recover into the plan.
Specialized hardware	Is there a need for USB-connected devices? Is there a need for COM devices? Note and plan for any other devices.
Special needs	Is there staff with special needs? What hardware and placement issues, such as an ergonomic or Braille keyboard, mouse or trackball placement, desk location, or other accessories, must be considered to meet their needs?

Regulatory Compliance

Once the system, network, and workstation architecture are defined, take the time to assess the eligible professional's regulatory exposure and compliance with current regulations. You might think that looking at regulatory compliance last is not the most ideal, but we believe it is more challenging to attempt to review the regulatory part prior to looking at the systems that will be deployed. We do offer that you should only implement systems that are in compliance with the current practice or hospital policies. However, we have found that most practices have implemented cookie-cutter policies, without much thought of their implementation needs or how to prove compliance to the policy. Here is where you can help. After looking at the technology required to implement the EHR, ask for a copy of the policies the practice or hospital has in place. Review them for compliance against HIPAA, HITECH, PCI, federal, and state regulations. The goal is not to show how ineffective their current policies are but to help them get to the point where the need to comply will ultimately increase their security posture. Remember, compliance doesn't equal security. Once the review of the policies is complete, do a complete GAP analysis on the policies. Here make sure that the three HIPAA safeguards, the privacy rule, and the HITECH Act are listed. Consider the following: skimping on any of these areas exposes the eligible professional to the maximum fine of $1.5 million levied by either the feds or the state. Add to the fine the cost of a breach expected to be $231, and the eligible professional could lose their practice.

Data Encryption and Key Management Compliance is more than just meeting the requirements on paper. Take the time to deploy encryption at every location data is used. This means the encryption of mobile devices, too. Full disk encryption will keep the business under safe harbor if a laptop or mobile device is stolen. If possible, encrypt the desktop as well. Certain antivirus manufacturers have purchased full disk encryption suites. Expect the agent that controls the updating of the malware and antivirus software to be the same agent that controls the disk encryption. Key management is critical here. If the end user forgets their key, then the information is lost unless there is a key repository. Of course, that key repository can grant access to any encrypted drive, so make sure to protect the key management system.

Data in Motion When meeting data encryption in motion requirements, use the technology outlined in NIST SP 80-113. This outlines the use of utilizing Secure Socket Layer or TLS as a transportation mode. FIPS 140-2 further outlines the use of secure transport layers to reduce the likelihood of having data viewed while in transit. Also, look at groups such as the Open Web Application Security Project (OWASP) when designing secure websites. They provide a framework for the development, implementation, and administration of secure websites.

Data at Rest   Data at rest might not be capable of sitting on a drive with full disk encryption. In these scenarios, it is important to implement database security methods, classify data, and encrypt the data to meet the criteria for data protection.

Authentication   Strong authentication assists in reducing the capability of an unauthorized user to gain access to data. When trying to verify who is who at the terminal, there are many methods for strong authentication. First are biometric devices. These devices look at some feature on the body, be it fingerprint, hand print, or retina. Another method is a proximity or tap card. These cards have an RFID or similar technology that, when in proximity with or touched by the device, causes an internal code to be read. This code, along with a username, grants the user access to the system. Some proximity and tap card readers require a password as well. A third method for authentication is a token. The token on the keyfob, plus a password and username, allows access to the system. We have recently also deployed technologies that use the user's phone number to authenticate.

Training and Staff Member Behavior   Pay special attention to the staff. Some staff might give signs of how they might behave after the system goes live. Some staff members might need additional training to prevent them from accidentally causing a data breach. More importantly, they might need training on the computers—just to become familiar with their use. Remember, if the staff is not comfortable with the technology, the EHR deployment will fail.

Security Audits   Finally, as you deploy the EHR, you might be wondering whether it is OK to also be the company that audits the security measure you put in place. Well, that is a tough question to answer. Plenty of companies have large engineering teams, and one group specializes in EHR deployments, while the other group handles the security aspects. If your business is too small to have a Chinese wall preventing the two groups from collusion, then seek a partner in the healthcare security space to look at the issues for you.

So, when we go through the office during one of the many visits that occurs during an EHR deployment, we find the regulatory compliance assessment checklist in Table 14.7 handy.

Table 14.7   Regulatory Compliance Assessment Checklist

Task	Additional Thoughts
Do they take credit cards?	Verify PCI compliance. Are paper transactions used? Does policy and implementation prohibit skimming?

Table 14.7 Regulatory Compliance Assessment Checklist *(continued)*

Task	Additional Thoughts
Do they comply with HIPAA regulations?	Is a security officer defined? Do they have the proper policy and procedures? Do they have physical safeguards? Do they document changes to policies? Does each user have a separate logon? Is there a warning screen at the time of logon? Is the data backed up? Is the data backup stored off-site? Do they meet privacy standards?
Do they meet HITECH?	Is the data encrypted per HITECH guidance?
Do they understand HITECH?	Do they understand the fine structure and penalties for noncompliance? Have they modified their BA agreements? Do they have a explicit breach notification procedure?
Do they comply with state regulations for privacy?	Know the regulations that are in effect in the state where you are deploying. Currently, California SB 1386 and Massachusetts CFR 201 are the toughest regulations.

Deploying the EHR

When looking at ways to deploy the EHR, a number of factors come into play. Based on the EHR selected, the specifications for the server, network, and workstation might be different from what is currently in use in the practice. We have even had specifications change for hardware in the middle of the project based on new requirements from the EHR vendor. Oversize it by a minimum of 25 percent for RAM, disk, and processor. If possible, purchase a system that has slots for additional processors. Investing up front in extra capacity reduces the need for the embarrassing conversation of hardware purchases every time the vendor upgrades the application. We always look at the current layout first. Then, once an EHR is selected, complete a GAP analysis to identify what must be changed.

Shared Space The size and number of offices included in the practice will help determine which systems to first review. While walking the offices, you can determine whether the space is shared with other medical practices or whether the practice is the only one in the space. To keep costs low, some medical practices sublease use of their office space to another medical practice when they are not on-site. When this occurs, it is important to understand both the physical risks and the connectivity challenges of where the EHR package sits.

Outsourcing   When the practice is small, the entire EHR package might be outsourced. If this is the case, it is critical to understand how the EHR system works, how support will be handled, and how data can be exported. The SaaS model is very useful when working with smaller medical offices.

Affiliated Medical Practices   Hospital systems are now also in the business of deploying EHR systems into their affiliated medical practices. These Independent Physician Associations (IPAs) are delivering an EHR in a box. The IPA works with a hosting company to install the brand of software they believe will meet the requirements of the greatest number of medical practices in the IPA. However, no single package is good enough for all specialties. When the IPA decides what application will be deployed, they also decide how the practices will gain access to it.

The VPN Tunnel   In most cases, the application is accessed via a secure VPN tunnel. The IPA runs a T-1 or higher-speed line into the practice and configures it to access only the data center where the application is hosted. To gain actual access, typically Terminal Services or Citrix XenApp is used as the application presentation layer. To reduce delay in accessing the application remotely, remember to configure the ICA client or Terminal Services Client appropriately. Never use 32-bit mode, and never enable the use of a background image or other high-use bandwidth settings such as cut and paste, drive mapping, port redirection, and sound redirection.

Customization, Updates, and Patches   Most eligible professionals are going down this road on their own. Here is where you can assist in deploying the right solution with a higher level of satisfaction because the application can be customized to meet the special needs of the practice. However, the closer to the vanilla installation, the easier it will be to update and maintain the application. Remember that each modification to the vanilla install must be tested by the vendor on top of the normal quality controls in place. We see that on average nearly 4,000 patches or special updates are applied by an EHR vendor.

Specialties   When selecting the product, the systems capability to be used by the particular practice is of utmost importance. Review what specialties are part of the medical practice. Include in your survey the number of clinicians, the number of supporting staff, and the type of modalities they will be connecting into the EHR.

Incentives   To determine which incentive program to participate in, make sure that the calculations for Medicare and Medicaid are done. The advantage to Medicaid is that the timeline to implement is longer. However, the rules are different and in our opinion much more complex than the Medicare requirements. The incentive reimbursement calculations can be found on the Health and Human Services website.

Workflow Assessments   The size of the practice will determine how many days are necessary to complete the workflow assessment. This assessment is one of the most critical steps in the successful implementation of an EHR system. In prior chapters, we talked about the different needs of the front-office, back-office, clinical staff, and lab systems. One study showed that only 11 percent of the benefit goes to the physician. Spend enough time getting comfortable documenting the process. Work with the staff to verify that what was documented in the workflow is correct. From there, work on optimizing the workflow for the EHR. Remember that simply putting the paper process in the EHR system will reduce the overall effectiveness of the application. Help the practice avoid at all costs the temptation to computerize their paper workflow.

After reviewing the front-office, back-office, and nursing staff, make sure you document how the physician utilizes the SOAP method when practicing medicine. Time how long it takes for the physician to read the chart, to question the patient, to understand the complete medication history, and to see the trend information from the lab work. Efficiency gains in this part of the workflow will increase their satisfaction at the time of implementation. Ask whether they would prefer to click check boxes or to chart freely. Remember that unstructured text is more difficult to report from.

TIP

If the medical practice is not supportive in any of the efforts we presented in this section, you might just want to walk away. It is better to save your reputation than to be associated with a failed installation. You can recognize that an EHR deployment is going south when the physicians refuse to meet regarding workflow, staff members fail to attend training, and confirming the designed workflow is more challenging than necessary. At the project meetings, go over the issues lists, identify the possible resolutions, and determine whether the project is still on target. When the practice fails to be supportive in removing roadblocks, it is time to cut the cord and move on.

Working with Physicians and Clinicians

No matter how much technology you want to implement, if it gets in the way of delivering patient care, the physicians will have nothing nice to say about the work you do. Before you have to walk away from a project, here is some guidance on how to work with the different personalities found in the medical practices:

Listening   We cannot overemphasize that listening is the most important trait to have. One conference attendee's grandmother use to say, "God gave you twice the number of ears, so you should use them twice the amount of time." That is sound advice for those who want to succeed in this business. Listening is not passive, either. For those with short memories, write the conversation down. To confirm what you have heard, use the drive-through technique. When a staff member tells you something, repeat it for confirmation. Repeat this cycle until you have properly understood the message. Once the message is confirmed, move on to the next item. Proceeding without full understanding can cause delays in the project later.

Interrupting   Another trait that we find in many IT staff members is interrupting the person speaking. This is most likely a new market for those of you reading the book; hence, you should be listening more than speaking. Interrupting shows that you are not listening and that you think you know more than the person who is talking. These are two really bad traits that must be overcome to be successful. The interruption doesn't even have to happen out loud. When you listen with an idea that you already know the answer, you will not hear the small nuance or issue the person is trying to relay to you.

Finding the Answer   Never tell your client that there isn't an answer. If you do not know the answer, tell them that you will seek it out. Let them know once you find the answer. Let them hear you state that you might not know everything but that you have the resources to answer the questions and address the concerns they might have. Clearly, they refer their patients to specialists when necessary, so they will understand when you have to do the same.

Lastly, the eligible professionals know that they are the reason that many people can earn a living. Let them know that you appreciate that fact and you are there to help them deliver their service in a way that will improve patient outcomes. Professionally, they are committed to improving the health of the populations they serve. We in the HIT space are in the same business, but we go about it differently. We help the eligible professionals improve their work by increasing reimbursement through more efficient coding and billing, increasing patient outcomes through data mining, and improving the amount of time they can spend with their loved ones.

Maintaining Sanity in Life

When writing a chapter about tying it all together, we would be remiss if we didn't talk about some techniques to maintain a balance between work, home, and life. Though we may not have perfected them yet, we would still like to share some thoughts on how to stay up-to-date on regulatory changes, meet the demands of this very demanding market, and meet the obligations for your life away from the office.

Keeping Current

First, there is a whole bunch to learn. In Chapter 2 we offered a list of places where you can connect and stay up-to-date on the changes within the health-care system—from small medical practices to hospital systems all the way to the largest society of Healthcare Information Systems Professionals. Both the beauty and the challenge of the healthcare market is that you must keep up with the technology as well as the industry. But, trying to learn too many topics at once has proven challenging for us.

Here is the way I (Patrick) personally overcame that challenge. I skim the RSS feeds that are sent to me daily. I also read the plethora of magazines in a way that I find very helpful. First I skim them for topical information. I rip out the pages that I believe I would like to read and put them into folders based on topics. I have topics that include regulations, staffing, networking, systems, security, industry news, and other. This exercise takes about 10 minutes per magazine. Then, I take a topic and focus on learning about it from the maga-zine or other material for the month. This means I might see networking as a study topic only twice a year. In general, that might be enough to stay current on that particular topic. When reviewing regulations, though, you might not want to wait that long. To keep the regulatory and security information at the front of my brain, I attend webinars or "lunch and learns" to stay abreast of those two topics in particular. I can recommend HIMSS; they might have an active regional chapter near you. If that is the case, spend some time at their meetings because they are typically very engaging.

Maintaining a Support Structure

Next you must have the support structure to allow you time off. If you are a one-person show, do not expect to ever have time off. Make arrangements with another local provider to provide phone coverage when you are away. Reciprocate when they ask. Having the local support enables your business to compete with the larger organizations.

Outsourcing   One method, which we have stayed away from, is com-pletely outsourcing your after-hours service to another company. We do not want to allow a third party to gain complete access to our customer's data. We believe that this would open us up to greater liabilities than nec-essary. If you do choose to partner with an outsourcing group, make sure you have a BA agreement with them and that your customer is aware of the situation.

Handling Multiple Customers   When you are working at a number of locations, you can run into a situation where you might be at one customer's site with a number of other customers calling. Remember that you want your customers to know that you care, and if at all possible, simply "flash" the phone to the other line letting the customer know you are there but helping someone else. When serving at a customer site, remember that you must focus on the customer there. They are paying you a rate to provide a service. You probably wouldn't like to have a doctor seeing two or more patients at once.

Using Toll-Free Numbers   Having the staff in place to handle 24/7 support might be too expensive. Many companies successfully use a toll-free number. Most toll-free providers allow multiple call trees. Typically hitting the 1 key sends the call to the on-call technician or team. The other lines are for other groups within the organization.

Hiring the Right Folks   Developing solid hiring practices will improve your capability to deliver services. Hire the wrong staff, and you will spend too much time training and firing staff. Hire the rights folks the first time, and you will have fewer problems. Even the best people need to have the right culture to thrive. Just because they are the best doesn't mean that there shouldn't be a training process for them.

Carrying the Right Insurance   Peace of mind also comes by having the right type of insurance coverage. Team up with a company that can provide you with the necessary coverage in case there is a breach caused by you or your staff. Also, if you have company vehicles, make sure you have the right coverage. The right coverage will be determined by conversations you have with your attorneys, advisors, and others.

Balancing Work and Life

There are three last topics that are intertwined. When work becomes our single focus, we have found that we communicate less effectively, burn out faster, and take no time to rest or enjoy the pursuits we once had. We bring this up as a word of caution for those who simply want to face the enormous challenge of understanding healthcare and how it is deployed to meet the demand. You should be aware that there is never enough staff to complete the work. By default, that means you can be pushed into working longer hours.

Burning Bridges   Burning bridges is one of the first signs when the work-life balance is a little off. Our community is a small one, and we need each other to survive. More importantly, we need each other to be successful, or the American public will not trust their medical records to the eligible providers, and the money to implement will simply dry up.

Burning Faster, Burning Out   Hundreds of pages of legislation come out on a yearly basis regarding healthcare, privacy, data security, or another facet of the healthcare vertical. Keeping up with the market without a plan will cause you to burn out. Sure, there is some adrenaline at first, but it fades over time. In my case, I (Patrick) have missed important events in the lives of my kids and family. While trying to grow a business, I have taken time away from sleep just to keep up with customer needs, legislative changes, and other demands. I can only tell you that I get more done when I have spent the time with my family and gotten a little exercise in.

Giving It a Rest Lastly, take some time to rest. As you ramp up on the regulatory and compliance aspect of the vertical, take some time to clear the brain. I (Patrick) believe God made a day of rest for us because we need it. Resting doesn't have to mean sleeping all day. Go shoot hoops, play a round of golf, take a mini trip with the family. Our developmental editor (Mary Ellen, aka ME) takes time to read a novel, garden, and play the dulcimer. The point is, do whatever it is that rejuvenates you! (Of course, if it's illegal, you are on your own.)

What's in Our Toolkit?

One way to maintain work-life balance is knowing what to put in your toolkit. The tools we use are not just systems tools but include a number of tools that facilitated our business's transition into healthcare. And just in case you think we are getting kickbacks from these vendors for mentioning their products, we are not. We use and recommend these tools. And, after reviewing our toolkit, you will probably think of something important that we forgot. You can participate in improving this book by letting us know about tools that you have found useful.

EHR Decision Tools

When talking about EHR decision tools, there are two separate varieties. First are the tools that help you analyze the medical practice. In our toolkit, we have the following:

CompTIA Physician Assessment This tool allows you to work within the practice by guiding some of the questions you might need to ask when determining the right EHR vendors to target. You must be a CompTIA member to have access to the tools. Once logged into `www.comptia.org`, you can find the tool under the healthcare community tab located in the top navigation bar.

Delmarva Foundation's Barrier Profile Tool This four-page documents helps you, as the VAR, ask the tough questions regarding the barriers to a medical practice's use of an EHR system. You can access the tool at `www.delmarvafoundation.org/providers/physicians/quality Improvement/workflow/documents/BarrierProfileTool.pdf`.

HIMSS There are so many tools available from the HIMSS website (`www.himss.org`) that it would take too many pages to document them all. Spend time on the site, and if you run into issues or difficulties finding what you need, contact the support team; they have always been very helpful when we were searching for items.

HITRUST   The HITRUST community has developed the HITRUST Common Security Framework (CSF), which allows a reseller to go into a practice setting to identify the compliance needs of the organization. The method is based on the size and revenue of the practice you want to analyze. We have found it to be extremely useful for security audits. You can find the tools at www.hitrust.org.

Network Analysis Tools

Network analysis tools, when properly used, will enable you and your team to complete a thorough analysis of the environment. A properly running network tool will pinpoint areas of congestion, outdated network operating systems, and network vulnerabilities. We use the following:

NetWitness   NetWitness Corporation was recently purchased by EMC Corporation. Focused on uncovering what is going on in the network, the company has a free tool (NetWitness Investigator Freeware, available for download from http://netwitness.com/products-services/ investigator-freeware) that allows you to collect 1GB of traffic. Once the traffic is analyzed by the application, you can see the protocols, the types of geographic destinations, and the classification of the risk per protocol and application type.

Wireshark   Whether you are in HIT or not, you need to have *Wireshark* in your kit. When installed, this tool looks at all incoming and outgoing traffic. It breaks apart the TCP/IP packets into consumable chunks. Though it does take time to learn, it will help you uncover those annoying network glitches (www.wireshark.org).

CACE Pilot and AirPcap   Never leave home without this wireless analysis and wireless promiscuous USB card. When running, the AirPcap card can intercept traffic, add packets to the network, and provide a wealth of information that allows you to get to the root cause of wireless network issues in the practices you will serve. Additionally, the CACE Pilot software produces graphics and analytics of the information just collected. The graphical representation allows for easier digestion of the data collected (www.cacetech.com).

Workstation and Server Troubleshooting Tools

Moving onto the workstation and server hardware troubleshooting, we know that there are so many tools out there. The challenge is that the more tools, the more challenging it is to master the ones that provide the biggest bang for the buck.

Tripwire   Knowing what files changed, and when, can help both in a forensics cases analysis and in troubleshooting a system down issue. Tripwire has been around for decades and provides an excellent view into changes made on a system. The tool is located at www.tripwire.org.

Microsoft Sysinternals   The Microsoft Sysinternals tools allow system administrators to do their jobs with amazing insight into what a Windows-based system is doing (`http://technet.microsoft.com/en-us/sysinternals/bb545021`). One tool in the package will uncover rootkits. Another looks at all open ports, both inbound and outbound. Yet another looks at all the processes and breaks them down into how much each process is using in CPU and memory and, if the application is running under svchost, what the actual executables are.

Microsoft Desktop Optimization Pack   When you are looking for recovery methods, the Microsoft Desktop Optimization Pack (MDOP) is the best solution we have found (`www.microsoft.com/windows/enterprise/products/mdop/default.aspx`). When Microsoft bought Winternals Software, the purchase included the emergency repair disk tool known as ERD Commander. Microsoft pulled the tool off the market and put it into the MDOP package. The ERD recovery disk allows you to boot into a complete OS and troubleshoot it. The disk comes with network drivers so that new antivirus updates can be downloaded, if necessary. This tool can also be used to recover passwords and fix some drive-related issues. To receive licenses for MDOP, consult with your Microsoft licensing reps. Currently only certain customers have access to MDOP. Access is based on the Microsoft license holder having purchased Microsoft Software Assurance.

SolarWinds   The Orion Network Performance Monitor and other SolarWinds products found at `www.solarwinds.com` reduce the amount of time it takes to get to the root of a problem. The tools look at both PC and network-related issues. The single console helps when troubleshooting more complex issues. In addition to the toolkit, LANSurveyor provides a view of the entire LAN by creating Visio diagrams of each node on the network.

Backup Tools

Nothing can save you like a good plan B. Plan B, in most cases, is recovery from backup. Here you need to partner with a company that allows any relevant system to be able to recover either data only or an entire machine. Not all backup solutions have that capability built in. For long-term backups, we recommend using an enterprise-capable backup such as Legato, Backup Exec, NetBackup, or Avamar. Since we do not travel around with those tools in our toolkit (because of the cost), we do have backup solutions for backing up a single system no matter the OS. Here is what we use:

Acronis True Image   The value here is that the drive you want to back up can be imaged to an external drive. From there, information on that drive can be ported to any other system and viewed. This is particularly useful when you are upgrading a system or adding a bigger drive to an existing system. Both servers and workstations can be imaged using True Image. The tools can be found at www.acronis.com.

A USB Drive   Sometimes the only data that is important is contained in spreadsheets and notes. A simple USB drive will meet this challenge.

Emergency Recover Pro   KnollOnTrack has a tool that is far cheaper than AccessData's Forensics Tool Kit. ER Pro can recover most data from nearly any type of drive. If you must recover the boot drive and do not have a spare computer to mount the drive from, this tool gives you the option to boot from a CD or floppy. The tools is located at www.knollontrack.com.

Network Monitoring Tools

Over the years, we have used a variety of monitoring tools—and have not been completely satisfied with any of them. To make your decision, you must first understand what you are trying to monitor. Once that is decided, you need to determine whether you want to host the monitoring yourself or have network monitoring externally hosted. Finally, you must decide how you want to be alerted. Not all systems support email, pager, cell phone, and audible alerts. Understand which are most important to you, and select the best tool. Remember, without this tool, you will be caught off guard—and that can cause longer-than-necessary downtimes. Of course, there are many systems, but just like any other tool, sometimes it is best to pick a tool and move on than to worry about the 30 other vendors with similar technology. We have used the following network monitoring tools:

PacketTrap   Now owned by Quest Software, PacketTrap focuses on the network side of management and monitoring. Recent investments have increased the capabilities of managing servers, workstations, and laptops. When deployed, an agent sits on the remote system and checks in every few seconds. The agent allows for a near-real-time understanding of what is occurring on the network. The tool is located at www.packetrap.net.

WhatsUp   WhatsUp network monitoring tools have been around since the 1990s. They are constantly being upgraded and tweaked and, thus, have a refined look and feel. Logs are constantly combed and sent back to a central repository. WhatsUp can also query applications to confirm that they are operational, such as a web server responding to a port 80 request. WhatsUp can be downloaded at www.ipswitch.com.

Nagios   The Nagios enterprise monitoring tool can be used to manage a plethora of system types. It requires that you know a little about Linux for configuration and to get the most power out of the system. Nagios can be found at www.nagios.org.

Zenoss   Zenoss enterprise monitoring and system management tools come in a number of editions. The Zenoss Service Dynamics tool includes event management, resource management, and analytics and optimization.

The way the tool is laid out allows for easier management of cloud-based resources, such as storage. Zenoss can be downloaded for free at `www.zenoss.com`.

Vendor Support Packages

Vendor support is often overlooked by IT professionals. Remember that the customer is paying for support on the hardware and applications. With this investment, you should take the time to contact the vendor if a system goes down and you simply do not know where to look. On average, a customer will spend 20 percent of the cost of the software and hardware on support per year. This means they will have paid for the software twice during the time that they use it in a five-year period. Use the support services your customer paid for, or you are simply fattening the vendor's bottom line.

One reason that some IT staff is reluctant to call support is that we believe that with the troubleshooting skills we have, our prowess in searching for answers online, and the pride we take in our work, we somehow should never have to involve support. Remember to put your ego aside when working on returning machines to operational status. If it gets the system up and running faster, you will not receive any demerits.

To maintain the support of the vendor, you must keep the application at a patch and release level that the vendor supports. When calling the vendor, one of the first questions they will ask is, what version of the application is having the issue? Here, it is critical to make sure you are running a recent version. Some vendors support only the last two versions, while others require a version within a set number of prior years, typically three.

Our Computers

We have not yet covered one of the most critical items in the toolkit, and that is a computer. Definitely a computer is necessary if you want to get any work done in this field. Depending on the type of work that you are planning to do, you might have to carry more than one. As an Apple user since 1985, I (Patrick) carry a MacBook in my bag. I can boot into multiple operating systems. However, my latest version of the MacBook does not include a COM port. I do carry a converter so that I can use it to configure networking or other RS-232 systems. Scott carries a Dell Latitude laptop with an extended life battery and an internal wireless broadband network card. This combination allows him to connect to our clients from anywhere he can get a cellular connection and resolve their issues without having to recharge.

You will need to define your requirements and select a system based on your requirements. Having a COM port is nice, although that typically means the system will be heavy. Make sure there is enough battery life to keep you operational for a few hours without being tied to an outlet. Make sure you have properly licensed software on the system, as well. Using hacked copies or improperly licensed software exposes you and your customer to unnecessary risk. Lastly, get the fastest CPU, most RAM, and best graphics card you can afford. These allow for faster password cracking and vulnerability testing when you are working on the security side of the healthcare vertical.

Deployment Tasks Based on Practice Size

We have covered a lot of material in this chapter. Let's now drop down from many of the high-level topics into the context of our three case studies. Although we have assigned priorities to the tasks and items for each type of deployment, we recommend that the entire list be addressed.

Small Practices

You will remember that Dr. Multisite is the fictional allergist with three offices and four staff members. They currently use Medical Manager, a proprietary system, and their selected EHR vendor has had verified success in extracting patient information from the system and importing the data into the relevant areas of an EHR. When we assisted in deploying an EHR system, we prioritized their needs high, medium, or low (H, M, L), as listed in Table 14.8.

Table 14.8   Small-practice EHR Deployment Tasks and Issues

Task or Item	Priority	Reason
Importing prior three years of patients	H	With limited staff, the amount of data rekeying was going to be a drawback.
Internet bandwidth	H	Moving from place to place and spending less than 35 percent at the main office meant that Internet bandwidth was important to either connect to the EHR or use a SaaS.
Current PM software	H	The cost of importing the patient demographic data is $20,000 into the SaaS provider. This is a high cost for the numbers of patients. Given the small number of staff, the provider might pay the cost.
Access points	H	Because two of the office locations are shared, the access point has to be portable from one location to another without configuration changes.

Table 14.8 Small-practice EHR Deployment Tasks and Issues *(continued)*

Task or Item	Priority	Reason
Security	H	Because of the doctor moving from one location to another, the possibly of theft of devices increases. A $1.5 million fine would bankrupt the business as well. Security for SSL.
PCI compliance	M	The have to comply, but because of how the credit cards are transmitted, the business has off-loaded the liability to their merchant services company.
State compliance with local and state law	M	Using SaaS has limited their need to build in compliance. The vendor must comply with the law and verify that the software complies. Ultimately, the practice is responsible for compliance, though the business carrying out the tasks to meet compliance is the vendor.
System monitoring	L	The SaaS vendor is responsible for monitoring the application and server.
Backup	L	The responsibility of the backup is that of the SaaS vendor. Ask for monthly backups so that if the vendor ends up bankrupt, there is a contingency plan.
Working with the physician	L	Typically since there is only a single physician, there are fewer decision challenges with the provider. The single decision point facilitates completing the EHR and hardware selection.

Midsize Practices

With Middleton Pediatrics, our fictional midsize pediatric practice, there are a number of challenges. Here, the focus is typically on getting the 10 physicians to agree on technology and workflow, while the high employee turnover requires a solid training program. The servers and intraoffice connectivity will also need special attention. When assisting this particular practice, we identified the task and items in Table 14.9 as H, M, and L priorities. We still recommend addressing the entire list as outlined in the chapter, though the following stood out.

Table 14.9   Midsize Practice EHR Deployment Tasks and Issues

Task or Item	Priority	Reason
30 percent staff rotation	H	Training is critical to continually onboard new staff. A team lead will be necessary to provide ongoing training. We recommended that the employee be trained in the higher-volume office to be exposed.
Number of physicians	H	With the high number of physicians, spend the time to get a few physicians to be the spokespeople for the group. If all 10 participate in decision making, implementation timelines are typically longer.
Number of locations	H	The higher number of locations will require VPN tunnels between the five locations. An advantage of the number of locations is that one site can be the primary and another site can be the backup location.
Network speed	H	Network bandwidth is critical to facilitate the number of connections to the server. DSL is not sufficient enough for the intraoffice connections. Using business-class circuits appropriately sized will increase the reliability of the network. We recommend using a Terminal Services or Citrix environment in a business this size.
Security	H	With the number of employees accessing data, having a security training program is important. Also, having tools to prevent the spread of viruses and malware will increase the uptime of the environment. Patch management will also improve the security posture.
Backups	H	This practice is in charge of their own servers and thus in charge of their own backups. Operationalize the procedures for backup and the testing of backups at least monthly.
Regulatory compliance	H	Work with internal staff or a third-party vendor to handle the security assessment required under HIPAA and HITECH. Typically given the size of a project, you will handle either the EHR deployment or the security assessment, not both.

Table 14.9   Midsize Practice EHR Deployment Tasks and Issues *(continued)*

Task or Item	Priority	Reason
Network	M	Install managed network devices that will allow easier troubleshooting.
Monitoring	H	Install network monitoring so that as a IT professional you are aware of a system issue typically prior to the provider.
Servers	M	We always recommend installing out-of-band tools that allow a server to be managed without the server being operational (of course, you need power).
Disk	M	Disk selection is important. Make sure that the spindle speed, RAID configuration, and size will meet the current and ongoing requirements of the system.
Current PM	L	In a project of this size with the need to have complete integration of the practice management software with the EHR, the PM is typically a module of the EHR. We would not recommend integrating an EHR with the PM in a practice of this size.
Deploying the EHR	L	When going live with the EHR and PM software, we recommend a two-stage approach: Install the PM first, letting folks become familiar with it, and then move to the EHR deployment after two to three months.

Hospitals and Large Practices

Our fictional North Community Hospital and Clinics is the acute-care facility with 160 beds. Their IT staff of 50 employees has experience managing applications but limited experience in deploying new systems. In the past, they relied heavily on the vendor and contractors for deployment services. They are opinionated and are willing to share the ways they expect the project will fail. The physicians and clinical staff are stuck using the selected data systems, so training on the new system will be important. Securing the PCs to prevent theft might be one way to approach the security, or deploying remote desktops or Terminal Services where the data never resides on the desktop might be the better option. Table 14.10 list the challenges for this deployment.

Table 14.10   Hospital- and large-practice EHR Deployment Tasks and Issues

Task or Item	Priority	Reason
Staff training	H	Training is critical to continually onboard new staff just like the pediatrics group. A team lead will be necessary to provide ongoing training.
IS staff	H	Pay special attention to those on the IS team who have vast knowledge but do not want to share it.
Number of physicians	H	With hundreds of physicians, the only way for the project to succeed is by using an executive steering committee.
Number of locations	H	A high number of locations requires EHR project staff to be mobile enough to get to meetings at the different locations. Pay special attention to the timing of meetings.
Network speed	H	Network bandwidth is critical to facilitate the number of connections to the server. The network bandwidth might need to be upgraded to support the number of connections. Their prior text-based application is not as bandwidth heavy as the new EHR.
Security	H	Help the hospital develop and deploy an ongoing HIPAA and HITECH training environment to keep employees up-to-date on the important changes in the law. Implement tools to secure the perimeter and segment off the data center from the rest of the organization. Have a third party conduct an audit if your IT shop is not large enough to handle the EHR and the security audit.
Backups	H	This hospital is in charge of their own servers and thus in charge of their own backups. Operationalize the procedures for backup and the testing of backups at least monthly. This particular site has computer operators who monitor the status.
Regulatory compliance	H	Millions of dollars flow via credit card transactions here. Spend time to verify that a PCI compliance audit has occurred. Verify the security of the areas where credit cards are taken. Video surveillance can be useful to reduce fraud.

Table 14.10 Hospital- and large-practice EHR Deployment Tasks and Issues *(continued)*

Task or Item	Priority	Reason
Network	M	Install managed network devices to reduce the time to troubleshoot.
Monitoring	H	Install network monitoring so that as an IT professional you are aware of a system issue typically prior to the provider.
Servers	M	We always recommend installing out-of-band tools that allow a server to be managed without the server being operational (of course, you need power).
Disk	M	Disk selection is important. Make sure that the spindle speed, RAID configuration, and size will meet the current and ongoing requirements of the system. Make sure that the backup system hits the disk directly, or the time to back up and recover will be increased.
Integration with ancillary systems	M	Each ancillary system will have the capability to send out information either in a DICOM format or in HL7. This will require interface mapping and programming expertise.
Current PM	L	Again, in a project of this size and the need to have complete integration of the practice management software with the EHR, the PM is typically a module of the EHR. Using HER and PM modules from separate vendors will complicate support and increase the number of interfaces necessary to talk between the two systems.
Deploying the EHR	L	When going live with the EHR and PM software, we recommend a two-stage approach. Install the PM first, letting folks become familiar with it, and then move to the EHR deployment after two to three months.
Importing patients	L	Though the need is high, typically the health information management system will have a way to extract the current dictation and reports. If the plan is to scan the chart, then this becomes a higher-priority task and very resource intensive.

Clearly there is more to each project, and depending on the situation, there will be different priorities. The previous is what we would have expected to experience based on our experience in deploying EHRs.

Terms to Know

802.11	802.1x
practice management (PM) software	SAS 70 audit

Review Questions

1. Which tool would you look to when trying to identify the security requirements a practice must comply with?

   A. HIMSS

   B. HITECH

   C. REC

   D. HITRUST

2. What type of map will show the strength of a wireless signal in a particular environment?

   A. Heat map

   B. Signal map

   C. Frequency map

   D. Strength map

3. When purchasing a computer for your work, what should you not put on it?

   A. System cracking tools

   B. Network monitoring tools

   C. Forensic analysis tools

   D. Improperly licensed software

4. What tool will sniff packets on the network?

   A. Nagios

   B. HITRUST

   C. Wireshark

   D. MDOP

5. How many multiples of ears do you have compared to your mouth?

   A. 0.5 times

   B. 1 time

   C. 0.25 times

   D. 2 times

6. Healthcare IT is a growing market. Which association has a practice and physician assessment tool?

   A. CompTIA

   B. MGMA

   C. MS-HUG

   D. HITRUST

7. What tool is a remote network and system monitoring tool?

    A. Sysinternals

    B. PacketTrap

    C. WhatsUp

    D. Wireshark

8. When the client wants to have remote access to the EHR, what is a good application to use?

    A. Packettrap

    B. Wireshark

    C. Terminal Services

    D. Citrix XenApp

Chapter 15

Selecting the Right EHR Vendor

The federal government has set aside more than $25 billion for building an information superhighway of clinical data called the National Health Information Network. Add to this that nearly 30 percent of the current users of an electronic medical/health record (EMR or EHR) solution will be switching it out this year. As an IT professional looking to advance your career in healthcare, knowing how to select an EMR package is critical. Emotions can run high during the selection process, so you must know how to systematically help the physician select the product and arrange an appropriate contract.

High-Level Overview

Implementing an electronic health record (EHR) system in either an acute or ambulatory setting can be one of the most challenging projects that an eligible provider or eligible hospital will go through. Some consider EHR deployments more complex than building out a new hospital or practice office, and the many personalities involved contribute to the situation. Operating rooms (ORs) are nearly the same in different hospitals, and exam rooms are probably nice enough to see a patient. However, a new EHR system touches every last crevice in an organization. It can show how undertrained the staff is for data entry, how unnecessarily complex software vendors have made an EHR, how clinicians feel they are beta testing software, or how the entire computer and network infrastructure needs to be replaced.

We have spent time reviewing how clinicians believe they are being forced to use technology that does nothing to improve patient outcome (the underserved will continue to be underserved), how reporting health information electronically seems a bit too Big Brother for patients, and lastly how the clinicians don't want to invest in technology and never receive the incentive payment. You can see how doctors are going to be a bit of a tough sell when you are trying to get an EHR system installed. Their colleagues are facing higher EHR startup costs, a drop in receivables as back-office staff members become accustomed to the EHR package, and an increase in the time the physician must spend away from patients. During a recent interview, a local doctor told us that adding an EHR increased his daily workload by two hours. Clearly, these are not the efficiencies doctors are looking for. Doctors want better outcomes for their patients, not better profits for the insurance companies.

However, with all of the challenges of getting an EHR deployed, there are a number of reasons why physicians will adopt an EHR system. Medicare and Medicaid are investing more than $27 million to advance the adoption of an EHR system. The government's investment in this technology is meant to improve the continuity of care for patients. By sharing lab results, insurance information, and other clinically relevant information, the government believes it will save billions of dollars. Increases in productivity and workflow can be a benefit to physicians. Back-office staff can increase reimbursements through improved coding practices. With certain applications or infrastructures, clinicians can access the information from any smart device, including iOS, Android, Linux, Mac OS X, and other devices. Advanced reporting is also a possibility and allows physicians to report on patient outcomes and procedures that have the best outcomes for all cases.

Figure 15.1 demonstrates the complexities in the workflow. The figure also shows how a holistic view of a patient can be gleaned from an EHR and how the complete view can improve patient outcomes and care.

Figure 15.1   Data flow in patient care

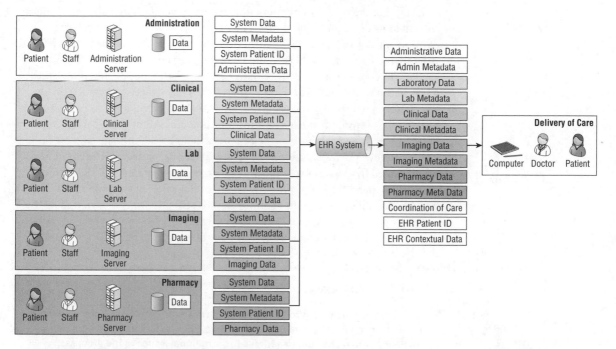

Compliance is another reason that physicians are looking to deploy an EHR system. HITECH requires that all business associates be HIPAA compliant. Fines of up to $1.5 million for any type of security breach could end up shuttering a smaller practice. To reduce the possibility of data breeches, some providers are looking at an EHR system as a method to allow business associates direct access to the data without the data ever leaving the data center of the business.

Controlling the EHR Blues

HITECH is pushing physicians and hospitals that have large Medicare or Medicaid patient populations to adopt an EHR system. Those who do not will face punitive reductions in Medicare and/or Medicaid reimbursements of up to 5 percent, depending on the EHR adoption rate among eligible professionals (EP) and eligible hospitals (EH). So, remember that when you approach a physician, they are not all happy about the incentive money. Some tell us that the EHR incentive was a way to appease the healthcare community and make sure the banks received their multibillion-dollar payout. Some physicians can review paper documents much faster than scrolling through screen after screen.

regional extension centers
Regional extension centers (RECs) are the EHR support infrastructure to help clinicians choose the right solution. The REC has the capability to support workflow design and additional improvements. RECs also provide ongoing training and marketing for the local clinical and medical staff. In the future, RECs might be required to validate EHR adoption rates. Get to know the RECs in your area by visiting the following website: http://healthit.hhs.gov/portal/server.pt/community/hit_extension_program/1495/home/17174.

Most physicians are jaded when it comes to deploying EHR systems, considering that the security of patient data could be in question. (Mind you, these same people don't understand that leaving patient records in the back of their car and transporting them from office to office is less secure than an appropriately secured EMR application.) The physicians also know that most of the benefit goes to someone other than the physician. Sure, the pharmacy sees gains because returned orders are reduced, the back-office staff can reconcile payments more quickly, and the front-office staff can send reminders with a click of the button, but what's in it for the clinician? All of these background emotions must be dealt with at the organizational level. Although the process and workflow are always addressed by the EHR analyst teams, the emotional stress caused by those changes are at the root of many failed EMR deployments. Therefore, spend time reviewing the behavioral aspects of the project before proceeding full-steam ahead. IT professionals will not always be viewed as the smartest people in the room, but be sure throw up red flags when the underlying emotional stresses of the project are not being addressed.

Emotional Baggage

EHR solutions are meant to improve workflow. A vast amount of time is spent developing, optimizing, and restructuring workflow to facilitate the adoption of an EMR package. Be sure to address the emotional issues of the process.

Challenges of Deploying an EHR System

Before we jump into the selection process for the EHR, we will cover a few challenges that should be at the forefront of your mind as an IT professional.

First, you have probably participated on an application deployment to support a business workflow. If the project was successful, the business unit that was going to use the application was actively engaged in deploying the application. If the project was treated as an IT-only project, you probably experienced significant challenges getting buy-in and decisions made. An EHR deployment is not an IT-only project. We cannot stress that enough. Without proper project planning, business support, and stakeholder involvement, the project will not be successful.

Another fantasy of an EHR deployment is when physicians believe they can manage the actual EHR project. Though they clearly play an important role, they should not be managing the project. Typically in smaller practices you will work with the practice manager. Include time for weekly (or more frequent) calls with the practice manager in your scheduling. Remember that physicians already have overcommitted their time. Deploying an EHR takes time and cannot be relegated to the last task at the end of the day.

Marketing by application vendors can also be a problem. As a trusted advisor to the clinician, you must be able to sift through the marketing brochures that doctors get at conferences and get to the actual data required to make a decision. One of the most successful ways to figure out what the application can do is to ask the vendor for references. Talk with customers and understand the challenges they face. Don't allow the vendor to be on the call; they will attempt to direct the conversation. In some vendor materials, we have seen promises such as "out of the box," "running within hours," and "15-day success guarantee." These statements could be true, but with understaffing being an industry-wide problem, we suggest you proceed with caution. Unless the physician is willing to accept an out-of-the-box application, they are likely to pay a premium. The ability to customize the application is important. Rarely is a physician able to use the application out of the box without configuration. If a practice under financial constraints must use an out-of-the-box EHR system, then they will need to spend time dealing with change management within the practice.

Not all EHR vendors are equal. Test the customer support line at all hours. Call during the day to see how long it takes to reach them. Call in the middle of the night to see whether they respond at all. Investigate how often the application is updated. If the updates come out every month, then you need to realize that the vendor runs an agile development shop. An agile development shop focuses on small, fast, iterative changes to the code. This can lead to application outages. Since quality-control steps must be taken with every upgrade or update, these vendors present more versions to test.

Finally, not all EHR systems can transfer data to and from other clinical applications. Spend time reviewing the protocols the application supports. At a minimum, the application should support HL7, X12N (if necessary), and structured data extracts such as CSV.

EHR Benefits

Depending on which vendor's Kool-Aid you decide to drink, there will be benefits that have been marketed to the provider and actual, real EHR benefits. Nearly every EHR vendor offers the following benefits:

Legible Records   One of the greatest benefits of an EHR system is the capability to read a doctor's notes. When used in combination with a shortcut-key application, the doctor can type less but still have the application represent what they mean. Legible notes give referring physicians, dictation staff, and others a much better idea of what the physician was trying to note. Some physicians are not comfortable with the keyboard and might need the assistance of a speech recognition application. Many of the standard speech recognition applications have dictionaries specifically designed for the medical community.

How many times have you gone to the pharmacy and found that the pharmacist could not read your prescription? We have had this happen on enough occasions that, when the medication order is not sent electronically, we ask that the nurse call it in. Especially during the height of the allergy or flu season, physicians have the worst hand writing; they are writing scripts all day long. We can't blame them—their hands do get tired. Electronically delivering the prescription to the pharmacy reduces these headaches. Some systems even check whether the pharmacy has the medication in stock and, if it doesn't, suggests the next possible pharmacy. EHRs extend beyond the medical office, because pharmacies and physicians receiving referrals do not need to call back to ask about an illegible prescription or referral.

Record Retrieval   Another benefit is that patient records can be found more easily. No more looking through rows of shelves of charts. In some locations, this is drastically increased because the physician might practice in many locations and the patient chart could be in any of the locations. With an EHR, the patient record can be searched on by date of birth, location of visit, attending physician, first or last name, address, and other search criteria. Productivity is increased since significantly less time is spent searching for the chart.

Multiple User Access   Multiple users can access the information about a patient at the same time. If the EHR is any good, they do not allow multiple users to write to a patient record at the same time. By not locking patient records, the billing staff can gain access for insurance information, the back-office staff can send the prescription to a pharmacy, and the front-office staff can handle payments while the patient is seen.

Security   Some folks believe that paper is more secure than electronically stored data. Clearly, physical access is required to steal the paper; however, properly secured networks and data infrastructures are far more secure. A paper chart is typically kept in one location. The data in an EHR can be replicated to a secure location and backed up to encrypted tapes. Imagine a fire that takes out the entire building. With paper charts, the business and patient are sunk. That's not the case with an EHR.

Improved Diagnosis   Staff members using an EHR typically have a number of data points that can be used to uncover the root cause of an ailment. Being able to see historical information or trending information on a single pane of glass gives them actionable information without having to hunt for it or do the calculations in their head. Sifting through papers to find the information is cumbersome and typically makes it impossible to catch all of the variances. Small changes in one lab that may not be considered abnormal may prove to be the key when looking holistically at the patient. When the patient has a chronic illness, a number of allergies, or a significant number of conditions, tracking each individually can be a challenge.

Office Efficiencies and Workflow Enhancements   Office efficiency is a key selling point made by a lot of EHR vendors. One of the top 10 vendors actually states in an ad that doctors can expect to have fewer coders on payroll because of the efficiencies of the system. Clearly, the coders are not going to be engaged when deploying that solution. Why participate in a project that will cost you your job? However, there are a number of office efficiencies that need to be mentioned without threatening anyone's job. One is that it will improve the number of patients a practice can see during the day. After about 45 days of using a system, the physician can see more patients because there is less time spent fumbling for paperwork, charts, medication lists, and possible drug-to-drug interactions. Most EHR systems display trending information and abnormal results on the first screen the doctor sees when working with the patient.

Workflow enhancements are also a possible benefit to the system. Prior to adopting the EHR system, a number of manual and paper-based processes permeated practices, such as having to sign for medication slips at the end of the day or double booking patients (though that is a scheduling module issue; most EHRs being deployed have practice management built in). Minimizing the manual filing of faxes, which are now received electronically, is another time-saver. The electronic fax still has to be organized, but using optical character recognition software can assist with filing the information to the right patient.

Review the office processes. When going live with the EHR system, make sure that only the minimal paper processes are still in use. Hanging on to paper processes can cause delays in the adoption of the EHR.

Stimulus Incentives   The citizens of the United States voted to elect a group to represent them in the House, Senate, and the Oval Office. In their infinite wisdom, they thought that the taxpayers should reimburse eligible physicians to the tune of $27 billion over the course of four years. The reason for this stimulus funding was to jump-start the economy by adding jobs and increasing the amount eligible physicians were spending on technology. The incentive funding, however, doesn't cover the cost of setting up an EHR system. Typically, the reimbursement covers about 30 percent of the cost of the EHR deployment over the life of the incentive payments.

Another impetus to go live is the negative incentive starting in 2015 when Medicare reduces payment to providers by 1 percent per year up to a total of 5 percent. Previously, the doctors fretted over receiving incentive payments. However, they are all to accustomed to the feds taking money away.

Reduced Outsourcing   With the amount of workflow that is outsourced to business associates such as transcriptionists, medical practices are looking for every possible cost savings when deploying an EHR system. Since the information about the visit will already be documented in a structured format, the physician is no longer in need of transcription services in most cases. Surgeons or other specialties might still have transcriptionists, because surgeons rarely document their work while performing an operation.

Reduced Staff Levels   Another benefit, typically after three to six months of EHR use, is the need for fewer staff. Though vendors tout this, we have seen this in only one installation. There really wasn't a reduction in staff; it was because of attrition because of the complexity of the product. As an IT professional, do not go into the office on the premise of reducing staff. This can be addressed when the practice or hospital brings it up to you. Remember that some staff in nearly all medical practices are related or have worked a long time for the eligible professionals, so it is a sensitive topic, but can have a positive impact on the bottom line.

Reduced Physical Space Requirements   Converting patient records and continuing forward electronically reduces the amount of space an office must maintain. A typical patient record takes roughly one-quarter inch of linear space. So, with 1,000 patient records, a medical office needs roughly 250 inches, which translates into 20.8 linear feet.

So, how many records does a typical physician have? The American Academy of Family Physicians (AAFP) has a calculator (www.aafp.org/fpm/2007/0400/p44.html) for defining how many patients can be seen by a single family physician, with each patient typically being seen by their general practitioner 3.19 times a year. But remember that for chronic-care patients, the number of visits per patient will be higher.) The next step is to figure out how many patients a physician can see in a year. A provider typically sees 24 patients a day. A physician works 240 days a year. The total then is $(24 \times 240)/3.19$, which equals 1,806 patients.

Pay for Performance   Pay for performance is a new method for how some insurance companies are reimbursing the physicians participating in their insurance program. The more information tracked about a patient, the better the quality metrics and outcome information can be gleaned from the system. By having this information tracked, the insurance companies can help translate that information back to the healthcare provider community, improving patient outcomes and typically lowering the cost of care.

Less Software Needed   EHR systems also allow inbound transactions relating to a patient's lab or X-ray results. Prior to an EHR, the provider would typically have to look at physical X-rays or pull up a website and use the imaging company's radiology imaging system (RIS). The challenge in reviewing the images online is that the imaging vendors typically use different picture archiving and communication systems (PACSs), requiring different versions of ActiveX, .NET, Java, or even full-blown clients installed. This complicates the access provided to the physician because of incompatible software. With the right EHR system and the right PACS system, the information can be sent electronically to the physician's EHR system without the additional client-side software.

Clinical Decision Support   Phase 1 of meaningful use requires using the EHR system for clinical decision support (CDS). The physician has the option of selecting which clinical decision support to use and only has to attest to its use. Though only one is needed to meet the Phase 1 requirements, a savvy IT professional will help the physician choose as many CDS flows that make sense for their particular practice. The better the outcomes for the physician's patients, the more time the physician has for new patients. A properly deployed CDS improves the bottom line.

Common Order Sets   Order sets are becoming the norm. As we mentioned in prior chapters, the book *Checklist Manifesto* is a call to arms of sorts for practicing physicians. As more and more physicians are moving to pay for performance, it is always best to standardize on the method for treating, post-op care, and the necessary care at home to improve the patient outcomes. Checklists are the norm in the airlines because of safety concerns. The safety of the population is also in the hands of the physicians, which is why we need standardized order sets.

Not all patients are unique. Given the wealth of clinical data now available, the proper mining of the data can uncover commonalities between patients and the best outcomes. Those commonalities are the basis for developing the common order sets. Without an EHR system in a small physician office, there is no way to uncover these commonalities. As an IT professional, when selecting the EHR make sure that the system allows for customized reporting without having to pay the EHR vendor exorbitant fees.

Data Exchange   Depending on how healthcare is delivered in the geographic region you plan on serving, there might be a common system used by the larger hospital systems and independent physician associations. In Northern California, one of the largest health systems offers a hosted EHR platform. This can improve interoperability of data when used properly. As mentioned in Chapter 11, "Operational Workflow: Clinician," having more than just the physician's practice changing data can cause operational challenges such as incorrect contact or payment information.

Patient Access   Patients are now demanding the capability to have their medical information available to them outside of the actual medical practice. These typically are folks with chronic diseases or who are taking care of their aging parents. Therefore, when looking at EHR options, confirm that there are export options into a standards-based format that allows for importing the information into a typical personal health record. This export functionality should be standard by the time the ONC releases the final phase of meaningful use.

Real-Time Tracking Practices can also see improvement in their bottom line now that the information is available to be tracked in real time. In the past, practice information was difficult to report on because it either existed in paper format or was not available because it wasn't tracked. One report that we have seen used more often than not is a tracking report of patients who fail to appear for their appointments. Initially, they were given a free pass when they missed the appointment. In the past five years, more and more physicians are charging cancellation fees. For some patients, it is even better if the practice no longer sees the patient.

With any reporting system, the information is useful only when acted upon. Writing reports where no action is taken is similar to having a meeting without an agenda and no follow-up. Take the time to interview the physician and office staff to uncover the right reports. Make sure the practice understands that the information is now available to be mined, thus improving the bottom line.

Remote Access We spent part of the chapter discussing the value of remote access. This is a benefit of an EHR only if it is available. As the IT professional, it is your job to make sure that remote access is a possibility. Some physicians will not ask for it initially but will want it later. Make sure the practice is aware of the costs to turn remote access on when the time comes. We have seen only one physician out of the hundreds who did not want remote access.

Table 15.1 lists other possible benefits that can result from deploying an EHR system.

Table 15.1 Other EHR Benefits

Workflow	Current	Possible
Chart delivery	20 minutes to 1 week if the record isn't on-site.	Less than 30 seconds.
Paper chart utilization	100% (all paper records).	Paper records reviewed in less than 30% of visits.
Third-party billing	Typically 5%–7% of total revenue.	No need for third party if built into the EHR.

Table 15.1   Other EHR Benefits *(continued)*

Workflow	Current	Possible
Remote/emergency access	Not available after business hours.	24/7 availability.
Referral documentation	One week.	Sent after doctor signs electronic chart (less than a day).
Medication errors (www.bbraunusa.com/index-A3866CA8D0B759A1E-395A615A2C006AD.html)	More people die because of medication errors than motor vehicle accidents (every 2 out of 100 patients).	This is reduced because of better drug-to-drug interactions, allergies, and right dosage for patient.
Income (MGMA study www.mgma.com/press/default.aspx?id=39824)	Under code by $100,000 per year per physician.	Higher productivity of nearly 50,000.

Pricing Models

Now that we have laid out the benefits of a properly deployed EHR system, it is time to uncover how to select one. There are many models, technologies, and costs. As with anything, the first question out of most physicians' mouths is about the cost. We will tackle that issue first, because if the physician is looking only at cost, you will need to spend more time talking about the benefits of the system, not the actual cost. Patrick's parents once bought a car in the middle of California's Central Valley without an air conditioner to save $700. The Central Valley has summers with temperatures in the 100- to 110-degree range. After the fact, we were able to convince them that was a really bad choice. You might be dealing with physicians who look at just the cost. It is your job to demonstrate the value of the EHR. When the medical group has a maximum they want to invest, just as my parents did with the car, you must make them aware of the pros and cons of that choice.

Pricing models differ tremendously across the market and include lump-sum, subscriptions, pay-per-encounter, and freeware plans. Since the passing of HITECH, a new model has emerged that we call a hybrid model.

> **Lump Sum**   Since leasing can be challenging to get on an EHR system, especially if it is not a nationally known vendor, many times leasing is not an option. When an EHR vendor requires a lump-sum payment, they are asking the physician to make an investment by paying the entire costs of the software up front. Lump-sum payments can be a zero-sum game. If

the EHR deployment is not successful over the long haul, the vendor goes out of business, or the vendor doesn't meet ONC-ANCB certification, then the physician's investment is lost. Remember that once the last check has been written and sent to the vendor, you have lost a lot of leverage. Since Phase 2 and Phase 3 requirements are not yet defined, make sure there is a provision in the contract allowing for full reimbursement if the EHR vendor fails to maintain compliance. Expect to pay maintenance costs once the software is installed under a lump-sum agreement. Typically maintenance is 20 to 23 percent of the cost of the software acquisition. Make sure that the cost of software upgrades are included in the maintenance costs. Also confirm that the system has a method for exporting its content so that it can be imported into another system. The EHR market is not yet mature, so betting on any single company is a gamble.

Subscription   Another payment model is a monthly fee based on the number of providers. Remember that not all providers in a practice must be utilizing an EHR system for a physician practicing in a medical practice to receive the incentive funds. When an EHR vendor offers a monthly provider fee, they are looking at building a long-term revenue stream. Your local gym operates that way. Operationally, the EHR vendor has a vested interest in keeping the physician happy, or the physician will no longer use the system. As a typical payment method, the costs are broken down on a three- to five-year cost basis. If the physician leaves prior to the three or five years, the EHR vendor doesn't recoup their costs. Because physicians can leave a practice or be bought out, make sure there is an out clause in the contract regarding career movement. Some contracts as written require the physician to pay even if they are no longer at the practice that is utilizing the system. This seems unfair, but basically because of the immaturity of the EHR space, the EHR vendor must become the leasing company, and they must be able to protect their money.

Cost per Encounter   Other EHR vendors are compensated on a cost per encounter. We typically see this model on the really low end and the ultra high end of applications. For physicians practicing just a few days a week, there can be some cost savings realized when paying on just the number of encounters. Larger health systems are also charged typically by the vendor based on the number of encounters. The largest EHR vendors see this as a calculation of the complexity of the environment and correlate it to the amount of work necessary to keep the acute and ambulatory settings operational. On top of the number of encounters, the vendor adds additional costs for the number of interfaces.

Hybrid   Federal funding is being paid back not as a lump-sum payment but as a yearly partial payment. Vendors have recognized this, and many have decided to charge a provider a monthly fee instead of the prior methods. Software updates, maintenance, and support are included in the monthly cost. EHR vendors typically do not care if the application is hosted internally or on-premise. With the monthly fee, the doctor typically does not end up owning the software, which is similar to a lease without a buyout option.

We prefer to refer to this payment model as an insurance model. Paying monthly, quarterly, or yearly insurance is the best analogy. The consumer loyalty can be comparable if the product is meeting the needs of the practice. As an IT professional, this model is very useful when trying to sell managed services in addition to the EHR package. You can include the costs of the hardware, hardware technical support, patch management, and other services with the EHR system.

Freeware   Freeware is a new model that is catching on. One of the hottest EHR systems is called Practice Fusion. It has more than 80,000 users and continues to grow. With free models, there can be additional integration costs when connecting to outside data sources such as a lab company. Many free systems are supported by advertisements being displayed, and to get rid of the ads, there is a nominal monthly fee.

The best part of the free model is that it frees up the $44,000 of incentive money to be spent on the necessary hardware upgrades or to be saved by the provider. Of course, since there is no cost, there is typically no reason not to get your feet wet to test the application. Most freeware vendors have a consulting or partner arm that you can participate in if the application meets the needs of your clients.

Narrowing the Selection

After looking at the possible specialties you would like to serve and whether the EMR vendor has a good reseller program, you might still have a few possible vendors to choose from. Narrowing the solution can be an exhaustive exercise. Spend the time to do it, because you will be investing a great deal of time, sweat, and money into working with an EHR vendor.

User Interface   In a side-by-side comparison, look at the vendor offerings. We are finding that applications with a greater number of shortcut keys improve the EHR adoption rate. Pointing a mouse and clicking is typically the method that physicians want to use to interact with the system, but pointing and clicking often is not the best interface. Imagine point-and-click on a laptop that's resting in your left hand all day! Spend some time with the provider. See when, where, and how they use their computer. You will know from that experience what is the best possible solution for that particular provider. We have seen great success when using ShortKeys, by Insight Software Solutions, for creating a short string of keys to represent a string of text. For example, the letters *sp* mean spirometer. When working with point-and-click EHR vendors, spend a great deal of time on the template design to minimize scrolling and excessive clicking. You don't want to be the instigator of carpal tunnel syndrome in the medical community!

Upgrades, Updates, and Changes   Another criteria for narrowing the selection is the upgrade/update path. If a physician requests modifications to the normal workflow of the application, as the IT solutions provider you will need to be able to explain those changes to the software as a service (SaaS) vendor, complete the change or upgrade request (if it is a local application), and finally test the application no matter the location. Every year expect to change workflow, especially when it comes to reporting requirements to the feds to meet meaningful use. Based on our experience, we recommend you look for vendors who patch no more than monthly and no less frequently than quarterly. If the application requires weekly or bi-weekly updates, the application vendor is typically programming too quickly to have consistently good-quality control.

Mobile Platform   Checking out vendors with a mobile solution that works across mobile device platforms should also help narrow the search. Tablets provide a weight savings much appreciated by the physicians. Typically doctors do not want to hold a six-pound device all day. Tablets with remote desktop connections will begin to fuel the migration from full-size tablet PCs to simply tablets. A company invested in the mobile space has a higher probability of being around than those still programming in systems no longer supported. Look at the new HP, Apple, and Samsung tablets or ultralight laptops.

Voice Recognition   The new rage is the ability to successfully have voice recognition. Nowadays, phones even support voice recognition. We find that nearly all of our customers who choose the voice recognition path use Nuanc's Dragon Naturally Speaking. This application can be purchased with a dictionary that is specific to the medical industry. The dictionary is constantly updated with new medical terminology, procedures, and medications.

Handwriting Recognition   Tablet handwriting recognition has a long way to go, but with newer tablets the handwriting software is getting better. However, most physicians who use a tablet do not use it like a paper chart or prescription pad. Given that most EHR systems are point-and-click driven, we haven't seen the adoption rate for handwriting recognition increase. Once the EHR vendors move away from forcibly structuring data with check boxes and radio buttons, there will need to be better handwriting solutions, though. And if the adoption rate of

EHRs is going to increase, we must provide the physicians who are set in their ways of documenting an encounter with a patient to continue their without a significant burden on how they process information. Some physicians want short bullets, while another once said that they liked having a story to ready. Many doctors are being forced to interface with technology, though they are uncomfortable with it. Handwriting recognition software will assist the doctors with poor penmanship and allow them to move information into a structured format more easily than pecking at a keyboard. Each tablet vendor has its own solution, so we cannot pinpoint a best-of-breed product at this time. Test any model you're considering with particularly sloppy handwriting prior to handing it over to a physician.

Data Migration   When you are looking to slim down the EHR selection to one vendor, take a look at how well they have done data migrations from older practice management software. Having integration with the top practice management applications (such as Medical Manager, Prime Clinical, NextGen, Sage Intergy, Medisoft, Centricity, and others) allows you to focus on selling the application, not finding customers with a particular practice management software. Anything that shrinks the projected market size for no real reason (such as a specialty), then they are the wrong EHR vendor to partner with. Data conversions are important, especially if the practice management software is no longer going to be used.

System Integration   Ongoing integration is another technology aspect where some vendors shine while others fade to black. Most EHR solutions have the practice management software as part of the solution. One hospital system we work with has 14 line-of-business applications being replaced with a single system. Although the hospital system felt they got the best-of-breed solution by integrating each one, they failed to understand how high the ongoing support costs (which were in the millions) would be. When selecting a vendor to partner with, make sure they have all the necessary parts and allow the practice to integrate into a single system. If the EHR your customer selects doesn't have a practice management component, you can add practice management capability through the user tools such as NeoTools, Oracle eGate Integrator, Orion Health Rhapsody Integration Engine, or the open source tools available from the Mirth Project. Mirth and NeoTools are the most cost effective for medical practices with fewer than 25 doctors. They can be used in huge hospital settings, as well. The high cost of the other platforms prevents tools such as eGate from being deployed in small practices or healthcare settings.

Interfaces to other entities such as labs should also be considered when working on shortening the EHR list. The more interfaces needed to keep the information flowing, the higher the costs of doing business, and the more likely the result is suboptimal care for the patients. Patients having to wait for care because of a downed system is an issue.

However, if the system provides an interface from the major labs in the area and the flexibility to handle transactions in X12N or HL7, then any future changes to the interface can be handled by the certified HL7 and X12N interfaces. Test the interface functionality, or work with a specialist before making the final selection. If you are not familiar with HL7 and X12N interfaces, hire a consultant to work on the areas you are not comfortable with. The consultant can also train staff and provide ongoing support.

Stage 2 and Stage 3 Requirements   Make sure the vendor has staying power. If the vendor is not able to meet the requirements of HITECH Stages 2 and 3, then investing time and money is a waste. More than 30 percent of all EHR customers replace their system. Spend time working with them to make sure the systems they choose are capable of delivering. The ONC/ANCB is the new certification entity, but take time to review older copies of the certification commission for healthcare information technology (CCHIT) to see whether the software was previously listed. Those companies have a higher probability of being around in a few years.

Online Reviews   If at the end you are still unsure, spend some time reviewing online sources. KLAS (www.klasresearch.com) is a really good source for customer-based responses to the vendors. This customer-driven research is not supported by vendors. KLAS reports are a good indicator of market penetration by an EHR vendor and their capability to serve the market. Other places to find out independent sources are EHR websites such as www.emrupdate.com or www.histalk.com, another site that provides an agnostic view of the EHR market.

Existing Deployed Solutions   When in doubt, take a look at the deployed solutions that are already in place. These might be the EHR solutions at practices with the same specialties that you, a health IT advisor, are looking to serve. Talk with the pharmaceutical reps. The reps will tell you everything you might want to know about the better solutions. They are with physicians daily, so they have a good feel for what is going on.

Vendor Staff Physician   Many EHR vendors have a physician on their staff. Sometimes the staff physician is also supplying the investment dollars to get the product launched. Having an active physician on the staff shows the businesses interest in keeping the product relevant. Review the physicians who are on the staff, and pay special attention to their specialties. Typically, the product will do very well in the specialties where the on-staff doctors are certified.

Installs by Specialty   Take a look at the number of installs one last time and notice the breakdown by specialty. Look for installs in the specialties where you want to work. If the number of EMR installs is high overall but the number within the specialty is low, then you might be selecting the wrong product. A customer of ours continues to have issues with their EMR package because they are the only practice in their specialty that is using the package. The EMR vendor is in the top 10, but that means little to the physicians who struggle with the application daily. Luckily for us, we were hired after the deployment and were able to ease the pain.

Table 15.2 lists several of the most popular EMR/EHR systems and gives an overview of the specialties they address, their installed base at the time of writing, and their capabilities.

Table 15.2   Summary of Common EHR Applications

Vendor	Specialty and Web Link	Installed Base	Capabilities
Allscripts MyWay EHR	Supports all but radiology, dentistry, and allergy. www.allscripts.com	180,000 doctors using Allscripts; the exact breakdown for MyWay users was not provided.	Mobile support for BlackBerry, iOS, and Android. Customized value packages which shorten deployment time-frames. Point and click, menu driven, and good reporting.
GE Centricity	Most specialties except radiology and dentistry; those specialties are included in another product. www.centricityforspecialty.com	30,000 physicians	System can handle most ambulatory specialties. The system is very point-and-click intensive. GE recommends using its PM software to get the most out of the product. Utilizes Windows-based servers. Terminal Services used to deliver mobile services.

Table 15.2   Summary of Common EHR Applications *(continued)*

Vendor	Specialty and Web Link	Installed Base	Capabilities
ChiroPad EMR	Chiropractic. www.lifesystemssoftware.com	Vendor would not disclose.	Paraphrase system for fast data input into system. Written by a chiropractor. In business for 20+ years. Supports credit card payments within application. Uses Terminal Services for mobile device use.
CPSI Systems Computer Programs and Systems	Community hospitals. www.cpsinet.com	650 hospitals in 45 states.	Wireless point of care for bedside drug verification. Chartlink CPOE for mobile devices via a web interface. Radiology imaging system and operating room management. This system is typically deployed in small to midsize community hospitals. We have heard that support and finding systems administrator talent can be challenging. Integrates with seven RHIOs.
eClinicalWorks	Has products from the single practice to hospitals. www.eclinicalworks.com	55,000 physicians.	Can be delivered as an SaaS for smaller practices. Supports Linux for running the application server. Mobile application supports eprescription, messaging, reviewing lab results, schedule checking. EHR and PM product combination is recommended for the best business workflow.

Table 15.2   Summary of Common EHR Applications *(continued)*

Vendor	Specialty and Web Link	Installed Base	Capabilities
Falcon EHR	Only for nephrology. www.falconehr.com	Not reported.	System has integration into DVA renal-specific laboratories. This improves renal patient care, because labs are directly input into the system. Supports doing hospital rounds for privately practicing physicians.
Greenway PrimeSUITE	Supports all specialties but radiology. www.greenwaymedical.com	33,000 physicians.	PrimeMOBILE for iOS devices. System is the basis of an offering by Synnex. Good customer support. Servers utilize Windows. Uses PrimeEXCHANGE for uploading information into an RHIO or HIE.
KeyChart	Retinal surgeons. www.keymedicalsoftware.com	Not reported.	Based on the Prism PM software. Though specialized, the business allows the documentation of retina images directly into the system. An image can be imported, and then the retinal doctor can draw on the image to indicate where the glaucoma or detached retina is located.

Table 15.2   Summary of Common EHR Applications *(continued)*

Vendor	Specialty and Web Link	Installed Base	Capabilities
NextGen EHR NextPen	Supports all specialties but allergy; radiology; dentistry; and ear, nose, throat. www.nextgen.com	1,600 clients. Number of physicians not reported.	NextPen captures handwriting and places it into the EHR. This can be helpful for those physicians who don't want to use computers. Has tight partnership with Dell to deliver EMRs. NextGen Mobile for iOS, BlackBerry, and Android operating systems. Utilizes Windows servers to support application. Reporting requires beefy servers.
Practice Fusion	Can be customized to meet needs. Ob/gyn, pediatric, psychiatry, internal medicine, and family practice are currently supported. www.practicefusion.com	100,000 physicians.	We believe this is the best free EHR available. Available only via hosted platform. Installed by certified consultants (such as you). Integrates with outside labs. Only been in business since 2005.
EpicCare EMR	Acute and ambulatory care. For large enterprises. www.epic.com	240 clients, used by 1 of 4 physicians in the United States.	iPad, point and click, integration with community, Integration with other Epic sites.

Computing Model

Selecting the best possible computer model is somewhat of an art. There are challenges to each platform that you must be aware of prior to recommending any of the three. The most common models are as follows:

- Client-server
- SaaS
- Hybrid

Explain the differences to the medical provider or practice you are working with to make sure they are aware of the pros and cons of each. Receiving the status of a trusted partner takes time to earn and is easily lost.

Client-Server Model

The most common installation you will find in a practice is the client-server model. Most providers have a practice management solution in place. These are typically client-server applications, but as recently as 2006, we were still replacing old amber-screen dumb terminals that were directly attached using serials connections. (Luckily, we are running into those less and less.)

The benefit of an on-premise client-server EHR installation includes the capability to customize the application with greater freedom. The complex workflow of doctors and other clinicians lends itself well to the client-server model. Since you can customize the workflow for a patient visit, the reports to referring physicians, and even different visit templates for each physician, solutions that are on-premise are typically best.

For larger or more data-paranoid eligible providers, having data off-premise is just too difficult to comprehend. Having the data stored locally can provide better levels of comfort since the physician physically controls the data. When hosting on-site, make sure that the data is protected from loss. Theft, fire, earthquake, and even a disgruntled employee are all possible ways to destroy the data that the physician so heavily relied on.

SaaS Model

An advantage of deploying the SaaS model is the physician typically doesn't have to make large investments in hardware. The cost of servers and backup hardware and the associated support costs are covered in the monthly fee of the SaaS vendor. This reduces the need for space as well. We have customers who have their servers under desks, in the employee bathroom, and even in the closet next to the water heater.

SaaS vendors handle the upgrades for hardware and software. Given their robust and typically multi-datacenter design, there is a minimal amount of downtime when the software is upgraded. When the data center is not owned by the vendor, make sure the hosting company has a good track record. As a trusted advisor, you wouldn't want to recommend an EHR vendor using a subpar hosting company that forgot to pay their electrical bill. Look at what happened to Exodus; they went into Chapter 11, forcing customers to change vendors, even though Exodus was sold during the bankruptcy proceedings. No matter what application, the SaaS provider and those vendors they rely on have to be managed to reduce the risk to the practice. The software used by the SaaS vendor to present the application to the customer, must also be upgraded periodically. Things to consider are if the application will require administrative access to install, does the anti-virus software consider the application malicious (like UltraVNC, VNC, and others), and when it will happen (at logon, in the middle of the night, or in the middle of updating a patient record). Either way, make sure the application is secured, patched, and available only to the appropriate users.

The most critical link is the link from the provider to the Internet. There are providers such as Speakeasy, now part of MegaPath, that provide reliable Internet connectivity with service level agreements (SLAs) at the top of the market. Another vendor, Internap, is available in certain locations. Internap provides access from the client's site to the point of presence (POP) where Internap has connections to the top-tier providers. To their customers, Internap gives an SLA of 100 percent uptime. Check your local area prior to settling on the local phone company or large Internet provider. There might just be better options.

Look for redundant connections to protect the customer. When working with the SaaS vendor, make sure there are other technical options to produce medical charts in the event of a prolonged outage. If the SaaS vendor requires access from predefined IP address ranges, make sure the second IP address has been preconfigured in the SaaS providers VPN, when failing over network traffic from the backup location. During the outage is not the time to do this work, as your customer will probably be one of many customers affected by the issue and trying to reach the SaaS support at the same time.

Where the SaaS and client-server model do not differ is the need to have a robust infrastructure. This includes business-class PCs. The PCs should be managed for patching, antivirus software, and remote control. Wireless access points should be business-grade (think higher than $200), and the network components such as routers, switches, and so on, should be capable of being managed remotely. A stable and large Internet pipe is always important, but it's even more so for SaaS solutions. If the physician wants to share the Internet with their patients, make sure to configure the public access point to constrain bandwidth to a reasonable amount for the patients; give preference to the practice.

Chiropractor on an Island

We have a customer located on an island off the coast of Washington. Internet connectivity was a bit of a challenge in the early 2000s when we first configured the customer's office. As the only provider on the island, the local telco provided limited services. The first DSL circuit available to the customer was just 128KB.

When we first noticed the slow speeds, we went to the main telco office, located just a few miles from the client's office. We spent a number of hours working through possible solutions to increase the available bandwidth but were unsuccessful because the capacity simply didn't exist from the telco.

The telco provider suggested using a modem to connect to the Internet instead of DSL since no one should ever need more than the DSL speeds they were providing. Of course, we found this laughable, since we were using much larger circuits.

The point is, we had forgotten to check the available connection options when installing the system. We should have known the constraints prior to our arrival. We would have operated with less frustration when remembering we weren't in Silicon Valley.

Hybrid Model

There is a major opportunity as a trusted advisor to be part of or create your own company that focuses on building a hybrid EHR computing model for medical practices. Most practices want the data locally for security and performance reasons, but would prefer to have the servers off-site processing against the local practice data. If you as a technology professional find this model appealing, then partner with a vendor with this capability.

Ongoing support fees to maintain the systems at the practice are another substantial revenue stream. Managed services that support the on-premise or hybrid model allow you as the VAR or trusted advisor to know what is happening on the customer's network and proactively support the eligible physician as they work with the EHR solution. Having remote access reduces the amount of time necessary to fix a problem, and typically when the right management tool is selected, the tool repairs the problem before the customer even knows about it.

Should You Partner with an EHR Vendor?

As an IT professional looking at breaking into this space, it is reasonable to ask yourself whether there is a need to select a single EHR vendor to go to market with or whether it is better to stay agnostic. As IT solutions providers focusing on healthcare, we have found that there is really no need to associate with a single EHR vendor. When we first started in this field, there were more than 1,200 EHR vendors. That number continues to drop as the market matures and as new federal certification costs cause vendors to seek a buyout or simply shutter their doors. As the market matures, we expect there to be between 30 and 50 EHR vendors. In the larger installations, we will most likely see no more than five because of the investment costs to develop an acute-care EHR system. The vendors serving the 1- to 25-doctor practices will ultimately acquire the technology that they need to build the different specialization modules.

To make the decision about whether to partner with an EHR vendor, ask yourself these questions:

◆ What is your target market?

◆ How friendly is the vendor you're considering?

◆ What kind of training is offered?

◆ How well does the vendor support demonstrations and presentations?

◆ How well does the vendor support new partners during deployment?

◆ What kind of partner tools are available on their portal?

◆ Will you be treated as a true partner?

◆ How often are patches and updates provided, and how are they supported?

Target Market   First, what is the target market you are trying to reach? If as a business you are targeting a type of doctor or specialty such as chiropractors, it makes more sense to partner with the best vendor in that particular specialty. The focus by you and your business lends itself well to choosing a single vendor. Make sure that your target market is underserved in the geographic region you will be marketing. It makes no sense to target a specialty with only a few practices in the area.

As a business, if it is your decision to sell into the entire healthcare space, then partnering with a single vendor will preclude you from selling into certain specialties. EHRs cannot be everything to everyone at this point. Partnering with a large EHR such as eClinicalworks, NextGen, and others forces you into serving the customer specialties that they as a vendor are capable of supporting. When the EHR vendors spend additional time and money to develop the remaining portions of their applications, they will become a better choice for a one-stop shop.

So, we recommend if your choice is to target the broader healthcare market, sell your services as a trusted IT advisor. Help the practice through the selection process, manage the vendor selection, and ultimately choose the right EHR vendor for each practice's needs.

Friendly Vendors   Vendors understand that the market for healthcare IT is huge. They also understand that they do not have the staff necessary to complete all of the installations they want. Therefore, many are reaching out to VAR community members such as yourself to increase their reach. The question really revolves around how easy or friendly the vendor is to the VARs. Some vendors require that the vendor sell only their EHR package. If that is a requirement, then we would consider that an unfriendly vendor. Some vendors require huge up-front investments to participate in the partner program. We have seen fees as high as $25,000 to participate on top of costs associated with training staff and market campaigns.

As an IT professional, it is important to know that if you go to market with an EHR vendor, you are going to make enough money to make it worth the time and energy spent. Partnering with a vendor that treats each customer as a customer-for-life is important. When the vendor is unfriendly to the customer, as a VAR you will take the heat for that. Customers in this space are "high touch" and require a great deal of care. When the culture of the vendor is to make sure each customer is referable and there for life, the true needs of the customer will be met.

Training   Take a look at the training programs made available to the partners. Is there mandatory training? Remember that if the VAR program is subpar and the product gets a bad reputation for difficult installation, your business will suffer. Word will get out among the medical community regarding the competency of the VARs implementing the EHR package. You only want to associate yourself with an EHR vendor that has a solid program and weeds out the bad VARs.

Training is also key in onboarding new staff. If you must train the staff on the product from the ground up, then you are making a huge investment in the EHR solution. While you are providing that one-on-one training, you are not able to be out marketing, selling, and installing the product.

When looking at the training department, make sure there is adequate training for the medical practice staff. Without training, they will be lost when you launch the product. As a trusted advisor, you must be able to assist when the vendor training doesn't cover the workflow or when the customer has a particular question about functionality. Just as the training must be there to provide a foundation for your employees, the same must be true for the end users. If there is no online training every time a medical practice hires an employee, the rest of the staff will have to train that employee, reducing the overall productivity of the practice.

Demo Support   Now that you and your staff are trained on the EHR solution, you must be able to provide presentations regarding it. To do this, the vendor typically gives the VAR an option of installing the software in a on-premise environment or the vendor has a demo system where each VAR can connect and provide a demonstration. Having the vendor responsible for hosting the demo platform is a two-edged sword. First, there is no maintenance on the part of the VAR that must be done. All upgrades are handled by the vendor—and so is support. Additionally, the platform might be more stable because the EHR vendor has a vested interest in keeping the system alive. The drawback to having the demo environment hosted is that there is typically limited access to make modifications or customize the application. Customized templates and reports are lost every time the vendor upgrades the application. Hosting the application internally allows for staff to become more familiar with the installation and maintenance procedures. The application can be customized and tailored to each unique demo scenario. The challenge when hosting demos internally include the maintenance, additional hardware expenses, and perhaps a licensing fee. Maintaining yet another system can add to the daily workload. Depending on the EHR vendor's quality assurance, the upgrades can also be very challenging. If at all possible, when installing the EHR demo environment, install it on a virtual guest operating system. That way, if an upgrade ever causes corruption, there is a quick recovery time.

New Partner Deployment Support   Partner with a vendor who can assist in the first few implementations until you and your business are able to confidently deploy the EHR. The type of assistance you will need is in workflow design, workflow improvements, and training. The vendor should have a staff member with prior healthcare work experience as either a nurse, practice manager, physician's assistant, and so on. With prior work credentials, they bring more credibility to the table when doing workflow design. If the eligible physician was told that their practice would be more efficient, it is critical as their trusted advisor to guide them through the design decision points.

For back-office needs, an EHR vendor who has people that were previously practice managers on-site for support will be better suited to tackle back-end workflow issues. The same is true for those EHR solutions that require a great deal of configuration or changes to the back-end workflow. The staff that initially was working with just paper might have a difficult time transition to electronic. Vendor support in coaching staff will increase the odds of a successful implementation.

When it is time to go live, the vendor must be available. The larger clients will need a command center. We have found that there is a need for roughly one implementation specialist per 20 employees at launch.

Portal Tools and Support   Some vendors simply take the partner fee and then throw the partner in front of prospective clients. The more successful EHR partner programs require training and staffing levels and generally are involved in helping develop the business plan for the space. An involved vendor will support go-to-market campaigns, hold web-based training seminars, and develop instructor-led training programs.

The partner portal should be chockfull of tools to support your jump into the healthcare field. There will be training about workflow, practices best suited for the EHR product, and the best business-to-business communities. The vendor should foster relationships among their partners. Each partner is unique, but they still can learn from each other.

Other support tools should include the pricing model. A method to register deals will reduce the amount of encroachment by other competitors. Other tools include deployment plans based on specialties, questions that you might ask as the trusted IT advisor, and lead generation. Spreadsheets including hardware sizing guides, projected cost savings, and check lists to verify that the preimplementation visits have uncovered all the necessary workflow. Most partner programs come at a cost, so it is important that the vendor simply doesn't look at the program as a revenue generator.

True Partners   The best EHR vendors treat the partner as a true partner and extension of their business. The partner is openly communicated with. Open communication must be the rule, especially as meaningful use requirements change, hardware requirements change after upgrades, and during the patching or upgrade process. The best vendors, such as Epic, have upgrade weekends where staff is on call all weekend free of charge to assist with the upgrade.

Patches and Updates   Depending on the solution, patches may come weekly, monthly, or quarterly. Any less frequently, and there is a chance that the changes to the application are so drastic that it could cause quality problems. Clearly, the greater number of the files changed, the greater the reliance on the EHR vendor's QA/QC staff to perform their tests properly. On the other hand, we also found that weekly or biweekly patch cycles demonstrate either a lack of understanding of a doctor's willingness to accept a high change frequency or an inadequate quality control of the application.

If the patches occur less often, make sure the vendor supports a way to do system health checks. The largest EHR solutions have their own built-in monitoring tools. These tools monitor the operating system,

application, log files, system response times, security access, and bottlenecks within the system. Many of these applications can "phone home"
to the EHR vendor as well as the local IT staff. When working with
smaller clients, it is critical to show the importance of monitoring the
system through health checks, on-site visits, and 24/7 monitoring. (For
smaller applications, you might have to set up third-party monitoring
tools to verify system reliability and uptime.) EHR systems are complex,
and the more data you have to show where a problem is, the quicker the
resolution, and the better your reputation as a trusted advisor is.

Standard Terms and Contract Language

In the past, you might have never been exposed to contract language or even
the contract dance that happens between the vendor and the client. Typically,
the contracts entered into between the EHR vendor and the client are much
more complex than the contract you have with the client. In some cases, you
may be representing the EHR vendor without any prior contract with the
company. The following are the most common contract terms that need to
be addressed. Most IT professionals are not attorneys, so we recommend you
consult an attorney when writing and signing contracts. Nothing in this book
should be construed as legal advice.

Reimbursable Costs　Reimbursable costs generally include the costs you
incur for integration, deployment, support, travel, and other expenses.
Make sure that the reimbursed costs are clearly delineated. Never assume
the other party knows what they will be paying for. Document it clearly
within the contract.

Provider Definitions and Terms　The definition of a provider can be an
issue. Is a provider a full-time employee provider? Can a provider who
works only three days a week pay only three-fifths the cost of the license?
Is a provider considered a provider when they access the patient record?
This definition is a bit troublesome, especially if on-call pager rotation is
shared among different provider practices in the area.

Payment Terms　Payment terms must be properly spelled out. Some
clients want to pay based on milestones. However, the milestones
might not be met if the practice doesn't get their part of the necessary
work done. We see projects fail based on lack of back-office staff or
physician involvement. Make sure you have defined payment dates
with a clause making sure you are paid no matter the commitment of
the group.

Business Associate Agreements　The EHR vendor is a business associate. Under HITECH, any business that can come into contact with PHI
must be covered under a business associates agreement. Make sure that

the vendor is under this sort of arrangement, or a breach of data caused by their poor programming skills can cause financial harm to the medical practice you are serving.

Service Level Agreements   Software and hardware support is a key area to have service level agreements defined in the contract. When a practice is investing any amount of money, they want to make sure that the software and hardware is supported. The contract from the vendor will be written in their favor. Coach the practice and make suggestions that put the customer in control of the support.

Application Warranty   The warranty of the application is another area that is written to the benefit of the EHR vendor. Make sure that the warranty includes language protecting the customer in the event the vendor is unable to pass the Stage 2 or Stage 3 certification process. Remember, if the vendor doesn't pass, your customer will not be able to receive the incentive funds.

Test Environment Licensing   Testing upgrades can be a challenge even for the largest vendors. Have a contract written that allows a no-cost license for installing a test environment. Without a test environment, each time you upgrade software, you run the risk of database corruption or application instability. Either can cause unnecessary downtime. Also include a clause for recourse in the event that the vendor fails to adequately test their software in QA.

Uptime SLAs   Uptime SLAs are important to include in contracts for SaaS vendors. We once saw a contract from an SaaS vendor reimbursing the customer only $250 a day for an outage. The application was to be used by 300+ employees, so the restitution for failing to meet the uptime SLA didn't cover the cost of lost productivity during downtimes. The SaaS vendor was not selected because of that clause in their contract (and because of a bug we found in the code that exposed patient data).

Vendor Consolidation   The consolidation of EHR vendors is inevitable. Every year the EHR solution must be certified to meet the new stage requirements. Hence, as a representative of the customer, it is important that a buyout clause be included to cover situations where the EHR vendor merges or is acquired by another business. The contract language, costs, and so on, should not change for the worse once the vendor is purchased.

Data Ownership   Never allow a contract to give ownership of the patient data to anyone but the medical practice. Ultimately, the research shows that roughly 30 percent of the medical practices will change EHR vendors at least once. If the medical practice doesn't own the data, they will be met with resistance when trying to export the information from one system to another.

Data Portability Information portability supports the previous requirement of data ownership. The practice may own the data, but if they are unable to extract it into a format that is consumable by a new EHR vendor or even to a format that could be used in a backup, the data ownership clause in the contract has little teeth. Once the data is portable, the practice has the capability to move between vendors to support the changing needs of the practice.

Schema Access The eligible provider or medical practice should also have access to the database schema as part of the contract. This allows the practitioner to have a understanding as to how the data is structured, thus providing them with a road map of the possible ways they can report on the data housed in their database. Knowing the database schema also supports the business requirement for switching vendors if necessary.

Custom Programming Lastly, we find that there is a need to include a clause that any programming paid for by the practice is owned by the practice. In many cases, the vendor will push back, but ultimately each practice should not have to bear the development cost of a feature that the vendor then profits from by selling to another customer. Some vendors, such as Epic, offer (at no additional charge) any new feature paid for by a customer to their other customers. Outside of reimbursement for sublicensing the features paid for by the customer, this free-to-all method is the next best deal for your customer.

Summing It Up

Over the past few hundred pages we have opened up our brains and dumped out as much information as we could. The information in this chapter is the culmination of the knowledge put into a checklist format that you can use. There is still a lot to learn as you define your role in the market. Remember to go into this market with eyes wide open, mind in learning mode, and the right tools in your quiver to get the job done.

Thanks for investing the time, money, and energy in reading this book. May your future be blessed by your investment in knowledge.

Terms to Know

KLAS   ONC-ATCB

Review Questions

1. Which healthcare research company is focused on the customers of EHR vendors?

   A. J.D. Powers

   B. KLAS

   C. EMR Updates

   D. HISTalk

2. Which two options are reasons to implement an on-premise EHR solution?

   A. Reliable Internet connectivity

   B. The physician has a complex workflow

   C. Data on local servers is more secure

   D. A and B

   E. B and C

3. Independent physicians who are on EMRs make roughly how much more a year, based on an MGMA study?

   A. $50,000

   B. $122,000

   C. -$17,000

   D. $37,000

4. What is the name of the certification body for EHRs?

   A. HHS

   B. CCHIT

   C. ONC

   D. ONC-ATCB

5. When researching your business model for EHRs, which of the following is a critical part of the plan?

   A. Selecting a vendor working with the specialties you are looking to serve

   B. The EHR vendor go-to-market material

   C. Selecting a target market

   D. All of the above

6. Is stimulus funding the best story to lead with when selling an EHR?

   A. Yes

   B. No

7. How big is the EHR market in terms of federal incentives?

   A. $27 million

   B. $270 million

   C. $2.7 billion

   D. $27 billion

8. Which computing model requires the highest SLA from the Internet provider?

   A. Client-server

   B. Hybrid

   C. SaaS

   D. On-premise

9. When prepping to select an EHR vendor, what contract language is best reviewed by an attorney?

   A. Service level agreements

   B. Definition of a provider

   C. End user license agreement

   D. Everything

Appendix

Answers to Review Questions

Chapter 1

1. Hippocrates and Galen are best known for their contributions to _____.

   Answer: A Hippocrates and Galen made significant contributions to the early study of medicine. The Hippocratic oath and some of the medical discovery Galen uncovered is still applicable.

2. When was COBRA coverage, as we know it today, established?

   Answer: C Although tax breaks for providing portable healthcare coverage for employees were first introduced in 1985, COBRA coverage as we know it today was established in 1996.

3. HIPAA has how many titles?

   Answer: C HIPAA has five separate titles. These titles were meant to simplify the portability of healthcare, provide administrative simplification, and allow taxation of coverage.

4. What are the three types or classes of safeguards for HIPAA?

   Answer: C Administrative, technical, and physical are the three types of classifications of safeguards used in the HIPAA legislation.

5. Which of the following standards is not used in electronic data interchange?

   Answer: B HL7 is the Health Level 7 data interchange standard used to exchange data between patient-care systems. DICOM is used to interchange diagnostic image files between systems. Flat files are used as a data extract method and then transmitted utilizing FTP or another protocol. FIPS-140 is a security standard.

6. HITECH includes provisions to increase financial penalties for security breaches affecting data to what amount and criminal penalty?

   Answer: D The HITECH Act calls for penalties to be increased to $1.5 million dollars maximum penalty per year. These breaches can carry criminal penalties for negligence up to and including jail time.

7. Which type of diagnostic imaging equipment causes no known harm to the patient?

   Answer: C Ultrasound sends sound waves through area being examined. The body is subject to sound waves constantly, unlike nuclear medicine or imaging that exposes the patient to radiation.

8. Which legislation requires that business associates comply with HIPAA?

   Answer: C HITECH requires that a business associate working for a covered entity comply with the HIPAA security and privacy regulations. Security consulting firms have just been handed a plethora of new customers.

9. How many core meaningful use objectives must be met by a eligible provider?

Answer: D Eligible providers, not hospitals, are required to demonstrate their compliance to meaningful use by meeting 15 core objectives and 10 objectives from a menu.

10. What healthcare society was formed specifically for healthcare information management professionals?

Answer: A HIMSS is the Healthcare Information Management Systems Society. It holds the largest healthcare event in the world each February where nearly 30,000 people attend to receive training and see the latest technology.

Chapter 2

1. Which national organization would you look to when trying to understand back-office procedures?

Answer: B The Medical Group Management Association is the national association for medical group managers. They have the best documentation for back-office workflow and procedures.

2. The healthcare market is constantly changing. What association or society can help keep the IT staff up to date?

Answer: A The Healthcare Information Management Systems Society is constantly updating its educational material supporting the health IT market.

3. Medical providers have been given a team of local EMR experts to go to for help. What is the group called?

Answer: C Regional extension centers were set up by the federal government to assist medical practices in selecting and installing an EMR.

4. What alliance has developed a framework for security audits?

Answer: C HITRUST is a Common Security Framework developed by an alliance of healthcare and professional consulting firms. This group has consolidated all major laws and regulations into a single security framework.

5. Which vendor sponsored or managed group focuses on the delivery of the medical information across multiple methods such as video, network, and voice?

Answer: A Cisco Connected Health is a vendor-managed group that trains and informs their members on how to best deploy network, video, and voice solutions.

6. Healthcare IT is a growing market. Which association is best set up to certify beginning healthcare IT professionals?

Answer: A CompTIA has built a name for developing IT certifications that are vendor neutral. In 2011, it will be releasing an HIT certification.

7. A medical specialty is hard for you to understand. What local resource would be the best to find out more about that specialty?

Answer: B Local medical associations have lists of doctors in the particular specialty you are searching for more data on. Many times a provider will spend time over lunch to talk technology with an interested party. If not, look for recently retired physicians or surgeons.

8. Which association hosts the largest IT meeting annually?

   Answer: B HIMSS hosts a weeklong IT conference that is attended by nearly 30,000 IT professionals yearly. It is now so large that only four cities in the United States can host it.

9. What resource would be used when looking for a personal view on a topic?

   Answer: D Blog are typically personal sites that reflect the opinion of the writer. Hence, you get a colored view of a particular topic. The view may be correct; just use caution.

10. Is HITRUST a common security framework based on three tiers of provider sizes?

   Answer: A Yes. The HITRUST is based on either patient volume or business revenue.

Chapter 3

1. What color code is used when alerting for a bomb?

   Answer: A Yellow is the color as developed by the HASC.

2. What color code is used for a person bearing a weapon?

   Answer: D Gray is the color the HASC chose for alerting for a person with a weapon.

3. In healthcare what does the acronym IDS stand for?

   Answer: C An integrated delivery system is a group of facilities and care organizations that provide a continuum of care for a certain demographic or region

4. What vowel is used to combine a medical root word and a suffix?

   Answer: D The letter *o* is used to combine a root and a suffix when making a word that starts with a consonant.

5. What does the suffix *ology* mean?

   Answer: A The suffix *ology* means "the study of."

6. If the root word *pod* means foot, adding the suffix *-iatry* would create a word meaning what?

   Answer: D Podiatry is the specialization of the foot. When you have something wrong with your foot, you go to a podiatrist.

7. An abduction of an infant or child is what color code?

   Answer: D The color code for the abduction of a child is pink as defined by the HASC.

8. What languages are used for most medical terminology?

   Answer: B Greek and Latin are the foundation for all medical terminology.

9. What is the best reason for having a standardized color coding system?

   Answer: D Standardization improves the bottom line. Staff is able to move from one facility to another without learning the unique codes for each hospital or care setting. This also has the added benefit of reducing errors when responding to a code alert.

Chapter 4

1. What electronic data interchange protocol or technology is used when transmitting admissions and discharges?

   Answer: B Health Level 7 (HL7) is the protocol used to transfer admissions and discharges. This technology is typically used when a real-time or near-real-time interface is needed between systems.

2. HIPAA was meant to reduce fraud and the administrative costs of providing healthcare. What percentage of healthcare coverage did the feds determine is wasted?

   Answer: A The federal government estimated that 31 cents of every dollar is spent on administrative tasks that could be automated and on fraudulent transactions being processed.

3. Workstation use belongs to which safeguard group?

   Answer: C The workstation use implementation standard is part of the physical security safeguards.

4. What government entity oversees medical privacy complaints?

   Answer: D The Office of Civil Rights has the responsibility of processing privacy violation complaints. They are becoming more aggressive in carrying out their responsibility recently. They just levied $4.5 million in fines to two hospital systems.

5. What type of encryption must be used to comply with HIPAA?

   Answer: D The HIPAA legislation doesn't define a particular encryption strength. That law came under HITECH.

6. Notices of privacy are required for which covered entities?

   Answer: D Medical practices and hospitals must have notices of privacy for patients to sign. The notice must include what the entity plans to do with the data and where to file a complaint.

7. A covered entity must have which one of the following identified as part of the administrative safeguards?

   Answer: B A security officer is part of the requirement for administrative safeguards. A privacy officer is necessary under the privacy rules and guidelines.

8. True or false? A workstation must be automatically logged off after 10 minutes.

   Answer: B The logoff timeout is not defined because this implementation standard is addressable and associated by each covered entity.

9. To track providers nationally, what identifier is used?

   Answer: C The national provider ID is the identified assigned uniquely to each provider.

10. The administrative simplification portion of the HIPAA Act requires the use of code and transaction sets. Which is not part of a code or transaction set?

    Answer: D HL7 is a method for transmitting patient information internally or between systems. It is not a transaction set or a code set.

Chapter 5

1. How many individual records must be breached before being required to immediately (within 60 days) report the breach to the HHS secretary?

   Answer: C   The HHS secretary must be notified immediately when there is a breach affecting more than 500 individuals.

2. What is the minimum number of individuals who must be affected by a breach of PHI before reporting it to the HHS secretary on a yearly basis?

   Answer: A   The HHS secretary must be notified annually when a breach has affected fewer than 500 individuals.

3. When reporting a breach, fewer than 10 of the affected people do not have current contact information. What must be done to reach those individuals?

   Answer: B   Publishing on the corporate website is an option for reaching the remaining affected individuals.

4. When a breach affects 500 or more individuals, which of the following is not required?

   Answer: D   A letter sent first-class or an email (if the individual agreed to electronic communications) must be sent outlining the breach within 60 days. The HHS secretary must be notified within 60 days. A message about the breach must be broadcast on media stations that the affected individuals are most likely to view or read. You do not need to offer credit monitoring services.

5. What is the new civil penalty for the negligent breach of PHI?

   Answer: C   The civil penalty can be as high as $1.5 million for a data breach.

6. Are business associates required to comply with the HITECH rules?

   Answer: A   Businesses are subject to the HITECH rules and must comply with the provisions that are relevant to their business.

7. Are business associates required to comply with HIPAA?

   Answer: A   HITECH now requires that business associates comply with the security and privacy portions of HIPAA.

8. When selling PHI, what is required?

   Answer: C   The consent of the individual is required when selling PHI.

9. When selling PHI, what is the maximum payment allowed?

   Answer: D   The CE can be compensated for what were considered reasonable expenses in creating the transmitted data.

Chapter 6

1. In Stage 1 of meaningful use, how many objectives must be met by an EP?

   Answer: C   The ONC has identified 25 meaningful use objectives that must be met by eligible physicians.

2. How many Stage 1 objectives must be met by an EH?

   Answer: C   The ONC has identified 24 objectives that must be met by an eligible hospital to receive EHR incentive funding.

3. For an EP who has a number of locations but has access to the EHR at only some of the sites, what is the minimum amount of encounters that must be recorded in the EHR?

   Answer: A   The EP would need to have 50 percent of their patient encounters where the EHR technology is available. Encounters used for reporting purposes are only for the encounters in the EHR.

4. How many CQMs are available in the additional set for EPs?

   Answer: D   There are 38 additional QM sets to choose from for an EP.

5. What is the last day for an EP to start using a certified EHR to meet meaningful use and receive full Medicare Incentive pay?

   Answer: B   October 3, 2012, is the last possible day for an EP to start to meet the required 90 days of continued use in a reporting year to meet maximum reimbursement.

6. What is the last year that eligible hospitals can receive EHR reimbursement under Medicaid reimbursement?

   Answer: D   Medicaid EHR incentive funding ends in 2021.

7. What percentage of unique patients seen by the EP or admitted to a CAH or EH must maintain an active medication list that has been entered as structured data?

   Answer: D   The ONC requires that the EP, EH, or CAH maintain an active medication list for 80 percent of their patients.

8. Is a security assessment required to receive EHR incentive reimbursement?

   Answer: A   Assessing the security and mitigating the findings of the assessment are both required. This is a huge boondoggle for healthcare IT professional specializing in security.

9. A requirement to meet Stage 1 meaningful use is to transmit data electronically with another facility or public health system. Is the transmission required to be successful to meet meaningful use?

   Answer: B   There is no requirement that the transmission be successful. There is a requirement to actually give it the good ol' college try, though.

10. What is the percentage of Medicare patients that a pediatrician must see to receive full reimbursement of ARRA stimulus funds?

   Answer: B   The government requires that the eligible professional must have at least 20 percent of their patient volume be Medicare patients to receive full reimbursement.

Chapter 7

1. How are businesses classified under the PCI-DSS standard?

   Answer: C   PCI classification is based on the number of credit card transactions processed a year.

2. What merchant level requires an annual on-site PCI Data Security Assessment?

   Answer: A   To meet PCI-DSS compliance, a Level 1 merchant must have an annual on-site PCI Data Security Assessment.

3. Which classification of company performs vulnerability scans?

   Answer: B   Approved scanning vendors (ASVs) are organizations that perform vulnerability scans that validate the target company's compliance against PCI-DSS standards.

4. Which PCI-DSS requirement establishes the need to change the default vendor-supplied password?

   Answer: C   Requirement 2.1 requires the change of all vendor-supplied passwords prior to installing on the network.

5. Which of the following is *not* a PCI-DSS control domain?

   Answer: D   Management assessment of internal controls is a SOX control objective.

6. According to Massachusetts 201 CMR 17.0, a breach of security occurs when which of the following happens?

   Answer: B   Unencrypted data that is accessed by an unauthorized person is a breach of security, unless that person is acting in good faith and for lawful purposes.

7. Technical feasibility takes reasonableness into account. Which of the following would be an unreasonable requirement for protecting personally identifiable information?

   Answer: D   A CISSP is not reasonable for a small medical practice.

8. Which of the following sections of SOX requires a public oversights board?

   Answer: A   The Public Company Accounting Oversights Board was created under Section 301.

Chapter 8

1. In addition to the fees a provider charges, what determines how much money a medical practice brings in?

   Answer: B   In addition to fees, the number of patients a provider can see determines the amount of revenue.

2. Why is scheduling and resource management important to a medical practice as a business?

   Answer: D   Scheduling and resource management are important aspects of the workflow process and determine how effective the provider is at moving patients through the practice. This in turn drives profitability and patient satisfaction.

3. During which process are the patient's vital signs recorded?

   Answer: A   The patient's vital signs are recorded during the intake process.

4. Which part of the examination process allows the patient to describe their symptoms?

Answer: A   The subjective component of the examination captures the patient's own description of their symptoms.

5. At the end of their visit, the patient is scheduled for a follow-up appointment. Which process typically handles this?

Answer: C   The checkout process is typically where the patient schedules a new appointment.

6. What is a process map used for?

Answer: D   Process maps help the medical practice to visually identify their workflow and timing in order to identify wasted effort or bottlenecks.

7. Name one key to a successful process.

Answer: B   Processes should be reviewed on a periodic basis to give the staff an opportunity to make adjustments based upon changing conditions.

8. Why is it important to measure your processes?

Answer: C   Process measurement provides ongoing feedback on your process performance.

9. Why is it necessary to certify that the staff understands the process when cross-training?

Answer: A   Having a staff member perform tasks they are unfamiliar with may introduce delays or errors during a busy time.

Chapter 9

1. Name two components of the revenue management cycle.

Answer: A   The revenue management cycle includes provider/payer contracts, medical coding and billing, collections, and dispute resolution.

2. What is the payment agreement between the provider and the payer called?

Answer: D   In the contract, the provider agrees to accept payment for their services from the insurance company at predefined rates called a fee schedule.

3. When is the medical code typically entered into the patient's record?

Answer: B   The medical codes are typically entered by the front-office staff; however, a really good medical biller might change or combine codes to get the maximum allowable benefit payment.

4. Which medical code describes the type of service rendered to the patient?

Answer: A   CPT codes describe every type of service a healthcare provider can deliver to patients. ICD codes are used to describe the diagnosis, and NDC codes uniquely identify medications.

5. What do the simplification provisions of HIPAA require HHS to do?

Answer: C   HIPAA Title II requires the Department of Health and Human Services to establish national standards for electronic healthcare transactions and national identifiers for providers, health plans, and employers.

6. What is a SuperBill?

   Answer: B   A is a tempting answer, but the correct answer is B. The SuperBill is the mechanism that providers use to submit claims to payers.

7. What is the purpose of the clearinghouse?

   Answer: D   The clearinghouse serves as the middleman between the provider and the payer. They accept the claim, sort it, and convert the claim into a standard EDI format before translating it into the specific EDI format required by the payer and securely transmitting it to the payer for processing.

8. What is an explanation of benefits form used for?

   Answer: C   An explanation of benefits (EOB) is a form or document that is sent to the provider and the patient by the insurance company that details what was paid on behalf of the patient.

9. Which of the following is an advantage of using a third-party billing service?

   Answer: D   The correct answer is all of the above. Depending on the size of the practice and the number of patients seen, a third-party billing company can lower operational costs, improve the quality of claims, and generate faster claims processing, which in turn could lead to improved cash flow for the provider.

10. As a percentage of revenue, what percent of the medical practice overall revenues typically are related to billing and collections?

    Answer: A   Studies have shown that medical practices that perform their own in-house billing function spend up to 14 percent of overall revenues on the billing and collections process when you factor in employee costs, training, overhead from business operations, and fees charged by collection agents when the bill goes unpaid.

Chapter 10

1. Which of the following is not an element of the nursing process?

   Answer: D   The five elements are assessment, diagnosis, plan, implementation, and evaluation.

2. What is an example of an administrative activity in the nursing workflow?

   Answer: A   Patient registration occurs in the preexamination room steps.

3. The goal of evidence-based practice is to do what?

   Answer: B   Evidence-based practice (EBP) or evidence-based medicine (EBM) is a growing trend in healthcare that applies a scientific decision–based approach to patient care.

4. What is the Health Information Exchange?

   Answer: D   Health Information Exchange (HIE) refers to the process of interoperable and reliable electronic sharing of health-related data in a manner that protects the confidentiality, privacy, and security of the information.

5. Which of the following is not a reason to participate in an HIE?

   Answer: C   It is usually not a good idea to increase costs, especially if it is on the manual delivery of patient data.

6. What percentage of all HIT projects fail because of lack of involvement and buy-in from users of the system?

    Answer: C   Studies have shown that up to 30 percent of HIT projects have failed because of a lack of involvement and buy-in from the users of the system.

7. Which of the follow helps ensure a successful systems implementation?

    Answer: C   Unlimited budget is a tempting answer, but the correct answer is C.

8. Nursing resistance is _____.

    Answer: D   The introduction of new technology into the nursing process must involve the nurses in every phase of the implementation in order to be successful.

9. Why is it important to get buy-in from the nurses when it comes to implementing technical solutions?

    Answer: D   All of these answers are valid reasons to seek input from nurses on technology solutions.

10. Nurses with access to electronic devices at the point of care show an average productivity increase of _____ percent?

    Answer: B   Nurses with the ability to use an electronic device at the point of care show, on average, a 24 percent increase in productivity.

Chapter 11

1. What are the common reasons for administrative staff turnover in a medical practice?

    Answer: B   Administrative staff members perform the same duties day-in and day-out at lower pay than the skilled positions.

2. How do medical practices compensate for patients who take longer getting ready for an exam?

    Answer: C   Medical staffs meet on a daily and weekly basis to discuss the patients and adjust the schedule as necessary.

3. Which of these is *not* a component of good communication between the clinician and their patients and staff?

    Answer: D   Detailed notes and orders, acute listening skills, and detailed observations are all components of effective communication.

4. To compensate for their slower than average typing skills, clinicians have _____.

    Answer: B   To compensate for their slower than average typing skills, clinicians have either reduced the number of patients they see in a day or kept patient levels the same and work an additional one to two hours each night catching up on their data entry.

5. Which of the following is *not* a clinician need that was identified in this chapter?

    Answer: C   Clinicians might argue that vacation needs should be included in the discussion, but we did not discuss these needs.

6. When helping a clinician choose a point-of-care compute platform, what factors should you consider?

    Answer: D   Support, replacement, and the size of the screen are all important considerations for the clinician's point-of-care compute platform.

7. Remote access to the EHR for the clinician should _____.

   Answer: B   Remote access can be secure and easy to use.

8. The primary goal for the RECs is to _____.

   Answer: A   RECs provide assistance to some 100,000 healthcare providers in their efforts to establish and meaningfully use EHR in their practices.

9. Whose role is it to coordinate REC services locally?

   Answer: D   The role of the LEC is to coordinate REC services in the local community with the help of service partners and vendor partners.

10. Which of the following is not a consideration when selecting a point-of-care device?

   Answer: C   Warranty, durability, and usability are all important considerations when helping a clinician select a POC device.

Chapter 12

1. A pharmacy dispensing system uses what protocol to communicate orders?

   Answer: A   Health Level 7 is the protocol used to transfer information in real time from one clinical supplication to another.

2. True or false: An RIS captures images from the radiology modalities.

   Answer: B   False. A radiology information system (RIS) can have images scanned into it but doesn't connect directly to the modality.

3. When running a search to look up the harmful effects of a cleaning detergent, what database would you be connected to?

   Answer: C   A toxicology database is set up to review any report of the consumption or exposure to something toxic.

4. Radiologists store images in which system?

   Answer: B   Images are stored in the picture archiving and communication system (PACS).

5. Cardiologists use which type of system to attach their findings to patient images?

   Answer: C   Cardiologists use the PACS to attach their findings to the patient images.

6. What California law requires medication bottles to have better descriptions?

   Answer: C   California law 292 requires labels on medication bottles or packaging to describe the color, shape, scoring, and other features of the medication.

7. Which is not a right of the patient who is receiving medication?

   Answer: B   The right size is not part of the patient's right for medication dispensing.

8. Pharmacy systems use data code set for identifying medications?

   Answer: D   D.0 is the national council for prescription drug program version for claims reimbursement for medication.

9. Encounter forms are used for what part of the clinical workflow?

Answer: D Encounter forms are used by clinicians to document why they saw a patient and what treatment codes are applicable.

10. When working with a toxicology database, what is the government database that the data is pulled from?

Answer: B Toxicology information can be found at `http://toxnet.nlm.nih.gov`.

Chapter 13

1. Why is it important to understand how applications are used in a healthcare environment?

Answer: B Supporting technology must be appropriate to ensure the application's peak performance no matter where it is deployed.

2. When is it necessary to test applications in a healthcare environment?

Answer: D Any of these changes could fail and cause an interruption to normal business activities.

3. HIPAA-compliant software _____.

Answer: A There is no such thing as HIPAA-compliant software. HIPAA compliance is achieved by the healthcare entity through adherence to the rules and regulations.

4. Which of the following is a key metric for measuring the billing processes?

Answer: C Days sales outstanding is an indicator measuring how long it takes for the medical practice to get paid.

5. Workforce management is _____.

Answer: B On-demand coverage, regulations, and patient safety demand that the organization has the right people in the right place at the right time.

6. Single sign-on refers to _____.

Answer: C Single sign-on refers to accessing multiple data sources across multiple systems using a single ID.

7. Which of the following technologies are not used in authentication technologies?

Answer: D HL7 is an interface standard for connecting data sources.

8. HIPPA regulations specify that patient medical records have a retention period of _____.

Answer: A HIPAA requires that PHI must be kept at least six years or two years after the patient's death.

9. Which of the following is an advantage to using a hosted solution?

Answer: D All of these answers are reasons to consider a hosted solution.

10. What type of certification should you look for from an ASP?

Answer: B An SAS 70 type II certification is a report issued by an independent auditor attesting that the ASP has the proper controls for managing their application and its associated delivery model.

11. Which of the following is the best place to put a server?

    Answer: C   If space allows, the obvious answer is a dedicated server room.

12. Multipayer portals serve what function?

    Answer: C   Multipayer portals give access to multiple payer information and processes from a single sign-on through a web browser.

Chapter 14

1. Which tool would you look to when trying to identify the security requirements a practice must comply with?

    Answer: D   HITRUST is a tool that consolidates the major legislation and industry-standard requirements that a healthcare entity must comply with.

2. What type of map will show the strength of a wireless signal in a particular environment?

    Answer: A   A heat map is a graphical representation of the signal strength of a wireless signal in an environment.

3. When purchasing a computer for your work, what should you not put on it?

    Answer: D   Improperly licensed software is one of the fastest ways to infect a network. Make sure that you obtain legal copies of all software prior to use.

4. What tool will sniff packets on the network?

    Answer: C   Wireshark will look at every packet on the network.

5. How many multiples of ears do you have compared to your mouth?

    Answer: D   You have twice the capacity to listen.

6. Healthcare IT is a growing market. Which association has a practice and physician assessment tool?

    Answer: A   CompTIA has built a name for developing IT certifications that are vendor neutral. In 2011, it released a tool to assess physician practices.

7. What tool is a remote network and system monitoring tool?

    Answer: C   WhatsUp is a network and systems monitoring tool. This tool has been on the market for decades and is currently on release 15.

8. When the client wants to have remote access to the EHR, what is a good application to use?

    Answer: D   Citrix XenApp offers the greatest level of flexibility when deploying an EHR and the devices that can connect to it.

Chapter 15

1. Which healthcare research company is focused on the customers of EHR vendors?

    Answer: B   KLAS is a national research company focused on surveying customers of EMR vendors.

2. Which two options are reasons to implement an on-premise EHR solution?

   Answer: D If the Internet connection is not reliable, deploying the SaaS solution will not work reliably. Most SaaS solutions allow for common workflows. More complex workflows require client-server solutions.

3. Independent physicians who are on EMRs make roughly how much more a year, based on an MGMA study?

   Answer: A The MGMA study found that independent physicians make roughly $50,000 more a year.

4. What is the name of the certification body for EHRs?

   Answer: D The Office of the National Coordinator Authorized Testing and Certification Body appoints qualified certification bodies such as CCHIT to certify EHRs.

5. When researching your business model for EHRs, which of the following is a critical part of the plan?

   Answer: C When looking at your business plan, it is most important to actually select your target market before selecting the EHR vendor.

6. Is stimulus funding the best story to lead with when selling an EHR?

   Answer: B No. The best story is about optimization, productivity, and access to information.

7. How big is the EHR market in terms of federal incentives?

   Answer: D The ARRA funding pumps roughly $27 billion into the healthcare marketplace.

8. Which computing model requires the highest SLA from the Internet provider?

   Answer: C. The stability of the Internet is important when utilizing applications not local to the network.

9. When prepping to select an EHR vendor, what contract language is best reviewed by an attorney?

   Answer: D You are not an attorney, so have the contract reviewed by one.

Glossary

0-9

802.11 A set of standards for implementing wireless local area network (WLAN) computer communication in the 2.4 GHz, 3.6 GHz, and 5 GHz frequency bands.

802.1x An IEEE standard for port-based network access control (PNAC). It is part of the IEEE 802.1 group of networking protocols. It provides an authentication mechanism to devices wanting to attach to a LAN or WLAN.

A

addressable implementation specification Part of the HIPAA implementation specifications. For addressable implementation specifications, covered entities must perform an assessment to determine whether the implementation specification is a reasonable and appropriate safeguard for implementation in the covered entity's environment.

addressable safeguards Part of the HIPAA security technical safeguards. The covered entity must assess whether the specification is a reasonable and appropriate safeguard in their environment. The covered entity is required to either implement the specification or document why it is not reasonable and appropriate to implement and the mitigating measures in place to meet the safeguard.

administrative safeguards Administrative actions, policies, and procedures to manage the selection, development, implementation, and maintenance of security measures to protect ePHI and to manage the conduct of the covered entity's workforce.

administrative simplification Provisions of HIPAA that require the Department of Health and Human Services to adopt national standards for electronic healthcare transactions and code sets, unique health identifiers, and security.

admission, discharge, transfer (ADT) Messages that carry patient demographic information for HL7 communications but also provide important information about trigger events (such as patient admit, discharge, transfer, registration, and the like). ADT messages are extremely common in HL7 processing and are among the most widely used of all message types.

ADPIE *See* nursing process.

American Recovery and Reinvestment Act (ARRA) of 2009 An economic stimulus package, enacted in 2009 by the 111th United States Congress, designed to save and create jobs. The act included direct spending in infrastructure, education, health, and energy; federal tax incentives; and expansion of unemployment benefits and other social welfare provisions. Healthcare spending totaled $151 billion. *See also* Health Information Technology for Economic and Clinical Health (HITECH).

approved scanning vendor (ASV) Organizations that validate adherence to certain DSS requirements by performing vulnerability scans of Internet-facing environments of merchants and service providers.

B

back office The nonpatient-facing part of the medical practice responsible for the administrative functions, including patient billing and accounting.

breach The unauthorized acquisition, access, use, or disclosure of PHI that can compromise the privacy and/or security of this information. *See also* protected health information (PHI).

breach notification A written notice informing someone that their personal or protected information has been accessed or disclosed to an unauthorized person. The notice generally includes a description of what happened, the date it was discovered, what information was disclosed, and what the covered entity is doing to rectify the situation.

business associate (BA)   A person or other business performing certain activities on behalf of the covered entity that requires access, use, or disclosure of protected health information. Most business associates are billers, lawyers, utilization review, reporting services, data mining services, or claims processing.

C

California SB 1386   A California law regulating the privacy of personal information, which mandates notification to any resident of California whose unencrypted personal information was reasonably believed to have been acquired by an unauthorized person.

Certification Commission for Healthcare IT   A recognized ONC-ATCB, which was founded by the American Health Information Management Association, national Alliance for Health Technology, and Healthcare Information and Management Systems Society (HIMSS) prior to being selected by HHS to be an ONC-ATCB. Founded in 2004, they have been certifying EHRs since 2006. As an organization, they developed certification criteria among the members and leaders, and tested the applications against the standards.

Chinese menu option   Slang that refers to the ARRA HITECH EHR incentive funding menu set objectives from which providers must choose five out of 10 metrics/objectives to demonstrate meaningful use. *See also* American Recovery and Reinvestment Act of 2009 (ARRA), electronic health record (EHR), and Health Information Technology for Economic and Clinical Health (HITECH).

clinical decision support system (CDSS)   An interactive decision support system (DSS) software package, which is designed to assist physicians and other health professionals with decision-making tasks, such as determining the diagnosis of patient data.

clinical quality measures (CQMs)   Measures of processes, experiences, and outcomes of patient care, observations, or treatments that relate to one or more of the domains of healthcare quality (for example, effective, safe, efficient, patient-centered, equitable, and timely). To qualify for EHR incentive funding, eligible professionals must record six quality measures consisting of three core set or three alternate core measures (if the core set is not applicable to the patient population being served), plus three of the remaining thirty-eight clinical quality measurements. *See also* CQM core set, CQM alternate core set, and electronic health record (EHR).

code sets   Under HIPAA, any set of codes used to encode data elements, such as tables of terms, medical concepts, medical diagnostic codes, or medical procedure codes. Examples of code sets include ICD-9, CPT-4, HCPCS, and NDC.

color code   Also known as hospital codes; short phrases—usually named after colors—that healthcare workers use to talk about serious issues quickly and clearly. By using a common language, workers can respond to emergency situations quickly, reduce errors, and improve care at the same time. Codes are also useful in alerting staff without alarming visitors and patients.

Committee of Sponsoring Organizations (COSO)   A comprehensive framework designed to help companies of any size improve their internal controls, mitigate risk, and detect and prevent fraud. COSO was developed by a private-sector organization, originally formed to study the causal factors of fraudulent financial reporting.

common security framework (CSF)   A certifiable framework that provides organizations with the needed structure, detail, and clarity relating to information security tailored to the healthcare industry.

computer-aided detection (CAD)   A technology designed to decrease observational oversights—and thus the false negative rates—by physicians interpreting medical images.

computer physician order entry (CPOE)   The process of electronically entering medical practitioner instructions for the treatment of patients (particularly hospitalized patients) under the medical practitioner's care.

Computing Technology Industry Association (CompTIA)   A nonprofit trade association and self-described voice of the global IT industry. CompTIA is a recognized authority for IT education and credentials and a primary advocate for IT businesses and workers.

Consolidated Omnibus Budget Reconciliation Act (COBRA)   A federal law that gives workers and their families who lose their health benefits the right to choose to continue group health benefits provided by their group health plan for a limited period of time under certain circumstances such as voluntary or involuntary job loss, reduction in the hours worked, or transition between jobs, death, divorce, and other life events.

continuity of care document (CCD)   An electronic document used for sharing patient summary information. Summaries include the most commonly needed pertinent information about current and past health status in a form that can be shared by all computer applications, including web browsers, electronic medical record (EMR), and electronic health record (EHR) software systems. *See also* electronic health record (EHR) and electronic medical record (EMR).

core objectives   The required subset of objectives that every participating provider must meet in order to demonstrate meaningful use. (Under ARRA, eligible professionals, hospitals, and critical-access hospitals must demonstrate meaningful use of EHR technology in order to qualify for incentive payments.) *See also* electronic health record (EHR).

covered entity (CE)   A business required to comply with HIPAA.

CQM alternate core set   Reference CQM alternate core set quality measurements include the following:

- Weight Assessment and Counseling for Children and Adolescents
- Preventive Care and Screening: Influenza Immunization for Patients 50 Years Old or Older
- Childhood Immunization Status

See also clinical quality measures (CQM) and CQM core set.

CQM core set   Reference CQM core set quality measurements include the following:

- Hypertension: Blood Pressure Measurement
- Preventive Care and Screening Measure Pair:
  - Tobacco Use Assessment
  - Tobacco Cessation Intervention
- Adult Weight Screening and Follow-up

See also clinical quality measures (CQM) and CQM alternate core set.

current procedural terminology (CPT) codes   Numbers assigned to every task and service a medical practitioner may provide to a patient including medical, surgical, and diagnostic services and that are used by insurers to determine the amount of reimbursement that a practitioner will receive from that insurer.

D

D.0   The new version of the National Council for Prescription Drug Program (NCPDP) standards for pharmacy and supplier transactions.

de-identified data   Health information that does not identify an individual and with respect to which there is no reasonable basis to believe that the information can be used to identify an individual.

Digital Imaging and Communications in Medicine (DICOM) standard   A standard used for the exchange of images and related information. The DICOM standard can be thought of as having several levels of support, such as the support for image exchange for both senders and receivers, the underlying information model, and information management services.

disease registries   Collections of secondary data related to patients with a specific diagnosis, condition, or procedure needed.

drug, toxicology, disease databases   A database that contains clinical information about drugs, toxicology, or disease. These databases are usually purchased through third parties that keep them up-to-date.

E

EHR incentive program   A federal program that provides incentive payments to eligible professionals, eligible hospitals, and critical-access hospitals (CAHs) as they adopt, implement, upgrade, or demonstrate meaningful use of certified EHR technology. *See also* electronic health record (EHR).

electronic data interchange (EDI)   A standardized method for transferring data between different computer systems or computer networks.

electronic health record (EHR)   The computerized record for all patient-related information, maintained without regard to the location of service and including demographics, allergies, prior medical history, immunization records, medication lists, lab results, and more. *See also* electronic medical record (EMR).

electronic master patient index (eMPI)   An electronic medical database that holds information on every patient registered at a healthcare organization.

electronic medical record (EMR)   The computerized record for a patient in a single location of service that includes prior treatment, demographic, immunization, lab, medication, prior history, and more, depending on the type of treatment. *See also* electronic health record (EHR).

electronic medication administration record (eMAR)   A point-of-care process that utilizes barcode-reading technology to monitor the bedside administration of medications.

Electronic Prescribing   The use of computers to review drug or formulary coverage for a patient, transmit patient prescriptions to a local pharmacy or printer. There are free e-Prescribing vendors which allow providers to meet e-prescribing Medicare requirements, or the functionality is available in certified EHR applications.

electronic record or data repository   A record in digital format that is capable of being shared across different healthcare settings, by being embedded in network-connected, enterprise-wide information systems.

electronic remittance advice (ERA)   A method of receiving your Medicare A/Medicare B remittance advice electronically instead of on paper.

emergency department (ED)   A medical treatment facility that specializes in acute care of patients who present without prior appointment, either by their own means or by ambulance.

encounter   A patient visit to a medical practice.

encounter form   A document or record used to collect data about given elements of a patient visit to a provider office or similar site that can become part of a patient record or be used for management purposes or for quality review activities.

eprescribing (eRx)   The electronic transmission of prescription information from the prescriber's computer to a pharmacy computer.

evidence-based practice (EBP)   The integration of clinical expertise/expert opinion, external scientific evidence, and client/patient/caregiver perspectives to provide high-quality patient care.

explanation of benefits (EOB) A statement sent by a health insurance company to covered individuals explaining what medical treatment and/or services charges were paid on their behalf.

F

fee schedule A list of maximum dollar allowances for medical procedures that apply under a specific contract with a payer.

Fibre Channel A gigabit or faster technology used for the transmission of data between computers and storage targets. When selecting Fibre Channel, you must deploy a separate fabric for the disk traffic to ride upon. Having a separate fabric can be extremely useful when working with high-bandwidth applications; however, advancements in the iSCSI and FCoE protocols have improved their capabilities and I/O response times on the IP networks that are deployed in most of the practices you will serve.

front office The patient-facing part of the medical practice responsible for the administrative functions, including scheduling, interacting with patients before and after treatment, and other administrative duties pertaining to healthcare.

G

Greek/Latin root words Root words that lend specificity that otherwise would be nonexistent if medical terminology simply employed prefixes and suffixes only. Some examples of root words from the Greek are *phleb-* (vein), *gastro-* (stomach), *crani(o)-* (skull), and *dermat(o)-* (skin).

H

health information exchange (HIE) The use of electronic healthcare information across disparate systems that maintains the meaning of the information being exchanged. Benefits include continuity of care across multiple providers, reduced expenses associated with duplicate testing, reduced time involved with recovering patient data, and analyses of the health of the population by public health officials.

Health Information Management Systems Society (HIMSS) A U.S. not-for-profit organization dedicated to promoting a better understanding of healthcare information and management systems.

Health Information Portability and Accountability Act (HIPAA) Enacted by Congress in 1996, the first comprehensive federal protection for the privacy of personal health information.

health information technology (HIT) The hardware, software, and integrated technologies, services, intellectual property, or packaged solutions sold as a service or services designed to support healthcare entities or patients for the secure creation, access, or sharing of health-related information. *See also* American Recovery and Reinvestment Act of 2009 (ARRA).

Health Information Technology for Economic and Clinical Health (HITECH) A part of ARRA that contains incentives related to healthcare information technology in general and contains specific incentives designed to accelerate the adoption of electronic health record (EHR) systems among providers. The act also requires covered entities and their business associates to provide for notification in the case of breaches of unsecured protected health information. *See also* American Recovery and Reinvestment Act of 2009 (ARRA), breach, business associate (BA), covered entity (CE), and electronic health record (EHR).

Health Information Technology Research Center (HITRC) A government agency authorized by the HITECH Act to gather information on effective practices and help the regional education centers work with one another and with relevant stakeholders to identify and share best practices in EHR adoption, meaningful use, and provider support.

Healthcare Information Technology Standards Panel (HITSP) The goal of the HITSP is to serve as a partnership between the government and commercial enterprises for the purpose of develop a set of standards which specifically enable interoperability among healthcare software, hardware, and other specialized vendors.

Health Information Trust Alliance (HITRUST)   A collaboration with healthcare, business, technology, and information security leaders who came together to form HITRUST and the Common Security Framework (CSF). *See also* Common Security Framework (CSF).

Health Level Seven International (HL7)   A not-for-profit, ANSI-accredited standards-developing organization dedicated to providing a comprehensive framework and related standards for the exchange, integration, sharing, and retrieval of electronic health information that supports clinical practice and the management, delivery, and evaluation of health.

I

informed consent   An agreement intended to ensure that both parties understand the activities being undertaken and the risks associated with them. This is often used in conjunction with a waiver or hold-harmless and indemnifying agreement.

integrated delivery system (IDS)   A network of healthcare providers and organizations that provides or arranges to provide a coordinated continuum of services to a defined population.

International Classification of Diseases (ICD) codes   A system defined by the World Health Organization (WHO) for coding diagnoses and procedures. Revisions are noted by adding a sequential update number after the code, such as ICD-10 for the 10th revision.

K

KLAS   A research firm specializing in monitoring and reporting on the performance of healthcare vendors. KLAS's mission is to improve delivery by independently measuring vendor performance for the benefit of healthcare provider partners, consultants, investors, and vendors.

L

laboratory information system (LIS)   A series of computer programs that process, store, and manage data from all stages of medical processes and tests.

laboratory management system (LMS)   Computer software that is used in the laboratory for the management of samples, laboratory users, instruments, standards, and other laboratory functions, such as invoicing, plate management, and workflow automation.

limited data set   Health information that excludes certain listed, direct identifiers. It also may include city, state, ZIP code, elements of date, and other numbers, characteristics, or codes not listed as direct identifiers.

local extension centers (LECs)   A local organization, working under the direction of a regional extension center (REC), to assist healthcare providers with the selection and implementation of electronic health record (EHR) technology. *See also* electronic health record (EHR) and regional extension center (REC).

M

Massachusetts 201 CMR 17.00   A Massachusetts state law establishing the minimum standards to be met in connection with the safeguarding of personal information for all residents of Massachusetts. The regulation applies to entities that own or license personal information about Massachusetts residents; it is important to note the regulations apply to all entities, wherever they are located.

maternal and infant systems   Systems that monitor the heart rate and temperature of the mother and child during delivery and post-partum. Infant systems are used after birth to control baby temperature, control airflow, and reduce exposure to the environment.

meaningful use   A qualification to receive federal funding for health information technology. For instance, if a health information technology (HIT) system is used in a meaningful way to provide better patient care, a health system can qualify to receive federal subsidies to help pay for the technology. *See also* health information technology (HIT).

Medicaid patient volume   The number of Medicaid patients a provider sees. This number is used to determine eligibility to participate in the Medicaid EHR Incentive Program.

Medicaid—Title 19   A federal/state entitlement program that pays for medical assistance for certain individuals and families with low incomes and resources. This program, known as Medicaid, became law in 1965 as a cooperative venture jointly funded by the federal and state governments (including the District of Columbia and the territories) to assist states in furnishing medical assistance to eligible needy persons. Medicaid, part of the Social Security Act, is the largest source of funding for medical and health-related services for America's poorest people.

Medical Group Management Association (MGMA)   A membership association for professional administrators and leaders of medical group practices. MGMA delivers networking, professional education and resources, and political advocacy for medical practice management.

Medicare Electronic Health Record Demonstration and Medicare Care Management Performance Demonstration (MCMP)   A three-year demonstration mandated under Section 649 of the Medicare Prescription Drug, Improvement, and Modernization Act (MMA) to promote the use of health information technology and improve the quality of care for beneficiaries. Doctors in small to medium-sized practices who meet clinical performance measure standards received a bonus payment for managing the care of eligible Medicare beneficiaries and reporting quality measure data to CMS from a CCHIT-certified electronic health record. The demonstration was implemented in California, Arkansas, Massachusetts, and Utah and ended on June 30, 2010.

Medicare Improvements for Patients and Providers Act (MIPPA) of 2008   Section 132 of the Medicare Improvements for Patients and Providers Act of 2008 (MIPPA) authorizes a new and separate incentive program for eligible professionals who are successful electronic prescribers as defined by MIPPA.

Medicare Physician Quality Reporting Initiative (PQRI)   A voluntary program that allows physicians and other healthcare professionals to report information to Medicare about the quality of care they give to people who have certain medical conditions and are covered by Medicare. Some physicians and other healthcare professionals provide the information by adding quality codes to the claims they submit to Medicare.

Medicare—Title 18   Entitled "Health Insurance for the Aged and Disabled" and commonly known as Medicare. As part of the Social Security Amendments of 1965, the Medicare legislation established a health insurance program for aged persons to complement the retirement, survivors, and disability insurance benefits under other titles of the Social Security Act.

menu set objectives   Under ARRA, eligible professionals, hospitals, and critical-access hospitals must demonstrate meaningful use of EHR technology to qualify for incentive payments. The menu set objectives includes 12 objectives, of which 10 apply to eligible professionals and 10 apply to hospitals. Eligible professionals and hospitals must choose 5 out of the 10 menu set objectives. Participants also must select one population and public health measure objective. *See also* American Recovery and Reinvestment Act of 2009 (ARRA) and electronic health record (EHR).

minimum necessary   A guideline where a covered entity must develop policies and procedures that reasonably limit its disclosures of, and requests for, protected health information for payment and healthcare operations to the minimum necessary. A covered entity also is required to develop role-based access policies and procedures that limit which members of its workforce may have access to protected health information for treatment, payment, and healthcare operations, based on those who need access to the information to do their jobs. However, covered entities are not required to apply the minimum necessary standard to disclosures or to requests by a healthcare provider for treatment purposes.

N

national drug codes   A unique 10-digit, 3-segment numeric identifier assigned to each medication listed under Section 510 of the U.S. federal Food, Drug, and Cosmetic Act. The segments identify the labeler or vendor, product (within the scope of the labeler), and trade package (of the product).

National Health Information Network (NHIN)   A set of standards, services, and policies that enable secure health information exchange over the Internet. The network will provide a foundation for the exchange of health information across diverse entities, within communities, and across the country, and it will help achieve the goals of the HITECH Act.

National Institute of Standards and Technology (NIST)   The government agency in charge of defining standards and technology. NIST has developed special publications with the standards for data encryption (SP 800-67 or FIPS 197), Transport Layer Security (SP800-52), storage encryption (SP 800-111), and media sanitization (SP-800-88)

national provider identifier (NPI)   A unique identification number for covered healthcare providers. Covered healthcare providers, all health plans, and healthcare clearinghouses must use the NPIs in the administrative and financial transactions adopted under HIPAA.

nursing process   A goal-oriented method of caring that provides a framework to nursing care. It involves five major steps commonly known as ADPIE:

- ◆ Assess (what data is collected?)
- ◆ Diagnose (what is the problem?)
- ◆ Plan (how to manage the problem?)
- ◆ Implement (putting plan into action)
- ◆ Evaluate (did the plan work?)

O

Office of the Nation Coordinator (ONC)   The ONC serves as the principal advisor to health and human services in the use, application, support, and design of health information technology, meaningful use, the NHIN, and for a yearly HIT plan. President Bush created this office in 2004.

ONC-ATCB   Office of the National Coordinator for Health Information Technology (ONC)–Authorized Testing and Certification Body (ATCB). This is an organization that has been authorized by the Office of the National Coordinator for Health Information Technology to perform complete EHR and/or EHR module testing and certification. These ONC-ATCBs are required to test and certify EHRs. At the time of this writing, six businesses were selected to handle the testing and certification of the many EHR applications on the market. Without ONC-ATCB certification, the eligible professional cannot receive reimbursement. There are exceptions for in-house applications.

OpenDNS   An Internet-based service that provides additional web security and content filtering for home, school, and business. The service is configurable and allows filtering based upon content, domain blocking, phishing filters, and typo correction.

operational safeguards   The review of documents containing policies and procedures from an operational perspective to ensure accuracy and consistency. Reviewed documents are usually kept for a minimum of six years.

P

pay for performance (P4P)   A method for paying hospitals and physicians based upon their demonstrated achievements in meeting specific healthcare quality objectives.

payer The entity that assumes the risk of paying for medical treatments. Examples include uninsured patients, self-insured employers, health plans, and health maintenance organizations (HMOs).

payer portal Internet sites used to collect reimbursement information. Many insurance companies use the Internet to interface with the providers who are trying to receive reimbursement. Payer portals are typically available after authentication as a specific user. Explanation of benefits documents are also available on most payor portals and can be used by back-office staff to determine whether a procedure is covered prior to the patient having the procedure done.

Payment Card Industry-Data Security Standards (PCI-DSS) The 12 requirements that must be met by companies who take credit card payments or process payments.

Personal health information As defined by HIPAA, is any information in any form recorded by a covered entity during the course of providing care, treatment, or payment, which can be used to identify the individual directly.

personal health record (PHR) Contains the medical and health-related background documents pertaining to a consumer. *See also* electronic medical record (EMR) and electronic health record (EHR).

PHI marketing Only for narrow circumstances is PHI allowed to be used for marketing purposes. The two exclusions are for the purposes of treatment and refilling medication orders. *See also* protected health information (PHI).

PHI sale HITECH privacy rules require signed consent of the patient whose PHI is sold for any purpose. The two exclusions are when the communication is for the purpose of treatment or for refilling medication. The payment must be commensurate with the cost of preparing and transmitting data. *See also* Health Information Technology

for Economic and Clinical Health (HITECH) and protected health information (PHI).

physical safeguards Physical measures, policies, and procedures to protect a covered entity's electronic information systems and related buildings and equipment from natural and environmental hazards and unauthorized intrusion.

physician assistant (PA) A healthcare professional trained and licensed to practice medicine with limited supervision by a physician.

picture archiving and communications system (PACS) A medical imaging technology that provides for the electronic imaging, storage, and transmission of medical and diagnostic images from multiple source machines.

point of care (POC) The location where the care of the patient occurred.

prescription label Identifying information affixed to the container for a licensed medicine that is regulated by legislation to require a medical prescription before it can be obtained. In California, state legislation requires that each prescription label include color, shape, scoring, brand, strength, national drug code, and delivery type (liquid capsule, pill) information.

primary care physician (PCP) The physician who is assigned the responsibility for a particular patient either by the health insurance company or as selected by the patient. In most cases, the patient is allowed to choose their PCP if the provider takes the patient's insurance coverage.

privacy notice A notification, required under HIPAA, given to the patients prior to the collection of PHI. This notice outlines the responsibility of the covered entity to protect the patient's information. Also included is contact information for the privacy officer for the entity. *See also* protected health information (PHI).

privacy rule   The HIPAA privacy rule establishes national standards to protect individuals' medical records and other personal health information. The rule applies to health plans, healthcare clearinghouses, and those healthcare providers that conduct certain healthcare transactions electronically. In 2008, the ONC released the Privacy and Security framework for electronic exchange of individually identifiable health information. This document can be found at http://healthit.hhs.gov/portal/server.pt/community/healthit_hhs_gov_privacy_security_framework/1173.

professional component   A billing modifier used by radiologists for the professional services component of a radiology study.

protected health information (PHI)   Individually identifiable health information that is transmitted by electronic media, maintained in electronic media, or transmitted or maintained in any other form or medium.

provider   A professional engaged in the delivery of health services, including physicians, dentists, nurses, podiatrists, optometrists, clinical psychologists, and the like. Hospitals and long-term care facilities are also providers. The Medicare program uses the term *provider* more narrowly to mean participating institutions: hospitals, skilled nursing facilities, home health agencies, and so on.

Q

qualified electronic health record   An electronic record of health-related information on an individual that includes patient demographic and clinical health information, such as medical history and problem lists, and has the capacity to provide clinical decision support and physician order entry.

qualified electronic health record technology
The ONC has identified six companies to complete the assessment of an EHR's functionality. Once certified, customers of the certified EHR solution

are allowed to seek reimbursement from the ARRA incentive money.

qualified security assessor (QSA)   Companies that have staff who have been certified by the PCI Security Standards Council, an open global forum that was launched in 2006. It is their business to act as vulnerability scanners and auditors for companies that handle credit card transactions. At the time of printing, there were only 266 qualified security assessors for PCI compliance.

R

radiology information system (RIS)   The system that handles the scheduling of patients, collects demographic information from patients, and in some cases calls patients to confirm the appointment. This system interfaces with the clinical applications and hospital billing systems for proper billing and assignment of studies to the right modality.

regional extension center (REC)   An organization that has received funding under the HITECH Act to assist healthcare providers with the selection and implementation of EHR technology. *See also* electronic health record (EHR) and Health Information Technology for Economic and Clinical Health Act (HITECH).

registered nurse (RN)   A clinical staff member who has graduated from a nursing program at a university or college and has passed a national licensing exam and is allowed to treat the patient, collect vitals, and other associated tasks.

required implementation specification   A required implementation specification is similar to a standard, in that a covered entity must comply with it.

S

Sarbanes–Oxley (SOX)   A federal law passed on July 30, 2002, after the Enron stock scandal that requires that companies larger than $75million have their CFO and CEO certify the veracity of corporate financial statements.

SAS70 Type II   An independent, third-party audit that verifies that a service organization's policies and procedures were correctly designed at a point in time and were operating effectively enough throughout the period (typically six months to one year) in order to achieve the specified control objectives.

security rule   The HIPAA security rule establishes national standards to protect electronic personal health information that is created, received, used, or maintained by a covered entity. The security rule requires appropriate administrative, physical, and technical safeguards to ensure the confidentiality, integrity, and security of electronic protected health information.

situation, background, assessment, recommendation (SBAR)   A technique that provides a framework for communication between members of the healthcare team. SBAR is an easy-to-remember, concrete mechanism useful for framing any conversation, especially critical ones, requiring a clinician's immediate attention and action.

SOAP note   A method used by many physicians to document their interactions with patients. SOAP stands for Subjective, Objective, Analysis, and Plan. Many EHR systems behave in the same manner in an effort to improve the EHR adoption rate.

T

technical component   Billing modifier used by radiologists for charges related to the equipment used during the radiology study.

technical safeguards   Technology and the policy and procedures for its use that protect health information and control access to it.

transaction sets   Used in EDI. A collection of data that contains all the information required by the receiving system to perform a normal business transaction. *See also* electronic data interchange (EDI).

triage system   A nursing intervention defined as establishing priorities and initiating treatment for patients. A triage system supports the intake of patients into the emergency department.

Two-Factor authentication   Utilizing two different factors such as: something you know (password, user ID, something you are (iris scan, fingerprint, hand print), or something you have (token, phone, smartcard), to identify that the entity, person, or process requesting access is who or what they say they are.

V

Vital Signs Technology   A healthcare IT solutions provider in the greater San Francisco Bay Area.

W

Wireshark   The prominent leader in the freeware space for network packet capture and analysis. The application, which is written for multiple operating systems, can capture data of the network in real time or for later processing. When properly analyzed, the data capture can point to the underlying problem.

workforce management   Having the right amount and kind of staff is important in high-cost labor industries such as healthcare. A workforce management system helps scheduling the right staff for the right times, notifying management of deficiencies in the number of staff, highlighting staff vacation schedules, and reporting what the labor costs are for any given area.

X

X12   The national standards group tasked with defining the transaction code sets for electronic data interchange. X12 also refers to the specific national standard that defines transaction code sets for insurance for which healthcare is a component.

Index

Note to the Reader: Throughout this index **boldfaced** page numbers indicate primary discussions of a topic. *Italicized* page numbers indicate illustrations.